MARK TWAIN

AND

JOHN BULL

The British Connection

Samuel L. Clemens in London, 1872

Mark Twain Papers

MARK TWAIN

A N D

JOHN BULL

The British Connection

Howard G. Baetzhold

INDIANA UNIVERSITY PRESS

BLOOMINGTON / LONDON

PS 1336
.B3

For Nancy, Barbara, and Howard King

*"Heroism, the Caucasian mountaineers say,
is endurance for one moment more."*

[George F. Kennan *to* H. M. Rogers, 7/25/21]

Contents

FOREWORD / xi
ACKNOWLEDGMENTS *(and a Note on Documentation)* / xv

1	*The Voyage Out (1872)*	3
2	*The Compleat Anglophile (1873–1877)*	11
3	*Europe Once More (1878–1879)*	33
4	The Prince and the Pauper *(1880–1881)*	48
5	*The Bright and the Dark (1882–1885)*	68
6	*Thunder and the Storm (1885–1889)*	102
7	A Connecticut Yankee: *Other British Literary Sources*	131
8	*The Road Back (1890–1894)*	162
9	*The World Tour and After (1895–1897)*	179
10	*Reconciliation and Reminiscence (1897–1900)*	196
11	*Literary Efforts: The Later Years (1895–1906)*	210
12	*The Final Honor (1907)*	241

POSTSCRIPT: *Mark Twain and British Authors* 254

I	*The Eighteenth Century and Earlier* / 254	
II	*Nineteenth-Century Poetry* / 276	
III	*Nineteenth-Century Fiction* / 293	
	AFTERWORD / 318	
	BIBLIOGRAPHICAL NOTE / 320	
	NOTES / 325	
	INDEX / 384	

Illustrations

Clemens in London, 1872   Frontispiece

Clemens with George Routledge, 1872   7

Olivia Langdon Clemens, about 1872   12

Poster advertising London lectures, 1873   17

Clemens about 1886, age 51   103

Clemens in 1896, age 61   168

Lambton Castle, Durham, England   168

Clemens at Dollis Hill, 1900   199

Clemens in London, 1899   212

Cablegram from Whitelaw Reid   243

Invitation to Garden Party at Windsor Castle   243

Clemens in his Oxford robes, 1907   243

Mr. Punch Toasts Mark Twain, drawing by
     Bernard Partridge   249

Clemens in his library, 1908 or 1909   253

Foreword

THE COURSE OF SAMUEL CLEMENS' RELATIONSHIP WITH BRITAIN was much like that of many intense friendships. From an initial warmth it passed through a stormy quarrel and a gradual reconciliation into a golden glow of mutual admiration. This study attempts to describe that evolution and its influence on the American author's art and thought. In doing so, it considers the part played by British writers in helping to shape the various stages in the development of Clemens' political, social, and philosophical ideas, especially those concerning the nature of man. More particularly, it endeavors to show how the humorist adapted specific elements from his reading to his own works. Finally, as a glimpse at the personal side of Anglo-American literary relations, it considers the author's associations with some of his British contemporaries. Much of the discussion of literary influence falls naturally into chronological narrative. What does not is treated in a Postscript.

When I first began this investigation more years ago than I care to remember, I suppose I envisioned treating the whole Mark Twain canon (insofar as it concerned the author's relations with England and British authors) in the sort of detail since so admirably employed in Walter Blair's *Mark Twain & "Huck Finn."* The impossibility of achieving that goal in any reasonable length of time (or manuscript) soon became obvious. Nevertheless, I hope that some of my discussions may serve as starting points for further inquiry, and that others may provide new lights and shadows for the still incomplete portrait of Samuel Clemens as man and writer.

For this sort of study a chronological approach is essential. Because Clemens' opinions varied so widely at different periods of his life, any other treatment results in confusion or distortion. A man of strong emotions, he was often inconsistent, but not so often as has been charged. A number of the seeming inconsistencies fade when they are seen in chronological perspective.

Many studies run aground because they take at face value some of the views expressed in ostensibly autobiographical works like *The Innocents Abroad* and *Roughing It*. As recent articles and books by John Gerber, Henry Nash Smith, and Franklin Rogers have clearly demonstrated, it is important to separate the man Samuel Clemens from the many "poses" of the writer Mark Twain. Such separation is often difficult, sometimes impossible. Nevertheless I have attempted wherever it *is* possible to distinguish between Clemens' own views and those belonging to his sometimes fictional narrator Mark Twain. This is why I use his real name more often than his pseudonym—and *always* do so when I am endeavoring to assess his actual opinions and his literary intentions.

An examination of the humorist's fluctuating attitudes toward England and of his reading in British literature serves to modify several widely accepted "images." Those who have preferred to see Mark Twain as the equalitarian voice of the American West, scoffing at tradition and all that Europe and England stood for, have overlooked or minimized significant opinions and reactions. Another image that has been a long time fading, is that of the unlettered "original" who sprang full-grown from the forehead of the frontier, tutored only by personal experience and the American humorists who preceded him.

For this latter legend, Clemens himself was partly responsible, though his official biographer Albert Bigelow Paine enthusiastically abetted it. For instance, as Paine has noted, the humorist told a British correspondent in 1890 that though his qualifications as a novelist were based on "a wide culture," all of it was "real," adding, "I don't know anything about books." Some years later, in speaking about his lack of appreciation of various writers, he declared: "I don't know anything about anything, and never did."[1]

Such denials may have resulted from an actual sense of intellectual inferiority. It is easy to see how a man who left school before his teens could feel that his own efforts to educate himself had been feeble. On the other hand, in playing up the fact that his talents owed nothing to books, he was also indulging in a form of self-aggrandizement. He enjoyed being considered an "original" just as he enjoyed the early posters proclaiming him "the greatest humorist in America,"[2] and the attention he later attracted with his famous white suit.

Clemens did read widely, however, not only in the histories, biographies, travels, and scientific works that he once admitted liking, but also in the novels, poetry, and theology that he professed to abhor. Moreover, on various occasions he admitted the possibility that he had "unconsciously" borrowed from other authors. Once, after telling his friend William Dean Howells how he had inadvertently stolen a story idea from Charles Dudley Warner, he even wondered whether he might not be "the worst literary thief in the world, without knowing it." To another correspondent he remarked that unconscious plagiarism ought not be considered a crime, but that if a man should knowingly appropriate ideas or language from another, he would be a thief. Still, at least once in 1876, he confessed to Howells that he often borrowed situations or ideas from other stories to weave into his own.[3]

That there was some justification in his mind even for conscious borrowing is suggested by marginal comments in a copy of H. H. Breen's *Modern English Literature: Its Blemishes and Defects* (1857). Most striking, perhaps, is the note "a good deal of truth"[4] placed beside the assertion of Dumas' view that the man of genius does not steal from other authors but rather conquers and annexes. Other reactions to Breen's discussions of literary indebtedness, as Walter Blair has pointed out, also indicate that the humorist not only admired writers who gave new expression to old ideas but believed that the materials so adapted and revised became the legitimate possessions of the borrower. How much of his own borrowing was "unconscious" and how much deliberate, no one can tell for certain. But borrow he did; and in most cases his borrowings served to enrich his own writing.

In considering Clemens' debt to British literature I have not attempted to compile a definitive list of all the works he may have known or referred to. Moreover, except in the cases of Thomas Carlyle and W. E. H. Lecky, I have emphasized his reading in *belles lettres,* though other literary categories receive some attention in the chronological narrative itself.

Acknowledgments

I N ANY STUDY OF MARK TWAIN, debts to other scholars pile up at
an alarming rate. I have endeavored to acknowledge my many
obligations either in the text itself or in the notes. If I have inadvertently failed to do so in any instance, I can only plead "unconscious absorption" and apologize. I should perhaps indicate, however, that except for direct quotations, I have not footnoted factual
material derived from Paine's *Mark Twain: A Biography* (1912).

Notes will be found at the back of the book, except for those
citing previously unpublished quotations from Mark Twain's writings. The latter, by requirement of the Mark Twain Company, will
be found on the pages on which they occur. Titles of frequently
cited works are abbreviated, as indicated in the list preceding the
notes. In quoting from previously unpublished works, I have written out Clemens' ampersands (in accordance with the practice followed in the new editions of Mark Twain's writings). Ampersands
have been retained, of course, in quotations from *published* works
in which they appear.

Of the many persons who have graciously provided help and en-
couragement, I wish especially to thank Frederick Anderson and
Henry Nash Smith for their generous answers to my numerous
questions; Walter Blair and John S. Tuckey, whose suggestions at
a number of points have been invaluable; Harry Hayden Clark,
whose kind words about my work led me, long ago, to undertake
this entire investigation, and Dorothy Wikelund of the Indiana
University Press, whose editorial suggestions have been at all times
kind, considerate, and extremely helpful. Acknowledgment of specific debts to others will be found in the notes.

For permission to examine and to quote from unpublished manuscripts and letters, and for other assistance, I am indebted to the following persons and libraries: Frederick Anderson, Regents of the University of California, and Trustees of the Mark Twain Company for materials in the Mark Twain Papers and elsewhere; Edwin H. Cady; Chester L. Davis, Secretary of the Mark Twain Research Foundation; the late John D. Gordan, Lola M. Szladits, and Trustees of the Henry W. and Albert A. Berg Collection, Astor, Lenox, and Tilden Foundations, New York Public Library; the Connecticut State Library, Hartford; Tyrus E. Harmsen and the Henry E. Huntington Library and Art Gallery, San Marino; Anne Freudenberg, C. Waller Barrett, and the Clifton Waller Barrett Library of the University of Virginia Library; Franklin J. Meine; Douglas Veale, Registrar of the University of Oxford; University of Wisconsin Library (custodian of the George Hiram Brownell Collection); George G. Tyler, literary executor of the Joseph Twichell Papers; and Donald C. Gallup and the Beinecke Library, Yale University (custodian of the Morse-Frear and Clemens-Twichell Collections).

I wish also to thank the following publishers who have allowed me to quote extensively from copyrighted works: The President and Fellows of Harvard College and the Belknap Press of Harvard University Press, publishers of the *Mark Twain-Howells Letters,* edited by Henry Nash Smith and William M. Gibson, with the assistance of Frederick Anderson; Harper and Row, publishers of *Mark Twain's Works* (Author's National Edition); Clara Clemens, *My Father Mark Twain; The Love Letters of Mark Twain,* edited by Dixon Wecter; *Mark Twain's Letters, Mark Twain's Autobiography,* and *Mark Twain's Notebook,* all edited by Albert Bigelow Paine; and Albert Bigelow Paine, *Mark Twain: A Biography.*

I am deeply grateful, also, to the American Philosophical Society whose grant from the Johnson Fund during the summer of 1958 permitted me to work with the Mark Twain Papers in Berkeley. I wish to thank the Trustees of Butler University and the Committee on Faculty Fellowships for a grant which permitted a reduced teaching load for one of the semesters during which I was conducting my research.

Finally, to my wife—whose joy in the fact that Mark Twain will henceforth be with us only as a frequent guest rather than a permanent boarder is exceeded only by my gratitude for her aid and

Acknowledgments

understanding during the many years of his residence—my deepest
thanks and much love.

H. G. B.

Butler University
July, 1968

MARK TWAIN

A N D

JOHN BULL

The British Connection

Chapter One

The Voyage Out

(1872)

WRITING ON JULY 21, 1872, TO JOSEPH BLAMIRE, the New York agent for Routledge and Sons, Samuel L. Clemens mentioned in passing that he might spend the following winter in England or in Cuba to collect materials for a new book. If he was angling, he proved himself a good fisherman. Or was he lured by Blamire's glowing descriptions of the enthusiasm with which the Routledges would greet a visitor to London, or by the assurances on August 6 that a book on England would create far more interest than one on Cuba? Whoever caught whom, Clemens' mind was made up by August 7. Two days later he was inquiring about steamship reservations. By the fifteenth he had Blamire's letter of introduction to the Routledges, and on the twenty-first was aboard the S.S. *Scotia* as she steamed out of New York Harbor.[1]

Clemens had thought of visiting England at least as early as March, 1870, when he wrote his American publisher, Elisha Bliss, of his "vague half-notion" to spend the summer there. But at the time the charms of a newly acquired bride were far stronger than the literary potential of the proposed trip. Only a month earlier the thirty-four-year-old author had married Olivia Langdon of Elmira, New York, and understandably, as he told Bliss, neither of them was anxious to leave their "delightful nest"* in Buffalo,

* Quotations from SLC to Bliss, 3/11/70, Berg Collection, New York Public Library.

[3

where Clemens was editor and part owner of the *Express*.

Within a year, however, illness in the household and increasing boredom with newspaper work had made the Buffalo nest less delightful. In the spring of 1871 Clemens sold his interest in the paper and took his family to the home of Olivia's adopted sister Susan Crane, Quarry Farm near Elmira, New York. There, during the summer, he worked on *Roughing It*. October saw the Clemenses moving to Hartford, Connecticut, which was to be their home for the next twenty years. And that fall Clemens arranged with the Routledges for "authorized" English editions of *Roughing It* and two volumes of sketches, which were to be published in February, May, and June, 1872, respectively.[2]

It was probably natural, then, that the negotiations with Blamire should transform into action the "vague half-notion" of two years before. Besides the opportunity to collect material for a new book, Clemens probably intended to survey England for a possible "raid," as he often called his appearances on the lecture circuit. Sometime earlier, in fact, he had sounded out Edward P. Hingston, an old friend from his Western days and longtime manager of Artemus Ward, about the feasibility of "giving an entertainment in London."[3]

The correspondence with Blamire in July, which had solidified his intention, had begun with a discussion of Clemens' revisions of *The Innocents Abroad* for another "authorized" volume to join *Roughing It* and the sketches in competing with the piracies of John Camden Hotten. These piracies had been considerable. Beginning in 1867 with *The Celebrated Jumping Frog of Calaveras County and Other Sketches,* Hotten by 1872 had taken advantage of the wide popularity of American humor in Britain to appropriate material for five additional volumes. Two of these, purporting to be entirely the work of Clemens, bore the charming titles, *Eye-Openers* and *Screamers*. Now that Clemens was associated with Routledge and Sons (who themselves had pirated *The Jumping Frog* in 1867 and Mark Twain's *Burlesque Autobiography and First Romance* in 1871), Hotten's "borrowings" more than ever rankled.

Actually, the humorist owed a great deal of his renown to British pirates, for through them, his works had become widely popular, not only in England but in India and Australia as well. *The Jumping Frog* was praised for its humor by the London *Saturday Review,* and by 1872 had appeared in three English and two Australian editions. Even more popular was Hotten's gaudy version of *The Innocents Abroad,* issued in 1870 in two volumes with separate titles: *The Innocents Abroad . . . The Voyage Out* and *The New Pilgrim's Progress . . . The Voyage Home.* By the time of Clemens' visit this edition and another one-volume version (issued in 1871) had been several times reprinted and were still selling well. But though the American was elated at first by English notices of his works, more practical considerations had prevailed. His connection with the Routledges, he hoped, would bring more tangible rewards than mere popularity.

The earliest English reviews of *The Innocents Abroad* had not reflected the general popular favor. The first one, in the *Athenaeum* (September 24, 1870), found an overall "boorishness" in the book, which even the possibility that the author was merely playing a part could not dispel. The *Saturday Review* two weeks later was slightly less critical. It did urge Americans who wished to find a welcome in England to absorb European culture and society so as not to "obtrude their national peculiarity upon us in any disagreeable form." But it also found a redeeming feature in the American tourist's ability to laugh at himself and in the "frankness and originality" of Mark Twain's comments. As the book became established, appreciation of its freshness and novelty of conception increased.[4]

Clemens himself was naturally concerned with the reception of his books in England. At an extremely busy time in Hartford he had undertaken to revise *The Innocents Abroad* for the "authorized" Routledge edition. A rather self-deprecating preface made a strong bid for English favor with its praise of England as "the mother country" and her people as "our kindred blood." In the text itself, he omitted certain exaggerations and a few items of purely frontier humor. Seeking to clarify the material for British readers, he substituted a number of English words for their American equivalents (*draught-board* for *checker-board,* for instance), and he also added a few explanations aimed either at clarification or at courting approval. One made clear that the "mildewed old fossil, the Smithsonian Institution" was "the National Scientific Institution at Washington." Another confessed that the organizers of the *Quaker City* Excursion to the Mediterranean, on which his book was based, had borrowed the idea from the British. Moreover, though the matter of potential sales was doubtless uppermost in his mind, the preface and kinds of changes he made also imply a desire to be respected in England as more than a mere "funny-man."[5]

When the *Scotia* docked in Liverpool, Clemens was naturally apprehensive. But soon, mightily cheered to find a fellow-passenger on the Liverpool-London train absorbed in a copy of *The Innocents Abroad,* he settled back to enjoy the scenery along the route. From this first sight of the fences, hedgerows, and green fields, the cottages, churches, and woodlands, there developed a love of the English countryside that never left him. A quarter-century later and half-a-world away, he would note that the beauties of exotic tropical lands could not compare with those of rural England. One of his short stories (not published during his lifetime) would state categorically that "England is the most beautiful of all the countries."[6]

But on the London train, the atmosphere did not remain serene. As the miles clicked by without a chuckle, or even a smile from the dour reader, the always changeable Clemens barometer swung from "Fair" to "Stormy." The clouds still hovered as he registered at the Langham Hotel and the next day sought out the Routledge brothers, who were to pilot him through the remainder of his maiden voyage.

The Routledges greeted him with all the cordiality that Blamire had promised. Luncheon, an afternoon of conversation, and an evening at the exclusive Savage Club rapidly dissipated the gloom; and the social events of the days that followed obliterated every trace of anxiety. Among the notables whom Clemens met that first evening were Tom Hood the younger, Henry Irving, and Henry M. Stanley, recently returned from his successful search for Dr. Livingstone. Invitations were soon forthcoming to the Whitefriars Club, the Guildhall Dinner given by the Sheriffs of London, and many London homes and country estates.

Glowing in this atmosphere of warm personal attention and praise bestowed on his books, Clemens decided to extend his visit and to bring his family from America to share in his triumph. A letter to Olivia, shortly before his return home, epitomized his current state of mind; he wrote of the Lord Mayor's dinner the night before: how flattering to be escorted through the crowd by "the Lord High Chancellor of England, in his vast wig & gown, with a splendid sword-bearing lackey, following him & holding up

Clemens with English publisher George Routledge
and one of the latter's sons, London, 1872

Franklin J. Meine

his train"; how pleasant to hear the Chancellor say that "when affairs of state oppress him & he can't sleep, he always has my books at
hand & forgets his perplexities in reading them!" and to have two
other "great state Judges of England" say the same thing; how
agreeable "to overhear people talking about me at every step, &
always complimentarily—& also to have these grandees come up &
introduce themselves & apologize for it."[7]

The one dark spot on Clemens' contentment, his anger at the
piracies of John Camden Hotten, was partially eradicated with the
appearance of the September *Spectator* about two weeks after his
arrival. This carried his attack on Hotten. It leaves little doubt that
a desire to advertise his new association with the Routledges
mingled with his anger at the piracies. Two early attempts to write
this piece had burned themselves out in their own excesses. The
first, in the form of a letter to the Superintendent of the Zoological
Gardens, offered for sale a rare creature called "John Camden
Hottentot"—the "missing link between man and the hyena."[8] The
second, much longer, began skillfully by pretending fascination
with Hotten's shoddy business practices and professing to bear no
malice toward this pitiable being who carried "only a 'fatty de-
generation' where his heart ought to be, and a hole in the place
where other people carry a conscience." But the irony soon gave
way to direct abuse of Hotten as "this creature, this vegetable, this
candle-end, this mollusk, this fungus, this bug, this pill, this verte-
brated and articulated emetic."*

The onslaught assumed a more subtle form in the published
letter. Speaking softly again, Clemens ironically pretended not to
be concerned with the then common practice of literary piracy (a
practice not really abandoned until the International Copyright
Act of 1891). The hurt had come, he said, when Hotten titled his
thefts with "so foul an invention" as "Screamers and Eye Openers."
Moreover, Hotten had inserted pieces written by himself or others
among those by Mark Twain. Such actions, Clemens said, made
him want "to take a broomstraw and go and knock that man's brains
out." Not in anger, he hastened to add, "but only to see, that is all."
Finally, he urged his readers to avoid the "unrevised, uncorrected,
and in some ways spurious" Hotten editions in favor of the authorized Routledge publications. "If my books are to disseminate either
suffering or crime among the readers of our language," he con-

* Paine 90, p. 3, Mark Twain Papers.

8]

cluded, "I would ever so much rather they did it through that house, and then I could contemplate the spectacle calmly as the dividends came in."[9]

If Clemens had really expected his attack to halt Hotten's piracies, he was disappointed. But after one more volume of sketches, *The Choice Humorous Works of Mark Twain,* was published early in 1873, Hotten's death in June of that year effectively accomplished what satire had not.

In restrospect that last effort of Hotten contributes an added bit of irony. Whether or not Hotten himself invented it, there appears in the preface the title of Mark Twain's proposed book, *Upon the Oddities and Eccentricities of the English.* Since some of the stimulus for Clemens' projected satire on England may well have come from his annoyance at Hotten's piracies, it is neatly ironic that the only extant notice of its possible title should appear in yet another piracy.

The flurry with Hotten had not really subdued Clemens' high spirits for long. His acquaintances among the great and near-great came to include Charles Reade and Charles Kingsley, who called on him at the Langham. Among his dinner companions at the home of Sir Charles Dilke were Robert Browning; Stopford Brooke; the Reverend Mr. Brookfield, chaplain to the Queen; the historian Alexander Kinglake; Riciotti Garibaldi, son of the Italian patriot; Lord Houghton (Richard Monckton Milnes); the statesman Charles Villiers; and Moret, the Spanish Minister.[10]

To the glitter attending such occasions, growing acquaintance with London itself and pleasant weekends in the countryside round about added their enchantment. More and more Clemens felt that he "belonged," an emotion which in turn quickened his innate love of tradition and nourished his increasing admiration for the British, in particular the British upper classes. One of his country weekends at "Walgrave-near-Henley-on-the-Thames," resulted in a letter to Mrs. Mary Fairbanks, his friend and counselor from the *Quaker City* voyage of 1867, recording the flood-tide of his happiness. "These English men & women take a body right into the inner sanctuary, as it were—& when you have broken bread & eaten salt with them once it amounts to *friendship.* . . . In about 4 weeks here, one learns to quit questioning people's motives & trying to hunt out slights. He finds that these folks do not doubt each other's truth, & that it does not occur to them to ascribe ill motives to each other.

[9

Of course this is by no means universal, but it amounts to the rule, I think."

The color and excitement of a stag hunt that weekend thrilled him, but not so much as dinner and breakfast with a "splendid fox-hunting squire named Broom in his quaint & queer old house that has been occupied 500 years." When it turned out that Broom was descended from the Plantagenet kings, Clemens told Mrs. Fairbanks, "it had all the seeming of hob-nobbing with the Black Prince in the flesh!—for this fellow is of princely presence & manners, & 35 years old."[11]

In London, visits to Westminster Abbey, the Doré Gallery, and the British Museum whetted Clemens' appetite for history and tradition. The latter, especially, with its vast holdings of "secrets of all the earth and all the ages" rendered him almost speechless. Wishing to share his enthusiasm, he urged his sister-in-law Susan Crane and her husband to join the Clemenses in England the next spring. "You will see a country that is so beautiful," he told her, "that you will be obliged to believe in Fairyland . . . and Theodore can browse with me among dusty old dens that look now as they looked five hundred years ago; and puzzle over books in the British Museum that were made before Christ was born; and in the customs of their public dinners, and the ceremonies of every official act, and the dresses of a thousand dignitaries, trace the speech and manners of all the centuries that have dragged their lagging decades over England since the Heptarchy fell asunder."[12]

Samuel Clemens had come a long way from Missouri and from his days of roughing it in the mining camps of Nevada and California. The applause from all over England from "self-elected committees of *gentlemen*" who wanted to extend their hospitality in return for their pleasure in his books was sweet indeed, and made him anxious, he told Livy, not to offend them in any way. "When *gentlemen* condescend this way in England," he said, "it means a very great deal. An English gentleman never does a thing that may in the slightest degree detract from his dignity."* To be sure, Mark Twain was accepted more as a personality than as a literary giant, but the "literary gods of New England" had accorded him no such enthusiasm as did the English lord mayors, lord chief justices, industrial magnates, and literary men.

* SLC to OLC, 10/25/72, Mark Twain Papers.

Chapter Two

The Compleat Anglophile
(1873-1877)

W HEN CLEMENS SAILED HOME IN NOVEMBER, 1872, to be with
his family for Christmas, he was already anticipating his
return to London. He had, in fact, written an open letter to *The
Times* announcing his intention to spend "the better part of next
year" in England and perhaps to lecture for a month during the fall
"upon such scientific subjects as I know least about and may conse-
quently feel least trammeled in dilating upon."[1] The following
May, with Olivia, fourteen-month-old Susy, and Clara Spaulding,
a life-long friend of Olivia, he was back.

The interim had been busy, for in the few months between
voyages Clemens and his Hartford neighbor, Charles Dudley Warner, completed the manuscript of *The Gilded Age* (1873). A pot-
pourri of farce, sentimental romance and slashing satire, the novel
struck at get-rich-quick speculation, political chicanery, and sentimentalism in literature. Though usually unfavorably reviewed, it
was to achieve a wide popular success; ultimately its title came to
designate an entire era of post-Civil War American history. More
important for the present purpose, however, its attacks on the
processes of government as they had developed in the United States
doubtless owed some of their vehemence to the contrast Clemens
had observed between England and his own country.

The general atmosphere of the book lay ready-made in contemporary American events. In recent years newspaper headlines had blazed with such scandals as the Black Friday financial panic of 1869, the break-up of the Tweed Ring in 1871, and the exposure of the *Crédit Mobilier* swindle of 1872. Boss Tweed himself received specific mention in the book as "Wm. M. Weed," who was "envied . . . honored . . . adored" for having "stolen $20,000,000 from the city."[2] More specifically, at the very time the book was being written, the climax for the political portion of the story and the model for the Honorable Abner Dilworthy came almost providentially to hand with the sensational revelation of vote-buying by Senator Samuel C. Pomeroy of Kansas.[3] Other phases of the satire found their inspiration in Clemens' own observations of Washington nepotism, Political Influence (he almost always capitalized it), and the abuses of privilege by government officials.

Much of the criticism in *The Gilded Age* proceeded from Clemens' growing conviction that corruption in government stemmed largely from the dangerous possession of political power by the ignorant and incompetent. That conviction, which had developed during the Western years, became almost a fetish during the rest of the decade. In the novel itself, the whitewashing of Dil-

Olivia Langdon Clemens, about 1872
Mark Twain Papers

worthy by his Senate colleagues brought a sneer at those who professed dismay: If those "good and worthy people" persisted in sitting home and leaving "the true source of our political power (the 'primaries') in the hands of saloon-keepers, dog-fanciers, and hod-carriers, they could go on expecting 'another' case of this kind, and even dozens and hundreds of them, and never be disappointed."[4]

Nor did the book extol the virtues of frontier America where the artificial caste lines of the effete East were supposedly nonexistent. On the contrary, Cattleville's eager willingness to accept as gospel Dilworthy's blatant hypocrisies, and the "distant Territory's" choice of saloon-keeper Higgins as its legislative representative, point up the crudity and stupidity of the frontier voters.

Some of the foregoing attitudes had spilled over into two articles on the proposed annexation of Hawaii, which appeared in the New York *Tribune* for January 6 and 9, 1873. Whereas in 1866 Clemens had almost fervently advocated such annexation,[5] he now saw the disadvantages to the Hawaiians outweighing the advantages to the United States. In concluding the second of the two pieces, he ironically summarized the benefits and improvements which would accrue to the Islanders. They would experience the novelty of all sorts of thieves—"streetcar pickpockets, municipal robbers and Government defaulters"—and men like Tweed and Jay Gould who bought Legislatures "like old clothes." Yes, he said, those "sleepy islands" *should* be arrayed in "the moral splendor of our high and holy civilization." To assist, "We can give them lecturers! I will go myself!"

To compare officials like the "great state Judges" of England, whom he had described to Olivia, with the Higginses and Dilworthys of his own country must indeed have given Clemens pause. In England—whose form of government he had been taught to consider corrupt, tyrannical, and oppressive toward the masses—it seemed that the "best" people, rather than almost the worst, occupied the positions of authority.

In the preface to the English edition of *The Gilded Age,* which he wrote in London the following December, Clemens' disillusionment struggled with his attempt to be hopeful about the future of his country. He and Warner, he told his readers, had found little pleasure in dealing with "the shameful corruption" which in a few years had "spread until the pollution has affected some portion of every State and every Territory in the Union." Progress *could* be made if the honest and straightforward people of the nation became sufficiently aroused to "attend to the politics of the country personally, and put only their very best men into positions of trust and authority." But considering Clemens' current state of feeling, it is difficult not to read something less than complete confidence into the exclamation, "That day will come." He was not merely striving for a laugh in his citation of recent hopeful signs when he recorded the "bliss" afforded by the sentencing of Boss Tweed to thirteen years at hard labor, and then added, "It will be at least two years before any governor will dare to pardon him out, too."[6]

Respect for England's conduct of affairs found its way also into his denunciation, in January, 1873, of what he considered one of the prime contributors to American political corruption. To the Hartford Monday Evening Club he lectured on "License of the Press." He bewailed the fact that the "horde of ignorant, self-complacent simpletons who failed at ditching or shoemaking and fetched up in journalism" should be so irresponsible in their moulding of "that awful power, the public opinion of a nation." More specifically, their scoffing at religion, and defending dishonest office-holders had created, he said (perhaps referring to the Pomeroy case), "a United States Senate whose members are incapable of determining what a crime against law and the dignity of their own body *is.*" But it was different in England, where such abuses of proper journalistic function did not occur: "The touchy Charles Reade can sue English newspapers and get verdicts; he would soon change his tactics here; the papers (backed by a public well-taught by themselves) would soon teach him that it is better to suffer any amount of misrepresentation than to go into our courts with a libel suit and make himself the laughing stock of the community." Such abuses of the freedom of the press, therefore, must be restricted: "There is too much liberty of the press in this country, and . . . through the absence of a wholesome restraint, the newspaper has become in a large degree a national *curse.* . . ."[7] Strong talk from a man who had grown up in the rough-and-tumble journalism of the West and whose own "restraint" was not his most noticeable characteristic.

On the twenty-second of the same month—this time for publication—Clemens again praised the English way of doing things. In a *Tribune* article entitled "British Benevolence" he urged the establishment of an American equivalent to the London Humane

Society. The generous care given survivors of a recent Cunard Line shipwreck he found typical of the English—their lavish but unostentatious support of "any high or worthy object needing help." Equally worthy of emulation was the efficient administration of the great benevolent societies, mismanagement of funds being a rarity.

When the Clemenses sailed for England in May, 1873, the author took along the completed manuscript of *The Gilded Age,* since simultaneous publication in England and America was planned for late summer. In London any clouds that had lowered over the author in his disillusionment with democracy soon dissolved in the glow of an even warmer reception than on his first visit. To the Langham Hotel rooms a great many distinguished callers flocked. From there, with Olivia or alone, Clemens made numerous forays to luncheons and dinners in his honor.

Late in June his newly stimulated interest in British tradition found special satisfaction in London's spectacular welcome to the Shah of Persia. In a report to the New York *Herald,* Clemens' real love of the elaborate trappings showed clearly through his raillery. He thrilled especially to the naval review in the Shah's honor, and to the firing of salutes by some of the famous warships of Britain's past. But it was to his Cleveland friend, Mrs. Fairbanks, that Clemens penned his most significant reaction to the Shah's visit and its attendant ceremonies. After complaining that the constant socializing had effectively forestalled both sightseeing and collection of material for his British book, he spoke of the naval reception and of Nelson's flagship: "I saw that colossal & superb old ship the other day, all beflagged in honor of the Shah, & with her old historical guns booming, & her old historical signal flying at her masthead once more . . . ," adding, "God knows I wish we had some of England's reverence for the old & great."[8] If the character Mark Twain was indeed the iconoclastic anti-traditionalist so often portrayed, the man Samuel Clemens during these years certainly was not.

The summer which followed saw Clemens' reverence for the old and great in full bloom. On the way to a vacation in Scotland, for instance, he recorded the excursion into England's past provided by a stopover in York. The town's half-timbered Tudor houses seemed to welcome the tourists to the age of Elizabeth. Crooked lanes, ancient walls, and the picturesque ruins of St. Mary's Abbey marked "the heart of Crusading times and the glory of English chivalry and romance," and the "outlandish names of streets and courts and byways" led them back to the days of Danish dominion. He even discovered hints "here and there of King Arthur and his knights and their bloody fights with Saxon oppressors round about this old city more than thirteen hundred years gone by." And at the avenue's end were "melancholy old stone coffins and sculptured inscriptions, a venerable arch and a hoary tower of stone that still remain and are kissed by the sun and caressed by the shadows . . . just as the sun and shadows have kissed and caressed them every lagging day since the Roman Emperor's soldiers placed them here in the times when Jesus the son of Mary walked the streets of Nazareth a youth, with no more name or fame than the Yorkshire boy who is loitering down the street at this moment."[9]

When, after brief trips to Ireland and France, the family returned to London early in October, Olivia was eager to get back to America. They had to stay in London long enough, however, for the humorist to fulfill a week's lecture engagements.

Soon dignified posters announced that beginning October 13 Mark Twain would present "Our Fellow Savages of the Sandwich Islands" to the London public for five evenings and a Saturday matinée. Scoffers said that George Dolby, the impresario who had so successfully managed Dickens' last reading tours, had badly overestimated the chances of filling the Queen's Concert Rooms. But Dolby apparently knew what he was doing. The first-night audience was excellent, perhaps motivated largely by curiosity. A judicious "papering" assured a successful second performance. And for the rest of the week, as the London *Daily News* said on October 19, "the holding capacity of the Hanover Square rooms [was] inadequate to the demand made upon it every night."

The recurrent waves of applause and laughter of those five days brought this second English visit to a fitting climax. At the final matinée, when the last chuckle had died, Clemens added a few words of farewell: "I simply wish to say that this is the last lecture I shall have the honor to deliver in London until I return from America, four weeks from now." Struggling momentarily with a lump in his throat, he finally continued: "I only wish to say I am very grateful. I do not wish to appear pathetic, but it is something magnificent for a stranger to come to the metropolis of the world

QUEEN'S CONCERT ROOMS,

HANOVER SQUARE.

Mr. GEORGE DOLBY begs to announce that

MR. MARK TWAIN

WILL DELIVER A

LECTURE

OF A

HUMOROUS CHARACTER,

AS ABOVE, ON

MONDAY EVENING NEXT, OCTOBER 13th, 1873,

AND REPEAT IT IN THE SAME PLACE, ON

TUESDAY EVENING, OCTOBER		14th,
WEDNESDAY	„	15th,
THURSDAY	„	16th,
FRIDAY	„	17th,

At Eight o'Clock,

AND

SATURDAY AFTERNOON, OCTOBER 18th,

At Three o'Clock.

SUBJECT :

"Our Fellow Savages of the Sandwich Islands."

As Mr. TWAIN has spent several months in these Islands, and is well acquainted with his subject, the Lecture may be expected to furnish matter of interest.

STALLS, 5s.   UNRESERVED SEATS, 3s.

Tickets may be obtained of CHAPPELL & Co. 50, New Bond Street; MITCHELL, 33, Old Bond Street; KEITH, PROWSE, & Co. 48, Cheapside; A. HAYS, Royal Exchange Buildings; Mr. GEORGE DOLBY, 52, New Bond Street; Mr. HALL, at the Hanover Square Rooms; and at Austin's Ticket Office, St. James's Hall, Piccadilly.

Poster advertising London Lectures, October 1873

Mark Twain Papers

and be received so handsomely as I have been. I simply thank you."[10] That he shared the regrets of the *Daily News* reviewer that this was the last lecture was evident. Here was success of the sort which a soon-to-be-conceived Tom Sawyer might dream of.

Upon his return to England, barely a month after he had left it, and after only a week in America, he undertook a new lecture series, beginning on December 1. The audiences again turned out in force. While the reviews and comments were not so universally favorable as Albert Bigelow Paine would have us believe, they were sufficiently laudatory to keep a keen edge on Clemens' enthusiasm. When adventures among "Our Fellow Savages of the Sandwich Islands" gave way on December 9 to "Roughing It on the Silver Frontier," cabs and carriages still rolled to Hanover Square. Neither attendance nor Clemens' happiness suffered when Mr. Punch, the presiding genius of the famous humor magazine, proclaimed his "philanthropic act of hereby encouraging and exciting his friends to go and hear Mr. Twain's new lecture."[11] All but crowing on January 5, Clemens wrote to his minister friend Joseph Twichell that he had cancelled plans to tour the provinces because of the dearth of sufficiently large halls. Then, pretending to minimize his successes: "I always felt cramped in the Hanover Square Rooms, but I find that everybody here speaks with awe and respect of that prodigious place, and wonder [*sic*] that I could fill it so long."[12]

December 16 brought a special thrill in the form of a note from Poet Laureate Alfred Tennyson thanking Clemens for the complimentary tickets he had sent. Tennyson was not sure he could attend, but said that the praises of some of his acquaintances made him long to do so. Like the most eager celebrity-hunter, the humorist gleefully reported to Livy the very same day that "an autograph from *him* is a powerful hard thing to get."* He would have been even more puffed up to hear that Tennyson some time later praised his writings and complimented the "*finesse* in his choice of words, his feeling for the just word to catch, and, as it were, visualize, the precise shade of meaning desired."[13]

Social success on this third invasion of London matched success on the platform. Charles Warren Stoddard, an author friend from San Francisco days, whom Clemens had hired as secretary-companion during this tour, later reported being kept busy answering

---

* SLC to OLC, 12/16/73, Mark Twain Papers.

multitudes of "friendly messages from foreign parts, invitations to dinners, suppers, drives, croquet and garden parties, and the persistent appeals for autographs."[14] The days and free evenings were more than sufficiently filled. Clemens was also awarded honorary membership in the Athenaeum Club, the most important of London's clubs devoted to literature and the arts. Inevitably, he found himself in the midst of the great and the successful. So as to avoid embarrassment on the numerous occasions when members of the nobility were present, he clipped from a small book (or had Stoddard do it) two pages containing "directions for addressing persons of rank."[15] He found time, also, to attend occasional sessions of Parliament and to wander about London with Frank Finlay, the editor of the Belfast *Northern Whig,* whom he had met in Ireland the summer before and had later described to an associate of the Routledges as "one of the closest friends I have."[16]

When the moment came to return to America, Clemens, this time, too, was obviously reluctant to leave.[17] After the three final lectures—in Leicester on January 8, and Liverpool on the ninth and tenth—a gloom descended that even the prospect of seeing his family again seemed unable to relieve. And once more he made plans for a speedy return to England.

Successive postponements were to prevent the realization of those plans for five-and-a-half years. But during that period, an important one in the development of Clemens' art and thought, the influence of the English visits is amply evident. Very probably, he also sought to emulate the hospitality of hosts who had entertained him in English country-houses when he held lavish "open houses" in Hartford.

One immediate effect was his abandoning the book on England that had been his chief motive for crossing the Atlantic in the first place. When the editor of the New York *Evening Post* inquired about the project, Clemens said that he still hoped someday to write the book but would not do so at present. "There may be no serious indelicacy about eating a gentleman's bread and then printing an appreciative and complimentary account of the ways of his family," he explained, "but still it is a thing which one naturally dislikes to do. . . ." As late as 1879 he would tell the Paris correspondent for the New York *World* that England was not "a good text for hilarious literature" since there was nothing to satirize—or at least nothing that was not just as bad at home. "A man with a hump-backed uncle mustn't make fun of another man's cross-eyed aunt."[18]

Although Clemens several times during his visits complained that social demands were preventing collection of literary materials, he still managed to amass several hundred manuscript pages. Most of these he transcribed into a journal furnished with carbon paper so that he could send an original copy to Olivia for safekeeping and still have a record for himself. Nor did all of the manuscript remain unpublished. In 1874 Clemens drew upon the English notes for three pieces—"A Memorable Midnight Experience," "Rogers," and "Property in Opulent London"—which he included in an American News Company pamphlet entitled *Mark Twain's Sketches*. Three others—"The Albert Memorial," "Old Saint Paul's," and "The British Museum"—have recently been published in *Letters From the Earth* (1962).

With very few exceptions, these and other reflections show the humorist's admiration of what he saw in England and bear out his comment that he found little to satirize. The "Memorable Midnight Experience" in Westminster Abbey mixes occasional humor with general reverence to show Mark Twain obviously captivated by the beauty, tradition, and literary associations of the Abbey. The record of a trip to Brighton praises the Zoological Gardens and the Aquarium, and pronounces the latter's exhibits especially fascinating in contrast to the "little toy affairs . . . with half a dozen goldfish and a forlorn mud-turtle"* that the author had seen in America.

His tone becomes sharper when he describes another kind of zoological garden at Brighton—the Royal Pavilion that George IV had built "for a menagerie of lewd women—the only kind of zoological garden he took any interest in." He observes with apparent satisfaction that Queen Victoria consistently refused to visit the palace because of its unsavory history. The satire is heavy-handed in "The Albert Memorial": the revelation that the magnificent monument in Hyde Park—with its life-size procession of poets, painters, and architects—was a memorial not to Shakespeare but to Prince Albert, came to the writer as a shock. For Mark Twain, Albert was "a happy type of the Good, and the Kind, the Well-Meaning, the Mediocre, the Commonplace," who had raised a large family, "dabbled in amateur agriculture, law and science, dis-

---

* DV 69, Mark Twain Papers. All quotations from the English notes are from this source unless otherwise indicated.

tributed prizes to mechanics' societies, and [given] a notable impetus to industry by admiring it."[19] The only conclusion the author could draw was that Albert must have designed the monument himself and presented it to England as a sign of his gratitude to a land that had given him so much for so little.

But this sort of sharpness is relatively rare in the English notes. The account of his visit to Old St. Paul's Cathedral reverts to typical *Innocents Abroad* nonsense, complete with satiric comment on guidebooks, tourists, and the Old Masters. In a description of the installation of the new Sheriffs of London and the dinner in their honor, spoofing gives way to a vivid recreation of the pomp and circumstance, the dazzling costumes, and the impressive administering of oaths of office "in the simplest and prettiest old-time langauge." For the Doré Gallery and its contents, too, Clemens had nothing but praise. In the longest passage of the English notes save for that on Westminster Abbey, he discusses the works displayed, naming Doré's *Christ Leaving the Praetorium* as his favorite. At the end of the sketch, perhaps to lighten the general seriousness of the discussion, he turns from the paintings to the patrons of the gallery. Sneering at the English use of the word "capetal" [his spelling] to indicate approval, no matter what the situation might be, he suggests that anyone who would apply that word to Doré's great painting (as one man had done) would probably "screw his window glass into his eye and admire the day of judgment." But the fat old lady, with a poodle under her arm, who had studied the picture for fifteen minutes and then remarked: "Well, it's 'ansome," he lets off with an affectionate, "the gentle old goose." In a later attempt to develop the episode, he imagined the frustrations of a return visit, when his efforts to enjoy the displays were constantly interrupted by vendors soliciting orders for engravings of the paintings.[20]

Many of the briefer passages intended for the book also point up the general nature of Clemens' reactions. There is a fulsome tribute to the treasures of the British Museum, an anecdote concerning an American thief who sought cover in London but revealed his nationality by staying at the Langham Hotel and almost immediately setting out for Stratford to visit Shakespeare's grave; also a comment on the public's change of attitude toward Henry M. Stanley when it was announced that Queen Victoria had invited him to a luncheon. Another short sketch extols the medieval beauties of Oxford's Magdalen College. A description of difficulties with an English waiter leads to a discourse on the tastelessness of English food and then to approving remarks on the ability of English ladies and gentlemen to maintain "their natural grave geniality and comfortableness," no matter how much they had imbibed. Gentle satire spices other comments on the awful crookedness of London streets, the complication of London addresses that had resulted from the city's growth from an amalgamation of separate villages, and the uselessness of the wall at Temple Bar now that the heads of criminals were no longer mounted there.

Three other passages, finally, besides introducing materials which Clemens would develop in other works, underline his current attitudes toward American shortcomings. In "Rogers," one of the sketches published in the 1874 pamphlet, the seedy title-character, like Colonel Sellers of *The Gilded Age,* poses as the cosmopolite companion of those in high places. He advises Mark Twain about hatters, tailors, and wine, and promises to introduce him to various noblemen. But again like Sellers, he concocts ingenious last-minute dodges to avoid proving his grandiose pretensions. Clemens' narrator, Mark Twain, suspicious of Rogers but still gullible, is a relative of the narrator of *The Jumping Frog* and even more closely of the narrator of the Whittier Birthday Speech of 1877. Just as the latter's self-importance is deflated by the old miner's suspicion that he is an impostor, so the Mark Twain of the London sketch, complacent about being "so celebrated in England," receives his "cruelest cut" when Rogers refers to him as "an unknown person."

The second passage, while bemoaning the red tape encountered at the American Consulate, introduces a detail that Clemens would later use in *Huckleberry Finn* to alleviate Huck's distress when Mary Jane asks him to swear on a book that his stories about England are true. Besides having to fill out blanks in triplicate and pay a fee for doing so, Clemens says, one must swear an oath and "kiss the book (years ago they found it was a dictionary)." And then he concludes: "We do hunt up more ways to save at the spigot and lose at the bung than any other idiotic government afloat," adding a reminder to himself to "speak of our diplomatic service."

Clemens' current political interests appear more clearly, however, in "Property in Opulent London," one of the other pieces published in the *Sketches* pamphlet of 1874. Though commenting satirically on the unjust tax burden placed upon the middle and lower classes as a result of the ridiculously low revenues from the great areas in London owned by noblemen, it also reveals his continued antipathy toward the principle of universal suffrage. In England anyone who rented or owned a home could vote, he explained—"that is to say, a man who pays rates, or taxes—for there is no law here which gives a useless idler the privilege of disposing of public moneys furnished by other people."

And near the end of the journal that he sent to Olivia he broke off his narrative to address her directly. After several "homey" notes he epitomized his appreciation of the British by a spontaneous exclamation: "I do like these English people—they are perfectly splendid—and so says every American who has staid here any length to time."

Possibly Routledge's letter in June, 1874, regretting that the publication of the three pieces in the American News Company pamphlet meant loss of English copyright and hence would damage the future book,[21] had something to do with the failure to complete the manuscripts. But at least equally responsible was Clemens' affection for the English, which made him unwilling to subject them to anything but gentle satire.

Not that he was above poking some fun at the British, even to their faces. In his address to the Savage Club on September 28, 1872, he had joked about the chaotic statuary in Leicester Square and, a bit more sharply, about the exclusiveness of Hyde Park, where none but private carriages were allowed to enter. Early in December, 1873, he wrote a somewhat audacious note to the London *Morning Post,* as a device to stimulate interest in his new lecture series. Because, he said, his performances had as yet lacked the distinction of being attended by notable government figures, he had contracted with a wax-works man for "a couple of kings and some nobility." But disaster had doomed the plan. In moving the replicas to the hall, the porter had fallen and smashed Henry VIII, and something had let go in William the Conqueror so that all the sawdust fell out. The several dukes that he had "collared," he was forced to give up, too, because they "were so seedy and decayed that nobody would ever have believed their rank." Begging for pity rather than censure for his failure, Mark Twain hoped that he "could get a king somewhere, just only for a little while," promising to "take good care of him, and send him home, and pay the cab myself."[22]

Anyone who sees serious satire either in the Savage Club Speech or in this publicity stunt is mistaken. Clemens was not specifically satirizing "the snobbish tendencies of the great British public," as the Belfast *Northern Whig* jubilantly announced in reprinting the piece.[23] (Perhaps, as Paul Fatout suggests, he actually hoped to attract some member of the royal family to his performance.) Basically the letter represents the same sort of fun he was to engage in at the Whittier dinner when he would dress the "literary gods of New England" in disreputable miner's clothing. In both instances, the narrator of the piece is intended to be the real butt of the joke. In this case, if many were offended by his treatment of nobility and royalty in the *Morning Post* sketch, the box office receipts for the remainder of his lecture series did not show it.

During the half-decade following his return home, Clemens' love for England and approval of the British system left their mark on public and private comments alike. He was now firmly convinced that the chief cause of all political ills in the United States lay in the "curse" of universal suffrage. That many of his friends in England, like Frank Finlay, were members of the Liberal Party and supporters of William Gladstone would not have affected this attitude. At this time few if any Liberals even those in that party's Radical wing, were advocating extending the vote to all the people. In seeking a cure for current abuses, Clemens did propose extension of the suffrage in one direction—to women. Whereas in 1867 he had written a series of letters to the St. Louis *Missouri Democrat* satirizing the movement for female suffrage, now in February, 1875, he treated his friends of the Hartford Monday Evening Club to a discussion of the advantages to be gained by allowing women to vote.[24] That same year, he devised a more nearly complete prescription for reform, which found its way into the October *Atlantic Monthly* as "The Curious Republic of Gondour."

Dismissed by some as mere whimsy, that article was eminently serious. Clemens insisted that it appear anonymously,[25] lest his pen name detract from its message. In the Swiftian guise of a first-hand report from a recent visitor, the sketch outlined the "curious" republic's eradication of governmental corruption.

First had come a revision of Gondour's voting system so as to remove control of elections from "the ignorant and non-taxpaying classes," largely by granting of from one to nine additional votes, depending upon the voter's educational qualifications. A citizen might gain additional votes in proportion to the increase in value of his property. But care was taken that educated men should always be able to outvote wealthy ones; since learning usually presupposed "uprightness, broad views, and humanity," the educated would protect the rights of "the great lower rank of society."

With governing power thus in the hands of those best fitted to exercise it, government service itself was soon revolutionized. Candidates for office submitted to examinations requiring broad general information as well as knowledge of the position sought. All civil service appointments and promotions were made subject to regular examinations and thus were no longer available through a "jump from gin mills" or to "the needy family and friends of members of parliament." The resulting improvement in the civil service immeasurably increased governmental efficiency, since minor officials and their staffs were retained even when changes in administration brought the appointments of new ministers and chiefs to the large departments. Additional continuity in government resulted from the fact that the Grand Caliph—the titular head of state —now held office for twenty years. He was subject, of course, like all public officials, to impeachment and dismissal for misconduct. Most of the real governing power, however, lay in the hands of the ministers and the parliament.

Clemens' debt to the British system is immediately apparent: the position of the caliph was virtually that of the English king, save that it was elective rather than hereditary. Even the length of term resembled that of a monarch's reign. The provision for competitive examinations, likewise, derived directly from procedures followed by the British Civil Service, which had fully adopted such tests in 1870, only two years before Clemens' first visit to England.

Not so obvious, but fully as derivative, was the design for extension of the suffrage. Clemens may have first encountered the idea of plural votes in the very similar proposals advanced by John Stuart Mill in the late 1850's and early sixties. More likely, he had read of the efforts of Disraeli to incorporate educational and financial qualifications for plural votes in the Reform Bill of 1867.[26] While in England he may well have heard British acquaintances who shared his fear of misuse of the suffrage still discussing the failure to include such provisions in the final version of the Reform Bill. As implied in "Property in Opulent London," he heartily agreed with the qualifications for voting that the Bill did include.

After "Gondour" Clemens continued to expound upon American failure in that direction with a vehemence that sometimes startled his listeners. One April evening in 1876, for instance, when the conversation turned to education and then to the country in general, he treated his guests to a vigorous restatement of the "Gondour" plan. To Annie Fields, wife of publisher James T. Fields, it seemed apparent that Clemens had "lost all faith in our government," and she quoted and paraphrased some of his explosion in her diary: "This wicked ungodly suffrage, he said, where the vote of a man who knew nothing was as good as the vote of a man of education and industry; this endeavor to equalize what God had made unequal was a wrong and a shame. He only hoped to see such a wrong and such a government overthrown. . . . 'It is too late now,' he continued, 'to restrict the suffrage; we must increase it—for this let us give every university man, let us say, ten votes, and every man with a common school education two votes, and a man of superior power and position a hundred votes if we choose. This is the only way I see to get out of the false position into which we have fallen.' " His "shame and confusion" was such, Mrs. Fields concluded, that he was seriously considering making England his home, at least for a time.[27]

Though discouraged, Clemens remained convinced that if only the best-qualified men could assume leading roles in government, a near-utopia would result. There were occasional rumblings of his later conviction that human nature itself created almost insurmountable obstacles to progress. But these rumblings were few.[28] When Rutherford B. Hayes in 1876 promised sweeping civil service reforms, he won Clemens' wholehearted and active support. At a September 30 rally in Hartford the humorist explained that he was abandoning his traditional indifference to politics because at last there seemed a chance for good government and "an honest and sensible system of civil service" to replace the "idiotic" procedures "born of General Jackson and the Democratic party. . . ." Developing his theme, he listed various qualifications for other occupations, concluding (as reported by the Hartford Courant): "We even require a plumber to know something (Laughter, and a pause by the speaker) about his business (More laughter), that he shall at least know which side of a gas pipe is the inside (Shouts). . . ." But still, he said, "we serenely fill great numbers of our minor public offices with ignoramuses." And again he cited specific instances.[29]

William Dean Howells, who had written Hayes' campaign biography and had often urged Clemens to speak out, was especially pleased with the performance. Writing about a week later, he moaned a bit over the limited sales of his *Life of Hayes* but rejoiced in his friend's achievement: "Your speech was civil service reform in a nutshell. You are the only Republican orator quoted without distinction of party by all the newspapers, and I wish you could have gone largely into the canvass. Lowell was delighted with your hit at plumbers."[30] Both Clemens and Howells applauded the outcome of the long and bitterly contested campaign.

But if they had anticipated immediate or lasting progress, they were to be disappointed. Hayes did institute examinations for some positions, but no real improvement resulted.[31] As his hope waned, Clemens' view of government in the United States grew more and more bleak, and he continued among his friends to preach what amounted to sedition.

The deepening of Clemens' disillusionment with democracy during the 1870's was also stimulated by his reading. During the early years of the decade he first encountered works of two British authors, Thomas Carlyle and W.E.H. Lecky, whose ideas he would continue to weigh for most of his ensuing life. At this period, he for the most part agreed with both; later, at times, he was to react violently against some of their views.

Clemens probably first read Lecky's *History of European Morals from Augustus to Charlemagne* in 1874, some five years after its first publication. Again and again in later writings, he introduced ideas derived from Lecky. These will be discussed in connection with specific works. But, generally, Lecky's panoramic account of man's age-long enslavement to superstition doubtless helped to solidify the humorist's current conviction that the common man was incapable of ordering his own political affairs wisely.

Perhaps more immediately stimulating was Clemens' introduction in 1871 to Carlyle's vivid history of the French Revolution, a book he would soon call "one of the greatest creations that ever flowed from a pen."[32] That first reading aligned Clemens with the Girondins, the moderate constitutional monarchists, whom Carlyle also favored. The historian's graphic portrayal of "the howling waste of the Sansculottic earthquake" must have supplemented his own growing distrust of the masses.[33] And Carlyle's recurrent wonder at the depths to which man could sink struck responsive chords that produced their echoes during these and later years.

"The Curious Republic of Gondour" arose out of similar emotions, echoing also by implication Carlyle's scorn for representative governments as they were usually constituted. The American surely found a kindred spirit in the Scotsman's denunciation of fumbling attempts by the French National Assembly to frame a constitution. "Is it," Carlyle asks, "the nature of National Assemblies generally to do, with endless labour and clangour, Nothing? Are Representative Governments mostly at bottom Tyrannies too? Shall we say, the *Tyrants,* the ambitious contentious Persons, from all corners of the country do, in this manner, get gathered into one place; and there with motion and counter-motion . . . *cancel* one another, like the fabulous Kilkenny cats; and produce for net result, *zero;*—the country meanwhile *governing* or guiding *itself,* by such wisdom, recognized, or for the most part, unrecognized, as may exist in individual heads here and there?—Nay, even that were a great improvement . . . ." How like Clemens' own pronouncements on legislative bodies is Carlyle's partial answer to his own questions: "One thing an elected Assembly of Twelve Hundred is fit for: Destroying. Which indeed is but a more decided exercise of its natural talent for Doing Nothing. Do nothing, only keep agitating, debating; and things will destroy themselves."[34] In a system like that of Gondour the wisdom in the "individual heads" mentioned by Carlyle would be utilized properly.

In another direction, Carlyle quite probably contributed to the vigor of Clemens' attack on journalistic irresponsibility in the "License of the Press" speech. Scorn for the "Fourth Estate" permeates Carlyle's references to "the thick murk of Journalism" with its "dull blustering" and its "fixed or loose fury."[35] Clemens' fear of "that awful power, the public opinion of a nation," had found eloquent expression in Carlyle. "What king or convention can withstand it?" he almost shouts; and shortly thereafter he pronounces the "deafening Force of Public Opinion, from the Twenty-five million windpipes of a Nation" to be all but irresistible.[36]

Probably it was Carlyle's attitudes toward the masses and toward representative government more than his portrait of revolutionary excesses, that most reinforced Clemens' own distrust of popular government. Even before reading *The French Revolution,* Clemens had not had much sympathy for the revolutionaries. In *The Inno-cents Abroad* (Chapter Sixteen) he had described the Faubourg St. Antoine as the "breeding place" of revolutions, the home of a people, who "take as much genuine pleasure in building a barricade as they do in cutting a throat or shoving a friend into the Seine." These are the "savage-looking ruffians," he said, "who storm the splendid halls of the Tuileries, occasionally, and swarm into Versailles when a king is to be called to account." At the same time he seems to have shared Carlyle's pity for France's beautiful Queen, for he mentions that the furniture in her quarters at Versailles was "just as poor Marie Antoinette left it when the mob came and dragged her and the king to Paris, never to return."

That compassion for Marie and the less than laudatory comment on the French slum-dwellers may actually have been inspired by Horace Walpole, whose letters (in the nine-volume edition of 1861–66) occupied a favored spot in Clemens' library. When he first read Walpole's accounts of contemporary events in France is not certain, but marginal comments and underlinings show his complete agreement with Walpole's abhorrence of revolutionary barbarism, and at least imply his sympathy with the Englishman's obvious pity for the French queen. He pencils "Amen," for instance, to Walpole's horror at the fearful massacre of the Swiss Guards during the debacle of 10 August. Next to an assertion that "the French, by antecedent as well as by recent proofs, have never been fit to be unchained at once, so innate is their savage barbarity," he writes, "Gospel Truth," adding his own emphasis by underlining Walpole's last nine words. In another place, too, he marks as if for future reference a vivid passage where Walpole follows a horrified account of the French "demons" beating an old lady to death while forcing her to watch her son being roasted alive on a spit, with the question, "If the French kings have been tyrants, what are the French people?"[37]

Surely Clemens had read Walpole's letters when in 1879 he wrote in his notebook: "The Reign of Terror shows that, without distinction of rank, the people were savages. Marquises, dukes, lawyers, blacksmiths, they each figure in due proportion to their crafts."[38]

But it was probably Carlyle who led him in 1876 and 1877 to undertake an extensive course of reading in the literature of the French Revolution. In addition to re-reading Carlyle's book he pored through a number of volumes of fiction, history, and biography, both French and English. Among the French works he included Taine's *The Ancient Regime,* Dumas' *The Taking of the Bastille,* and another novel illustrating "the march of the rioters on Versailles, the massacre upon the Champ de Mars, the frightful scenes of the 10th of August & 2d of September, &c." An unidentified story by Mme. de Genlis and "a small history of France," both in French completed the list. From England came Sabine Baring-Gould's *In Exitu Israel,* which Clemens found to be a "very able novel," and a two-volume *Life of Marie Antoinette* by Charles D. Yonge.[39]

Yonge's book was perhaps responsible for Clemens' eventual loss of sympathy for Marie Antoinette, the only apparent change of attitude resulting from his studies of the revolutionary era. In his opinion, the biographer's attempt to make the reader a "pitying & lamenting friend" of the Queen succeeded only in making him loathe her and rejoice at her execution.

In reporting these various reactions, Clemens also noted that only Carlyle, Dumas, and some of Taine had been very valuable for his "subject." Significantly, Dumas, and even Taine, were in some ways as conservative as Carlyle in stressing the atrocities committed by the revolutionaries. Dumas' hero, Dr. Gilbert, is a moderate, who realizes that France is not ready for democracy. And though the novel mentions the suffering inflicted by the aristocracy, it not only dramatizes, but specifically condemns, the excesses of the mobs. Taine, though severely critical of the nobility, deplores the naïveté and savagery of those who would destroy an entire building in attempting to admit light and air, much as those elements might be needed. Moreover, he also stresses the need for controls and the necessity of educating the people to understand the responsibilities of citizenship.

Such considerations influenced Clemens' current opinions far more than did the several portrayals of aristocratic abuses during the *ancien régime.* At the same time, given his affection for England during these years, the humorist surely responded sympathetically to Taine's frequent quotations from British historian Arthur Young to illustrate the superiority of conditions in eighteenth-century England to those in France. He would also have shared Taine's admiration for the participation in public life by England's upper classes, who understood the difficulties of leading and controlling men, and for the resultant creation of an atmosphere in which revolutionary ideas did not take strong hold.

Even more specifically, Clemens would have found *The Ancient Regime*—his edition was that of 1876—almost echoing the words of his own "Gondour" of the year before. Not only did Taine make clear his conviction that the Third Estate was not equipped to rule, but in denouncing Rousseau, he especially attacked the latter's insistence that "neither birth nor property, nor function, nor capacity are titles to be considered; high or low, ignorant or learned, a general, a soldier, or a hod-carrier, each individual of the social army is a unit provided with a vote; wherever a majority is found, there is the right."[40]

Clemens' own feelings on this subject had coalesced in the summer of 1876 into one of the most successfully scathing passages of irony he ever wrote. His contempt for the general mass of voters spilled into Chapter Six of *Huckleberry Finn* in which the despicable, ignorant, verminous Pap announces his displeasure with a "govment" so ill-run as to let a Negro vote:

"They said he was a p'fessor in a college," Pap says to Huck, "and could talk all kinds of languages, and knowed everything. And that ain't the wust. They said he could *vote* when he was at home. Well, that let me out. Thinks I, what is the country a-coming to. It was 'lection day, and I was just about to go and vote myself if I warn't too drunk to get there; but when they told me there was a State in this country where they'd let that nigger vote, I drawed out. . . . The country may rot for all of me—I'll never vote ag'in as long as I live." Here, in one vivid flash, was the prototype of the masses of voters as Clemens had come to see them.

Although his "subject" of 1876–77 was chiefly the era of the French Revolution, Clemens did extend the range of his reading to consider other efforts to establish representative government. On a vacation trip to Bermuda in 1877 he had begun John Lothrop Motley's *The Rise of the Dutch Republic*. The effort was not a pleasant one, however, for he ended by so cordially despising "those pitiful Dutchmen & their execrable Republic," that he wanted to throw the book into the sea.[41] His conclusions about republics in general, we shall see in a moment.

The stay in Bermuda brought a new bloom to the American's love for things British. He applauded the sight of "the British flag flying," as "a symbol of efficient government and good order," and growled in mock fury at "the spectacle of an entire nation groveling in contentment."[42] At home again, he did not have to wait long for an unfortunate contrast to that efficiency and order.

Some three months after his return, a newspaper item announced that a small schooner, the *Jonas Smith,* was adrift in the Gulf Stream. Amazed, he remembered that his own ship had provided food and water to that very vessel on the homeward voyage. He was annoyed at the stupidity of the sailors, but thought that the United States government should come to their aid. Attempting to stimulate action, he wrote a long letter on September 19 to the Hartford *Courant* and another on the same day to William Dean Howells, condemning the ineffective procedures of the revenue cutter *Colfax* which went "a little way" the other day to search for them, "& then struck a fog & gave it up." Almost as an afterthought, he added that the *Colfax* had sought the *Jonas Smith* on the assumption that "there was mutiny or other crime aboard." But, he continued, "it occurs to me now that since there is only mere suffering & misery & nobody to punish, it ceases to be a matter which (a republican form of) government will feel authorized to interfere in further. Dam a republican form of government."[43]

But the climactic pronouncement of his current political opinions Clemens had penned to Mollie Fairbanks, the daughter of his Cleveland friend, the month before the *Jonas Smith* incident. After discussing his reading of the past year (which had included the books on the French Revolution), he said: "You may easily suppose that I hate all shades & forms of republican government now—or rather with an intensified hatred, for I always hated them." His reading of Motley's *Dutch Republic* had only increased that hatred further. Then, winding up his blast, he thundered: "Mind, I believe this: Republican government, with a sharply restricted suffrage, is just as good as a Constitutional monarchy with a virtuous & powerful aristocracy; but with an unrestricted suffrage it ought to . . . perish because it is founded in wrong & is weak & bad & tyrannical."[44]

Here at the peak of Clemens' abhorrence of universal suffrage, such a statement of political belief, and especially the conviction that a republic with a sharply restricted suffrage was *"just as good"* as a Constitutional monarchy, underscores the extent of his approval of the British system. As always, his desire was for the best possible government for his own country, and at this period and for the remainder of the decade, his model very clearly was England.

Chapter Three

Europe Once More

(1878-1879)

I

THE YEAR 1877 WAS NOT HAPPY FOR CLEMENS. The brightness
of the springtime Bermuda vacation faded as literary failures
and personal unpleasantnesses deepened the shadows of his general despondency. A double discouragement attended collaboration with Bret Harte on the play *Ah Sin*. Not only did the play
die after brief autumn runs in Baltimore, New York, and on the
road, but ten years of friendship with Harte perished with it.
Clemens' own play, *Cap'n Simon Wheeler, The Amateur Detective*, was stillborn for lack of a producer. But the nadir was ahead.

When William Dean Howells asked the humorist to be one of
the principal speakers at the dinner on December 17 commemo-
rating John Greenleaf Whittier's seventieth birthday, he gladly accepted. Some fifty-eight of America's most famous men of letters
were to be official guests of the *Atlantic Monthly;* other guests, including ladies, would be admitted for the postprandial speeches.
Much larger than the gathering at the *Atlantic* dinner two years
earlier (at which he responded to one of the toasts) this affair provided a splendid opportunity for the humorist to win from the literary elite of his own nation the same sort of applause that the
British had so generously bestowed.

[33

The speech proved a fiasco. Though the listeners laughed a good deal, Clemens must have sensed that they were not wholly appreciating his farcical anecdote about the three card-playing, whiskey-drinking tramps who impersonated Emerson, Longfellow, and Holmes. His "hideous mistake" (as Howells called it) left him desolate. Newspaper reviews, hurling charges that he had grossly insulted the nation's literary idols, compounded his dismay.[1]

Not the least among the causes of his distress was the ignominy of failing at home when he had succeeded so well in England. There he could joke about seedy dukes and stuffed kings without serious repercussions. But in America the aura surrounding the "Brahmins" was apparently such that to disturb it in any way was blasphemy. Small wonder that the humorist clipped for his scrap-book one of the pieces that appeared in mid-January in the London *World's* series, "Celebrities at Home." For there, in glowing contrast to the sneers at the "Backwoods bull in the Boston china shop," were plaudits for the "rare artistic taste" of the Clemens home and for the acute political opinions and excellent literary taste of its owner.[2]

The Whittier dinner with its aftermath was something of a "last straw" on the load of political exasperations, literary disappointments, business "responsibilities and annoyances," and multitudes of letters from "well-meaning strangers," all of which had been plaguing Clemens for some time. Money problems had also become acute, for the style of living to which the family had grown accustomed devoured funds at an alarming rate. The "badgered, harassed feeling" resulting from all of these irritations[3] served in turn to frustrate any current literary efforts. Among other projects, *The Prince and the Pauper* fell by the wayside sometime in February or March, with only a few chapters completed.

The only way out seemed to lie in another European trip. Clemens had planned such a voyage several times during the preceding two years, but each time important matters had interfered. Now he could scarcely wait to sail. It would be good, he wrote on March 28, to "breathe the free air of Europe and lay in a stock of self-respect and independence" and to cease feeling "so cowed . . . so deferential to all sorts of clerks and little officials."*

The sea voyage itself brought little peace, or perhaps it was Clemens' own mood which made him overly conscious of crying

* Notebook 12, TS, p. 4, Mark Twain Papers.

babies, noisy children, the pounding of the propeller, and the jangling of an "old cracked kettle of a piano." And when the ship steamed through the English Channel en route to Hamburg, memories of his earlier visits crowded in, and he found it "heartbreaking" to see "the lovely shores of England" without being able to land there.* But once the family was established in Germany, he forgot that disappointment in a "deep, grateful, unutterable sense of being 'out of it all.' " Germany seemed to him a paradise of cleanliness, contentment, prosperity, and good government, and Kaiser Wilhelm I, a "splendid old hero."[4] With the end of June he was able to announce to Howells the cessation of another source of strain. *"We've quit feeling poor!"* he exulted, underlining the sentence for emphasis.

These euphoric moods lingered for a time, but again passed away as the party toured Germany, Italy, and France during 1878 and early 1879. As minor annoyances grew into major ones, work on the new book was sporadic at best. In January, 1879, Clemens responded a touch irascibly to Howells' anticipation of the sharp satires on European life that he would be presenting. Satire required a "calm, judicial good-humor," he said, but he was never in "a good enough humor with ANYthing to *satirize* it"; he merely wanted "to stand up before it & *curse* it, . . . or take a club & pound it to rags & pulp."[5]

If any embers of joy in being in Europe still glowed through the several illnesses of Olivia and the children, and a few bronchial attacks of his own, they flickered only fitfully during the damp, cold spring of 1879 in France. Out of the ashes rose smoking diatribes directed principally at French manners and *mores,* vivid enough in the published versions of his notebook and of *A Tramp Abroad,* but pallid and sparse there compared with lengthy comments ultimately omitted from both. "France has neither winter nor summer nor morals," he wrote in one of the published notebook entries, and added ironically, "apart from these drawbacks it is a fine country."[6]

But there seemed a chance that the glow might be rekindled as the time approached for the Clemenses to leave France for a month in England. Earlier in the year the author had jotted down some complimentary notes concerning the comfort of English railways, the trustfulness of London merchants, and the voluminous reading

* Ibid., p. 10

matter in the London *Times*. Among the few things he had found to complain of were such momentous matters as colors in English dress, "execrable" toast, and the fact that the only thing in the world which one could not buy in London was a good potato.[7] When Reginald Cholmondeley, who had entertained the Clemenses in 1873, invited them to spend a week at Condover Hall, his country estate near Shrewsbury, the prospect of revisiting England was more than ever attractive.

Although this English visit lasted so short a time, Clemens renewed many old acquaintanceships and made some new ones. He complained occasionally about the bad weather which had followed the family from France, but there is little reason to infer that the visit as a whole was unpleasant. The gatherings at Condover Hall included Sir John Millais and his wife, "numerous relatives, and other delightful company." At a dinner in London the Clemenses met James Whistler and Henry James; the latter Olivia found "exceedingly pleasant and easy to talk with." She did not find Whistler equally charming, but Clemens apparently thought enough of him, or at least of his work, to ask Andrew Chatto, the publisher, to secure one of Whistler's etchings as a gift for Clara Spaulding.[8]

On another evening, Clemens was delighted to learn that Charles Lutwidge Dodgson was among the dinner guests. A long-time admirer of Lewis Carroll, he was anxious to hear what the author of "the immortal *Alice*" might have to say. Unfortunately, that author said almost nothing, his excessive shyness apparently preventing him from offering more than brief answers to questions directed at him. "The stillest and shyest full-grown man I have ever met except 'Uncle Remus' [Joel Chandler Harris]," Clemens later called him. The experience did not alter his respect, however, for he would tell an Australian reporter in 1895 that he had always regarded Lewis Carroll as " a true and subtle humorist."

Dodgson was not so disappointed as Clemens in the encounter. One may be sure that a considerable portion of the "lovely talk" that he noted in his diary issued from the lips of Mark Twain. If he was really as reticent as Clemens thought, his further entry doubtless represents something of an accolade: "Met Mr. Clemens (Mark Twain), with whom I was pleased and interested."[9]

Two side-trips that August proved especially fascinating for the Clemenses. On the first, the humorist told Livy that they were going to the village of Epworth. When they reached their destination, a carriage met them at the station and drove them to a small church. There, to Livy's joyous astonishment they were shown a gravestone bearing the famous epitaph that begins, "Good friend for Jesus' sake forbeare . . . ." Clemens' pleasure in the success of his subterfuge made them relish even more the chance to visit the many Stratford landmarks which they had read about so often. The second excursion, on August 19, Clemens recorded in his notebook: "Went up Windemere [*sic*] Lake in the steamer. Talked with the great Darwin."[10] Unfortunately, no indication of the content of that memorable conversation has survived, though Clemens was again to recall the occasion late in May, 1882, concluding that he was "glad to have seen that mighty man."*

With this visit the year-and-a-half of roving neared its end. Four days later the family was aboard the *Gallia* bound for home. From New York City, where they docked on September third, they traveled directly to Elmira. There, after a trip to Fredonia, New York, to see his mother, Clemens was finally able to relax for a few days before plunging again into the long-in-progress history of his "tramp" abroad.

II

The trip had benefited Clemens in one respect. He came home with a much kindlier feeling toward his own nation. Largely responsible for that softening was the antipathy toward France which had developed during his stay there, and possibly, a lessening of his former affection for England. Basically, however, his political views remained unchanged.

It was primarily in the area of manners and morals that the United States took on new respectability. His many diatribes against the French, both past and present, leave no doubt that an essential element of Clemens' antagonism was what Walter Blair has so aptly called "the un-American attitude of France toward sex."[11] In these deliberations also may be seen the first serious signs of the author's tendency to equate sexual morality with "civilization" as well as with political morality. This tendency, in turn, was to become a major influence on his subsequent attitude toward England and on the genesis of *A Connecticut Yankee*.

* Notebook 16, TS, p. 36, Mark Twain Papers.

Two notebook entries from the summer of 1879, when Clemens was still in Paris, reveal his current mood. After observing that France had usually been governed by prostitutes, he professed to be comforted by a backward glance at history, for it showed him that "bad as our gov't is, it is a mighty improvement on old times."[12] A few pages later he was more explicit. Scoring French "savagery" and immorality in general, he concluded that by and large America was the "most civilized of all nations," that pure-minded women were the rule "in every rank of life of the *native-born*," and that American men, too, were clean-minded "beyond the world's average."*

Such an identification of purity (or at least feminine purity of mind) with "civilization" does not, however, necessarily indicate excessive prudishness in Clemens. Rather it reveals him as a firm advocate of the Victorian code which sought to spare the fragile feminine mind from coarseness of any sort, especially from anything smacking of sex. The humorist was no scorner of ribaldry or bawdry in its "proper" place. One need only remember that three years before this entry his fascination with the frank indecencies of some "ancient English books" had produced *1601. Conversation, as it was by the Social Fireside, in the time of the Tudors.* But that had been strictly for private male consumption, as had his speech to the Stomach Club in Paris, "Some Thoughts on the Science of Onanism." It was *public* coarseness and indelicacy, contemporary or historical, that was so offensive to him.

Some of the beginnings of his cooling toward England may have arisen from the same sort of reflections on manners. The only really serious criticism of the British in *A Tramp Abroad,* in fact, resulted from the American's having felt obliged to defend his countrymen against European charges of crudity. Angered at one point when a young English dandy in Geneva insolently lounged into the path of a young lady, causing her to interrupt her stroll, the humorist sarcastically ventured to claim "one little matter of superiority" in American manners. Whereas in America, he said, an unescorted lady might come and go as she pleased, in London, for example, she was likely to be accosted and insulted even at noon—"and not by drunken sailors, but by men who carry the look and wear the dress of gentlemen."[13]

Clemens was not at this time, however, much concerned with

* Notebook 14, TS, p. 29, Mark Twain Papers.

matters of rank and caste in England. In his notebook attacks on the French in June, 1879, he said that only their basic savagery could have allowed the handing down of such "atrocious privileges" through many generations—"England could not have done it."* Yet, just after arriving in Paris the preceding February, he had written that the English should not piously proclaim their superiority to the Zulus, "for it is very plain that they have been better for no more than a hundred years." Now they were a "fine and pure and elevated people," but between the Roman invasion and a hundred years ago they had been but "a small improvement" on the Shoshone Indians.[14]

The apparent contradiction fades when one notices that though the reference to the Zulus was perhaps inspired by a newspaper report, the underlying stimulus was again very likely a moral one arising directly out of Clemens' current literary pursuits: his most recent reading was Henry Fielding's *Tom Jones*. In the note immediately preceding the comment on the English, in fact, Clemens had described Fielding's novel as "disgusting." What he found most distasteful was Tom's "gambling and whoring and beggary . . . ," and he doubtless considered such activities typical of English life in past centuries. A month later he was to say in so many words that the memory of times like those pictured in *Tom Jones* and *Roderick Random* defiled literature and was not fit to be preserved.** He had not, however, carried over any of that moral stigma to contemporary Englishmen as the "Shoshone" quotation clearly indicates. The seeds of antagonism toward contemporary Britain which apparently sprouted during the voyage home were nourished chiefly by his irritation at English manners.

A long notebook passage which he wrote aboard the *Gallia* shows the humorist torn between respect for England and her people and resentment that England did not properly appreciate America and Americans. For the latter attitude he blamed the English press. "All English individuals are kind and likable," he said, but "the newspapers are snobbish, pretentious . . ." Their scoffing at America or, worse yet, contemptuously ignoring her was bound to undo the efforts of English religious and political leaders to insure mutual respect and friendship between the two countries. "The nations are at their friendliest now," he said, "—the widening apart has

* Notebook 14, TS, p. 26, Mark Twain Papers.
** Notebook 14, TS, pp. 4, 12, Mark Twain Papers.

begun—the separation will be complete in a generation."[15] In that last opinion, he was to prove a better prophet of his own future feelings than of the course which Anglo-American relations themselves were to take, save that his estrangement would take place in less than a decade.

There was an element of personal pique in Clemens' attack, for in at least one instance the British press had been less complimentary than he doubtless thought it should have been. His continuing notebook entry criticizing the British failure to appreciate American literature and America in general, seems almost an answer to a piece in the London *Daily News* of January 29, 1879. Commenting on one of Bret Harte's current lectures in London, the reviewer described Harte's humor as "much more English and less thoroughly Yankee" than that of his contemporaries and as more "humane" than the "amazing paradoxes of Mark Twain." Such implied praise of his old-friend-turned-enemy would have been irritating enough, but the reviewer also went on to cite *The Innocents Abroad* as an example of how American humor inevitably failed. He concluded, moreover, that its lack of sympathy and reverence would prevent this humor from ever reaching the heights of that of Dickens and Thackeray.[16] The latter remark, especially, must have rankled.

This *Daily News* review stung Clemens enough to make him clip it and paste it into a scrapbook. And in the notebook entry just referred to, he growled that the growing American tendency to "praise everything English and do it affectionately" would soon cease because of the English failure to meet his country even half way. Broadening his range in a burst of boosterism, he noted that English criticism no longer hurt as it had when America was smaller; that presently we would be "indifferent to being looked down upon by a nation no bigger and no better than our own." Finally, after listing various examples of American superiority in technology and invention, he returned to literature to proclaim that "Nobody writes a finer and purer English than Motley, Howells, Hawthorne and Holmes."

It is possible that the stay at Condover Hall also helped kindle the spark that flickered here. In one of the never-finished attacks that Clemens wrote against Matthew Arnold in 1888 in answer to charges that Americans lacked culture, he catalogued certain acts of boorishness observed at an English country house "several years

ago": a squabble at dinner over precedence in seating arrange-
ments, ironically solved when all "bowed meekly" to the arrival of
an earl's daughter; the rudeness of a baronet's asking if there were
any such thing as an American gentleman; supposedly cultivated
ladies dominating conversation with topics obviously unfamiliar
and uninteresting to many of the guests.[17]

Yet if Condover Hall had been the scene of these unpleasantnesses, or if Clemens had been thoroughly disturbed at the time, it
seems strange that a blast had not immediately found its way into
a notebook or letter. Perhaps even in his private jottings he was
adhering to a code which he presumably tried to follow:—"that
when a man takes you into his house, he tacitly takes you into his
confidence, and it would be a graceless thing to abuse it."[18] But it
is more likely that he regarded the incident as annoying but unimportant and was reminded of it only when Arnold's citation of
American faults stung him into responding in kind.

With all this, however, Clemens' political views remained relatively unchanged.[19] He had arrived in Europe in the spring of 1879
with an idea for *Captain Stormfield's Visit to Heaven* freshly written down. He instructed himself to "have some people dissatisfied
because Heaven is an absolute monarchy, with many viceroys, when
they expected a leatherheaded Republic with the damnation of
unrestricted suffrage." Six months later in Munich the explanation that Switzerland had reinstated capital punishment because it
was cheaper to hang a criminal than to feed him during current
hard times evoked a sneer: "Go way with your monarchical statesmanship, only republics have real statesmanship." Sometime during the trip, too, in a chapter intended for *A Tramp Abroad* but
later omitted, he had returned to a favorite theme, this time proposing that by virtue of "the awful curse of an unrestricted suffrage," the United States was the only really absolute monarchy
remaining in the world. For there "The Majority" is king and
rules by "the right of possessing less money, less brains and more
ignorance" than his competitor for the throne, "The Minority."
This Majority, Clemens concluded, "*always* represents the mass of
the Ignorance and Incapacity of his land, for these he *is*, they are
his body's substance."*

In Paris there had been a new burst of interest in the French

---

* Notebook 12, TS, pp. 16–17; Notebook 13, TS, p. 30; DV 4, Mark Twain Papers.

Revolution, Clemens again read widely in French history and, with Dickens' *A Tale of Two Cities* and Carlyle's vivid chronicle as principal guides, took his family to see landmarks made famous by the Reign of Terror. The readings in Carlyle and other authors in 1876–77 had pretty well established Clemens' scorn for the revolutionary mobs, though he had not been indifferent to the evidences of ruling class tyranny and oppression. Now, in 1879, he was struck anew by the savagery of the whole French nation, not only "the lower classes, for that goes without saying—but the uppers." Still, the commoners often fared worse than the nobles as in his March 21 emendation of the famous motto of the Revolution: "Liberty (to rob . . . burn and butcher)—Equality (in bestiality)—Fraternity (of Devils)."*

For his view of the Revolution itself, Clemens seems still to have drawn heavily upon Carlyle. In a long passage retained in the final version of *A Tramp Abroad* (Chapter Twenty-six), as well as in passages ultimately omitted, he fully espouses Carlyle's moderate view. Like the Scotsman, he characterizes the Revolution as "beneficent but hideous," condemns the vacillations of King Louis, scorns the raging mobs, and admires the strong, forceful leader.

Speaking of the tragic September massacres of 1792, for instance, Carlyle had vividly painted the paradoxical blend of beneficence and horror when he described the month's "two most diverse aspects"—"all of black on the one side, all of bright on the other"—and saw "Sansculottism reigning in all its grandeur and in all its hideousness." The "blackest Consummation" of that hideousness had come for Carlyle with the December *"noyades"* at Nantes when men and women were stripped naked, tied together in a "Marriage Republicain," and flung into the river. No doubt it was the Scotsman's description which prompted Clemens' special mention of that quaint ceremony in "The French and the Comanches," one of the passages later discarded. Moreover, in that same passage, the author all but echoed Carlyle when he referred to the French as embodying "the littlest littlenesses conceivable, and the greatest greatnesses."[20]

In discussing Louis XVI's part in the massacre of the Swiss Guards on August 10, 1792, although other sources doubtless contributed some details, Clemens closely followed Carlyle's lead. To

* Notebook 14, TS, pp. 26, 10, Mark Twain Papers.

stress the complete inadequacy of the French ruler, he emphasized Louis' stubbornness as much as his irresolution. Yet here he also had a precedent in Carlyle, for the latter pointed out that with all his softness the King was not without "elements of will . . . spurting at times from a stagnating character."[21] As Mark Twain put it, King Louis "could not be persuaded to do a thing while it could do any good . . . but as soon as the thing had reached a point where it would be positively harmful to do it, do it he would, and nothing could stop him."

Mark Twain's Marie Antoinette, however, was not Carlyle's. If he had ever shared the Scotsman's sympathy for Marie, he had lost it in 1877. Now he accused her of equal responsibility with Louis for the fall of the French monarchy. Perhaps recalling his reactions to Charles Yonge's sentimentalized portrait, he ridiculed the efforts of even present-day biographers to make almost a saint of this "foolish" queen, who had contributed the one "calamitous instinct" her husband lacked, the ability to "root out and get rid of an honest, able, and loyal official, wherever she found him."

But in describing the blood-bath of 10 August, the American was back in the camp of Carlyle. The Scotsman considered the episode one of the most painful in the whole "history of carnage" and Louis' failure to support the Swiss Guards against the vicious mob an action totally unworthy of a king. Mark Twain calls the event "the most pitiable spectacle" in "a most unroyal career," charging Louis with "sentimental treachery" in ordering the Swiss heroes to cease firing on the "red-capped mob of miscreants." Then, almost as if remembering Carlyle's pointed reference to Napoleon's presence among the onlookers and the Corsican's opinion that a competent commander could have led the Swiss Guards to victory, he commented that had Napoleon been in charge that day instead of "merely a casual and unknown looker-on," there would be no Lion of Lucerne to commemorate the slaughter, but rather "a well-stocked Communist graveyard in Paris."[22] For Clemens, as for Carlyle, Napoleon was one of the great heroes of history.

Carlyle's treatment of history almost solely in terms of biography may also have helped solidify Clemens' own tendency to treat it similarly. It should immediately be added, however, that Clemens was at all times more capricious than Carlyle in assigning to individuals the responsibility for group or national faults. In this case, he concluded his castigation of the French monarchs with the sweeping charge that had it not been for Louis and his queen, the "hideous but beneficent French Revolution would have been deferred, or would have fallen short of completeness, or even might not have happened at all . . . ."

So vehement is the whole passage in its abhorrence of the revolutionary excesses and in its implication that reforms might best be instituted from the top, that one might well imagine Clemens urging Louis to action as Carlyle had done: "Summon the National Assembly to follow you, ... Thunder over France . . . commanding, not entreating, that this riot cease." And then rule "with utmost possible Constitutionality; doing justice, loving mercy;" and be "Shepherd of this indigent people, not Shearer merely. . . ."[23] Certainly, the American writer at this time was still far from his Connecticut Yankee's paean to the "ever memorable and blessed Revolution."

Obviously, Clemens had come home from this European trip with a broader conception of the frailties of mankind and a deeper conviction of man's need for the right kind of direction. Perhaps the most significant fictional representation of his current attitudes may be seen in yet another piece which he had intended for *A Tramp Abroad,* but published only in the March, 1879, *Atlantic Monthly* as "The Great Revolution in Pitcairn." In this wild yarn he shows how an American named Butterworth Stavely, by clever manipulation of several factions among Pitcairn Island's ninety inhabitants, engineers his own election as chief magistrate, a declaration of independence from England, and his coronation as Butterworth I. As a next step Stavely establishes orders of nobility and appoints ministers, generals, admirals, chamberlains, equerries-in-waiting, and the like. Inevitably factional jealousies arise; some rebellion occurs and is suitably punished. One newly "developed" Social Democrat even tries to assassinate the emperor with a harpoon, but "fortunately with such a peculiarly social democratic unprecision of aim as to do no damage."

But Butterworth I does not remain in power. Driven too far, the people finally revolt. Rehoisting the British flag and reinstating the British "tyranny," they reduce the nobility to the condition of commoners, and return to their "old useful industries and the old healing and solacing pieties." As for Stavely, when he restores a "lost" legal document, explaining that he had stolen it only to further his political projects, not to injure anyone, all is forgiven. His lands and his title of chief magistrate are returned to him. Even so, there is a final turn in Stavely's fortunes. When both he and the Social Democrat are sentenced, they are allowed to choose either perpetual banishment from church services or perpetual labor as galley slaves in the Island's one whale-boat. The fact that they choose banishment from services leads the people to believe that "the poor fellows' troubles had unseated their reason," and so they decide to confine them "for the present."

Some have argued that "The Great Revolution in Pitcairn" should rank high among Mark Twain's indictments of monarchy and class privilege. Far from it. Rather it is a condemnation of hypocritical piety and meanness of motive on the part of the mass of mankind which allows tyranny to prevail. Walter Blair is correct, I think, in assuming that Clemens meant this tale to be "a history of civilization in miniature."[24] In the sketch the dull-minded majority is continually manipulated by arguments well-calculated to exploit its weaknesses and vices. It is true that the people rebel when they are pushed too far, but the implication remains that another Butterworth Stavely would have little difficulty repeating the process. Indeed, the tale is closely akin to another long passage omitted from *A Tramp Abroad,* probably written some time later. Speaking of the many abuses suffered by the French people before the Revolution, the author says, "Even France rose at last," but "would have returned to its warren again quite contented with a cuff and a bonbon if the foolish King had offered them." Since it was not his style to do the "needful thing at the needful time," however, the opportunity passed.[25]

"The Great Revolution in Pitcairn" does foreshadow in some ways works like *A Connecticut Yankee,* "The Man that Corrupted Hadleyburg," and even *The Mysterious Stranger.* But more important is its revelation of how deeply ingrained certain of its author's pessimistic attitudes had become during the late 1870's. Ironically, this was the half-decade which DeVoto thought was probably the happiest period in Clemens' life. And it came just *before* the decade which has been lauded as the zenith of the humorist's espousal of equalitarian democracy and worship of the nineteenth-century doctrine of progress. But now, if the abuses of the *ancien régime* repelled him, abhorrence was balanced, or even outweighed, by distrust of the ignorance and incapacity of the masses. During the late 1880's a hatred of monarchy and aristocracy were to tip the balance drastically, but Clemens' disillusionment with mankind was to remain a force which would have striking results in his fiction.

As for *A Tramp Abroad,* which the author was wrestling to complete in Elmira and then in Hartford during the fall and early winter of 1879–80, still further items ultimately omitted from the published version illustrate best some of his chief concerns during the late seventies. Some of these passages he discarded in the interest of artistry, for in Elmira, and even before that, he realized that many of his political and social comments would not fit the book as he had originally conceived of it.[26] Therefore, as he told Twichell in September, he cut out a number of chapters, not because they were faulty or unimportant, "but merely because they hindered the flow of the narrative."[27] Very likely the reason the long passage on the August 10 massacre escaped the shears was that the visit to Lake Lucerne in Switzerland, where the sculptor Thorwaldsen's famous "Lion of Lucerne" commemorated the sad event, permitted the material to be introduced naturally into the flow of the narrative.

Yet, with much cut out, *A Tramp Abroad* still reflects Clemens' bitterness. As many have noted, the exuberance and buoyant enthusiasms of *The Innocents Abroad* seem to have vanished, leaving here a sense of painstaking effort. There are great moments of humor, to be sure, in such famous passages as Jim Baker's "Blue-Jay Yarn" and Mark Twain's futile battle with the baffling intricacies of the German language. But even the "Blue-Jay Yarn" carries a sharp commentary on the frailties of mankind, especially in its catalogue of traits possessed in common by jays and human beings.

Nevertheless, the autumn of 1879 had some bright spots, two of which were especially pleasant even though they further delayed the book's completion. A November speech in Chicago at a banquet given by the "Army of the Tennessee" to honor General Ulysses S. Grant was a rousing success. There were residual benefits, too, for the humorist's meeting with Grant led ultimately to his securing publishing rights to the General's memoirs. In December Clemens was again a featured speaker, this time at a Boston breakfast for Oliver Wendell Holmes. Obviously hoping to rectify his mistake at the Whittier dinner, he had accepted Howells' invitation to the breakfast only on condition that he be allowed to say a few words. No doubt some of his listeners were apprehensive, for most of them had been present at the dinner in 1877. But the sincere and gracious tribute to Holmes soon dispelled their fears. And their cordial response, in turn, doubtless helped erase some of the speaker's own black memories of the earlier fiasco.

Back at work on *A Tramp Abroad,* Clemens finally finished on January 8, crowing to Howells that he was "as soary (& flighty) as a rocket, to-day," with the joy of getting "that Old Man of the Sea" off his back after more than a year and a half.[28] That sense of relief, coupled with the successes in Chicago and Boston, made the outlook for the new decade a good deal brighter. Now the author turned enthusiastically to his first full-length book with an English setting, *The Prince and the Pauper.*

Chapter Four

The Prince and the Pauper

(1 8 8 0 - 1 8 8 1)

The Prince and the Pauper HAD BEEN ON CLEMENS' LIST of literary projects for almost four years.[1] As he later remembered it, he was browsing in the library at Quarry Farm one summer afternoon in 1876, picked up one of Charlotte M. Yonge's popular English juveniles, and, inspired by its charm, decided to try his hand at a historical tale of his own.

Albert Bigelow Paine was mistaken in naming Miss Yonge's *The Prince and the Page* as the stimulus, though the title perhaps was influential. Or possibly Clemens had actually mentioned that title to his biographer. Still, as Paine himself was quick to admit, the adventures of the teen-age page of Prince Edward (later Edward I) do not at all resemble those of Tom Canty and Edward Tudor. But another of Miss Yonge's books, *The Little Duke*, which recreates the boyhood of Duke William of Normandy (grandfather-to-be of William the Conqueror), contains parallels in both situation and character relationships to the novel that Clemens several times called "The Little Prince & the Little Pauper."[2] The association of the two boys, Richard and the more worldly Alberic de Montemar, and Osmond de Centeville's role as Richard's protector (and later, rescuer) foreshadow Prince Edward's relationships with Tom Canty and Miles Hendon. Some of Richard's reactions to court ceremonies, his attempted escape in disguise from the French king's guards (like Edward's ejection in pauper's rags from the palace at Westminster), and the coronation scene strongly suggest similar details in *The Prince and the Pauper*. Clemens was not (as Paine charged) the victim of a faulty memory in 1908 when he credited "that pleasant and picturesque little history book, Charlotte M. Yonge's 'Little Duke' " with providing his initial inspiration.[3]

The time for a new literary venture was right, too. Clemens needed a new project. After finishing reading proof for *Tom Sawyer* during July and the first week in August, he had begun *Huckleberry Finn*, only to have interest or inspiration, or both, fail after about four hundred manuscript pages.[4] No doubt the somewhat disappointing sales of *Sketches New and Old* (1875), as well as his desire to be considered a "literary" figure rather than merely a "funny-man," also encouraged him to seek other fields.

All these possibilities lead to the conjecture that it was actually Sir Walter Scott who influenced the decision to try a historical novel. Clemens' boyhood enthusiasm for Scott's works had by this time given way to a strong aversion to certain of their characteristics, particularly their florid style and overly romanticized adventures. In a savage mood early in January, 1870, following a lecture that had been poorly received, he had regaled Olivia in a letter with a burlesque synopsis of *Ivanhoe*, advising her not to bother reading the book.[5] He was not merely entertaining his fiancée, for his tone on the whole was gloomy. The probability is great that the thought of the widespread popularity of Scott's flowery rhetoric and the lack of appreciation for his own lecture, so carefully designed to seem casual and colloquial, irked him considerably. Sometime in 1876, in notes for a speech or essay, he specifically turned to the matter of style, including Scott as a prime example of the sort of writer whose excessive and inexact verbiage ruined the effectiveness of his literary efforts. After citing several examples of forceful yet unostentatious diction—like the Bible's "shadow of a great rock in a weary land"—he concluded that Scott, whose language was always "riding the high horse," could not have conveyed the idea "in anything short of four chapters."[6]

Even so, Clemens respected Scott's use of historical detail. In study notes for *The Prince and the Pauper*, he twice considered the possibility of incorporating examples of chivalric combat from *Ivanhoe*, and also jotted down page numbers from *Kenilworth*, *Quentin Durward*, and *The Fortunes of Nigel* where he might find

descriptions of dress and armor, the wording of "a stately proclamation," and an account of Alsatia (Whitefriars) as a place of refuge
for criminals.[7]

Since *Ivanhoe* was on Clemens' mind on these several occasions,
it is likely that some of the advice in Scott's introduction to the novel
had hit home. Explaining why he had abandoned Scottish subjects
for an excursion into the world of chivalry, Sir Walter there notes
that the greatest danger to an author's literary fame was to be regarded as a "mannerist" capable of working only in "a particular
and limited style," and a little later he concludes that to confine
himself to Scottish subjects would not only weary his readers but
also limit his ability to afford them pleasure—or, one is tempted to
add, to sell them books.

In his "Dedicatory Epistle to the Rev. Dr. Dryasdust," which also
prefaces *Ivanhoe,* Scott discusses the problems of a historical novelist in making his work seem authentic. He (or rather his *persona,*
Laurence Templeton) advises authors not to collect large numbers
of obsolete words, but rather to concern themselves with the
"grammatical character" of the language, its "turn of expression,
mode of arrangement." In the area of "sentiment and manners," he
applies the same principle, noting that in both instances the author
must of course take care not to introduce details inconsistent with
the manners of the age described, nor language that might betray
"an origin directly modern." Otherwise, the author would be making no very serious error to mingle the manners of two or three centuries in his medieval tale, for the general reader would not notice
them and experts in the field would "probably be lenient in proportion to their knowledge of the difficulty of [the author's] task."

Whether or not Scott's advice sent Clemens to those "ancient
English books" (mentioned before as the tangential source of *1601*)
for practice in archaic language, he followed the precepts Scott set
down. Probably that same summer he compiled the list of "Middle
Age phrases for a historical story" preserved in the Mark Twain
Papers.[8] It is interesting also, in the light of Scott's emphasis on
authenticity of manners and costumes, that Clemens' later study-
note references to the Waverly novels dealt primarily with details
of dress, armor, and local color.

The remainder of 1876, however, saw few tangible results of
these investigations besides *1601* and the list of phrases. The following summer began hopefully enough, with Clemens reminding

himself in May to take along the appropriate volumes of English history by Froude and Hume on the annual trek to Elmira. But other literary interests soon claimed priority—the longish story of the Bermuda trip that spring (later published in several *Atlantic* installments as "Some Rambling Notes of an Idle Excursion"); the ill-fated Simon Wheeler play, and revisions of *Ah Sin,* both before and after its July 31 opening in New York. At the end of the summer, therefore, though the stockpile was richer by some reference notes and a few suggestions for possible episodes, Tom Canty and Prince Edward had still not met.

Finally, in the late fall or early winter of 1877 the way seemed clear. On November 23 a synopsis of the author's current plan found its way into his notebook: "Edward VI and a little pauper exchange places by accident a day or so before Henry VIII's death. The Prince wanders in rags and hardships and the pauper suffers the (to him) horrible miseries of princedom, up to the moment of crowning in Westminster Abbey, when proof is brought and the mistake rectified."⁹ By February 5 Clemens was telling Mrs. Fairbanks of "a historical tale of 300 years ago" that he was writing "simply for the love of it." He was reveling, too, in the enthusiasm of his family and his Saturday Club of teen-age girls for the portions he read to them. But then the "badgered, harassed feeling" and preparations for the European trip had moved in to halt the novel shortly after the point (in Chapter Eleven) where Miles Hendon first leaps to Edward's defense before the gates of the Guildhall.¹⁰

While in England, Clemens supplemented earlier studies of a pocket map of London with visits to the actual localities his characters would frequent. But before doing so, he had repeated the practice begun in Paris earlier in 1879 of reading about places of interest before going to see them. His guides this time were works like John Timbs' *Curiosities of London* (1855) and Leigh Hunt's *The Town* (1848), both to be cited as documentation for specific details in *The Prince and the Pauper,*¹¹ and John Stow's *Survey of London* (1598, 1603).

Home again, and finally freed from the burden of *A Tramp Abroad* in January, 1880, he relaunched his book with all flags flying. February saw him "grinding away . . . with an interest which amounts to intemperance." By March 5 he had added 114 pages, bringing the total, as he told Howells, to 326. Even with the many interruptions which always plagued his literary work in Hartford, he finished eighty-seven more pages by mid-June. With summer and the greater leisure of life at Quarry Farm, the book almost reached port. In fact, on September 15 Clemens announced enthusiastically to Thomas Bailey Aldrich that he had completed the story the day before. But as so often happened, the huzzah was premature, for suggestions by Howells in December resulted in some additional revisions, notably the omission of the whipping-boy's story of the bull and bees. While revising, too, the author decided to expand "the prince's adventures in the rural districts" by some "130 new pages of MS." But finally, by January 21, 1881, *The Prince and the Pauper* was ready for the printer.[12]

From the beginning, Clemens intended this novel to be serious. Until Howells' enthusiasm encouraged him to "publish intrepidly instead of concealing the authorship," he had planned to follow the example set with "The Curious Republic of Gondour." His desire to be "authentic" had led him to many sources. As his "study notes" reveal, he turned to Pepys' *Diary* and Shakespeare's historical plays (especially *Henry IV*) for archaic language. Besides looking at several of Scott's novels, he scoured Froude and Hume for appropriate references to events, personages, and other pertinent details. More specifically he used the volumes by Timbs and Leigh Hunt that he had consulted in England; J. Heneage Jesse's three-volume, *London: Its Celebrated Characters and Remarkable Places* (1871); *The English Rogue,* a seventeenth-century compendium of English low-life by Richard Head and Francis Kirkman (1665; facsimile reprint, 1874); *A Classical Dictionary of the Vulgar Tongue* (1785); and his Hartford friend J. Hammond Trumbull's *The True Blue Laws of Connecticut and New Haven* (1876). From these sources and from Hume he sometimes quoted directly in the text, and further to "authenticate" various incidents, followed the practice of both Scott and Miss Yonge by appending to his novel explanatory notes based on most of these works.

Trumbull's defense of New England's "blue-laws" against charges of excessive harshness probably became most important to *The Prince and the Pauper* after Clemens' European trip, though he doubtless had known the book since its publication in 1876. It perhaps even helped to cause the slight shift in purpose that seems to have occurred when he resumed work on the novel in 1880. The original notebook plan of November, 1877, had suggested that Tom Canty and Prince Edward were to receive approximately equal emphasis as they learned how inaccurate their respective concepts of court and common life had been. But when Clemens told Howells about his project in March, 1880, his mind was on Edward's adventures. "My idea," he said, "is to afford a realizing sense of the exceeding severity of the laws of that day by inflicting some of their penalties upon the king himself & allowing him a chance to see the rest of them applied to others—all of which is to account for certain mildnesses which distinguished Edward VI's reign from those that preceded & followed it."[13] In the notes to the book itself he cited chapter and verse from Trumbull to justify the episodes involving the man sentenced to death by boiling, the girl and her mother condemned as witches for having caused a storm by pulling off their stockings, and the scene in prison where Edward observes at first hand the victims of other harsh laws.

The English Rogue proved another rich mine.[14] In it Clemens found historically accurate dialogue for his beggar band, and an ample vocabulary of cant terms (both of which he supplemented from *A Classical Dictionary of the Vulgar Tongue*). More specifically, he borrowed the last six lines of a rousing "Canting Song" and several examples from the catalogue of frauds perpetrated by the beggars upon their unwary victims. Among these were instructions for producing a "clyme" or false sore, which he introduced into Chapter Twenty-two, where Edward barely escapes being subjected to the process. More important, immediately following those instructions in *The English Rogue* Clemens discovered most of the details for his next episode—Edward's arrest on a charge of pig-stealing, and his narrow escape from death at the subsequent trial.

Several particulars of the theft and concealment of the pig also suggest that Clemens here received an assist from Pepy's *Diary*, which he had known and loved for some years.[15] On August 22, 1668, Pepys notes that while passing through Leaden Hall, he "did see a woman catched, that had stole a shoulder of mutton off a butcher's stall, and carrying it wrapt in a cloth in a basket." In this case, however, the culprit was not arrested, a fact which caused the diarist to sneer that the owner was "so silly as to let her go that took it, taking only the meat." Such implicit callousness (for if the owner had pressed charges, the penalty would have been as severe in Pepys' day as in Tudor England) perhaps underscored for Clemens both the cruelty of the age and the harshness of the laws.

Edward's experience at the trial—he was saved from hanging only when the woman reduced her valuation of the pig below "thirteen-pence ha'penny"—gives him his first real insight into the sufferings of his subjects under the harsh legal code. Hence the episode was an important one for developing the book's major theme. Moreover, it effectively prepares the way for Edward's full comprehension of human suffering when shortly thereafter he sees the two kindly Baptist women burned at the stake.

When Clemens announced to Howells that he hoped "to afford a realizing sense" of the harshness of life in Tudor times by exposing Edward directly to some of the unjust laws, he was echoing a concept derived from still another British author—William Edward Hartpole Lecky. From his first encounter with Lecky's *History of European Morals from Augustus to Charlemagne* (probably during the summer of 1874), he had read, marked, and inwardly digested many of its arguments. Often he noted marginally his agreement or disagreement with what the historian said, or even with how he said it. But at one point, after revising several clumsy constructions in the text, he revealed an abiding affection: "It is so noble a book, & so beautiful a book, that I don't wish it to have even trivial faults in it."[16] And he would continue to borrow ideas and incidents from it for the remainder of his writing career.

In his own works, one may perhaps mark the beginnings of his fascination with the historian's graphic analysis of medieval ascetism in Chapter Thirteen of *Tom Sawyer* (written in 1874), where Huck Finn ridicules the habits of hermits described by Tom. By 1876, as Walter Blair has shown in detail,[17] ideas stimulated by Lecky had permeated the chapters of *Huckleberry Finn* written that summer.

In *The Prince and the Pauper* Lecky's influence seems three-fold, stemming from the historian's examination of the conflicting moral theories of the "intuitionists" and the "utilitarians"; his emphasis on education as a stimulus to the imagination; and his portrait of man's subjection to fear and superstition down through the ages.

The first two of these elements appear in the historian's long opening chapter. Because they were to be important to Clemens' future works, as well as to *The Prince and the Pauper,* they deserve discussion in some detail.

For many years to come Clemens would implicitly carry on what Walter Blair has called his "discussion with Lecky" concerning the relative value of the two systems of moral theory characterized by the historian as "the stoical, the intuitive, the independent or the sentimental" and "the epicurean, the inductive, the utilitarian, or the selfish." The "intuitive" view, which Lecky espoused, argues that moral choices are governed by an innate moral sense, a "power of perceiving" that some qualities (like benevolence, chastity, or veracity) are better than others. A natural accompaniment to this power is a sense of *duty,* an obligation to cultivate the good qualities and suppress their opposites. This sense, in turn, becomes "in itself, and apart from all consequences," a sufficient reason for following any particular course of action. The "utilitarian" theory, to which Clemens was increasingly drawn over the years, *denies* that man possesses any such innate perception of virtue. Rather, his standards of right and wrong, his consideration of the "comparative excellence of . . . feelings and actions," depend solely on the degree to which those feelings and actions are conducive to happiness. That which increases happiness and lessens pain is good; that which does the opposite is evil. Hence it is external forces rather than intuitive perceptions of good or evil which determine moral choices.[18]

A number of marginal comments reveal Clemens' attraction to the utilitarian side. On page five of the history, for instance, Lecky summarizes the utilitarian position as follows: "A desire to obtain happiness and to avoid pain is the only possible motive to action. The reason, and the only reason, why we should perform virtuous actions, or in other words, seek the good of others, is that on the whole such a course will bring us the greatest amount of happiness." Besides heavily underscoring the whole statement, Clemens bracketed the "should," underlined the "us" a second time, and wrote in the margin: "Leave the 'should' out—then it is perfect (& true!)." In several other places he challenged Lecky's agreement with the intuitionists that man's moral perceptions were innate. At one point he contended that "all moral perceptions are acquired by the influences around us," and that since those influences begin in infancy, "we never get a chance to find out whether we have any that are innate or not."[19]

This is not to say that this was the humorist's first encounter with the idea that man's moral choices depend largely on forces outside himself. During his days as a cub-pilot he had absorbed the teachings of Tom Paine's *Age of Reason,* with its emphasis on the immutability of natural law. The notion that man's character and actions were molded primarily from without was doubtless reinforced also by some of Oliver Wendell Holmes' musings on hereditary and environmental influences in *The Autocrat of the Breakfast Table,* which Clemens and Olivia used as a "courting-book" in 1869. Even more important was Clemens' interest in nineteenth-century evolutionary theory.[20]

Because of a fragmentary essay by Clemens that Albert Bigelow Paine included in *Mark Twain's Autobiography,* it has generally been accepted that the author's first instruction in the mysteries of evolution came from a Scotsman named Macfarlane, who preached his own version of the theory in a Cincinnati boarding-house "fourteen or fifteen years before Mr. Darwin's *Descent of Man* startled the world."[21] It now appears, however, that the piece was intended as a magazine or newspaper article and that "Macfarlane" was probably a *persona,* a means of presenting Clemens' own current views of man's pettiness and conceit without publicly committing himself to opinions that might well prove unpopular. It could be that "Macfarlane" owes something to the author's association with J. H. Burrough, his literary-minded St. Louis roommate of 1854-55, who was also at least partially the model for Barrow, the boarding-house philosopher of *The American Claimant* (1892). But until additional evidence becomes available, one must accept the likelihood that Clemens' interest in evolution came primarily from a knowledge of Darwin's writings themselves, or from discussions of those works in contemporary periodicals.

Whether the humorist read *The Origin of Species* (1859) is not certain, but marginal notations in his copy of *The Descent of Man* (1871) show that he may well have been among those whom the book "startled." He thoroughly accepted the theory of evolution, and would later in his own *What is Man?* adapt specific ideas and details from *The Descent of Man.* Yet he apparently was not entirely satisfied with Darwin's attempts to support, on purely evolutionary grounds, the argument that the moral sense was the most important characteristic separating man from the lower animals. He was more impressed, it seems, by Darwin's reference to the notion that the impulse to relieve the sufferings of others stemmed not from altruism but from the desire to alleviate one's own painful feelings which the sight of suffering aroused. For in the margin beside that latter comment he wrote: "Selfishness again—not charity nor generosity (save toward ourselves.)"[22]

These years also marked the beginnings of Clemens' lifelong

fascination with Edward FitzGerald's *Rubaiyat of Omar Khayyam.* The haunting quatrains first enchanted him shortly after his return from Europe in 1879, when the Hartford *Courant* quoted a number of them in its front-page review of the new fourth edition of the "translation," published in England that August. From then on, the *Rubaiyat* became his favorite poem, one of the few examples of literary expression that he considered "perfect."[23] Though the effects were to be more obvious later on, particularly during the 1890's, there is little doubt that the deterministic overtones of Omar's discussion of morality and personal responsibility added their elements to Clemens' considerations in the late 'seventies and early 'eighties.

The fact remains, however, that in Lecky he probably first encountered a systematic development of the utilitarian and intuitionist arguments. And for many years his works would show that even though strongly attracted to the utilitarian position, he did not wholly accept it. The "discussion with Lecky" would continue for most of his life.

One of the matters on which Clemens partly agreed with Lecky at this time concerned the nature of the conscience. The historian agreed with the intuitionist view that the conscience was an "original faculty," arising from man's innate perceptions of good and evil. The utilitarians, on the other hand, regarded it simply as an "association of ideas" based on the pleasure-pain theory and society's standards of right and wrong.

To show the inadequacy of the utilitarian concept, Lecky argues that the operation of the conscience does not really fit the view that "self-interest" is the one ultimate reason for virtue. What one "ought or ought not" to do cannot depend merely upon "the prospect of acquiring or losing pleasure." For, if a man had a tendency toward a certain vice, he might well attain happiness by a "moderate and circumspect" indulgence of that vice. But if he sins, his conscience judges his conduct, and "its sting or its approval constitutes a pain or pleasure so intense, as to more than redress the balance." This would happen whether the conscience were an "association of ideas" or "an original faculty."

But (the argument continues) conscience is more often a source of pain than of pleasure, and if happiness is actually the sole end of life, then one should learn to disregard the proddings of conscience. If a man forms an association of ideas that inflicts more pain than

[57

it prevents, or prevents more pleasure than it affords, the reasonable course would be to dissolve that association or destroy the habit. "This is what he 'ought' to do according to the only meaning that word can possess in the utilitarian vocabulary." Therefore, a man who possessed such a temperament would be happier if he were to "quench that conscientious feeling, which . . . prevents him from pursuing the course that would be most conducive to his tranquillity."[24]

Clemens had dramatized this very theme in "The Facts Concerning the Recent Carnival of Crime in Connecticut," written in January, 1876, and published in the June issue of the *Atlantic Monthly*. As the story opens, the narrator muses over efforts of friends and relatives to keep him in the paths of virtue. Suddenly, his Conscience appears in the form of a "nauseating" dwarf, resembling the narrator himself but covered with a greenish mold. ("Considered as a source of pain," Lecky says, "conscience bears a striking resemblance to the feeling of disgust.") The two discuss at some length the function of the Conscience as tormentor. Finally, a recitation of his many sins goads the narrator into throttling the dwarf, tearing him to pieces, and throwing the "bleeding rubbish" into the fire. Having thus followed Lecky's advice to obliterate his conscience, the narrator embarks on a career of "unalloyed bliss," committing all sorts of heinous crimes without a moment's remorse.

Fantastic as the piece is, it nevertheless parallels Lecky's discussion almost exactly. Certainly Clemens' own experiences with a tormenting conscience, which must have been one of the keenest in literary history, had led him here to agree with Lecky's assertion that the reproaches of conscience often prevented a man from following a course that might be "most conducive to his tranquillity." And since the proddings of conscience obviously could *not* be so easily dismissed, Clemens at least implicitly agreed that Lecky had found a fallacy in the utilitarian reasoning.

Echoes of this idea of "quenching" the conscience occur also in the chapters of *Huckleberry Finn* written in 1876. Furthermore, Huck's struggles with his conscience about turning Jim over to the authorities show Clemens agreeing with the historian in a slightly different way. The climax of that conflict in Chapter Thirty-one, when Huck decides to "go to hell" rather than reveal Jim's whereabouts was not to be written for several years. But the struggle itself was clearly established in 1876, especially in Chapter Sixteen, when Huck decides to paddle ashore "and tell," but then recants and lies to the slave-catchers about the color of the man on the raft. Some years later, in a notebook plan for an elaborate "lay sermon on morals and things of that stately sort," Clemens proposed to use that very chapter from his novel to show how "in a crucial moral emergency a sound heart is a safer guide than an ill-trained conscience."[25] Though Clemens here was obviously regarding the conscience as an "association of ideas" rather than an "original faculty," both this passage and Huck's later decision not to write to Miss Watson dramatize the triumph of Huck's "sound heart" over his community-trained sense of right and wrong. This "sound heart" is first cousin, if not brother, to the "innate moral perceptions" championed by Lecky and the intuitionists.

The second major concept derived from Lecky involves the interrelationship of imagination and compassion, and the influence of education upon both. Shortly after his analysis of the two conflicting moral theories, the historian devotes a long passage to explaining how society's progress from barbarism to a high degree of civilization had depended upon "the strengthening of the imagination by intellectual culture." Defining imagination as "the power of realisation," he argues that men pity suffering only when they "realise" it, and that the intensity of their compassion is directly proportionate to the extent of that "realisation." That is why the death of an individual "brought prominently before our eyes" elicits greater compassion than any account of battle, shipwreck, or other catastrophe. Therefore, if benevolent feelings thus depend upon prior "realisation," then any influence that can increase the range and power of the imagination (the "realising faculty") will help to develop sympathy and compassion. And of all such influences, education is the foremost.[26]

Besides the echo in Clemens' letter to Howells, that idea finds a direct statement early in *The Prince and the Pauper* when Edward vows (in Chapter Four) to make Christ's Hospital a school for "mental nourishment" rather than "mere shelter" so that poor boys may develop the "gentleness and charity" which education encourages. More important, the concept underlies the subsequent education of Edward and, in some measure, that of Tom Canty.

The plot structure of this most carefully wrought of Clemens' works shows that the author clearly intended Edward's "education" to be primary. Each of the boys gets almost equal space until the end of Chapter Thirteen. But then the spotlight begins to focus on Edward, as Miles Hendon discovers the disappearance of his protégé, who has been lured from the lodgings on London Bridge by a mysterious message from John Canty. After three chapters describing Tom's experiences at court following the death of Henry VIII, the next twelve are Edward's (save for the two that relate Hendon's family troubles). Of the final five, two are again Tom's; one is shared; the fourth is largely Edward's; and the unnumbered "Conclusion" briefly summarizes the subsequent careers of the principal characters, with emphasis on Edward's good works as king.

Prince Edward's schooling begins immediately upon his ejection from the palace grounds when the group of boys from Christ's Hospital mock and beat him. His promise to make the institution into a school, like his initial befriending of Tom Canty, springs from his own innate "gentleness and charity." But he is to achieve real compassion and understanding only near the end of his wanderings. As Franklin Rogers has noted,[27] when Edward first leaves the city via London Bridge, he is still an arrogant aristocrat. He has demanded all the niceties of court etiquette from Miles Hendon and has sworn to have Tom Canty hanged, drawn, and quartered for usurping his throne. Only gradually does the basic soundness of heart, which Hendon recognizes as "the sweet and generous spirit that is in him" assert itself. Finally, after the burning of the Baptist women who befriended him, Edward (in Chapter Twenty-seven) declares that the horror will remain in his memory and his dreams for the rest of his life. Hendon then underscores the change of character by noting how gentle Edward has become; earlier he "would have stormed at these varlets, and said he was king, and commanded that the women be turned loose unscathed."

Other inhumanities in the prison complete the educational process, and Edward swears he will amend the harsh legal code, concluding: "The world is made wrong, kings should go to school to their own laws at times, and so learn mercy." Now he is ready to re-cross London Bridge, a merciful monarch. Subsequently, in righting earlier wrongs, he often stresses the importance of his personal experience, subduing objections by reminding his courtiers that *they* know little of suffering and oppression. And recognizing the tendency of human beings to forget important lessons, he often repeated his story so as to "keep its sorrowful spectacles fresh in his memory and the springs of pity replenished in his heart."

Besides paralleling Lecky's description of the "realisation" process, then, Edward's development reveals a "soundness" of heart like that of Huck Finn. From the first instinctive kindness to Tom, through the sloughing off of the aristocratic arrogance engendered by his upbringing, he proceeds to a conscious kindness. Had he not been innately good, however, it is more than likely that the abuse and ridicule to which his travels exposed him would have far outweighed his pity for the sufferings of others.

To say that *The Prince and the Pauper* is chiefly Edward's story should not, of course, minimize the importance of Tom Canty's "education." In the first place, once Tom loses his fear of being found out, he begins to discover how false were his dreams of kingly pleasures. Concern over the impending execution of Norfolk, the embarrassment of his first court dinner, and the tedium of business and ceremony successively engulf him until, in Chapter Fourteen, he almost begs to be freed from the "affliction" of kingship. Soon, however, his innately kind heart and sound common sense allow him to initiate a slight amelioration of the harsh laws.

Faced with the prospect of the execution of the alleged poisoner and the two "witches charged with controlling the weather" (Chapter Fifteen), he reacts with instinctive compassion. As Roger Salomon has observed, he faces something of the same conflict of heart and society-trained conscience as both Huck Finn and the historical Edward VI portrayed by David Hume. Of Edward, Hume says that training and "the age in which he lived" qualified his "mildness of disposition" and his "capacity to learn and judge," and thus caused him to "incline somewhat to bigotry and persecution." In a case involving the supposed heresy of a young girl, for instance, the king at first reacted compassionately, refusing to sanction the execution. But his advisers prevailed, and he finally signed the death warrant, though "with tears in his eyes."[28]

Tom Canty, as king, finds himself in a similar position. Like Hume's Edward he is sympathetic. Then, though he grants the "poisoner's" request to be hanged rather than boiled to death, he considers the seriousness of the crime and says with a sigh, "Take him away—he hath earned his death." Fortunately, he decides to review the case further, and when additional questioning reveals the flimsiness of the evidence, reason enters the picture, and Tom frees the man. In the case of the alleged witches, the "influence of the age" again is evident in Tom's superstitious shudder at their presence, a reaction natural in a time when everyone dreaded encountering those possessed by the devil. But whereas the real Edward consented to the execution of the young girl, in this case Tom's sound heart and common sense (again like Huck's) triumph over his trained conscience. Sorry for their plight, Tom reasons that a mother would do anything to save her child, and so offers them freedom and his own protection if they will repeat their magic. When they still protest their inability to create a thunderstorm, he pronounces them innocent and dismisses the charge.

Yet those episodes also affect Tom adversely. On realizing that his word truly *is* law, he begins to relish his position and power. Periodically, however, he is plagued by a different sort of conscience —more akin to what Lecky would call an "original" faculty than a community-trained "association of ideas." Tom's shame and guilt arise from two sources: the knowledge that he is usurping Edward's rightful place and his fear that his mother or sisters might appear to thwart his pleasure by exposing him. Though he almost succeeds in following Lecky's advice to quell a troublesome conscience, his guilty feelings continue to torture him. When his pride finally leads him to reject his mother during the coronation procession, all the glamor of kingship falls away as remorse overwhelms him. Edward's appearance in Westminster Abbey brings welcome relief, and Tom is only too glad to relinquish the throne.

One might argue that here Clemens has accorded a purely utilitarian function to the conscience; that Tom's restoring the throne to its rightful occupant and himself to his own family is an action that will ultimately result in the greatest happiness for himself. So it does. But his feelings evolve basically from his natural goodness —his concern for Edward and his love for his family, rather than from a fear of the consequences of being exposed. The miseries of conscience which destroy his happiness and make him glad to give up the throne reflect the kindness and gentleness that he exhibited even at the height of his pleasure in his kingly position. Thus Clemens still seems to side with Lecky.

From Lecky's discussion of the influences of superstition in human affairs at least two other episodes derived support, if not their original inspiration. In Chapter Seventeen, Edward learns of the sad plight of certain husbandmen and of the once-prosperous farmer, Yokel, whose property has been confiscated because his mother was convicted of witchcraft. In a sarcastic harangue to Hugo's outlaw band, Yokel describes his experiences with "the merciful English law": when he had turned to begging as his only recourse, he had for successive offenses been whipped, deprived of both ears, branded, and finally enslaved. "Do ye understand that word!" he shouts; "An English SLAVE!" And then he explains that he has fled from his master and, if caught, will hang.

At that point the horrified Edward cries that the law shall be revoked that very day, whereupon he is robed, crowned, sceptered, and dubbed "Foo-Foo the First, King of the Mooncalves." To keep the historical record straight, the author contributes a note to this passage which explains that the peasant was "suffering from this law *by anticipation*," for the statute "was to have birth in this little king's own reign." But, he adds, "we know, from the humanity of his character, that it could never have been suggested by him." Presumably, this law was to be among those which Edward (in the novel) would later repeal.

This chapter in Edward's education may well have been fathered by Lecky's discussion of the concept of Christian charity, and specifically, of how the establishment of charitable institutions had in many cases actually increased mendicancy rather than relieved it.[29] The paradox resulted, Lecky says, from the superstition that the donor of charity would reap spiritual rewards. The prospect of such rewards produced an anxiety to give. Increased giving, in turn, led to increased begging, even by those who might otherwise be able to engage in productive labor. Finally, in England and elsewhere, the problem of begging became so severe that the harshest sort of legislation was invoked.

Two of the laws cited by Lecky to illustrate his point are especially significant. The first, from the reign of Henry VIII, provided increasingly severe penalties: for a first offense—whipping; for second—whipping and loss of part of an ear; for a third—death. On the other statute, Lecky says: "*Under Edward VI., an atrocious law, which, however, was repealed in the same reign* [italics mine], enacted that every sturdy beggar who refused to work should be branded, and adjudged for two years as a slave to the person who gave information against him." If he fled during that period, he was condemned for a first offense to perpetual slavery, and for a second, to death.[30] Taken together, the two laws describe the experiences of several of the husbandmen and almost exactly the fate of Yokel.

Edward's visit to the insane hermit shortly after his escape from the beggars suggests one further debt to the *History of European Morals*. Immediately preceding the discussion of the relationship of charity and mendicancy, Lecky traces a number of historical attitudes toward insanity. Immediately following it, he embarks upon the long discourse on medieval asceticism from which Clemens was to borrow heavily for *A Connecticut Yankee*. The crazy recluse who claims to be an archangel and mutters about personal visits to Paradise is certainly a blood brother to Lecky's generic ascetic who, "delirious . . . from solitude and long-continued austerities," mistakes his hallucinations for "palpable realities." But there is a more specific model. In contending that for many centuries most madness assumed a theological cast, the historian cites, among others, the case of a Spanish lunatic who thought himself "the brother of the archangel Michael . . . destined for the place in heaven which Satan had lost" and, like Edward's hermit, claimed to have visited freely between this world and the next.[31]

If Clemens had originally intended Edward's encounter with the "archangel" to awaken a sense of sympathy for the hermit, who had been made homeless by Henry VIII's seizure of his monastery, he failed badly. At best the recluse is an object of horror as he whets his butcher-knife and chuckles over his intended revenge on Henry's heir. At worst he is ridiculous. Whatever the original intention, Clemens' treatment clearly reflects the mingled horror and disgust with which Lecky viewed religious mania.

In some respects Clemens' attacks on superstition point toward *A Connecticut Yankee,* where Lecky was to play an even larger role. Edward's travels among his people, too, foreshadow the similar journey of King Arthur. Nevertheless, many commentators have read *The Prince and the Pauper* under too strong a glow from *A Connecticut Yankee*. DeVoto's conclusion, for instance, that the author was attacking as much as he could manage of the "modern perpetuation" of the harsh Tudor law,[32] is warranted neither by Clemens' political and social attitudes at the time of composition nor by the book itself. First, the novel was conceived when Clemens' admiration for England, her traditions, and her government was at its zenith. At that time he may well have thought of the many examples of religious persecution and severe treatment of prisoners (gathered mainly from Hume in 1877) as "local color" which would illustrate the hardships to be observed by the little king in contrast to the "horrible miseries of princedom" to be borne by Tom Canty. Nor had his conviction of the common man's incompetence in government changed much as a result of the European trip of 1878–79. Nowhere in his personal utterances of these years, nor in *The Prince and the Pauper* itself, is there any sign of his later contention that all monarchies should be overthrown. Tudor law was oppressive, to be sure, and bespoke a system sorely deficient in respect for human rights. But it was man rather than monarchy that needed reform; first the rulers and then the people themselves must be rid of false notions. DeVoto's suggested title, "A Missouri Democrat at the Court of Edward VI" is thus inaccurate, and ascribes ideas to Clemens that he demonstrably did not hold when he wrote the book.[33]

In the book itself there is relatively little satire of monarchy and aristocracy. The sharpest thrusts at court ceremony occur in the ludicrous picture of grown men stumbling and fumbling as they attempt to clothe one small boy. Balanced against this sort of burlesque is an obvious fascination with the traditional pomp and display associated with other ceremonies, such as the coronation. Even in the exposure of the more striking legal atrocities of the age, Clemens' target is not the iniquity of the system which produced them but the ignorance and superstition of the age.

Finally, much as it points toward Clemens' later application of Carlyle's clothes-metaphor in *A Connecticut Yankee,* the often-cited picture of Tom and Edward standing naked before a mirror, amazed at their identical appearances, cannot really be read as proof of Clemens' current belief in social or political equality. Barring the fact that the plot itself demanded such physical similarity, other evidence seriously weakens any argument that Clemens had freighted *The Prince and the Pauper* with an "equalitarian" message. In fact, when the novel was in full swing and nearing completion in August, 1880, the author was planning still another episode for *Captain Stormfield's Visit to Heaven* with opposite implications. As the notebook sketch indicates, Stormfield was first to be charmed with the idea that the residents of Paradise lived in a world completely free of social barriers. But when a Negro, a Fiji Islander, an Eskimo, and various politicians, tramps, and other pariahs began inviting themselves to dinner and calling him "Brother Stormfield," he was to grow progressively less enthusiastic. Finally, he would become disgusted by this enforced association with "all sorts of disagreeable people," and would resolve to move from heaven.* Such a plan, though not ultimately used, shows that Clemens in 1880 and 1881 had not deviated far from his social and political opinions of the 1870's.

The "message" of *The Prince and the Pauper,* then, was not that British monarchy was evil, not even that monarchy in itself breeds injustice. It was rather that the cure for political and social ills might be achieved through the paternalistic rule of those best qualified to rule, whose qualifications should include innate kindness, intelligence, and the "realisation" provided by "education." The book is much closer to "The Curious Republic of Gondour" with its mistrust of the masses and plea for qualified public officials, or to *Huckleberry Finn* with its belief in the efficacy of the "sound heart," than to the Yankee Hank Morgan's proposal to demolish and then recreate on an equalitarian basis the institutions of a nation. Nevertheless, its exposure of ignorance, superstition, and unreason does reflect a further deepening of Clemens' disillusionment with human nature. And the careers of its protagonists show Clemens a step closer to the proposition that environment and circumstances alone determine the course of life.

Though Clemens thus weighted *The Prince and the Pauper* with serious implications, the novel unfortunately fails to transcend the limitations of time, place, and melodramatic action. Hence, it lacks the universality which allows *Huckleberry Finn,* or even *Tom Sawyer,* to grip the minds and imaginations of adult readers. The book continues to be read, certainly, but its appeal is chiefly to children and to students of Clemens' literary development, rather than to "young people of all ages."

In the novel's own day, however, most American critics praised it. Some applauded the emergence of a new and superior Mark Twain; a few, like Howells, contended that the book merely presented clearer evidence of the underlying seriousness in all of Mark Twain's works. Enthusiastic as he himself was about the story, Clemens no doubt found these plaudits especially heartwarming. But when the far less enthusiastic first reactions from England

* Notebook 12, TS, pp. 16–17, Mark Twain Papers.

reached him, he must have felt a very different kind of warmth—that of anger.

The critical barbs from Britain flung at *A Tramp Abroad* had not hurt much. Clemens' own impatience with the laborious task of finishing the book had deadened their sting. Now, however, with a labor of love under fire, he could not have remained unruffled. What perhaps irritated him most was the reviewer's advice in the *Athenaeum* for December 24, 1881, that Mark Twain should stick to his proper sphere as "a brilliant and engaging humorist" rather than attempt a genre in which he became only a "dull and painful romancer." If not that, then the opinion that the "disastrous and amazing" effort to achieve a serious book had resulted only in "some four hundred pages of careful tediousness, mitigated by occasional flashes of unintentional and unconscious fun." Clemens may not have seen the *Academy* for the same date, which characterized *The Prince and the Pauper* as "a ponderous fantasia of English history," bathed "in a misty atmosphere of Scott's chivalry." If he had, he would not have appreciated the comparison, especially in view of the pains he had taken to be "authentic."

The more favorable comments in January of the *Quarterly Review* and the *Spectator* probably salved the wounds somewhat, when the latter commended his skillful working out of an "ingenious idea" and the former praised his "fun and satirical chaff, his mingled humor and pathos, his fine perception of human nature, and his nimble fancy." But Clemens was more sensitive to slights than to praise, and he seems almost to protest too much in a letter to Andrew Chatto in March which pooh-poohed the adverse criticisms of the *Anthenaeum* and *Saturday Review*. "Here we consider that neither of those papers would compliment the holy scriptures if an American had written them," he said.* The unfavorable reviews had surely rankled, however, and they probably helped to aggravate whatever antipathy had developed during the English visit two years before.

* SLC to Chatto, 3/3/82, Morse-Frear Collection, Yale University.

Chapter Five

The Bright and the Dark

(1882-1885)

THE FIVE YEARS FOLLOWING THE PUBLICATION OF *The Prince and the Pauper* saw Clemens' prospects at their brightest. No period in his life was busier or more productive. Multitudes of interests from politics to patents to the business side of publishing vied with literary projects for his time and attention. In April and May, 1882, a long-planned trip[1] on the Mississippi River provided relaxation, but also helped him complete two more books. By the end of 1883, *Life on the Mississippi* was off the presses and *Huckleberry Finn* was in its final stages of revision (though publication was delayed until December of the following year). In 1884, convinced that his publishers had always taken advantage of him, Clemens established his own publishing company, under the management of his nephew, Charles L. Webster. By 1885 that venture glittered in the light of mounting sales of *Huckleberry Finn* and the promise of even greater returns from the *Personal Memoirs of General Ulysses S. Grant*. Clemens' hopes were running high, also, for the imminent completion of the Paige typesetting machine (in the works since 1881),[2] which was to revolutionize the printing industry and make its owner one of the world's richest men.

With these actualities and dreams sparkling before him, Clemens could easily forget the several abortive investments that had cost a mere thirty or forty thousand dollars. "I am frightened at the proportions of my prosperity," he said to a friend in 1885. "It seems to me that whatever I touch turns to gold."[3]

Yet under the surface enthusiasms of these busy years, the current of gloom that was as much a part of Clemens' nature as his buoyant confidence flowed strong, even deepened. Business commitments harrassed as well as stimulated him. His "discussion with Lecky" continued, with Clemens leaning more and more strongly toward the deterministic philosophy of the utilitarians. On the debit side of the ledger may be entered the aphorism: "The man who is a pessimist before he is forty-eight knows too much; the man who is an optimist after he is forty-eight knows too little."[4] Clemens was forty-eight in November, 1883.

Though the springtime voyage had its many pleasant moments, Clemens' return to the river seems to have contributed significantly to the deepening of his pessimism. There was a profound sense of loss—the world he had known in its "blossoming youth" now was "old and bowed and melancholy," and the "romance of boating" was gone. Shaking hands with former friends, perhaps for the last time; seeing their faces "scarred with the campaigns of life, and marked with their griefs and defeats" obviously troubled him.[5] Despair as well as sadness marked such reactions as the notebook comment that the careers of Will Bowen and other boyhood friends made "human life appear a grisly and hideous sarcasm."*

Along with this mood, other memories of tragic incidents—the drownings of Lem Hackett and "Dutchy," the death of an old tramp in a jail fire—found their way into *Life on the Mississippi*. That Clemens had been greatly shaken by these boyhood experiences is obvious from his several references to them in other, more serious, contexts.[6] In each instance the emphasis is upon the pangs of conscience, the sense of guilt that he himself had experienced.

In *Life on the Mississippi* the author presents the material humorously, pointing out how rapidly he had been able to shuck his fear and guilt once other considerations intervened. Doubtless he intended to satirize the eagerness with which human beings dodge moral responsibility. At the same time, his attempts to make humorous capital of events that were so important to him suggest the same motives that underlay "Facts Concerning the Recent

* Notebook 16, TS, p. 27, Mark Twain Papers.

Carnival of Crime in Connecticut." In the episode of the calaboose fire, as in "Facts," there seems to be an implicit denial that the sense of guilt *could* be dissipated that easily. If so, Clemens was still partly agreeing with Lecky that the utilitarian philosophy did not properly provide for the operation of the conscience.

On the other hand, the utilitarian position was becoming more attractive to Clemens during these years. Notebooks show that he was pondering the matter of individual responsibility during the river trip.[7] Once back in Hartford, he continued his speculations and in February, 1883, with *Life on the Mississippi* finally off his hands, he treated the Monday Evening Club to a chapter of his "gospel" (as he later called it). Partly a sketch, but "mostly talk," the paper sought to answer the question "What is Happiness?" Arguing that man was "merely a machine automatically functioning," therefore not entitled to either praise or blame for his actions, Clemens also asserted that since a machine was incapable of originating ideas, all man's inspirations must come from without. Denying the existence of free will and the notion of self-sacrifice, he took the utilitarian side against Lecky and the intuitionists, maintaining that a man does a duty, not for duty's sake, but for the personal satisfaction he derives from doing it, or "for the sake of avoiding the personal discomfort he would have to endure if he shirked that duty."[8]

Though many of the ideas were not then finally formulated, the essay contained the gist of what the author was later to expand into *What is Man?* And the fact that this new attraction to the utilitarian point of view followed close upon his consideration of the conscience and its pangs in *Life on the Mississippi* suggests still further that at this point he was subconsciously, if not consciously, searching for a rational way to rid himself of that annoying "monitor" of human actions.

Other aspects of the human condition observed during the voyage had disturbed him. Earlier opinions of the South's woeful backwardness were vividly enforced. Much impressed by the material and cultural progress of the towns north of St. Louis, he was appalled that the South should still be living in "the romantic Dark Ages."*

In *Life on the Mississippi*, attempting to explain the South's failure to keep pace with nineteenth-century progress, the writer

* Paine 259, Mark Twain Papers. TS of Roswell Phelps' notebook.

fixed upon the Southern obsession with the trappings of chivalry as a primary cause.[9] And since, like Carlyle, he tended to see history largely in terms of the actions and influences of individuals, he found a convenient whipping-boy in Sir Walter Scott, whose novels had long been a staple of the Southern literary diet. Much as *A Tramp Abroad* had blamed Louis XVI and his queen for the French Revolution, *Life on the Mississippi* charged that the "Sir Walter disease" had brought about the sorry state of the American South.

Two major explosions (Chapters Forty and Forty-six) deplore the absurdity of a "jejeune romanticism" still existing in the midst of the "genuine and wholesome" nineteenth-century civilization. The "pathetic shams" of Southern architecture with its grandiose "castles" and its wooden pillars that sought to capture the romance of Grecian marble; the "inflated" speech of most Southerners; the deplorable affectations of Southern journalism and Southern litera-ture; the love of titles that made every man a "Colonel" or "Judge," and the continued existence of the duel—all were tangible evidence of how Sir Walter's romanticizing had caused the South to cherish traditions long outgrown by the rest of the world. Thoroughly warmed up—though he immediately labeled the proposition a "wild" one—the humorist contended that "Scottism" was "in large measure" responsible for the Civil War. Finally, he concentrated his fire still more to name *Ivanhoe* the chief culprit. Though Cer-vantes' great masterpiece, *Don Quixote,* had swept away the world's admiration for "mediaeval chivalry-silliness," *Ivanhoe* had so ef-fectively restored it in the American South that Cervantes' good work was "pretty nearly a dead letter" there.[10]

It should be stressed, however, that Clemens' real target was not so much Scott himself as the South's insistence on continuing in outworn traditions. His reminding himself to turn to Scott's novels for *The Prince and the Pauper* shows that he had retained a good deal of respect for the novelist's handling of historical detail. More-over, he was soon to borrow (though perhaps unconsciously) several important details from *Quentin Durward* for *Huckleberry Finn.* And though his long-time aversion to Sir Walter's high-flown rhetoric was intensified by the effusions of the master's imitators, he called the Southern efforts "travesties" of Scott's style and method. He even granted that the Waverley novels, though out of place in the more realistic present, had been appropriate for the era in which they appeared. In the same vein, the sham castles were harmful, not in themselves but in their evocation of a sentimental and debilitating romanticism, devotion to which effectively prevented progress.

In *Life on the Mississippi* as originally written, the "Sir Walter disease" was less the complete villain than it appears in the published version. The finished book portrays the present-past conflict almost entirely in terms of backward South versus progressive North, with Scott the chief cause of the backwardness. But several chapters which Clemens ultimately deleted provide a broader comparison and a clearer indication of the author's current view of human flaws, flaws not limited to the South.[11]

To help him develop his contrast between past and present, Clemens called upon other British authors—Captain Marryat, Basil Hall, Francis Trollope, and others who had "filed marveling through the land" in the decades following the War of 1812. To Mrs. Trollope, his favorite, he devoted almost an entire chapter, intending it to follow Chapter Twenty-nine (which deals with progress in Memphis, Tennessee). Noting that the reader "could not have endured" the civilization that Mrs. Trollope had found in America, he praised the justness of her observations. Her indignation against "slavery, rowdyism, 'chivalrous' assassinations, sham godliness, and several other devilishnesses" was amply warranted. The "prejudices" for which she was so heartily despised seem to have been simply those "of a humane spirit against inhumanities; of an honest nature against humbug; of a clean breeding against grossness; of a right heart against unright speech and deed."

Another chapter dealing primarily with British tourists was to follow Chapter Forty, "Castles and Culture," which introduces the author's first attack on Scott's "contributions" to Southern architecture. Near the end of Chapter Forty, Clemens had returned to the tourist's reactions, quoting both Mrs. Trollope and Basil Hall while describing the river between Baton Rouge and New Orleans and, as a conclusion, had provided a list of some sixteen travelers (all British save Tocqueville) whose writings had flooded the United States between 1816 and 1850. The new chapter then further characterized the "civilization" observed by the tourists, noting that it was really "good rotten material for burial," and went on to describe significant improvements that had since occurred.

Had the author stopped there, the contrast of past and present would have been maintained and the superiority of the present established. But the same sort of honesty for which he commended the British observers seems to have inspired him to devote another chapter to certain "noticeable features of that departed America" which had *not* disappeared. After a long list of those flaws, including his old bugaboo Congressional ineptitude and lack of regard for the public welfare, particularly in its refusal to reform the Civil Service, he once more blasted the South's ridiculous perpetuation of the duel and mock tournament. And in closing, he fired a broader salvo at the general lack of moral courage which made most men renounce their principles rather than face up to opposition. Therefore, in thus exposing contemporary flaws, this chapter serves to undercut the praise of progress elsewhere and also to weaken the North-South contrast.

Finally, in still another chapter presumably designed to amplify the attack on Scottism, he elaborated on the tendency of human beings to bow to social pressures.[12] He flayed the irrational devotion to one political party that had created the epithet "Solid South." He sneered at the general fear of thinking and acting independently, and the fact that, in spite of such conformity, the citizens failed to unite to uphold the law or to demand the sort of justice in their courts that would prevent lynchings. Yet in comparing these characteristics with those of the average Northerner, he discovered only a slight superiority in the latter, namely a greater respect for the law and a better control of temper. Again, the emphasis both here and later in the chapter on the lack of moral courage exhibited by most men serves to extend the comment beyond the borders of the South. Since within a few months he was to associate these qualities with *all* men in *Huckleberry Finn,* the characteristics embodied in these chapters may justly be regarded as (in Henry Nash Smith's words) Clemens' current "metaphor for the human condition."[13]

Though the author yielded to James Osgood's suggestions that these several chapters be deleted from the final version of the book,[14] the material was important to him. He incorporated some of the "tourist" matter into an appendix. Sometime during the proof stage he added a long footnote in Chapter Forty citing instances of Southern "shooting affrays" (including the vivid Mabry-O'Connor incident) as ironic documentation of the claim in a Southern school's promotional "blurb" that the South afforded "the highest type of civilization this continent has seen." More significantly, he adapted much of his criticism of the South and of the average man generally to several episodes in *Huckleberry Finn*. The view of humanity which there emerges further suggests that the musings engendered by the river trip in 1882 indeed contributed to an increasingly dark mood.

Neither the attack on Scott nor the treatment of the British tourists, however, reveal any indication of a growing animosity toward England. At one point, in fact, Mark Twain allied England with the enemies of that "girly-girly romance" which the South held so dear. Noting that the Mardi Gras would surely fail in the North or in London because its original spirit of fun had been replaced by kings, knights, titles, and other "romantic mysteries," he added: "*Puck* and *Punch,* and the press universal, would fall upon it and make merciless fun of it, and its first exhibition would be also its last."[15]

As for the British tourists, even when one grants that the author's primary purpose in introducing their remarks was to stress the progress America had made since the "uncivilized" times of their visits, his approval of their attitudes is surprisingly strong. Marginal comments in his personal copy of Mrs. Trollope's *Domestic Manners of the Americans* demonstrate further that the favorable opinions in his book were not merely a pose to enhance his presentation of the present-past conflict. Among minor negative remarks he observes that American men no longer kept hats on or remained seated in the presence of ladies, as Mrs. Trollope had charged. He criticizes her report of the conversation of an impudent maidservant not for her attitude toward the girl (as might have been expected), but for her inaccurate representation of the vernacular idiom. In fact, he applauds as "a fair shot!" the traveler's amused observation that hiring servants was always referred to in Ohio as "getting help," since calling a free citizen a servant was regarded as "more than petty treason to the republic." More significantly he exclaims, "She hit it," next to the opinion that the chief distinction between Americans and Englishmen is the lack of refinement of the former. Later, when Mrs. Trollope concludes that whatever freedoms Americans enjoy beyond those permitted to the English are "enjoyed solely by the disorderly at the expense of the orderly," he concedes that the situation is "true yet."[16] No concern for the injustices of the British caste system here.

The Bright and the Dark (1882–1885)

Seldom had the British travelers in America received treatment as sympathetic as that in *Life on the Mississippi*. Traditionally, their comments had been greeted by choruses of self-righteous wrath and wounded pride. Even as late as the 1880's their names were seldom mentioned without a grimace. Only the successful reading tour of 1867 had allowed Charles Dickens to win back the affection that his *American Notes* (1842) had lost for him. But Clemens obviously respected their criticisms. And along with his surface desire to demonstrate the superiority of contemporary American life (except in the South), there runs the implication that instead of wallowing in hurt pride, Americans should have turned the British criticisms to constructive purposes.

Shortly after he finished *Life on the Mississippi*, however, there came other criticisms from England that he could not treat so generously. January, 1883, saw British periodicals up in arms over Charles Dudley Warner's report of a recent trip to England in the *Century* magazine for November, 1882. During 1882 there had been a general increase in British-American bickering, stimulated in part by Matthew Arnold's "A Word About America" in the May *Nineteenth Century*.[17] One such reaction appeared the same month as Warner's article, when George William Curtis—obviously with Arnold in mind—devoted his *Harper's* "Editor's Easy Chair" column to arguing the advantages of democratic institutions over those stressing rank and caste. Of British critics who retaliated to Warner, the editor of *Blackwood's*, having evidently taken special offense, sneered at the American's opinion that satires by Irving and Lowell surpassed anything in that genre since *Gulliver's Travels*, "gasping" at the implication that American writers could not properly be judged by British standards. Such provincialism, he snorted, would tend to set American authors "above criticism or comparison." Not only would it detract from the admiration of truly meritorious achievement, but it would establish "the public taste" or the "fashion of the moment" as the only possible standards for judging literary works.[18]

If Clemens had seen Arnold's remarks in "A Word About America" they had seemingly not irritated him. But since Warner was a personal friend, and since another friend, Howells, had also endured some less than laudatory comments from the *Blackwood's* critic, such insults could, apparently, not go unremarked. Using the *Blackwood's* article as a point of departure, Clemens began

[75

constructing a missile designed to shatter the British sense of superiority.

After general ridicule of the British for raising such a silly furor, he seized upon one condescending observation that America should be pitied both for her sad lack of accomplishment and for the "folly and evil" of her system of government. Britain was in no position to throw stones, he said. Ruled almost exclusively by foreigners, she had had only one short period of "native respectability"—under Cromwell, whose genius, ironically, was not appreciated "by the land he made so great." There had been two-thirds as many American presidents as British kings. But whereas only three or four presidents had really merited scorn, there had been only four or five English monarchs during the whole eight hundred years since the Battle of Hastings who had *not* deserved censure. Two alone had been without blemish—Victoria, and the boy Edward V—"and Richard III went and smothered him in the tower!" Therefore, the famous ruddy English complexion was really an "inherited blush," that "with sturdy English honesty" the British had even put "into their flag."*

So far, Clemens was well on the road to the sort of diatribe his Connecticut Yankee would be launching some four years later, but this one proved to be only a momentary flare-up. When the author came to defend other areas of American government, and, especially, to answer English criticisms of the civil service system, his missile sputtered out. Its roar faded into the weak claim that though corruption existed, America would correct her faults more rapidly than the British had done, and it finally died in a large "if." Just as England's present eminence as the greatest of nations had resulted from the pluck and inherent strength of the British people, the United States, too, was sound—"if we scrape off our American crust of shabby politicians."**

Apparently the outlook for America proved sufficiently bleak to extinguish Clemens' wrath, or at least to drain the power from his argument. It is almost as if he were recalling some of the omitted chapters of *Life on the Mississippi,* or even illustrating his answer in 1879 to the correspondent who had asked why he had not finished the book on England. "You couldn't satirize any given thing in England in any but a half-hearted way," he said, "because your

* Paine 91, Mark Twain Papers.
** Ibid.

conscience told you to look nearer home and you would find that very thing at your door."[19]

The generally favorable British reception of *Life on the Mississippi* early that summer probably also helped soothe his irritation. Reviewer Robert Brown told readers of the *Academy* for July 28, 1883, that the book did not contain a dull page. Nor did English critics seem offended at the attack on Sir Walter Scott, though one objected mildly.[20] What must have pleased Clemens most, however, was Howell's letter from England reporting that novelist Thomas Hardy had praised the book at a recent dinner party and had said: "Why don't people understand that Mark Twain is not merely a great humorist? He's a very remarkable fellow in a very different way."[21]

During that spring and summer, if Clemens' respect for English nobility and royalty changed at all, it rose rather than fell. The faults of monarchical government troubled him very little in May when he accepted the invitation of Canada's Governor-General, the Marquis of Lorne, to be his guest at a series of meetings of the Royal Literary and Scientific Society. From Government House at Ottawa he sent home a glowing tribute to the graciousness of his hosts, especially of the Marchioness, Princess Louise (fourth daughter of Queen Victoria). In August, when Howells wrote that he had given a letter of introduction to shipboard acquaintances, the Earl of Onslow and his wife, Clemens was hardly displeased. Answering that the family would be happy to receive them, he added: "And much obliged to you, too. There's plenty of worse people than the nobilities."[22]

That same summer Clemens' longtime fascination with English history manifested itself in a new form. One day in July, having struck a snag in his work on *Huckleberry Finn*, he tossed aside his pen and turned to mapping out a game that would both amuse his children and help them learn the important periods of English history. Along the Quarry Farm roadway he drove stakes (allotting one foot per year) to represent the respective reigns of British monarchs from William the Conqueror to Victoria. The children loved this learning-of-dates-made-easy, and Clemens himself was no less fascinated. He set about devising an indoor version that could be played on a board. For several months his enthusiasm bloomed into Sellers-like proportions as he foresaw his game creating a worldwide hunger for historical knowledge. He would satisfy that hunger by producing countless other games featuring not only monarchs, but statesmen, churchmen, and various celebrities of all nations. Like so many others, this dream never went beyond the dream stage, though a version of the original game was ultimately printed and patented.[23]

Something of the same fascination with history went into *Huckleberry Finn* to color Huck's dissertation on the nature of kings in Chapter Twenty-three, written during that spring or early summer. And this passage is relevant in another way to Clemens' current attitude toward England. Huck's remarks about kings, along with some of the King's and Duke's nefarious schemes, have customarily been cited as evidence of Clemens' deep hatred of monarchy and aristocracy and, somewhat less frequently, of his antipathy toward England itself. Few would argue, certainly, that monarchy and aristocracy appear in a favorable light. Perhaps something of Clemens' momentary anger at the attack on Warner's article touched his portrait of the con-men and Huck's comments on kings. But the conventional view places too strong a nationalistic interpretation on the novel. What some have seen as a satire on institutions foreign to "the American Way" is really a broader castigation of human nature in general, and of ignorance and prejudice in particular. Critics who have insisted on seeing Huck's comments as direct expressions of Clemens' democratic antagonism toward rank and caste have not sufficiently considered the matter of dramatic propriety.

A glaring instance of that sort of error regarding a later episode may serve to clarify this point. At least one critic has argued that Huck's conversation with Joanna Wilks in Chapter Twenty-six contains an attack on the British class system.[24] But when the dramatic situation is examined, the contention that Huck's remarks directly reflect the opinions of his creator does not hold up.

At the Wilkses' Huck has been passed off as the "valley" of the King and Duke, who are posing as the English brothers of the dead Peter Wilks. When Joanna questions Huck about life in England, he naturally has a difficult time, enmeshing himself in contradictory accounts of sea baths at the inland city of Sheffield, acquaintanceship with King William IV, and other matters which reveal to the reader, if not to Joanna, that he is completely ignorant of England. When Joanna asks whether servants in England were better treated than American slaves, his answer—"*No! a servant ain't nobody* there. They treat them worse than dogs,"—cannot be taken seriously as a statement of Clemens' social views. Or at least not as a direct statement.

The satire here is much more searching. The villain is not English social injustice but the nationalistic ignorance exhibited by Huck and Mary Jane. With no knowledge of the actual situation, Huck concludes that the position of a servant in another country *must* be worse than that of a slave in the United States. From such an attitude it is only a step to the bigotry and hypocrisy which, extolling democratic ideals, could yet condone slavery. This scene, therefore, is actually a close relative of the powerful one from the 1876 portion of the novel in which the despicable Pap Finn protests against a "govment" so corrupt as to allow a Negro to vote, by vowing never again to honor it by casting his own ballot. It reflects also the portrait of the average man in the deleted portions of *Life on the Mississippi*.

Huck's discussion of the nature and activities of monarchs (just after the King and Duke have swindled Bricksville with their performance of "The Royal Nonesuch,") reveals some of the same sort of provincial ignorance. His comments are just the kind a boy with his background would be likely to make if he knew any history at all. Especially reminiscent of schoolroom "boners" are his mixed-up examples of the "orneriness" of kings, when he credits Henry VIII not only with inspiring the 1,001 tales of Scheherazade (later published as the "Doomsday Book"), the Boston Tea Party, and the Declaration of Independence, but also with drowning his father, the Duke of Wellington, in a "butt of mamsey."

Again, as in the conversation with Joanna Wilks, the satire goes deeper than a jibe at monarchical institutions. What is being castigated is not so much the tyranny of kings as the tendency of human beings to seek their own advantage, to usurp and abuse privileges. Rationalizing his predicament with the Duke and Dauphin, Huck says, "We've got them on our hands, and we got to remember what they are, and make allowances." But then he adds—the italics are mine—"*Sometimes I wish we could hear of a country that's out of kings.*" He further decides that to tell Jim the two "noblemen" are imposters would serve no purpose: "It wouldn't a done no good; and, besides, it was just as I said, you couldn't tell them from the real kind."

That notion of the fundamental similarity of all men is actually one of the novel's primary themes. Beginning with Huck's realization at the end of Chapter Nineteen that the King and Duke are frauds, the author subtly underlines the essential baseness of men at all levels of society. Huck had quickly decided to be practical and not try to challenge the humbugs' claims, for as he says, his life with Pap has taught him that "the best way to get along with his kind of people is to let them have their way." That resolve, in turn, establishes an implicit connection between kings, con-men, and that lowest level of society represented by Pap Finn.

Huck's experiences in Bricksville furnish other links between commoners and kings. As the group arrives at the shabby Arkansas town (in Chapter Twenty-one) Huck describes the slothfulness and senseless cruelty of the loafers who line the main street and calls them "a mighty ornery lot." Two chapters later, when he tries to explain to Jim why the King and Duke have behaved so reprehensibly, he refers to the "real" kings of history in exactly the same phrase.

The Sherburn-Boggs episode and its aftermath (Chapters Twenty-one and Twenty-two) delineate more fully the "mighty ornery lot" that constituted the several levels of society in Bricksville and dramatize the overwhelming influence of community-bred opinions on the ordinary individual. Especially significant in Colonel Sherburn's defiance of the lynch-mob is the fact that Sherburn's scorn for the hypocrisy and essential cowardice of the average man represents Clemens' own views as expressed in the chapters deleted from *Life on the Mississippi*. Most critics agree that the Colonel's diatribe is one of the rare instances in the novel where the author's voice breaks through that of his narrator to speak directly to the reader.[25]

To help him dramatize some of these qualities in man, Clemens seems to have called upon several favorite British authors (and one less-than-favorite) for important ingredients. Echoes not only of Carlyle's *French Revolution* but possibly of his edition of Oliver Cromwell's *Letters and Speeches* enliven the action following the death of Boggs; Charles Dickens' *Tale of Two Cities* provides significant details for that and other episodes; Sir Walter Scott's *Fortunes of Nigel* furnishes a vivid descriptive detail, and *Quentin Durward,* a memorable characterization. The *Diary* of Samuel

Pepys, besides contributing to the portraits of the King and Duke, enhances—if it did not actually inspire—the humorist's depiction of the essential similarity of all men.

Just when Clemens first became acquainted with Pepys' great chronicle of Restoration England is not certain. His enthusiasm for "glorious old Pepy's Diary" in an 1873 letter to Joe Twichell[26] suggests that this was not the first time he had traveled through seventeenth-century London with Pepys as a guide. Personal memoirs of all kinds fascinated Clemens, but Pepys was his odds-on and life-long favorite among British diarists, and very likely the inspiration for the humorist's own numerous attempts at fictionalized diaries. In later years Clemens remembered writing part of his first such effort—the diary of Shem—when he was visiting in Edinburgh in July, 1873, just a month after the letter to Twichell. About 1876, too, he "translated" a portion of "Methuselah's Diary," the style of which greatly resembles Pepys'.[27]

What chiefly attracted Clemens was the Englishman's ability to bring to life the people and events he recorded—the great Plague and Fire; the colorful Charles II and his brother James, Duke of York; Nell Gwyn; and other famous and infamous characters of the day. Of special appeal were the insights into the character of the diarist himself as he marched among the great and near-great, rarely missing an opportunity to improve his situation.

Pepys was much on Clemens' mind during the summer of 1876 when he finished most of the first sixteen chapters of *Huckleberry Finn*. As noted earlier, the diary was doubtless among the "ancient English books" that he consulted in search of authentic language for the embryo *Prince and the Pauper*.[28] Moreover, in the headnote to *1601*, his "extract" from the diary of Queen Elizabeth's cupbearer, written that same August, he called his diarist "the Pepys of that day."

In that piece, properly titled *Date 1601. Conversation, as it was by the Social Fireside in the time of the Tudors*, the humorist endowed his narrator with Pepysian traits beyond a mere propensity for diary-keeping. His own main interest, as he later said, lay in the revelation of the cup-bearer's character through his outrage at having to serve such "low" persons as Shakespeare and the other literary men, and his contemptuous reactions to the conversation. Often these snobbish remarks sound much like some of Pepys' reactions—

his complaint of May 1, 1669, for instance, that the presence of hackney coaches in the Park prevented those of gentlemen from receiving proper notice.[29]

As Clemens remembered the genesis of *1601*, his rummaging among the old books had turned up a brief conversation between ladies and gentlemen whose "frank indelicacies of speech" had suddenly come to life for him. Until then he had looked on the various grossnesses in earlier writers like Rabelais merely as literary devices rather than as reflections of actual conversational usage. But with this new realization that such language must actually have been employed in polite company, he felt almost compelled to embody his own "archaics" in a piece that would "out-Rabelais Rabelais." And he decided to send it first to his minister friend Joe Twichell.

Though Paine attributed that inspiration directly to Pepys, he was probably wrong. The *Diary* often refers to lewd language, but there is no scene that really fits Clemens' description. Still, it is very possible that one passage not only sent the humorist to another source that does contain such conversations but may also have suggested addressing his exercise in ribaldry to a minister. In his entry for January 20, 1667/68 Pepys tells of dining with a minister named Case, who told "a pretty story of a religious lady, Queen of Navarre." An editor's footnote at that point adds that the "pretty story" was "doubtless from her Heptameron, a work imitating in title and manner that of Boccaccio."

Clemens would not have needed that identification of Marguerite of Navarre, for he had just added a copy of the *Heptameron* to his library in 1875, the year before he wrote *1601*.[30] Being more familiar with its tales than with Marguerite's religious writings, he would certainly have been amused by the reference to "a pretty story of a religious lady" and especially to its being told by a minister. Furthermore, Clemens was obviously thinking of the *Heptameron* while writing *1601*, for in the latter Sir Walter Raleigh attributes his concluding anecdote (in which a maiden foils an attempted rape by "an olde archbishoppe") to "ye ingenious Margrette of Navarre." Though Raleigh's story was apparently original with Clemens, it nevertheless reminds one that the Heptameron abounds with references to clerical assaults—successful as often as not—on maidenly and wifely virtue.

Most of the *Heptameron* stories evoke entertaining discussions among the ladies and gentlemen present. Many might have struck

Clemens as highly suggestive, but in two of them, especially (Tale 52, Eighth Day, and Tale 12, Third Day), both the language and an emphasis on odors make a connection with *1601* likely.[31] Perhaps one of these was the indelicate conversation Clemens had in mind when he brought his garrulous group together at Elizabeth's fireside to utter his own "frank indelicacies," which began, after a few preliminaries ,with the cup-bearer's comment that "one did breake wind . . . yielding an exceding mightie and distresful stink, whereat all did laugh full sore."

Though flatulence at the courts of kings and queens—and elsewhere—has often been the subject for humorous comment, Walter Blair has shown that this initial explosion and its immediate aftermath seem to echo two songs in *Wit and Mirth, or Pills to Purge Melancholy* (1716), the collection of Thomas D'Urfey, a younger contemporary of Pepys. Titled respectively "The FART; Famous for its Satyrical Humour in the Reign of Queen Anne," and "The Second Part of the FART; Or the Beef-eaters Appeal to Mr. D'Urfey," the songs tell of a similar explosion at the Court of St. James, various accusations, and the final revelation of the culprit—all of which find their parallels in *1601*.[32]

Some such delvings in Pepys, the *Heptameron,* and D'Urfey, then, doubtless provided the foundations on which Clemens built his bawdy tale of crepitation and conversation "as it was . . . in the time of the Tudors." Of the three, Pepys' *Diary* is perhaps the most important in having inspired both the form of the piece and the character of the cup-bearer. Clemens' fascination with creating the character of the old nobleman as an exercise in maintaining a restricted point of view is in turn significant, coming as it did at the time he was beginning *Huckleberry Finn.*

Pepys' *Diary* was important to *Huckleberry Finn* in a number of other ways. Though Clemens' notions of his two famous charlatans who enter Huck's story at Chapter Nineteen doubtless derived from many sources both in literature and in life, indications point also to Pepys' portraits of Charles II and his brother James. The diarist was seldom happier, it seems, than when he could recount his personal associations with that royal pair, who appear and reappear in the *Diary,* often together—roistering, conniving, and sometimes quarreling—and often referred to simply as "the King and Duke."

One passage in Pepys not only parallels the humorist's introduction of his King and Duke, but also dwells upon the similarities of Royalty to lesser men. When the two American rapscallions come splashing along a creek (pursued by bloodhounds) and board Huck's canoe to be paddled to the island, where the raft is hidden, it seems almost as if the author were dramatizing Pepys' report of his excursion in the royal barge on July 26, 1665, which begins: "To Greenwich, to the Park, where I heard the King and Duke are come by water this morn from Hampton Court." The remainder of the entry is even more significant. Elated at being in the presence of royalty, Pepys nevertheless reveals his hurt pride at being the only one of the group not invited to dine with the king that noon, the others all having the rank of knight or higher. Admitting that he could not "in modesty" have expected the honor, he still was moved to add, "yet, God forgive my Pride! I was sorry I was there, that Sir W. Batten should say he could sit down where I could not." Of the afternoon's trip in the royal barge he notes that he especially enjoyed hearing the King and Duke converse. But then, with an apologetic "God forgive me!" he admits that though he admires the pair "with all the duty possible," the more "one considers and observes them, the less he finds of difference between them and other men." Then he further qualifies his audacity by adding, "though blessed be God! they are both princes of great nobleness and spirits."

Huck, on the raft, undergoes a similar experience, with overtones that become even more ironic if Pepys was indeed Clemens' source. He, too, is much impressed with the "quality" of the visitors, when the younger reveals his *true* identity as the Duke of Bridgewater and his companion proceeds to top his story by claiming to be the "lost Dolphin" of France. Huck and Jim gladly accord the King the services proper to royalty and do not "set down in his presence" until asked to do so. But soon the observant Huck recognizes the kinship of *his* King and Duke with ordinary men—notably his Pap.

The characterization of these two charlatans shares several other elements with Pepys' *Diary*. From the first attempts of the King and Duke to surpass each other's lies, there is a good deal of tension between them. Though they realize the necessity for cooperation in their swindles, they often quarrel over money matters and over the Duke's tendency to direct activities. The frequent bitterness between Charles and James stemmed primarily from the same causes. In his entry for December 30, 1667, for instance, Pepys notes one such controversy, quoting Sir George Carteret's observation that though "the King and Duke do not in company disagree," he doubted "that there is a core [accord?] in their hearts. . . ."

By itself that comment is perhaps not significant, but in the same entry Pepys also speaks of the trouble stirred up by the King's decision (which the Duke opposed) to dismiss a number of his Councillors, among whom was "my Lord Bridgewater." Other references to the Earl of Bridgewater would likewise surely have caught Clemens' eye, especially the one in which Pepys also mentions Nell Gwyn, smiling from a Drury Lane doorway "in her smock sleeves and bodice" and calls her "a mighty pretty creature."[33]

As is perhaps almost inevitable, the "Dolphin" immediately corrupts the name Bridgewater to "Bilgewater," a change that becomes entirely appropriate when the Duke looses the full flood of his rhetoric. It also recalls the fact, however, that in *1601*, itself partly inspired by Pepys, Clemens had placed a Duchess of Bilgewater among the fireside group. Clemens had played with the comic possibilities of the name "W. Bilgewater" as early as 1865, and had mentioned a "Colonel Bilgewater" in *Roughing It* (1872).[34] But even if he had not read Pepys by that time, it is still probable that the references to the Earl of Bridgewater in the *Diary* reminded him later of the name that he bestowed on both Duchess and Duke.

Making "Bilgewater" a duke rather than an earl again possibly points to his relationship with Pepys' Duke of York. One of Huck's comments in Chapter Twenty-three may also imply a subtle relationship to the duke who was soon to become King James II. While agreeing with Jim that their Duke is not quite so obnoxious as the King, Huck adds that he is not *very* different, since "when he's drunk there ain't no near-sighted man could tell him from a king."

A much closer parallel in that same chapter shows that Clemens was almost certainly thinking of Pepys. In the discussion of kings and their ways, Huck cites "Henry the Eight's" habit of taking a new wife every day and executing her the next morning. Among Henry's short-lived brides he names three—Nell Gwyn, Jane Shore, and "Fair Rosamun" (Rosamond Clifford). No doubt Clemens knew something of these mistresses of Charles II, Edward IV, and Henry II from other reading in English history. But in few historical works does "pretty, witty Nell" appear more frequently than in the *Diary*. In another vivid passage, which also touches on themes already discussed, Pepys himself mentions both of the other lovelies in a context that Clemens would again have been sure to notice.

Writing of his attendance at a religious service at Whitehall on March 25, 1664, Pepys first notes that because of the crowded chapel he had pretended to be a member of the court, so as to sit in a reserved pew. Though certain "great persons" at first questioned his right to be there, his story apparently satisfied them. Later, recalling several impressive portions of the sermon, he described an especially bitter passage in which the minister, speaking directly to the king and the ladies, observed that skeletons of the dead exhibited no differences: that "for all the pains the ladies take with their faces, he that should look in a charnel-house could not distinguish which was Cleopatra's, or Fair Rosamond's or Jane Shore's."

Clemens' obvious knowledge of the grave-digger's scene in *Hamlet* would also have called his attention to this passage. He not only knew the play well but had drawn upon it himself for much of the Duke's burlesque soliloquy two chapters earlier. At any rate, Clemens' introduction of Jane Shore and Fair Rosamond immediately before Huck's comment that monarchs are "a mighty ornery lot" and that he wishes there were some country "that's out of kings," suggests that Pepy's report of the sermon had made a strong impression.

Pepys may also have provided one other minor detail in the Bricksville chapters. Sometime during the proof-stage of the novel Clemens changed the title of the King's ridiculous "dramatic" performance from "The Burning Shame" (as it appears in the manuscript) to "The King's Camelopard, or The Royal Nonesuch." The addition of the subtitle especially augments the satire by stressing the aspect of royalty, and makes the title more descriptive of the real nature of both the performance and performer. As Walter Blair has shown, both the title and the incident itself contain interesting parallels to one of Poe's tales, "Four Beasts in One, or the Homocameleopard."[35] The subtitle, however, may well have occurred to Clemens while he was leafing through Pepys' *Diary,* where the name "Nonsuch" occurs several times. Besides various memoranda about visits to Nonsuch House, the temporary home of the Exchequer in 1664, Pepys refers in his entry of March 19, 1669 to a quarrel between a Dutch Captain, "who commands 'the Nonsuch'," and one of his lieutenants, and calls the altercation "a drunken kind of silly business." Since few descriptions could be more appropriate to the "Dolphin's" antics, Pepys may well have helped inspire the change of title.

If Clemens borrowed these details from Pepys, they helped him dramatize an important phase of his novel's study of man and society. The connection of the passages from Pepys with the King and the Duke and with Huck's comments on the monarchs of history underlines both the essential kinship of all men and the fact that fraud, hypocrisy, and cowardice are the qualities that seemed to him to motivate most human actions.

In the Bricksville episodes the author also called upon Thomas Carlyle for help in illustrating some of the same qualities of man, and for other elements as well. Consistently fond of *The French Revolution,* Clemens in 1882 and 1883 had experienced a new burst of enthusiasm for Carlyle's works, and had added several to his library. During the summer after the river trip he tackled the massive biography of Frederick the Great. By the following May he had burrowed through the five volumes of *Oliver Cromwell's Letters and Speeches,* taking note of an incident that he was later to adapt for a short story, "The Death Disk."[36] He also owned Froude's biography of Carlyle, the first two volumes of which appeared in 1882. In 1883, the year of its publication, he bought and read Froude's three-volume edition of the *Letters and Memorials of Jane Welsh Carlyle, Prepared for Publication by Thomas Carlyle.*

From the latter work, if not from the biography, Clemens apparently adopted Froude's portrait of Carlyle as an erratic and selfish misanthrope. But the jaundiced view of Carlyle's personality did not diminish his appreciation of the Scotsman's artistry nor his affection for the works. As late as 1909, he would agree with Paine's description of Carlyle as "a fervid stump speaker," who pounded his fists and shouted at his audience. "But," he added, "he is the best one that ever lived." Only minutes before he died in 1910, he would turn again to his much-worn copy of *The French Revolution,* seeking escape from his worry and pain by reading once more Carlyle's brilliant recreation of those tumultuous times.[37]

The spurt of special interest in Carlyle in 1882 and 1883 left its mark on the final episode of *Huckleberry Finn.* Parts of Tom's elaborate scheme for freeing Jim in Chapters Thirty-nine and Forty lean heavily on Carlyle's account of the French Royal Family's abortive flight to Varennes. The inspiration for Tom's reference to "mullet-headed" captors and his use of "nonnamous letters" was almost certainly Carlyle's account of the "glassy-eyed" commandant Gouvion's failure to discover the absence of Louis and Marie, even after a certain "false Chambermaid" had told him of their suspicious preparations. Not until the investigation of a "patriot Deputy, warned by a billet" was the escape discovered. Tom, gloating over the "elegant" success of his adventure, again refers indirectly to Carlyle's episode when he vows that if they had "had the handling of Louis XVI., there wouldn't a been no 'Son of Saint Louis, ascend to heaven!' wrote down in *his* biography; no, sir, we'd a whooped him over the *border*. . . . and done it just as slick as nothing at all, too."[38]

In these passages, as well as in some of the details of activities of Tom's robber gang which Carlyle's account probably helped furnish,[39] the humorist used his source chiefly for the purpose of burlesquing Tom's romantic dreams. And Tom's vernacular rendering of the events gives the humor a special emphasis. In the Sherburn-Boggs episode, however, addition of details from Carlyle's picture of Paris under the Terror serve a more serious purpose. Added to the elements already discussed, they helped Clemens to portray the savagery and cowardice of his average man.

The reaction of the crowd after the shooting of Boggs—their "scrouging and pushing" to catch a glimpse of the body; their headlong rush, "whooping and raging" toward Sherburn's house—is a searching study of mob psychology. Since few of the books that Clemens read have as impressive mob scenes as *The French Revolution,* perhaps the most likely progenitor of the Bricksville mob is that which jammed the Place de la Guillotine to watch the execution of Robespierre. There, "in one dense stirring mass" of morbid fascination, the Parisians crowd all windows and other vantage points—"the very roofs and ridge-tiles budding forth Curiosity, in strange gladness." To help satisfy that curiosity, the gendarmes point at Robespierre with their swords "to show the people which is he." As the guillotine falls, there is "shout on shout of applause."[40] In *Huckleberry Finn* the same elements are present, but Carlyle's implied disapproval becomes ironic satire when Bricksville's sensation-seekers refuse to yield their places to those pushing from behind, and the latter seek satisfaction of their morbid curiosity by pleading: " 'Taint right and 'taint fair for you to stay thar all the time . . . ; other folks has their rights as well as you."

Carlyle's gendarmes who point out the intended victim so that the onlookers may fully savor the execution find a counterpart in the lanky Bricksvillian who demonstrates exactly how Boggs had been murdered. The crowd greets his performance with the same sort of "strange gladness" that brought the shouts of applause for the Paris executioner's dispatching of Robespierre. Their "treating" him with drinks as a reward for having "done it perfect," added to the earlier demands for fair play, help to make Clemens' picture more powerful than Carlyle's.

Clemens also seems to have borrowed from Carlyle for Sherburn's subsequent defiance of the lynch mob. Many of the details of the crowd's motion and the actual picture of a forceful figure haranguing a mob were common to a number of the works Clemens had read dealing with the French Revolution. But a direct question by Carlyle in one passage and the military imagery he employs seem to have furnished at least part of the inspiration for the Colonel's "slow and scornful" address to his would-be lynchers. "Is it not miraculous," Carlyle asks, "how one man moves hundreds of thousands; each unit of whom, it may be, loves him not, and singly fears him not, yet has to obey him. . . ." And later in the same passage he notes that "military mobs are mobs with muskets in their hands," and that to the soldier "revolt is frightful and, oftenest perhaps, pitiable. . . ."[41]

In Bricksville, Sherburn's contempt for the mob is monumental. "The idea of *you* lynching anybody!" he sneers. "It's amusing. The idea of you thinking you had pluck enough to lynch a *man!* . . . Your mistake is, that you didn't bring a man with you. . . ." Calling a mob "the pitifulest thing out," he compares it to an army whose members "don't fight with the courage that's born in them, but with courage that's borrowed from their mass, and from their officers." But without a *man* at its head, a mob "is *beneath* pitifulness." And then, raising his shotgun, he orders them to leave.

The crowd's dispersal is immediate, and even Huck beautifully reflects their mood as he says, almost with a swagger, "I could a stayed if I wanted to, but I didn't want to."

There is little doubt that Carlyle's admiration for the strong man supplemented Clemens' own inclination toward hero-worship. Such comments as that about Mirabeau—"Honour to the strong man, in these ages, who has shaken himself loose of shams and *is* something"—surely struck a responsive chord in the man who had lauded the same qualities in Ambassador Anson Burlingame and all but rhapsodized about the "more than regal power" of the old-time Mississippi pilot.[42] Colonel Sherburn, facing down the mob, is partly such a hero, his cold-blooded murder of Boggs notwithstanding.

The actual shooting of Boggs was based chiefly on Clemens' own memory of the death of "Uncle Sam" Smarr at the hands of a Hannibal merchant, William Owsley.[43] The records do not show, however, that any sort of mob action followed that incident. I should like to suggest, in fact, that still another passage in Carlyle not only might have jogged Clemens' memory of the Owsley-Smarr fracas but might even have inspired him to add to *Life on the Mississippi* the footnote describing the almost parallel Mabry-O'Connor shooting in Tennessee. In his reading of Carlyle's *Letters and Speeches of Cromwell* late in 1882 while he was finishing *Life on the Mississippi* and perhaps also working on *Huckleberry Finn,* Clemens would certainly have been interested in Carlyle's summary of an incident in which the Puritan leader snuffed out rumblings of dissension among his troops. Ordering eleven chief mutineers from the ranks, the Great Protector condemned them "by swift Court-Martial to die; and Trooper Arnald, one of them, was accordingly shot there and then; which extinguished the mutiny for that time." What makes it doubly certain that Clemens knew the incident is that Carlyle used it also in *The French Revolution,* less accurately, perhaps, but much more colorfully. There, to underscore his contention that a leader seeking to maintain control during troublous times must act quickly and decisively, Carlyle cited Cromwell's sure touch: "When that Agitator Sergeant stept forth from the ranks, with plea of grievances, and began gesticulating and demonstrating, as the mouthpiece of Thousands expectant there," the leader "discerned with those truculent eyes of his, how the matter lay; plucked a pistol from his holsters; blew Agitator and Agitation instantly out. Noll was a man fit for such things." Clemens would at least have said "Amen!"[44]

Whatever the exact stimulus for the Bricksville scenes, Clemens obviously still agreed with Carlyle (as he had in the 1870's) about the essential nature of the masses, particularly when formed into mobs. The chief emphasis in the Sherburn incident falls on the cowardice of the average man. Admiration for the bravery of Sherburn in defying the mob outweighs the censure aroused by his killing of Boggs. Yet Clemens could hardly be condoning a cold-blooded assassination. Hence Sherburn, too, becomes a representative of mankind in general. In many ways one of the highest types of individual in the novel, he is still capable of ruthless murder. Here the author seems to be saying that in the rare case when a man is not a sheep-like follower, then he is likely to be the sort of "hot-head" who takes the law into his own hands.

The sympathy created by the introduction of Boggs's sorrowing daughter underlines the cruelty of Sherburn's deed, and at the same time reveals another bond with Carlyle. Huck's pity for her, like that for Buck Grangerford earlier, and even for the tarred-and-feathered King and Duke later on, resembles Carlyle's for Louis, for Marie Antoinette, and even for Robespierre.[45]

To complete the record, it should be noted that one earlier episode parallels still another passage in Carlyle. Since the chapters relating Huck's visit to the Grangerford plantation (Seventeen, Eighteen) were probably written between October 1879, and June 1880, the attack on sentimentalism embodied therein may well have been stimulated by Clemens' re-reading of *The French Revolution* early in 1879. For, consciously or not, in presenting Emmeline Grangerford's lugubrious poetry and painting, followed by the much more serious and vicious feud, the author dramatizes one of Carlyle's denunciations of Jean Jacques Rousseau's pernicious influence. Sarcastically noting the usefulness of sentimentalism "for weeping with over romances and on pathetic occasions," the historian terms it "twin-sister to Cant, if not one and the same with it." *Cant* he defines in turn as "the *materia prima* of the Devil; from which all falsehoods, imbecilities, abominations body themselves; from which no true thing *can* come."[46]

Walter Blair correctly suggests that our introduction to the Grangerfords is a sympathetic one. Colonel Grangerford, the friendly children, and even the garish parlor inspire affection. So does the satire of Emmeline's "crayons" and poems (derived principally from the wonderfully awful poetry of Julia A. Moore, the "Sweet Singer of Michigan").[47] But just as Carlyle's equation of Sentimentalism with Cant passes from the harmless "weeping over romances and pathetic occasions" to the *"materia prima"* of falsehood, imbecility, and abominations, so Clemens takes the reader from the appealing ridiculousness of parlor, painting, and poetry to the vicious and senseless feud and the death of Buck Grangerford. Small wonder Huck feels so sick that he almost falls out of the tree in which he is hiding.

Charles Dickens' *Tale of Two Cities* also added much to *Huckleberry Finn*.[48] Like Carlyle's *French Revolution* (to which Dickens, too, admittedly owed a great deal), *A Tale of Two Cities* abounds with details like those used by Tom in directing the activities of his "robber gang" and the escape of Jim from the Phelpses' farm. Tom's directions to Huck for procuring and paying a doctor parallel the experiences of Doctor Manette in being summoned to treat the victims of the St. Evrémondes' violence. Earlier in the book, the argument of Jim and Huck about the French language (Chapter Fourteen), shows both assuming much the same attitude as that which the British-to-the-core Miss Pross held toward the French (Book Three, Chapter Thirteen). Jim sees "no sense to" the French way of speaking; Miss Pross regards learning French as "nonsense." Huck, responding to Jim's "stubbornness" by deciding it is no use to waste words because "you can't learn a nigger to argue," suggests the sort of superiority-feeling that Miss Pross exhibited. That same feeling of superiority blinds Huck entirely to Jim's point of view—a logical one when Jim's simple ignorance is taken into account—and he is disgusted. Hence, in this episode, Dickens may have contributed important elements to the characters of Jim and Huck as well as helped to depict the relationship between them. The subsequent changes in that relationship, of course, constitute a major part of the novel's purpose.

Those passages are largely humorous, but more serious overtones are present in other incidents in which Dickens' influence seems evident. In Chapter Five Pap Finn's browbeating of Huck for the "airs" he has acquired from the Widow Douglas is cut from the same cloth as Jerry Cruncher's blasts at his wife for activities harmful to his career as an "honest tradesman."[49] Just as the piety of "the Aggerawayter" is an affront to a man engaged in grave-robbing, so Huck's cleanliness and literacy enrage the filthy and ignorant Pap. Again, from a technical point of view, both scenes are important in establishing the characters of their respective participants and the motivation for subsequent action. Clemens' adaption of Cruncher's tirade to the person of Pap Finn allows the reader better to understand Pap's later disillusionment with a "govment" which would grant a Negro college professor equal rights with himself. It also makes clearer the resentment of his own inferiority which drives him to prove himself "Huck Finn's boss" by taking him to the hut on the Illinois shore, from where Huck's downriver wanderings soon begin.

Less humorous, but no less effective use of details from Dickens may be seen in Clemens' picture of mob action in Bricksville, supplementing those which Carlyle furnished. In one scene from *A Tale of Two Cities,* in particular, the Londoners seem close counterparts of the Bricksvillians. A cry of "Spies!" in a crowd following a funeral procession touches off a near riot as all immediately join in the shouting. When someone yells "Pull 'em out there!" the mob rush to comply, turning the single mourner out of his coach, and then, at the suggestion of one of their number, taking over the conduct of the entire funeral. This travesty accomplished, they seek "other entertainment" and again conform when someone conceives "the humour of impeaching casual passers-by as Old Bailey spies and wreaking vengeance on them." But when a rumor spreads that the Guards are coming, the crowd, Dickens says, "gradually melted away . . . and this was the usual progress of a mob" (Book Two, Chapter Fourteen).

In Bricksville, the mob's "progress" parallels that in London. After Boggs's death, the people crowd around, trying to see the corpse, and the "lanky man" entertains them by reenacting the murder. Then someone shouts Sherburn should be lynched, and "in about a minute everybody was saying it; so away they went, mad and yelling, and snatching down every clothes-line they come to to do the hanging with." The mob's "washing back sudden" and "breaking all apart" in the face of Sherburn's defiance also reflects the "melting away" in London, though here, too, the mob scenes of Carlyle and other writers on the French Revolution doubtless helped.

Thus, as Walter Blair has noted, the materials from Dickens are skillfully absorbed into the very heart of the book. The discussion of the French language delineates character, emphasizes an early stage of the book's central relationship, and contributes through its humor to the depiction of the idyllic life on the raft. The speeches of Pap Finn not only serve to characterize him and motivate important actions, but also ironically to castigate the prejudice, ignorance, and hypocrisy of mankind. The lynching episode not only reconstructs the life of the period, but also explicitly pronounces one of Clemens' harshest denunciations of the human race.

In view of the attack on Sir Walter Scott and romanticism in *Life on the Mississippi,* it is not strange to find a similar antagonism in *Huckleberry Finn.* Among several minor details, the humorist embellished Tom Sawyer's romantic nonsense in Chapter Three by having him dispatch a boy to run through town with a blazing stick as a signal for the gang to assemble—a device that echoes details in both *The Lay of the Last Minstrel* and *The Lady of the Lake.*[50] In Chapter Three he hit Scott's "decayed" romanticism more obliquely by naming the wrecked steamboat the *Walter Scott.* And from Huck's reading of books salvaged from that steamboat arises his first conversation with Jim about the nature of kings.

During his description of the characteristic slothfulness of monarchs (Chapter Fourteen), Huck makes a comment so natural that one would scarcely suspect a literary origin. Kings just "set around," he says, unless there happens to be a war; then they go. But "other times they just lazy around; or go hawking—just hawking and sp—." At that he hears a noise and does not finish the pun. It could be that the humorist was merely having Huck make a natural association with the word "hawking." Yet in Chapter Thirty-six of the *Fortunes of Nigel,* a book which Clemens had referred to in his study notes for *The Prince and the Pauper,* one finds the "artificial" Sir Walter using the same play on words when the rake Dalgarno soothes the fears of Nelly Christie, the ship-chandler's wife who has eloped with him. Painting the delights which await her, he adds as a special attraction the promise that she shall "ride a-hunting and hawking with a lord, instead of waiting upon an old ship-chandler, who could do nothing but hawk and spit." By bestowing upon royalty this crude characteristic which Lord Dalgarno had sneeringly applied to the commoner John Christie, Clemens here again, consciously or not, has Huck turn the tables on the aristocratic attitudes portrayed in Scott's works.

But not all of Clemens' borrowings in *Huckleberry Finn* attack Scott's romanticism. For all his complaining about Scott's flowery rhetoric and faulty character-drawing, the humorist had one real favorite among the Waverly novels, *Quentin Durward.*[51] He had consulted that book while planning *The Prince and the Pauper* and had transferred some details of a suit of Milanese armor described by Scott into his own novel. For *Huckleberry Finn,* he seems to have borrowed most of the details for the undertaker who managed the Wilkses' funeral "orgies" in Chapter Twenty-seven.

While reading *Quentin Durward* Clemens could hardly have helped being struck by Scott's characterization of Oliver Le Dain, the hypocritically obsequious barber and favorite councillor of Louis XI. At his first appearance, in Chapter Eight of the novel, Le Dain is described as a "little, pale, meagre man," who characteristically concealed his penetrating and quick glances "by keeping his eyes fixed on the ground, while, with the stealthy and quiet pace of a cat, he seemed modestly rather to glide than to walk through the apartment." On this occasion, after a few words to Count Dunois about the King's current wishes, he "glided quietly out of the room." As the assembled courtiers respectfully made way for him, he acknowledged this civility "by the most humble inclination of the body," except in a few instances when he made one or two the envy of all "by whispering a single word in their ear." At the same time he skillfully dodged both their replies and the "eager solicitations" of favor-seekers by "muttering something of the duties of his place." At another point (Chapter Twelve) Scott emphasizes Le Dain's skill in managing the King. Entering the audience chamber, the barber "glided on with his noiseless step until he had just crossed the line of the King's sight, so as to make him aware of his presence, then shrank modestly backward and out of sight, until he should be summoned to speak or to listen." Later in the same episode the author again compares Le Dain to a cat, both in the "purring affectation of officiousness and humility" that he usually exhibits, and the "watchful, animated and alert" readiness for sudden exertion that characterizes his conversations with King Louis.

Here, almost surely, was Clemens' model for the stealthy undertaker in *Huckleberry Finn.* As Huck describes him, that worthy "slid around in his black gloves with his softy soothering ways, putting on the last touches, and getting people and things all ship-shape and comfortable, and making no more sound than a cat." Without a word, he moved people around, squeezed in latecomers, and opened pathways through the crowd—"and done it with nods, and signs with his hands," and then this "softest, glidingest, stealthiest" man that Huck had ever seen "took his place over against the wall."

When the minister commences, a barking dog interrupts the

service; the undertaker makes a sign to the preacher "as much as to say, 'Don't you worry—just depend on me.' " and glides out. There is a whack, and "in a minute or two here comes this undertaker's back and shoulders gliding along the wall again; and so he glided and glided, around three sides of the room, and then rose up, and shaded his mouth with his hands, and stretched his neck out towards the preacher . . . and says in a kind of coarse whisper, *'He had a rat!'* Then he drooped down and glided along the wall again to his place." This pleased the people, Huck says, because naturally they were curious. "A little thing like that don't cost nothing, and it's just the little things that makes a man to be looked up to and liked. There warn't no more popular man in town than what that undertaker was."

The dog-and-rat incident, as Walter Blair suggests, probably derived either from an actual experience involving Captain Duncan of the *Quaker City* or from an undertaker yarn that Clemens had thought of working into *A Tramp Abroad*.[52] But the "softy soothering" undertaker himself is the image of Oliver Le Dain. Just as Le Dain controls the self-seeking courtiers with only "the most humble inclination of the body," the undertaker manipulates the sentimental sensation-seekers at the funeral simply by small signs. His confident motion to the minister and his "drooping" back against the wall after dispatching the noisy dog finds its special parallel in Le Dain's gliding into the King's line of vision, and then shrinking "modestly backward" until the King might need him. Though Le Dain was feared rather than liked, his access to King Louis made him perhaps the most "popular" man at court. His brief words to a favored few likewise have their counterparts in the undertaker's small services which, as Huck puts it "didn't cost nothing," but made him the most popular man in town.

In view of his immense influence with the King, Le Dain's gliding obsequiousness becomes sinister. Clemens turns that characteristic to splendid comic effect as he plays with the words "gliding" and "glided" almost (but not quite) to the point of absolute absurdity. Yet a sinister note is also present (for the reader at least) in the great prestige accorded this oily creature and also in the townspeople's absorption in the sodden sentimentality of the "orgies" he conducts. In addition, the transfer of Scott's obsequious manipulator of public affairs from a royal court to a small Arkansas town itself provides another tacit comment on the essential similarity of all mankind. Thus, though Clemens again created something new from his borrowed materials, his portrait gains in richness when the source is considered.

The portrait of the "human condition" that emerges in *Huckleberry Finn* is largely a pessimistic one. Again and again the "good" people as well as the "ornery" ones reveal themselves as either perpetrators of violence or willing victims of fraud, sham, and social pressure. The goodness of Huck himself seems always beset by almost insurmountable obstacles. The ideal situation for its operation, symbolized by the association of Huck and Jim on the raft, is difficult to maintain. Huck has to go ashore, and on the shore are the forces of society with their artificial values. During the 1870's Clemens had believed that the masses, though ignorant and gullible, could be comforted, corrected, and uplifted by enlightened leaders who would purify the corrupt institutions. Now he was moving toward the notion that man was all but incapable of improvement.

Huckleberry Finn of course stops well short of that view. Though weighted on the negative side, the novel indicates that Clemens had as yet become neither an avowed determinist nor a complete pessimist. His "discussion with Lecky" continued, and the final triumph of Huck's "sound heart" over his "ill-trained conscience" in Chapter Thirty-one dramatizes the fact that Clemens had not yet entirely lost faith in the existence of innate moral perceptions.

Once back in Hartford after the summer of 1883 at Quarry Farm, which saw the first draft of *Huckleberry Finn* completed, Clemens was busy as ever. In the midst of the many problems involved with plans to establish his own publishing company, he spent a good deal of time trying to market his history game. Soon he was also collaborating with Howells on "Colonel Sellers as a Scientist," the play that would later be the basis for *The American Claimant* (1892).

In November, 1883, he and Olivia gave a tea for Matthew Arnold, who was currently regaling American audiences with his famous triad of lectures: "Numbers," "Literature and Science," and "Emerson." In a journal entry on the nineteenth, Joseph Twichell noted that Arnold, his wife, and his daughter made "a most favorable impression" at the Clemenses, and that the critic himself was "a gentler, more sympathetic person than his writings would lead some people to expect."[53] Though it has generally been assumed that Clemens' antagonism toward the ideas of Matthew Arnold arose during these years, Twichell's comment suggests a pleasant relationship. Further studies of the unfinished manuscripts attacking the English critic also show that the battles with Arnold did not begin until the later 1880's.[54]

Though Clemens was apparently not yet overly annoyed by British notions of rank and caste (of which Arnold would later become a major symbol), he plunged that same month into work on a new novel embodying one of the other themes that would recur in *A Connecticut Yankee*. Except for fragments totalling seventeen pages, the manuscript has not survived, but other evidence shows that Clemens was again pondering ideas which he very likely derived from Lecky's *History of European Morals*.

The novel, set in Hawaii, was based on the life of Bill Ragsdale, a half-caste interpreter whom Clemens had known during his 1866 visit to the Sandwich Islands. According to a reminiscence in *Following the Equator* (Chapter Three), Ragsdale had been an exceptionally intelligent man, who discovered just before he was to be married that he had leprosy. Though he could have concealed the fact for many years, he chose to exile himself to the colony on Molokai rather than subject his intended bride to life with a leper. There he ultimately died "the loathsome and lingering death" typical of the disease.

As Clemens outlined his plot to Howells in a letter of January 7, 1884, he would begin at the point when Ragsdale was twelve and his sweetheart four, in the days of "the ancient idolatrous system, with its picturesque & amazing customs & superstitions." Three months later the missionaries would arrive to erect "a shallow Christianity" on the foundations of the old paganism; the children would be educated as Christians and become "highly civilized." Then he would "jump 15 years & do Ragsdale's leper business." The "hidden motive" of the story, he further explained, would illustrate a fact not often considered: that whatever "religious folly" one is born into, he will *die* in that belief, "no matter what apparently reasonabler religious folly may seem to have taken its place meanwhile & abolished & obliterated it."[55]

Very probably, as Fred W. Lorch has suggested, the book would have presented a contrast between the old and new civilizations in the islands, with the proponents of the old superstitions resisting the efforts of the Christian missionaries. The old would win, in a way, for Clemens doubtless intended to have Ragsdale revert to the ancient beliefs during his dying days in the leper colony.[56]

The various histories of Hawaii cited by Lorch furnished the author with important background materials, but the story's theme seems to have come directly from Lecky. Though the historian aligned himself primarily with the intuitionist philosophers, he also stressed the importance of environmental influences, and especially the combination of superstition and religious training. In one of many illustrations of the harmful effects of such training even upon the "bold enquirer" who sought to break away from the Church's teachings, he makes exactly the point that Clemens had defined as his "hidden motive": "Our thoughts in after years flow spontaneously, and even unconsciously, in the channels that are formed in youth. In moments when the controlling judgment has relaxed its grasp, old intellectual habits reassume their sway, and images painted on the imagination will live, when the intellectual propositions on which they have rested have been wholly abandoned." In times of weakness, illness, and anxiety, "when the mind floats passively upon the stream, the phantoms which reason had exorcised must have often reappeared, and the bitterness of an ancient tyranny must have entered into his soul."[57]

The Hawaiian story, then, marks another step in Clemens' progress toward a wholly deterministic philosophy. Presumably innate moral perceptions—the "sound heart"—here did not enter the picture, unless they might somehow be connected with Ragsdale's decision not to inflict his burden upon his bride. As indicated in the letter to Howells, Clemens' primary interest was obviously in the proposition that superstitious beliefs inculcated in childhood far outweighed the influence of later training.

What happened to the novel is not known. On January 24 Clemens wrote Mrs. Fairbanks that he had finished the book the week before and was now revising it. Soon after, he turned his attention to adapting *Tom Sawyer* and *The Prince and the Pauper* for the stage. But after two other letters to Howells in February about turning the Hawaiian story into a play, the project vanishes.[58]

During the remainder of 1884, Clemens moved from scheme to scheme. Besides the attempts at playwriting, he was seeking a producer for "Colonel Sellers as a Scientist," seeing *Huck Finn* through the presses, and investigating the possibilities of marketing a pair of grape-shears invented by Howells' father. He also became deeply involved in the Blaine-Cleveland presidential campaign, bolting the Republican Party to proclaim himself a Mugwump, and urging his Republican friends to do the same. Among other results of this political activity was his eventual agreement with Cleveland's free-trade policies. Whereas he had vigorously supported the Wood tariff bill in 1880,[59] he was soon to announce a wholehearted opposition to "protection" that he continued to voice for many years, even in his fiction.

With the handsome scale of living in Hartford now augmented by the expenses of a publishing company that had yet to earn any money, financial relief was imperative. The plans for storming the New York stage with the several dramas proved as abortive as the book on Hawaii. But the next few months provided the means of easing the ever-present strain on the family purse. From early November, 1884, through the following February, Clemens and George W. Cable toured sixteen states, the District of Columbia, and eastern Canada, presenting some 104 performances of readings from their works. So favorable was the response that Clemens wrote Andrew Chatto about the possibility of attracting sizable audiences in England with the program. The tour likewise provided literary benefits, for on December 6, 1884, while browsing in a Rochester, New York, bookstore, Clemens unearthed a copy of Sir Thomas Malory's *Le Morte Darthur,* which in turn supplied an idea for the story that ultimately became *A Connecticut Yankee in King Arthur's Court.*[60]

By the time the tour ended in February, 1885, prospects for the publishing company were bright. *Huckleberry Finn* had been issued in the United States that month, and sales were such that by mid-March Clemens was pronouncing it a success—"& from the standpoint of my own requirement."[61] Near the end of February, also, he and Charles Webster had concluded negotiations for General Grant's *Memoirs,* and orders soon were rolling in. With these successes Clemens was riding high. Now, at mid-decade, his mood was that mentioned earlier—awe at his apparent acquisition of the Midas-touch.

Under the surface exuberance, however, his outlook was not so sanguine. It was also in 1885, for instance, that he recorded a text for another Monday Evening Club paper: "The *insincerity* of man —all men are liars . . . moral sneaks." Yet, in his next sentence he contradicted himself by citing the lives of individuals like Luther and Christ as evidence that "when a merely honest man appears, he is a comet—his fame is eternal—needs no genius, no talent—mere honesty. . . ."[62] Obviously he was still seeking a faith in the essential goodness of man.

As for his current relations with England, all was apparently serene. He no doubt was pleased with the treatment of *Huckleberry Finn* in the *Saturday Review*. Even if he knew that the unsigned article was the work of an American, Brander Matthews,[63] the sanctioning of so favorable a review by an English journal would have resulted in friendly feelings. But the storm that culminated in *A Connecticut Yankee in King Arthur's Court* was not far off.

Chapter Six

Thunder and the Storm
(1885-1889)

N O RUMBLINGS OF ANIMOSITY TOWARD ENGLAND accompanied
the first stage of the novel that became *A Connecticut Yankee*.
Clemens' initial inspiration for the book resulted primarily from
his fascination with the archaic diction and the chivalric derring-do
that he found in Malory. Some of the passages in *Le Morte Darthur*
remained his favorites for life. The tale of Arthur's passing he considered "one of the most beautiful things ever written in English,"
and Sir Ector's lament for Launcelot no less than "perfect." But the
knightly adventures appealed likewise to his sense of the ridiculous.
During the remainder of the reading tour, he and Cable often
badgered their friends and each other in Malory's "quaint language," with Clemens gleefully dubbing Ozias Pond, brother of
their tour manager, "Sir Sagramore le Desirous."[1]

The first notebook "germ" for the Connecticut Yankee's adventures in King Arthur's England emerged from a similar mood of
raillery and burlesque sometime that December of 1884: "Dream
of being a knight errant in armor in the Middle Ages. Have the
notions and habits of thought of the present day mixed with the
necessities of that. No pockets in the armor. [No way to manage
certain requirements of nature.] Can't scratch. Cold in the head—
can't blow—can't get a handkerchief, can't use iron sleeve. Iron
gets redhot in the sun—leaks in the rain, gets white with frost and

Clemens about 1886, age 51

McClure's Magazine

freezes me solid in winter. Makes disagreeable clatter when I enter church. Can't dress or undress myself. Always getting struck by lightning. Fall down and can't get up. [See Morte Darthur.]"[2]

Though Clemens later said that he immediately began to make mental notes for the book, he did not get the story itself under way until late in the fall of 1885—almost a year later. Among the note-book entries at that time, one set down a format and a possible conclusion. The Yankee's story was to be preserved as a journal written on ancient yellowed parchment—a palimpsest with "remnants of monkish legends" showing through. The final chapter, however, was to be on new paper, embossed with the British coat-of-arms and the current year's date, 1885. At the end, perhaps as a sort of parallel to the pathos of King Arthur's death in Malory's eloquent account, Clemens envisioned the Yankee back in modern England, distressed by the changes he saw there. Mourning his "lost land," so "fresh & new, so virgin before," and now "old, so old!" he was to lose all interest in life and be "found dead next morning—suicide."[3]

By early February, the writing was well begun, though business pressures constantly threatened to tear the author away from his work. When they finally did so, near the end of February or beginning of March, he had managed to finish "A Word of Explanation" and the first three chapters (as they appear in the published book). But then the time-traveler from Hartford languished in Arthur's castle for almost a year and a half.[4]

Clemens did rouse him briefly on November 11, 1886, for an appearance at the Military Service Institution on Governors Island in New York Bay. There, to an enthusiastic audience of high-ranking military officials and their guests, the author read "all that was then written" and then presented an "outline" of his hero's subsequent adventures.[5] Detailed reports of the performance in the next day's New York *Sun* and *Herald,* and a squib in the *Tribune,* show that the part he read followed the final version of the book through Chapter Three, describing the inventive superintendent of the Colt Arms Factory, his awakening in Arthur's England and capture by Sir Kay; the festivities in Camelot, highlighted by the lies of the boastful knights; and finally, Merlin's putting the company to sleep by telling his "old story for the thousandth time." The remainder of the story as outlined was, however, far different from the final version.

Probably echoing Clemens' own statement of his purpose, the *Tribune* noted that the tale was "intended to bring into sharp contrast the days of the 'idyls of the king' with the present system of life." A few days later the author himself wrote Mrs. Fairbanks that the new book was not going to be "a satire peculiarly" but "more especially a *contrast*" [his italics] between "the daily life of the time & that of today." Taken together, the first three chapters and the "outline" suggest that this contrast would play upon the humorous clashes between the bumptious and somewhat vulgar modernity of the Yankee and the romantic world of chivalry as conceived by Malory, Scott, and Tennyson.[6] As a brash "operator," the Yankee would turn his superior wits and inventive skill primarily to his own profit, like the allegorical Sir Wissenschaft in "The Legend of the Spectacular Ruin" (*A Tramp Abroad*, Chapter Seventeen), who slew the local dragon with a fire-extinguisher invented for the purpose, demanded a monopoly on the sale of spectacles as his reward, and grew rich on the proceeds.

From the Yankee's awakening in Arthurian England through the end of Chapter Three, the published novel shows this burlesque contrast of ancient and modern dominating the action.[7] The few signs of medieval cruelty that do appear, seem to be there primarily as local color rather than as an attack on the feudal system itself. The Yankee's bruised and battered fellow-prisoners are not representatives of the downtrodden peasantry, but are knights—"big boobies," whose stoicism deserved neither admiration nor pity since it resulted from mere "animal training" rather than essential bravery. The attitude implied in the description of these knights and also of the animal-like peasants, seems much like that expressed in Clemens' article "The Tournament in A. D. 1870" where he had commented: "The doings of the so-called 'chivalry' of the Middle Ages were absurd enough, even when they were brutally and bloodily in earnest, and when their surroundings of castles and donjons, savage landscapes and half-savage peoples, were in keeping . . . ."[8] The Arthurian town itself, with its "naked brats, and joyous dogs and shabby huts," and the hog wallowing in the street, resembles the Bricksville of *Huckleberry Finn*, whose wretched inhabitants had received little of the author's pity.

In these three chapters, too, more than in the rest of the book, the favorable side of Clemens' initial reaction to Malory is apparent. The castle at Camelot, as the Yankee describes it, is itself "full of loud contrasts." Above the snarls and growls of dogs fighting for scraps flung from the banquet tables sounds the "gracious and courtly" speech of knights and ladies. Though childish and gullible, the knights exhibit a "manliness" and a certain "lofty sweetness." More specifically, the Yankee notes "the majesty and greatness" of Launcelot's glance and bearing and "the noble benignity and purity" which characterize Arthur and Galahad. The disrespectful rat in Chapter Three who climbs on the sleeping King's head during Merlin's story and dribbles crumbs in his face "with naïve and impudent irreverence" was not added to the manuscript until much later.

Clemens was not merely soft-soaping Mrs. Fairbanks, then, when he assured her that he intended to leave "unsmirched & unbelittled the great & beautiful *characters* drawn by the master hand of old Malory," and at the same time reiterated his pleasure in certain passages in *Le Morte Darthur*.[9]

As for the actual tales from Malory quoted or referred to in these early chapters, their primary purpose was to emphasize the readiness of this "childlike and innocent" lot of people to accept as gospel any account of chivalric exploits, no matter how extravagant. The fact that Merlin's story puts the audience to sleep reflects not on the tale itself, but on the fact that the garrulous magician has told it so many times. For here Merlin is not presented as a sinister force but as a bumbling egotist, whom the clever Yankee will have little trouble outwitting.

The "outline" of the subsequent episodes with which Clemens entertained his Governors Island audience shows that the Yankee (here called Sir Robert Smith) would have continued to exploit his native shrewdness and knowledge of tools and machinery to win wealth and power for himself. Finding that he could not dodge Arthur's commission to rescue sixty captive princesses from a neighboring ogre, he would decide first to "compromise" with the ogre rather than resort to direct combat, and finally, to ignore the mission entirely and merely "tell a majestic lie about" it "like the rest of the knights." His illustration of what "an educated man of the nineteenth century can do in the lofty realms of that art," in turn, would make his rapid rise to power all but certain.

Within a year, Sir Bob was to be running the entire kingdom "at a moderate royalty of forty percent." Within three and a half, he would have cleared away all the "fuss and flummery of romance," and put the kingdom on a "strictly business basis." Launcelot would be conducting "a kind of Louisiana lottery," the quest for the Holy Grail would give way to a search for the Northwest Passage, and the 140 knights of Arthur's Court would form a Stock Board, with seats at the Round Table selling for $30,000.[10]

Sir Bob's skill at prevarication, his "moderate" forty per cent royalty, and his other manipulations indicate that certain contemporary practices were to be fair game for Clemens' burlesque along with the "fuss and flummery of romance," though the latter would, of course, provide the primary target.

Among the "germs" for other episodes that were later expanded, Clemens mentioned the possibility of Sir Bob's using a lasso to defeat his cumbersome competitors and later employing an electrically charged barbed wire fence and battery of Gatling guns to halt "squadrons" of hostile knights. But in the early version, the guns and electricity were pressed into service not to destroy the whole chivalry of England, but merely to win a victory over King Arthur's enemies in one of the great tournaments.

Clemens apparently did not tell his audience of his plan for the Yankee's eventual suicide in modern England. Either he had already abandoned the idea or preferred not to reveal the entire plot. He was probably not greatly concerned with the ending at this time, for in the letter already mentioned, he told Mrs. Fairbanks that he intended to find his "holiday entertainment" for thirty years in writing just three chapters of the novel each summer.

When he picked up the story the next summer, however, he did not stop at three chapters but wrote more than *sixteen*—Chapters Four through Twenty and part of Twenty-one (except for Chapter Ten, "The Beginnings of Civilization," which he inserted in 1888). Therefore, by mid-September, despite several delays resulting from business worries, he had seen the Yankee through his rise to Bossdom, introduced the demoiselle Alisande la Carteloise (Sandy) into the further-elaborated quest for the captive princesses (now forty-five rather than sixty), and had brought the wanderers through the horrors of Morgan le Fay's castle to the portals of the Valley of Holiness.[11]

But sometime between the Governors Island reading and the summer of 1887, Clemens' concept of the story of the Yankee's role seems to have changed drastically. Instead of merely profit for himself and for the king's treasury, the Yankee's primary goal became no less than total reform of political and social evils in Arthur's kingdom. Instead of dodging the encounter with the ogre, he would carry the quest through to its vivid conclusion that the princesses (and by implication, all royalty and nobility) were hogs. And instead of using his Gatling gun and electrified fence simply against Arthur's enemies, he would ultimately add the devastating power of dynamite and turn his weapons against the whole chivalry of England and the "superstitions" for which it stood.

The reasons for the shift in purpose doubtless were complicated ones. In some respects, of course, the change made the novel a much more logical next step from *Life on the Mississippi* and *Huckleberry Finn* than the original contrast would have been. Its examination of the influences of chivalry and of the effects of slavery of various sorts embody some of the most serious concerns of the earlier books. But new emphases are also apparent. In the discussions of the advantages of free-trade over protection, for instance, the author would embody his admiration for the policies of Grover Cleveland. More important, during these years Clemens developed a new sympathy for equalitarian democracy.

The breakdown of his earlier mistrust stemmed partly from his interest in the activities of the Knights of Labor in 1886. Intrigued by the group's potentialities for improving conditions for the masses, he had treated the Monday Evening Club meeting of March 22, 1886, to a flowery eulogy that hailed the workers as "The New Dynasty." Admitting that power inevitably resulted in oppression, he argued that because this dynasty would be concerned with the nation's good rather than with the selfish interests of a small clique, it need not be feared. Rather, it would form a permanent defense "against the Socialist, the Communist, the anarchist, the tramp, and the selfish agitator for 'reforms,' " and "against all like forms of political disease, pollution and death."[12] Many of the attitudes and comments of that speech Clemens would transfer almost verbatim to the *Yankee* a year and a half later.

But given the difference between the "outline" at Governors Island and the new themes that emerged the following summer, something else must have contributed to this change. Whatever other elements helped produce the critical mass, Clemens' growing antagonism toward England was a major catalyst to the explosion.

In examining the events of these months and the immediately succeeding years, it is important to note that Clemens' quarrel with

England did not result in a broadside blast at *all* English attitudes. Rather, he directed his fire only at those that seemed obstacles to progress and the preservation of human dignity. In becoming a Mugwump he had moved closer to the views of the British Liberal Party, for as Louis J. Budd has said, the Mugwumps "were well-defined politically as the American branch of middle-class Liberalism."[13]

Clemens had kept in fairly close touch with developments in England ever since his visits during the 1870's. Besides reading newspapers and periodicals, he corresponded with British friends like Frank Finlay, a long-time member of the Liberal Reform Club. At various times during the middle and late 1880's, reports from abroad evoked direct reactions in his notebooks. In 1885, for instance, he speculated briefly at one point on the future of the Liberal Party and the possibility that Lord Rosebery might become the next Prime Minister. In July, 1888, he would applaud the progress of the Local Government Bill, a Liberal measure hotly debated for several years in both Parliament and the press. Copying a July 1 news report from London that the Liberals were welcoming the bill's passage through committee as "almost a revolution, which transfers control of county affairs from the privileged few to the people," he added his own cheer: "There—the handwriting on the wall! There's a day coming!"[14]

As Budd has correctly observed, many of the "improvements" that the Yankee came to propose for Arthurian England were those which Britain's Liberals—and especially the party's Radical wing—were currently advocating. In an unpublished essay of 1888 or 1889, also, Clemens' listing of major steps in England's "slow climb from chattel slavery" all but summarized the principles for which the Liberals had been fighting over the years. Yet it was a new sense that the evils of monarchy and aristocracy had continued into the present, even in the England he had loved so well during the 1870s, that accounts for most of the themes in *A Connecticut Yankee* not envisioned in the earlier "outline."

The outlook for Liberal legislation in 1886 and 1887 was less than bright. In the spring of 1885, the fall of Gladstone's ministry had aroused great interest in the United States, and many had watched with deep concern the general election that followed. American public opinion very largely reflected that of the New York *Herald* and other newspapers. For them Gladstone was the champion of progress, staunchly opposing the obstructionist tactics of the British aristocracy and landed gentry. Many were dismayed, therefore, when even those whom the Liberals' Reform Act of 1885 had recently enfranchised, flocked in large numbers to vote the Conservative ticket.

Though Clemens' reactions to the sweeping Conservative victory had apparently not jelled sufficiently by November, 1886, to find their way into his "outline," other irritants soon stirred him up. Reports that autumn of Welsh riots against enforced tithing led to a notebook blast at this "frightful tax" which so harassed the poor. From those reports, too, he gleaned an incident about a poor woman's reaction to the tithe-collector priest, which he would incorporate into the *Yankee* the following summer. Very likely he also read about the use of government troops to disperse the crowds who had gathered in Trafalgar Square to protest against unemployment, and about the Scottish crofters' demonstrations against their landlords for setting aside grazing lands as private deer-parks.[15] If not, England was still specifically on his mind during these months, for another notebook entry proposed that he write up a comparison of "the Englishman 100 years ago" and "the Englishman of To-Day."*

Other rumblings sounded early in 1887, when Matthew Arnold's opinion of General Grant's *Memoirs* came to his attention. Though the review (which first appeared in the January and February issues of *Murray's* magazine) was more complimentary than critical, Clemens did not let its few objections go unchallenged. He was no doubt ruffled a good deal by Arnold's repetition of his objections to American boasting, especially now that the criticism was implicitly aimed at Grant.

With both the defense of a friend and possible book sales at stake, Clemens welcomed the opportunity for counterattack provided by an invitation to address a reunion of the Army and Navy Club of Connecticut on April 27, the anniversary of Grant's birthday. Concentrating on Arnold's criticisms of certain grammatical constructions, he drew for logistical support on H. H. Breen's *Modern English Literature: Its Blemishes and Defects* in order to "prove" that the general's grammatical faults were no more numerous nor serious than those of many universally acknowledged literary masters.

---

* Notebook 21, TS, pp. 32–33, Mark Twain Papers.

Finally, after firing at certain stylistic flaws in the review itself, he flung Arnold's charges of American chauvinism back in his face with a flowery tribute to the grandeur of the *Memoirs* and their soldier-author, "who, all untaught by the silken phrase-makers, linked words together with an art surpassing the art of the school-men."[16]

A more important stimulus to the *Yankee*'s change of direction, however—perhaps the primary one—was a book sent by an English acquaintance, which arrived in May, 1887, barely a month before Clemens resumed work on the novel. This bit of potential dynamite, *The People's History of the English Aristocracy*, was the work of another British correspondent, a London printer and Radical propagandist named George Standring, who edited his own magazine, *The Republican* (later called *The Radical*), and also wrote for several other Liberal and free-thought journals.

Clemens' acquaintance with Standring seems to have begun early in 1886 with a note of thanks for the complimentary review of Mark Twain's life and works which the Englishman had contributed to the *Progressive* magazine as part of a series on American humorists. Thereafter the two exchanged letters occasionally, with Standring sometimes sending *The Republican* and copies of other articles that he thought might be of interest. The pair met personally at least once, for Standring's letter of December 5, 1905, congratulating Clemens on his seventieth birthday, recalls a pleasant visit at Dollis Hill in 1901.

Clemens had first encountered *The People's History* during its serial publication in the *Republican*. The parts that he read had so intrigued him that he wrote sometime during the summer of 1886 to ask for a copy of the entire work, and offered a complete set of his own books in exchange. Still waiting for it the following April, he wrote again requesting Standring to "step around and kill" Andrew Chatto for neglecting to forward the book. In reply, a letter dated May 7 brought profuse apologies for delays at the bindery and the news that the volume had gone to Chatto for trans-shipment the evening before.[17]

If *The People's History* did not actually inspire Clemens to give new directions to *A Connecticut Yankee,* it at least crystallized his decision to do so. In its vivid expression of the most vehement strains of current Liberal and Radical sentiments, it treated many of the same themes which came to dominate the *Yankee*. Standring's major premise was that England's only hope lay in replacing the monarchy with a republic. He charged particularly that the vast wealth of the aristocracy allowed it to control not only the House of Lords, but also the mercantile interests, the professions, the military services, and even "that one bulwark which the nation is supposed to possess against tyranny—the House of Commons." Among the causes of this deplorable situation, he isolated two principal evils: the feudal laws of primogeniture and entail, and, almost more important, the British devotion to the "fetish of nobility," which kept the commoner in a state of slavery more hopeless than if his chains were real ones.[18]

As evidence that the nobility was completely unworthy of respect, much less of loyalty and devotion, Standring presented the "case histories" of most of England's noble families, tracing them from their beginnings to the present day. Emphasizing those that had originated in the guilty amours of kings and courtesans, he marshalled an amazing catalogue of "crimes," both serious and petty. And to hammer home his point, he almost invariably capped each recital with a sarcastic jibe like that following an account of the misdeeds of Thomas Howard, Third Duke of Norfolk: "Yet this is the stock to which our nobility point with pride when they prate over their long descent."

Clemens' wide reading in English history had made him familiar with much of Standring's "evidence."[19] But nowhere in one place and in such detail had he found the intimate stories of so many of England's noble houses. He was so enthusiastic about *The People's History*, in fact, that soon after its arrival in May, he proposed to publish it with some of his longtime favorites in a high-priced edition, to be called "Royalty and Nobility Exposed." St. Simon's *Memoires* and "the English printer's little book" would come first, with Taine's *Ancient Regime* and Carlyle's *French Revolution* following almost immediately, and then, sometime later, "The White Slave—Mining Life in Wales—Margravine of Bayreuth."*

Though that project (and also several later plans for introducing *The People's History* to American readers) failed to materialize,[20] there is no doubt that Standring's book served as an important agent in focusing Clemens' attention on aristocratic abuses in En-

* Notebook 21, TS, p. 49, Mark Twain Papers.

gland. Furthermore, its very position in the proposed edition, preceding even such old friends as Taine and Carlyle, not only testifies to Clemens' high regard for the volume, but shows him placing England squarely alongside France as a perpetrator of the ancient evils. No longer was he affirming (as he had in 1879) that the British lacked the essential savagery which had allowed the French to continue the "atrocious privileges" of the nobility down through the ages. Here was firsthand evidence from a native-born Englishman that British slavery to a totally corrupt ideal was far from dead.

If Standring's vituperations had not totally convinced Clemens that the "fetish of nobility" was still potent in England, the reports that June of Queen Victoria's Jubilee would certainly have completed the job. Seldom had adulation reached such a peak as in the crowds who lined the streets on June 20 to cheer the parade to Westminster Abbey. According to contemporary newspaper accounts, no fewer than three kings (of Denmark, Belgium, and Greece) marched in the colorful procession, along with "the Crown Princes of every throne in Christendom, and of some outside Christendom."[21] The particular cortege which followed Victoria's carriage—her three sons, five sons-in-law, and nine grandsons and grandsons-in-law—provided an eloquent reminder that Victoria's numerous progeny had linked Britain with most of the other thrones of Europe. Whether it was the descriptions of the Jubilee, or merely the sneers of Standring and other Liberals which impressed him, Clemens himself was to allude to Victoria's fertility in his novel, not once but twice.[22]

Less than two months later, struck by how radically one's attitudes could change without one's being conscious of the alterations, Clemens described to Howells the progress of his own ideas regarding monarchy and aristocracy since his first reading of Carlyle's *French Revolution* in 1871, at which time he had sided with the moderate Girondins. "Every time I have read it since, I have read it differently—being influenced & changed little by little, by life & environment (& Taine & St. Simon): & now I lay the book down once more, & recognize that I am a Sansculotte—And not a pale characterless Sansculotte, but a Marat. Carlyle teaches no such gospel: so the change is in *me*—in my vision of the evidences." Obviously Clemens had come by this time to regard the French Revolution, despite its excesses, in much the same terms as he later described it (again to Howells)—as "the noblest & the holiest" event in history next to the Fourth of July and its aftermath. Yet he was also convinced that its "gracious work" was not yet finished—"nor anywhere in the remote neighborhood of it."[23]

In the novel itself, signs of the storm that was about to break appeared almost immediately in Chapter Four. Following Sir Dinadan's hoary jokes and Sir Kay's lies about capturing the Yankee, a sharper tone begins to emerge as the narrator turns his attention to Arthurian morals. Where earlier he had spoken of "gracious and courtly speech," he now describes the knights' and ladies' "language that would make a Comanche blush." More significantly, he adds that reading *Tom Jones, Roderick Random*, "and other books of that kind" had convinced him that bawdy conversation "and the morals and conduct which such talk implies" were common among English ladies and gentlemen "clear into our own nineteenth century . . . ."

Some critics have denied that these remarks indicate a shift in the novel's tone, or at least that they can be attributed to any new antagonism toward England. Clemens had, to be sure, said much the same thing about the coarseness of *Tom Jones* in 1879. But in terms of *A Connecticut Yankee* itself, the comments on language and morals are more sharply critical of the Arthurians than those in the preceding chapters. The connection of the crudity and immorality with later centuries, including the nineteenth, also implies a considerable extension of the scope of the novel's satire. Furthermore, the immediate inspiration for the Yankee's remarks very likely came from Standring's *People's History*. Around the time he wrote the passage, Clemens made a list of some fourteen sources that could be included in an appendix, to support his charges that laxity in language and morals had lingered far beyond the medieval era.[24] Of those included, he had probably read Standring's book most recently and could hardly have failed to note such vivid examples of aristocratic elegance as the Duchess of Marlborough, whose "volleys of oaths and streams of foul language would have done credit to a Billingsgate fish-fag," or the subsequent remark of a law-clerk that though he did not know her, he "was sure she was a lady of quality, *as she swore so dreadfully*" [Standring's italics].

The People's History also contributed at least supporting evidence for the later extension of these observations on morals in the Yankee's comment (Chapter Fourteen), that the "squaws" of these

Arthurian "Comanches" were always ready "to desert to the buck with the biggest string of scalps at his belt." Was he thinking of various ladies in *Le Morte Darthur*—like the damsel (in Book Ten, Chapter Eighty-three) who became the property of Sir Epinogris, Sir Helior, and Sir Safere, in rapid succession? (But most of Malory's females are passive and submissive.) Standring's anthology of aristocratic misdeeds, on the other hand, not only cites the "flood of filth and garbage" from English divorce courts as representing "the daily life of the Modern English Aristocracy," but also records how Lady Shrewsbury, disguised as a page, attended the duel between her husband and George Villiers, second Duke of Buckingham, and *"when her husband lay cold and dead on the ground . . . rode off with his murderer"* [again Standring's italics].[25] The possible play on the first syllable of *Buck*ingham's name in Clemens' Indian metaphor is also intriguing.

The immediately following episodes, too, give important indications of Clemens' current antagonisms (which will appear in another context), but he managed to remain pretty well detached from his protagonist through the destruction of Merlin's Tower in Chapter Seven. With the Yankee's first direct diatribe against English reverence for rank and pedigree in Chapter Eight, however, the mask slips considerably. Invoking the same sort of scorn which Standring had so often heaped upon British bondage to the "fetish of nobility"—and in much the same language—the author makes the Yankee sneer at the "inherited ideas" that made ostensibly free Englishmen into slaves, proud to grovel before king, Church, and noble, and grateful even for the snubs which invariably greet their devotion. "*Any* kind of royalty, howsoever modified, *any* kind of aristocracy, howsoever pruned, is rightly an insult," Hank Morgan says. Thereafter, the humorist makes the connection with the present even more obvious with the Yankee's ironic observation that in Arthur's Britain, "just as in the remote England of my birth-time, the sheep-witted earl who could claim long descent from a king's leman . . . was a better man than I was."

Earlier in the same passage, in emphasizing the importance of "hereditary ideas" (one of the novel's primary themes) Clemens made especially effective use of a line from the works of his British contemporary, W. S. Gilbert. Fond of the Gilbert and Sullivan operettas, he had no doubt seen many of them either in New York or in Boston, where the Boston Ideal Opera Company had been formed in 1879 to produce *H. M. S. Pinafore* (1878). Some years later he was to mention his awe at Gilbert's talent for "saying not only the wittiest of things," but for "saying them in verse." As recently as April, 1886, he had taken Olivia and some Hartford friends to one of the first-run New York performances of *The Mikado*.[26]

Pinafore obviously came to the humorist's mind while he was composing the Yankee's blast at British reverence for titles and heritable ranks. In Act II of the operetta one of Little Buttercup's songs both foreshadows revelations to come and pokes fun at shams, deceptions, and the unreliability of appearances:

> Things are seldom what they seem,
> Skim milk masquerades as cream;
> Highlows pass as patent leathers;
> Jackdaws strut in peacock's feathers. . . .

In attacking the notion that rank and pedigree merit a respect that mere natural ability and intelligence cannot command, Clemens had the Yankee say: "I had inherited the idea that human Jackdaws who had no more self-respect than to consent to strut around in the silly peacock feathers. . . ." At that point he reconsidered, crossed out "silly peacock feathers" and continued: " peacock-shams of inherited dignities and unearned titles, are of no good but to be laughed at."* Sometime before publication he was to revise the passage again, perhaps to make his borrowing less obvious, and referred this time to the "human daws who can consent to masquerade in the peacock shams of inherited dignities. . . ."

Clemens thus forged Little Buttercup's thrust at pretense into a more powerful satiric barb by concentrating his stroke on the particular deception involved in equating titles with intrinsic worth. At the same time he broadened its metaphoric range by the changes from "strut around" to "masquerade" and "peacock feathers" to "peacock shams."

When he returned to this chapter somewhat later to expand on the role of the Church in establishing these "superstitions of rank and caste," the humorist inserted additional charges that the "poison" of this sort of reverence had continued into the nineteenth century to infect "even the best of English commoners." As an-

---

* Ms. I, 145. All citations from the manuscript of *A Connecticut Yankee* are from the holograph in the Berg Collection, New York Public Library.

other crack at contemporary Englishmen, he had the Yankee assert that some "dudes and dudesses"[27] in his own country sought to imitate "English high society dress and grossness of manners, mispronunciation and appetite for the compliment of a snub from a noble."*

Ultimately, however, the author toned down that latter remark by omitting the direct reference to British dress and manners and leaving only the comment that the reverential taint was "restricted to dudes and dudesses." He likewise deleted a phrase naming "Charles the Second's scepter-wielding drabs," the "revered mothers of English nobility." Both of these changes were perhaps among the "darlings" that he regretfully came to destroy because (as he was to tell Howells in 1889) they represented "blasts of opinion . . . so strongly worded as to repel instead of persuade."[28] He may well have thought, also, that the "revered mothers" phrase was too close an echo of Standring's many sneers. On the other hand, he may simply have realized that both comments had repeated essentially what the reference to "the sheep-witted earl" had said more subtly.

In the attack on the Church as the force behind the illogical reverence for rank, the Anglican was certainly under fire as well as the Roman. The Yankee's conviction (in Chapter Sixteen) that "any Established Church is an established crime, an established slave-pen" points a direct finger. His plan to create numerous sects which could police each other, first introduced in Chapter Eighteen (since Chapter Ten was not written until 1888), and the charge that the *raison d'être* of an Established Church was solely political, reflect the current agitations for Disestablishment in England and Wales. But even more pointed is the author's adaptation of the tithing incident recorded the preceding fall. In Chapter Twenty, after the swineherd cites his wife's plea that the priest take one of their ten children, since his taking one of their ten pigs had robbed them of the means of feeding the child, Hank Morgan notes the "curious" fact that the same thing had happened in Wales in his own day—"under this same old Established Church, which was supposed by many to have changed its nature when it changed its disguise."

Other episodes which Clemens wrote that same summer carry contemporary implications not quite so obvious to many twentieth-

* Ms. I, 147a.

century readers. The young farmer on Morgan le Fay's rack for killing a deer in the royal preserves (though the animal had actually been ravaging his own fields) might have reminded some Englishmen that until the Ground Game Act of 1880, tenant farmers were forbidden to hunt or trap even the rabbits or other "vermin" which might wander onto their own plots of ground. Others would recall that despite the Crofters' Act of 1886, agitations against the Scottish landlords (as well as the tithe-riots in Wales) continued through 1887, with the tenants pleading starvation as their excuse for raiding the deer-forests. Clemens himself, in 1891 would again exclaim, that "game stands next to God in English reverence," and would note a contemporary case of the traditionally cruel treatment accorded to poachers by the English law courts.[29]

Some readers might even see in Morgan le Fay's summary dispensations of justice a reflection of the judicial powers of the local squirearchy which the proponents of the much-debated Local Government Bill (finally passed in 1888) sought to curtail. Many more would certainly have read Clemens' emphasis on the coarseness and brutality of language and action as aimed directly at Tennyson's idealized Arthurians, for the last of the *Idylls* had appeared as recently as 1885. A few might recall that the ridiculous advertisement for "Peterson's Prophylactic Tooth-Brushes—All the Go" on Sir Madok de la Montaine's sandwich-board had also appeared in 1885—in a British newspaper.[30]

Given the setting of *A Connecticut Yankee,* it is not strange that there are so few contemporary references, but that there are so many. Those who see no shift in the novel's intention in 1887, or contend that Clemens' current displeasure with England was not a shaping force for the chapters written that summer, have not adequately accounted for these references and implications.

Work on the novel lagged in late August or early September, though the author still hoped to complete the book that fall. But once back in Hartford, he soon gave up. "This kind of rush is why parties write no books," he complained to Mrs. Fairbanks on November 25, after listing some of his recent business and social activities.[31]

During that fall and winter his animosity toward England continued to make itself evident, and several incidents furnished specific impetus for later chapters of *A Connecticut Yankee.* In November, suspiciously close on the heels of a visit from Charles Dickens (the novelist's son) and his daughter, Clemens growled that a "cessation of hospitalities to traveling English" had occurred "because English manners could not be endured." Shortly thereafter, another notebook entry suggested that "English Breeding as Exhibited in the United States" was "a prodigious theme," well-calculated to make "all England blush." Obviously, there was little left, by this time, of the tolerance shown to critical English visitors in *Life on the Mississippi*. The following spring Clemens reacted even more vigorously to Matthew Arnold's "Civilization in the United States" which appeared in the April issue of *Nineteenth Century*. Touched off by a request for a rebuttal from *Forum* editor Lorettus D. Metcalf, the outburst was nonetheless sincere. Early in April a single notebook sentence proclaiming that "Matthew Arnold's civilization" was *"superficial polish"* began a barrage whose reverberations would echo through scores of notebook and manuscript pages during the next two years.[32]

Whether the outraged American immediately plunged into the furious fragmentary replies that remain among the unpublished manuscripts in the Mark Twain Papers (one of which specifically mentions an editor's request) is not certain. By June 13, however, he had projected a future book entitled "English Criticism on America, Letters to an English Friend," and a week later was filling his notebook with ammunition that could serve equally well for that book or for the attack on Arnold.

Though Clemens never did complete his article for the *Forum,* his various fulminations found their way into several drafts of some half-dozen essays, mostly unfinished, but altogether totalling more than a hundred manuscript pages. Repeatedly he lambasted Arnold's definition of "civilization," and above all the Englishman's insistence that "a spirit of reverence" was the quintessential element of any truly civilized society. He was particularly irked, also, by Arnold's charge that the deplorable lack of reverence among Americans stemmed not only from an irresponsible press, but from their unfortunate "addiction to the 'funny man'."

Yale University provided the platform for his only public reference to Arnold that summer. In accepting their honorary Master of Arts degree, he answered the slur on American humorists, and at the same time all but defined the purpose which had come to dominate *A Connecticut Yankee* in 1887. The degree, he said, rep-

resented a tribute to all humorists, a tribute made all the more
"forcible and timely" by "the late Matthew Arnold's sharp rebuke
to the guild of American 'funny men' in his latest literary delicacy." It would remind the world of the humorist's real purpose:
"the deriding of shams, the exposure of pretentious falsities, the
laughing of stupid superstitions out of existence. . . ," a purpose
which made him "the natural enemy of royalties, nobilities, privileges, and all kindred swindles, and the natural friend of human
rights and human liberties."[33]

This is the mood in which Clemens took up Hank Morgan's
story again soon after the ceremony in New Haven. Though the
battle lines had long been drawn, Arnold's essay obviously had
made him more determined than ever to laugh those "stupid superstitions" out of existence.

More specifically, the long notebook diatribes which began late
in June by charging that the "absence of an irreverent press" had
permitted Europe to exist for a thousand years "merely for the advantage of half a dozen seventh-rate families called Monarchs, and
some hundreds of riffraff sarcastically called Nobles,"[34] help to determine the point at which Clemens resumed Hank Morgan's adventures. Just at the paragraph in Chapter Twenty-one where
Sandy assembles the "princesses" in the castle dining room (and
both paper and handwriting change in the manuscript), Hank
echoes his creator's renewed antagonism toward English subservience to rank and caste. Observing the ironic picture of Sandy waiting personally upon the hogs, he comments that her attitude manifested "in every way the deep reverence which the natives of her
island, ancient and modern, have always felt for rank, let its out-
ward casket and the mental and moral contents be what they may."

Arnold was not the only new stimulus for the book, nor for
Clemens' conviction that the ancient superstitions still lingered
strong. Important among them was a British novel, Mrs. Humphry
Ward's *Robert Elsmere,* which enjoyed phenomenal popularity
after its publication in April, 1888.[35] Clemens had read this best-
seller chiefly because he knew that his friends and acquaintances
would ask his opinion of it. But once into it he had found "the
grace and beauty of the style" enchanting. It was as if "a singer of
street ballads were to hear excellent music from a church organ,"
he said. "I listened, and I liked what I heard."[36]

It would have been strange if he had not liked the novel. The realism of frequent references to recent events and living people, some of whom he knew personally,[37] surely appealed. In Elsmere's unsuccessful battle to reconcile his Anglican faith with the new teachings of science and the Higher Criticism, Clemens would have seen an extremely persuasive argument against the "miraculous" elements of Christianity. But in his current mood, he must have been even more intrigued by Mrs. Ward's sharp portraits of snobbish aristocrats, and especially of Squire Roger Wendover's indifference to the plight of the wretched tenants on his huge estate. This was not the feudal lord of ancient Britain or France. This was a modern aristocrat, vastly learned, intellectually acute, but still almost wholly insensitive to human suffering—another vivid reminder that the old evils had by no means vanished from modern England.

Clemens could hardly have helped seeing reflections of his own experiences and interests in those of the young minister. Not only would Elsmere's intellectual struggles have hit a responsive chord, but his love of history and "passionate sense of the human problems which underlie all the dry and dusty detail" were exact counterparts of the humorist's own feeling for the past. He must likewise have appreciated Elsmere's artistry in capturing the imaginations of his audience during public readings. An even closer link existed, perhaps, in the various domestic relationships created by Mrs. Ward. The bond between Elsmere and his vivacious, witty mother; Elsmere's deep love for Catherine Leyburn and ultimately for their daughter; the close-knit Leyburn family with its three daughters, one of whom was exceptionally talented in music—all had their exact parallels in Clemens' own life.

As for the novel's style, part of what Clemens no doubt enjoyed was the author's considerable skill in capturing the speech patterns of her various characters, the Westmoreland rustics in particular. But other phrasing from the novel seems also to have lingered in his mind. In one episode, Langham, the Oxford aesthete, attempting to explain his own lackadaisical approach to life, shows Elsmere a passage from Senancour's *Rêveries* which depicts life as a series of disillusionments and man as powerless to accomplish anything truly significant. "Fools!" the passage concludes, "Will all these resounding projects, though they enable us to cheat ourselves, enable us to cheat the icy fate which rules us and our globe, wandering forsaken through the vast silence of the heavens?" Not only would

Hank Morgan eventually experience much the same sort of disillusionment, but his author, when revising the "training" passage in Chapter Eighteen, used almost the same metaphor, adding the phrases "this plodding sad pilgrimage, this pathetic drift between the eternities" to Hank's description of human life. Some fifteen years thereafter, part of the same image would reappear in the "dream" ending which Paine tacked on to the "Eseldorf" manuscript as the concluding chapter of *The Mysterious Stranger,* where Clemens describes his narrator as a vagrant thought "wandering forlorn among the empty eternities."

With these parallels, and Clemens' admitted fascination with the novel, the likelihood increases that Elsmere's visit to the Leyburn home in the remote valley of Long Whindale may have struck Clemens as a modern equivalent of the Yankee's visit to the Valley of Holiness. Besides devoting a good deal of space to local superstitions, Mrs. Ward comments that Elsmere's conversations brought something of "the beat of the great currents of English life and thought" into the "deep quiet" of the Westmorland countryside. Both Hank and Elsmere recuperate from illnesses while in their respective valleys. Clemens originally planned, in fact, to devote a whole chapter to Sandy's nursing of Hank, assisted only by "one lovely Sister" from the local convent.[38] In *Robert Elsmere,* Catherine Leyburn not only assists in Elsmere's recuperation, but finds her chief occupation in caring for the sick and needy. Moreover, a sense of oppressive "holiness" seemed to dominate Long Whindale. Catherine had all but buried herself in community service out of devotion to the memory of her father, a fundamentalist minister. To her own lovely sister, Rose, who longed to leave their isolated home to study music in London, Catherine's life had assumed all the characteristics of a rigid monasticism—"the most scrupulous order, the most rigid self-repression, the most determined sacrificing of 'this warm, kind world' with all its indefensible delights, to a cold other-world with its torturing, inadmissible claims." The busybody Mrs. Thornburgh, deploring Catherine's seeming perversity, reemphasized that spirit on another occasion: "It was all because she would not be happy like anybody else, but must needs set herself up to be peculiar. Why not live on a pillar, and go into hair-shirts at once?"

St. Simeon Stylites, whose perching atop a high pillar made him an excellent symbol of the ridiculous excesses of medieval asceticism, was to be the most colorful inhabitant of Clemens' Holy Valley. Clemens had encountered references to the hermit both in Carlyle's description of Marat as "the lone Stylites" isolated on his pillar, and in Lecky's *European Morals,* from which he borrowed specific details of St. Simeon's appearance and actions.[39] But meeting the hermit again in this derogatory reference to the ascetic ideal undoubtedly supplied an additional stimulus. And the fact that Clemens almost certainly drew other details from *Robert Elsmere* for later episodes[40] further suggests that Mrs. Ward's novel helped to inspire Hank Morgan's invasion of the remote, superstition-bound, monastic Valley of Holiness.

The Valley episodes reflect other issues currently receiving much attention in England, as does Chapter Ten, "The Beginnings of Civilization." Clemens wrote Chapter Ten sometime late in the summer of 1888, when he apparently realized he had not adequately prepared for various details like the appearance of the telephone and newspaper in the Holy Valley.[41] There he established a four-year period between the tournament of Chapter Nine and the beginning of the quest with Sandy, and summarized the Yankee's accomplishments. Besides a network of telephone and telegraph lines and the newspaper (with Clarence as editor), the Yankee creates technical schools, a "teacher-factory," and military and naval academies, revises the revenue system, and establishes a "complete variety" of protestant sects. In addition he underlines the Church's commanding role by stressing the need to keep all these projects (except the newspaper and revenue systems) secret for fear of ecclesiastical opposition.

Traditionally, the Yankee's plans for improving England have been seen in terms of American technological and industrial development. Yet along with ideas derived from Lecky's works (to be considered presently), recent discussions in English newspapers and journals very likely contributed to the picture. Clemens was no doubt aware, for instance, that the matter of public education, especially technical education, was a vital issue in England during 1887 and 1888. In 1887 various members of Parliament had introduced into the House of Commons a bill for publicly supported technical education, only to see it by-passed in favor of other legislation. In another area, certain British Liberals had for some time advocated a reduction in Church control of English schools. A Royal Commission was appointed to study the matter. But when this essentially Conservative group reported, it recommended only a few changes, primarily in teacher training and the methods of paying salaries. Moreover, besides voting 15–5 in favor of maintaining the voluntary (private) school system rather than increasing public support of education, it suggested that religious instruction be increased rather than decreased.[42]

The efforts of journalists to draw public attention to the need for reform increased. During 1888 the *Nineteenth Century* alone devoted some twenty articles to educational problems. Of these, ten dealt specifically with the need for increased technical education. In the February number, Thomas Henry Huxley declared his disappointment that the Technical Instruction Bill had been dropped, and another writer called the lack of action on that bill one of the most important Parliamentary failures of the preceding year. But, though many in England would have sided with the opinion of the anarchist Prince, Peter Kropotkin, who declared in June that technological training was the boon that would usher in a "reign of plenty," there were those who demurred. In July, for instance, a British nobleman, Lord Armstrong, argued that the workingman would benefit far more from additional instruction "of a religious and moral nature" than from technical education. And despite all the arguments in favor of improving technical training in British schools, those who agreed with Lord Armstrong temporarily prevailed, for the Education Act did not come before the Parliament again until 1889 (after *A Connecticut Yankee* had been completed). That the Yankee established public schools, the "teacher-factory," and other training schools for technical skills therefore probably reflects more than merely a tribute to American know-how.

Some of the Yankee's specific technological achievements can also be read as satiric thrusts at England's backwardness. Though Edison had invented the incandescent lamp in 1879 and New York had completed the world's first central power plant for electric lighting two years later, it was not until 1888 (again the very year in which Clemens wrote most of his novel) that house-to-house lighting became practicable in London. Before that, each electrical installation had required its own separate power plant, and even in 1888 the two companies formed that year confined their activities chiefly to areas where theaters, clubs, and hotels assured sufficient consumption to make the operation profitable.

The Yankee's long-distance telephone system was also ahead of that in the England of Clemens' own day. There had been service between Brighton and London as early as 1882, but Londoners were not able to talk with friends or business associates in Birmingham, Liverpool, and Manchester until 1890. As a recent visitor to the United States informed readers of the *Nineteenth Century* for March, 1888, "certain modern inventions, such as the telephone," were in "much more common and practical household use" in America than in England.[43]

Even the introduction of the newspaper, whose first issue caused such a stir in the Holy Valley, may itself have carried an additional contemporary sting. Clemens' immediate inspiration probably lay in his desire to strike back at Arnold's objections to the "irreverence" of American newspapers (and perhaps partly in Lecky's assessment of the power of the press to influence public affairs). He achieved one of his neater bits of irony, in fact, by having Hank Morgan admit that the flippant headlines of the paper sent "a quivery little cold wave" through him because he had become so used to this "clammy atmosphere of reverence, respect, deference." Yet one wonders if Clemens might not also have seen a parallel in the fact that London's first half-penny paper, the *Star*, had begun publication in January 1888.[44] Designed both in price and in content to appeal to the working-classes, and staffed by such models of reticence and propriety as the young Bernard Shaw, the *Star*, too, probably caused a few "quivers"—of rage, if not of fear—among British Conservatives.

Among other hotly debated subjects during the middle and late 1880's were the inadequacies of Britain's military establishment, the excessive costs of royal grants and pensions included in Victoria's Civil List, and the role of the House of Lords and the Church in government affairs. George Standring and others had for some years been railing at the inefficiency of the armed forces and the great expense of maintaining an officer corps consisting primarily of incompetent nobles, whose commissions represented little more than sinecures. During 1887 and 1888, too, English newspapers and magazines carried numerous discussions of weaknesses in Britain's military and naval defenses. The *Nineteenth Century* reflected this concern in no fewer than eight articles in 1888 alone.

Clemens, sometime near the point where he had stopped work

on the *Yankee* in September, 1887, had copied Standring's statistics from *The People's History* on the vast over-supply of high-ranking, highly paid officers in the army and navy. Later he echoed Standring again when he commented: "Rank in the army is still restricted to the nobility—by a thing which is stronger than law—the power of ancient habit and superstition. Let a commoner become an officer—he will be snubbed by all his brethren, ostracized, driven out."[45]

As for the House of Lords, the Liberal and Radical press in recent years had become increasingly irritated by the tendency of the Upper Chamber to oppose reform measures. Some critics took special exception to the vast powers afforded to the Established Church by the presence of the twenty-four bishops, who formed a potent voting bloc. Others sneered at the creation of new peerages, especially those bestowed on such entrepreneurs as Messrs. Bass, Allsopp, and Guinness, the proprietors of Britain's great breweries.[46]

In the early months of 1888, at least three proposals for reorganizing or even abolishing the House of Lords came to the floor of the Parliament. Arguments from both sides again graced the pages of the *Nineteenth Century*. In the April number (that which also contained Arnold's "Civilization in the United States"), one Frank H. Hill forcibly opined that the inefficiency, negligence, and general lack of intelligence of most of the peers made reform imperative. In May, on the other hand, Lord Lymington denounced another of the current proposals, minimized the faults of the House's present structure, and stressed the appeal of long and hallowed tradition.

Clemens was surely aware of some of these discussions just as he was of the debate over the Local Government Bill, whose passage through committee that July he applauded so heartily. Such opposition to change as Lord Lymington's, or objections to the Local Government Bill as Lord Thring's (in the June *Nineteenth Century*), no doubt further convinced him that British nobility was battling progress wherever possible. His opinion of the Church's characteristic opposition to reform he made graphic, also, in his comment on the failure of the "Deceased Wife's Sister's Bill" the following May: "24 Bishops in House of Lords & 27 majority against the bill. Without the Established Church the bill would have had a majority."[47] If he could have known that it would be

1907 before the proponents of that bill would muster enough votes to legalize marriage between an English widower and a sister of his deceased wife, he would have been even more irritated. He aimed his most direct blast at the House of Lords as an institution in one of the unfinished essays. If the Upper Chamber always sought to promote the best interest of the nation as a whole, it would indeed merit the reverence it received. But, he said sarcastically, it did not deserve such esteem because just "once in awhile" it took care "of Number One to the neglect of the rest of the numerals," and thus proved itself to be "only the common run of clay after all."*

Almost all of these elements—technological backwardness, aristocratic opposition to education, abuses in the military system, reverence for hereditary rank, and the close association of Church and State in matters of aristocratic prerogatives—Clemens molded especially skillfully into the Chapter Twenty-five episode in which the Yankee's West Pointer and two young nobles compete for a lieutenancy in the newly established army. Though the humorist's long-time aversion to corrupt practices in the American civil service system may also have added its bit, England was the primary target.

Along with W. E. H. Lecky's pointed comment (in *The History of England in the Eighteenth Century*) that in most areas of competition, aristocratic lineage invariably overshadowed intellectual eminence,[48] any number of Standring's acid remarks could have served as the immediate inspiration for this episode. But Clemens probably also remembered W. S. Gilbert's vivid spoof of Parliamentary obtuseness in *Iolanthe* (1882). The fact that he had already adapted the "Jackdaws strut in peacock feathers" line from *Pinafore* for Hank Morgan's earlier blast at aristocratic pretensions doubles the temptation to see in the Arthurian contest echoes of Strephon's "shocking proposal" (in Act II) to "throw the Peerage open to Competitive Examination," and Lord Tolloller's rejoinder that "with a House of Peers with no grandfathers worth mentioning, the country must go to the dogs."

Clemens' barbs fly thick from the very beginning of the episode. Some Americans might miss the shaft in Hank's identification of the chief examiner as "the officer known to later centuries as Norroy King-at-Arms." But English readers would immediately recognize the allusion to the Herald's College, the authority since 1483 in all matters of noble genealogy.[49] The Church's concern with heredi-

* Paine 102b, Mark Twain Papers.

tary rank is also assailed, both in the Yankee's remark that of course the examiners were all priests, and in the vivid passage where Hank is rebuked for questioning the requirement that candidates for commissions prove that they are descended from at least four generations of nobility, When the chief examiner tells him that his query "impugns the wisdom of our Holy Mother Church herself," since a similar rule applies to the canonization of saints, Hank hammers home the basic likeness between the aristocratic and ecclesiastical "superstitions" with the only overtly satiric comment in the episode: "In the one case a man lies dead-alive four generations—mummified in ignorance and sloth—and that qualifies him to command live people . . . and in the other case, a man lies bedded with death and worms four generations, and that qualifies him for office in the celestial camp."

The humorist's principal source for his attack on the "four-generation" rule for Army officerships was Carlyle's *French Revolution* which cites the requirement as the brain-child "in comparatively late years" of a French Minister of War, who sought to reduce the excessive number of requests for commissions. Carlyle explains, too, that this solution to the immediate problem had had a more serious effect. By establishing a barrier between the old and the new nobility, as well as by increasing still further the gulf between commoner and noble, it created a harsher contrast between classes in France.[50] This concept Clemens put to excellent use, first in King Arthur's explanation that the rule prevented peers "of more lofty lineage" from scorning military service because of the presence of those "of too recent blood," and later in the Examining Board's final choice between the candidates.

As the examination begins, the Board eliminates the Yankee's West Pointer immediately, refusing at first even to question him when they discover that his father was a weaver. But then it relents enough to let Hank Morgan conduct the examination into the cadet's other qualifications for officership. The youth's obvious skill and his fund of technical knowledge of course count for nothing compared with the "real" qualifications of the two nobles. Though the first, Sir Pertipole, is thoroughly stupid and the second is his "twin, for ignorance and incapacity," both possess the requisite four generations of nobility.

In the Board's final choice of Sir Pertipole's rival, Clemens adapted Carlyle's distinction between the "old" and "new" nobility so as to create a double irony. Sir Pertipole's great-grand-father had been elevated to "the sacred dignity of the British nobility" as first Baron of Barley Mash, for having built a brewery. But though the author here subtly supports the contemporary objections to the "beerage" in England, this fact is not what disqualifies Sir Pertipole. Presumably he means to imply that the "beer peerages" are just as legitimate as any others. What does win the place for the other young noble is the character of the wife of his line's founder. Sir Pertipole's ancestress had been a chaste and gracious gentlewoman. But when his rival reveals that *his* great-great grandmother had been "a king's leman" who climbed "to that splendid eminence by her own unholpen merit from the sewer where she was born," the examiner proclaims this lineage to be "the true nobility . . . the right and perfect intermixture . . . the blood all Britain loves and reverences."

In thus defining the "old" nobility, the humorist once again underlined the pet aversion he shared with George Standring—the unwarranted pride of most British aristocrats in their noble heritage and the irrational slavery of British commoners to the "fetish of nobility." In reconsidering the passage later, he may have thought, in fact, that the final phrase of the examiner's accolade resembled some of Standring's sarcasms too closely, or at least considered it too direct a statement, for he ultimately deleted it from the manuscript.

Clemens' biting satire of the young nobles in this episode is likewise identical in spirit with Standring's snorting indignation over such anomalies as one of Nell Gwyn's sons being commissioned Colonel of a cavalry regiment at age fifteen, even though (as Standring adds) "like many royal and aristocratic officers of today, he did nothing besides drawing his pay."[51] Such observations doubtless lay behind the Yankee's subsequent scheme to establish the King's Own Regiment, exclusively for nobles, and with absolute independence in time of war. With the nobles flocking to such an infinitely attractive company, the rest of the army could then be officered by "nobodies" like the West Pointer, "selected on the basis of mere efficiency." In the conclusion of this "Competitive Examination" chapter Clemens took a final fling at the aristocratic code, scoring the inequities in the awards of pensions and allowances, especially as these came to members of the Royal Family. Here again he parallels Standring.[52]

There is a fascinating possibility that the timely arrival on bicycles of Launcelot and his five hundred knights (in Chapter Thirty-eight) carries a contemporary implication. In 1888 some of England's local Volunteer companies, whose role in their country's defense system received much discussion, were introducing cycling into their maneuvers. But, as one historian has said with almost classic restraint, "the high bicycle did not lend itself well to such uses."[53] Did the thought of soldiers in full military gear pedalling furiously down the highway so overwhelm Clemens that he could not resist enhancing the absurdity by having his cumbersome armored knights mount similar steeds?

Once the Valley episodes were finished, progress on the novel during September and October was more rapid. The book was going so well, in fact, that on October 5 Clemens hopefully named October 22 as the date when both the novel and the Paige typesetter might be finished. Again his calculations proved over-optimistic. But by some time in March[54] the holocaust of the Sand-Belt had burned itself out, and the author had brought the Yankee back to die in modern England, not by suicide as in his original plan, but still, in a way, yearning for his "lost land."

Chapter Seven

A Connecticut Yankee:
Other British Literary Sources

I MPORTANT AS WERE THE VARIOUS "CONTEMPORARY" BRITISH influences in changing the story's direction from burlesque "contrast" toward more serious satire, one should not conclude that *A Connecticut Yankee* was intended solely, or even primarily, as an attack on England. Though the author himself emphasized that intention in an interview at the time of publication, other factors suggest that he intended his book to have a much broader scope. He owed much to several British authors, and a look at some of them may help to clarify certain underlying concepts of this confused and confusing novel.

Actually, the sources from which Clemens drew his materials for *A Connecticut Yankee* represent most of the ages of Western history from Roman times until his own. The major ones alone cover the ground fairly well. As its title indicates, Lecky's *History of European Morals* deals primarily with the interval "from Augustus to Charlemagne," but its allusions and footnotes extend the range well beyond those limits. Malory's *Le Morte Darthur* by implication represents the whole Age of Chivalry. Writers on the French Revolution and its antecedents—notably Taine, St. Simon, Carlyle, and Dickens *(A Tale of Two Cities)*—furnish documentation for seventeenth- and eighteenth-century France. Lecky's *History of England in the Eighteenth Century* (published in six volumes in 1887 and 1888), besides supplementing the materials on the French Revolution, furnishes many examples of English "evils" during the so-called Enlightenment and often describes their continuation into the nineteenth century. Along with the "contemporary" elements already described, Charles Ball's *Slavery in The United States* (first edition, 1836) and George Kennan's articles on Russia in the *Century* magazine (especially those of June, 1887, and May, June, July, 1888) bring the frame of reference up to the time of the novel itself. Other minor sources, including such unlikely ones as Tennyson's *The Princess,* provide implicit references or allusions to medieval England, Scotland, and Ireland; Renaissance England, France, and Italy; seventeenth-, eighteenth-, and nineteenth-century England, France, Germany, and the United States.[1]

The fact that the "medieval" practices and abuses Clemens satirizes were drawn from so many different eras is significant. Most of the borrowings illustrate man's subjection to the combined religious and secular "superstitions" underlying the concepts of monarchy, aristocracy, and the Established Church. That subjection, furthermore, is consistently equated with actual slavery in later eras, as in the case of the "freemen" (Chapter Thirteen), King Arthur's attitudes in judging law cases (Chapter Twenty-five) and the peasants' support of their lord at Abblasoure (Chapter Thirty). The author's use of his sources, therefore, suggests that he intended the novel to serve as an implicit examination of man's "slavery" to "superstition," not only as it existed in medieval times but as it had persisted down through the centuries into his own age. The Yankee's effort to reform the system and "train" the "slaves" for their proper roles as independent citizens of a republic, of course, provides the conflict.

Of the novel's major sources, Malory's *Le Morte Darthur,* though it added important elements, contributed less to the attack on "medieval" ideas than might be expected. Its influence pervades the novel, of course, through the names of its characters and places, so skillfully introduced that any reader familiar with Malory (or with Tennyson's *Idylls of the King*) feels pretty much at home. But as Robert Wilson's study points out,[2] the more extensive borrowings (including quotations of several lengthy passages[3]) occur in the first half of the novel, and, for the most part, are adapted to the author's original intention of burlesquing chivalric combat and its glorification of physical prowess over brains. After Sandy's long-winded stories in Chapters Fifteen and Nineteen, which constitute the humorist's most effective adaptation of *Le Morte Darthur,* Malory reappears only in the names and in bits and snatches of phraseology until Chapter Forty-two, when Clarence's report of events leading to the break-up of Arthur's kingdom quotes from Malory's account of the last battle and of the passing of Arthur (Book Twenty-one, Chapter Four).

In one important instance, however, Clemens combined a quotation from *Le Morte Darthur* (Book Seven, Chapter Twenty-eight) with a passage adapted from Scott's *Ivanhoe* to launch one of his attacks on the cruelty and immorality of the chivalric ideal, as well as on its ridiculousness. Presented as the apprentice effort of a priest turned newspaper reporter, the excerpt from Malory (in Chapter Nine, "The Tournament") serves primarily to burlesque the style of its author.[4] Yet in the long list of who "brake his spear" upon whom, some of the senseless violence still comes through, especially when coupled with the description of the attitudes of the spectators —which Clemens borrowed from Scott's great tournament at Ashby-de-la-Zouche.

In *Ivanhoe* (Chapter Twelve), while describing the crowds at Ashby, Scott expresses surprise that the brutal tournaments should evoke such enthusiasm not only from "the vulgar," who would naturally revel in horrible sights, but even from the "ladies of distinction, who crowded the galleries." Here and there, he says, "a fair cheek might turn pale, or a faint scream might be heard, as a lover, a brother, or a husband was struck from his horse." But most of the time the ladies cheered the knights on, waving veils and kerchiefs and "exclaiming 'Brave lance! Good sword!' when any successful thrust or blow took place under their observation."

Sir Walter's mild wonder at such an attitude, Clemens turns to comedy, but comedy with a bite. As the Yankee tells it, the "banks of beautiful ladies, shining in their barbaric splendors" at Camelot would not think of fainting when a knight sprawled from his horse "with a lance-shaft the thickness of your ankle clean through him and the blood spouting." Instead, they "would clap their hands and crowd each other for a better view." Occasionally one did "dive into her handkerchief and look ostentatiously broken-hearted," and "then you could lay two to one that there was a scandal there somewhere and she was afraid the public hadn't found it out."

The Yankee's description satirizes both the Age of Chivalry and its Scottish chronicler. Besides suggesting the fundamental viciousness of the feudal ideal, the emphasis on the immorality, as well as the bloodthirstiness of the fair spectators undercuts Scott's obvious admiration for the color and glamor of the feudal age. Moreover, the conciseness of scene and the broad vernacular of the language implicitly mock Sir Walter's lengthy descriptions and elaborate diction.[5]

Structurally, the Chapter Nine tournament not only provides the motivation for the Yankee's later "Fight with the Knights" (Chapter Thirty-nine) but establishes the period of time for his intervening adventures. Sir Sagramor, taking offense at a chance remark, challenges Hank to a joust "three or four years in the future" when the knight is to return from seeking the Holy Grail. That joust then develops into a battle with the whole Round Table Company.

The later contest also reflects elements from Scott. Like Ivanhoe at Ashby, Hank Morgan meets and masters five opponents in succession (at which point the knights decide to send their greatest champions against him, again to no avail). Much of his advantage derives from the agility of his horse, just as the cleverness of Ivanhoe's steed allows its master to evade the simultaneous charge of three adversaries during the tournament's second day. In stressing the Yankee's own agility, the humorist may also have remembered how Quentin Durward's nimbleness of foot and comparatively light armor enabled the Scot to harass his opponent "by traversing on all sides, with a suddenness of motion and rapidity of attack, against which the knight, in his heavy panoply, found it difficult to defend himself without much fatigue" (Chapter Four). Here Clemens would probably have fumed at Sir Walter's rhetoric, but he still would have admired Quentin's skill and courage.

By far the richest source of both details and controlling ideas, however, was that "so noble & so beautiful" book, *The History of European Morals*. Besides the grounds for portraying the Church as the primary "villain" of his tale, Clemens probably found therein the rationale for his Yankee's development from selfish opportunist to reformer. And Hank's dissertation on "training" in Chapter Eighteen suggests that Clemens' own "discussion with Lecky," was still going on. Whether or not Clemens had consciously turned to Lecky before reminding himself (in a planning note at the beginning of Chapter Fifteen) to use certain details for a future incident,[6] echoes from *The History of European Morals* occur as early as the eclipse segment (Chapters Five and Six) and are especially vivid in the Chapter Eight diatribe which places the responsibility squarely upon the Church for establishing both ecclesiastical and secular tyranny.

Though Clemens' concept of the Church as villain was probably not inspired by Lecky alone,[7] in *A Connecticut Yankee* he drew most of the ammunition for his assaults from the historian's well-stocked arsenal. He was obviously fascinated by Lecky's analysis of the Church's "almost absolute empire" over the minds of men from the fall of Rome to the Renaissance. In his own copy of *European Morals,* for instance, he drew a heavy line next to a passage which concludes: "A boundless intolerance of all divergence of opinion was united with an equally boundless toleration of all falsehood and deliberate fraud that could favor received opinions." With credulity taught as a virtue, and all conclusions dictated by authority, "a deadly torpor sank upon the human mind, which for many centuries almost suspended its action, and was only broken by the scrutinising, innovating, and free-thinking habits that accompanied the rise of the industrial republics in Italy."[8] At another point Clemens emphasized by heavy underscoring the explanation that for many centuries during the Christian era men had failed to question even the most "grotesquely extravagant" histories, principally because of *"the theological notion that the spirit of belief is a virtue, and the spirit of scepticism a sin."*

That last statement occurs in a long catalogue of ancient superstitions which Lecky assembled in order to demonstrate how fertile a field lay ready for the Church's domination of the gullible through her own "miracles," and her "apparently perfectly unscrupulous forgery of a whole literature." Additional underlinings (and borrowings for later episodes) show that this compendium was one of Clemens' favorite sections of the book.[9]

Though *A Connecticut Yankee* early stresses the astonishing credulity of the Arthurians, that gullibility is depicted, in the first three chapters primarily in the courtiers' ready acceptance of the knights' wild lies. But with the eclipse and its aftermath,[10] the "spirit of belief" takes on the *religious* tinge of Lecky's discussion. The Yankee's image of churches, monasteries, and convents overflowing with "praying and weeping poor creatures who thought that the end of the world was come" is in the exact spirit of the historian's catalogue. So is Hank's succinct comment that when the eclipse passed, the terrified Arthurians "not only believed . . . but never dreamed of doubting" that he had saved the earth from destruction.

With the attack on ecclesiastical influence in Chapter Eight, the effects of Lecky's repeated emphasis on the Church's success in enforcing "passive, unreasoning obedience" become much clearer.[11] As Clemens first wrote the passage in 1887, the Yankee merely mentioned that the Church's "awful power" had enabled it in only two centuries to convert "a nation of men to a nation of worms." But sometime the same summer he added an explanation of how that conversion had been accomplished. Perhaps the decision to expand the attack may have been partly inspired by his current reading in the literature of the French Revolution, for both Taine and Carlyle comment forcefully on the Church's role as a political power.[12] Nevertheless, the Yankee's flood of irony and outright sarcasm clearly reflects ideas from Lecky. As Hank Morgan puts it: before the Church became supreme, "men were men, and held their heads up, and had a man's pride and spirit and independence." Fame and position depended upon achievement, not accident of birth. But then the Church subtly took control by inventing "divine right of kings" and wrenching the Beatitudes from their good purpose to fortify that evil concept. "She preached (to the commoner) humility, obedience to superiors, the beauty of self-sacrifice; . . . meekness under insult; preached (still to the commoner, always to the commoner) patience, meanness of spirit, non-resistance under oppression." To bolster the monarch's position still further, she "introduced heritable ranks and aristocracies, and taught all the Christian populations of the earth to bow down to them and worship them." At this point, as indicated in the last chapter, the humorist traced the "poison" of that reverence for rank down into modern times.

Besides the repeated emphasis on humility and obedience, the reference to the proud and independent spirit of man "before the day of the Church's supremacy" seems to condense comments on the Stoic ideal from several passages which Clemens marked in his copy of *European Morals*.[13] In charging the Church with grinding her own axe by introducing the "divine right" theory and "heritable ranks," he echoes Lecky's explanation of how the Church had established this "consecration of secular rank" so as to maintain her control of affairs when she saw her power beginning to wane. In his current mood, too, Clemens would have found support in the historian's conclusion that the theory of divine right was one of the most "enduring and influential" superstitions—one which had still "not wholly vanished from the world."

Following his identification of this "holy alliance" of religious and secular tyranny, Clemens often introduced details from Lecky to help illustrate man's bondage to the "superstitions" of rank and caste. In comparing the lot of Arthurian commoners to that of French peasants during the *ancien régime* (Chapter Thirteen), he stressed the Church's role in their "slavery" by making their feudal lord a bishop rather than a secular noble, by accentuating their acquiescence to the priestly assurances that their hard lot was "ordained by God," and by again naming the Established Church an enemy of free thought and expression.

As marginal notations suggest, he was also interested in the historian's summary of theological and political attitudes toward suicide.[14] Though he did not mark them specifically, he would certainly have noted the observations that England had not abandoned the practice of burying suicides in the public highway until the reign of George IV and that English law still provided for confiscation of the suicide's property (though Lecky did admit that this "monstrous injustice" was no longer enforced). In the novel, the author turns Lecky's prosaic summary into a colorful climax. As a final irony, after listing the atrocities borne by the "freemen," the Yankee notes that if a poor wretch, unable to bear his suffering any longer, sought release in suicide, "the gentle Church condemned him to eternal fire, the gentle law buried him at midnight at the cross-roads with a stake through his back, and his master the baron or the bishop confiscated all his property and turned his widow and his orphans out of doors."

Throughout the rest of the book, Clemens continued to rely on Lecky for additional examples of evils that intended to "enslave" men's minds and bodies. It should perhaps be noted, however, that in attacking the Church, the satirist almost entirely disregarded the historian's efforts to remain objective. Fascinated by what Lecky called (in another marked passage) the "abyss of depravity into which it is possible for human nature to sink," he obviously saw the Church's insistence on subservience and reverence for rank as a major cause of that descent into depravity. At one point he greeted Lecky's assertion that Rome's servile classes had gained new dignity through the Christian emphasis on humility, patience, and resignation with a brusque marginal sneer: "Christianity, then, did not raise up the Slave, but degraded all conditions of men to the Slave's level." The nearest thing to a compliment came with the Yankee's admission (Chapter Eighteen) that some parish priests were sincerely devoted to relieving human suffering. But even this situation effectively deterred progress since (as the Yankee says) it was "just the sort of thing to keep people reconciled to an Established Church." A final notation at the end of Lecky's second volume, likewise, seems to imply Clemens' wry exasperation with the historian's efforts to present both sides concerning the Church's influence. "If I have understood this book aright," he says, "it proves two things beyond shadow or question: 1: That Christianity is the very invention of Hell itself; 2 & that Christianity is the most precious and elevating and ennobling boon ever vouchsafed to the world."[15] If by "Christianity" the author meant organized religion, *A Connecticut Yankee* obviously leans far toward the first premise alone.

Besides the basis for much of the novel's anti-clericalism, Clemens seems to have found in the *History of European Morals* a rationale both for Hank Morgan's development from "operator" to humanitarian, and for his plans to reform Arthur's kingdom. Despite some obvious flaws in the Yankee's characterization, that development follows closely the process outlined in Lecky's discussion of "realisation" and compassion already cited in connection with *The Prince and the Pauper*.

In that passage, besides identifying the imagination as the realising faculty" and education as the primary means by which its sensitivity is developed, Lecky defines three levels of imaginative response. At the first level—the "earlier and feebler stages"—the imagination is "wholly unable to grasp ideas, except in a personified and concrete form" and so "concentrates itself on individuals." At this level, most cruelty (as distinct from vindictiveness) results from callousness, "which is simply dulness of the imagination." Next, imagination may progress to an understanding of the more abstract concept of "an institution or well-defined organization." Finally, it may reach the most advanced stage at which it can fully grasp "a moral or intellectual principle." Moreover, each stage is characterized by its appropriate "moral enthusiasm," which Lecky names "loyalty," "patriotism," and "attachment to a cosmopolitan cause."[16]

A Connecticut Yankee reveals ample evidence of the author's interest in that analysis. He had echoed it, perhaps unconsciously, when he told Mrs. Fairbanks in 1886 that he wished to "get at" life in Arthur's England, "to see how it feels & seems."[17] In the eclipse episode of Chapter Six, he adapts it almost verbatim, when Hank, faced with death at the stake, declares: "The mere knowledge of a fact is pale, but when you come to *realize* [Clemens' italics] your fact, it takes on color. It is all the difference hearing of a man being stabbed to the heart, and seeing it done." Some fourteen chapters later, the concept enters in a different context, when Hank deplores the villagers' astonishing complacency toward the sufferings of their fellow-townsmen in Morgan le Fay's dungeons. Emphasizing the village people's complete degradation, Clemens envisions an even lower step than Lecky's "dulness" of imagination. "Their very imagination was dead," Hank says: "When you can say that of a man, he has struck bottom, I reckon; there is no lower deep for him."

Such explicit parallels support the conjecture that Clemens intended the Yankee to follow a similar three-stage development—from self-concern to concern first for the Arthurians' material welfare, and then for their political and social welfare. As he reached the last stage he would, in turn, endeavor to raise the Arthurians from their blind loyalty to Church, king, and noble, to a true patriotism (loyalty to the country itself instead of to its political "clothing") and then to the "cosmopolitan cause" of freedom under a democratic government.

Clemens obviously never really succeeded in reconciling the Yankee's initial role as bumptious vernacular "operator" with that of the relatively intellectual would-be political savior. Both qualities are implicit in a later comment to his daughter Clara that Howard Taylor's inept dramatization of the novel captured only the "rude animal side," the "circus side" of Hank Morgan's character, leaving the "good heart & the high intent" unrevealed.[18] In the novel, when the inventive "ignoramus" expounds upon history, economics, politics, and morals, the "circus side" vanishes and the language slips out of Hank's vernacular to become that of the author. On the other hand, that "circus side" reappears periodically in the Yankee's love of Tom Sawyerish "effects" and his continued sharp eye for a fast profit, often to the detriment of serious mood or effective satire. Nevertheless, revisions in the manuscript suggest that Clemens was at least partly aware of the problem and sought, however unsuccessfully, to suggest a gradual development from "operator" to humanitarian.

In the novel as originally written (i.e. without Chapter Ten, "The Beginnings of Civilization," added in 1888), the Yankee's concern for the political and social welfare of the Arthurians was not revealed until the meeting with the freemen in Chapter Thirteen. And not until two chapters later does Hank ponder how he will "banish oppression from this land and restore to all its people their stolen rights and manhood." Following his "control" of the eclipse, he is still chiefly concerned with his own personal glory. His destruction of Merlin's Tower in Chapter Seven seems motivated primarily by a desire for self-aggrandizement, and even the blast at reverence for rank in Chapter Eight results largely from the Arthurians' failure to respect his personal merits as well as his position. Plans for financial gain still bulk large.

Presumably to maintain the Yankee's original point of view still further, the author at some point during the summer of 1887 altered the beginning of the second paragraph in Chapter Eight. Originally he had included a sentence in which the Yankee vowed to use his newly won power for the benefit of the entire nation "from the King down."* In revising, however, the writer omitted that sentence, with the result that Hank's schemes seem less altruistic than they otherwise would. Even when he added "The Beginnings of Civilization" chapter, he maintained essentially the "operator" point of view, though he did indicate the importance of public schools and teacher training along with his emphasis on technology and industrial development. Hence, in terms of the plot, it is primarily the encounter with the freemen in Chapter Thirteen that brings Hank to a real concern with changing the political and social life of the kingdom.

The planning notes in the manuscript at the beginning of that chapter furnish additional evidence that the author's own anger at political and social abuses was running strong. He had obviously already decided to have the "princesses" turn out to be hogs and thus to satirize monarchy and aristocracy, as well as to ridicule aspects of the knightly quest itself. Yet, almost as if warning himself not to let his sentiments interfere, he followed his proposal to have

* Ms. I, 137, Berg Collection, New York Public Library.

Hank and Sandy meet the freemen with a parenthetical admonition: "Not too much talk about the corveè" [*sic*]. But at the end of
the note, as if he could no longer contain his feelings, he wrote: "No
nobility or royal family was ever created by a people's consent—
hence all such that exist are lies and frauds. Takes the hogs."*

In the chapter itself, however, despite an outburst about the
"ever blessed and memorable" French Revolution, there are indications that Clemens was trying to tone down his own "sansculottism" (as reflected in the Yankee's desire for a violent revolution)
and also to make the passage more consistent with his narrator's
basic "shrewdness." As he originally wrote it, the Yankee, on discovering that one man showed signs of understanding the concepts
of democracy, had commented that with a thousand like him he
would overthrow the government.[19] "I consider myself a super-loyal
citizen," he said, "and in my creed a citizen's first duty, under a bad
system, is to get up a revolution." Then, for the first time, Hank was
to admit that "in his secret heart," he was already beginning to plot
against the government. Yet even in the original version Clemens
played down the possibilities of violence with the Yankee's conclusion that his revolution was to be a peaceful one and that he had
"no serious doubt" about his ability to "work it out on that line."**

In revising the passage, the author modified Hank's temptation
to violence even more. Omitting the reference to overthrowing the
government, he altered the sentences to read merely that with the
backing of enough men of that sort, the Yankee would strive to
prove himself the nation's "loyalest citizen" by making "a wholesome change in its system of government." In addition, he further
emphasized his narrator's "shrewdness" by having Hank explain
his reasons for not attempting to incite an insurrection. Anyone
who did so without first "educating his materials up to revolution
grade" was almost certain to fail. Therefore, since he himself was
not accustomed to "getting left," he did not talk "blood and insurrection" to that one "man" among the "mistaught herd of human
sheep," but merely sent him to Clarence to be educated.

Thus the author's delay until Chapter Thirteen in revealing
Hank's decision to reform the government, together with the revisions in that chapter and the Yankee's subsequent ponderings on
how he could "banish oppression" and restore the people's "stolen

* Ms. I, 207, Berg Collection, New York Public Library.
**Ms. I, 220, Berg Collection, New York Public Library.

rights and manhood," all suggest Clemens' intention that Hank Morgan's progressive "realisation" of the dreadful conditions under which the common people lived should follow the stages outlined by Lecky. In addition, the emphasis on education in the revisions of Chapter Thirteen, along with Hank's insistence that his revolution is to be a peaceful one, enhances the irony of his eventual conclusion that only through violence can he even begin to shake the people's unthinking "loyalty" to the "superstitions" of rank and caste.

The probable connection with Lecky's theory of "realisation" further suggests that the "miracles" by which Hank exploits the people result not only from his "circus side" but from the premise that in their "feebler" state of imagination the Arthurians could comprehend only such concrete acts. Ironically, this is exactly the sort of manipulation that Lecky charged the Church with employing in order to bring barbarian peoples into the fold. But since the Yankee ultimately sought to free the Arthurians rather than keep them "enslaved," Clemens would probably have argued that his kind of exploitation was justified, especially since Hank employed the "true" miracles of science rather than the fraudulent ones perpetrated by the Church.

Clemens' agreement with Lecky on the importance of education and training and on the evils of Church influence did not mean that he also had completely agreed with the historian's view of the moral nature of man. On the contrary, one of the incidents at Morgan le Fay's castle specifically suggests that he had grown much closer to the utilitarian philosophy. After the Queen murders a page boy who chances to brush against her while serving, the Yankee is at first astonished by her callous rationalization of the act.[20] But then, considering the matter of motivation (and speaking more in his creator's voice than in his own) he declares that "training is everything; training is all there is *to* a person," and that what men call *nature* is "merely heredity and training," all thoughts and opinions being "transmitted to us, trained into us."

So far he is wholly in the camp of the utilitarians. But then he hedges slightly: "All that is original in us, and therefore fairly creditable or discreditable to us, can be covered . . . by the point of a cambric needle." And he proceeds to stress the importance of that infinitesimal bit of originality, asserting that his sole concern will be to "save that one microscopic atom in me that is truly *me. . . .*" In that fragile tie with "originality," Clemens, perhaps almost despite himself, maintains a tenuous link with Lecky and the intuitionists.

There is an additional suggestion of that connection in the Yankee's subsequent comments on the nature of the conscience as a detriment to contentment. After deciding to aid Morgan's prisoners rather than obey his first inclination to leave without bothering about them, he admits that the conscience "certainly does a great deal of good," but concludes that "it would be much better to have less good, and more comfort." As far as comfort is concerned, one might just as well prize an anvil, if he happened to have one inside him. Here again, Clemens seems to be agreeing—as he had in *Huckleberry Finn* and "The Recent Carnival of Crime"—that if the conscience resulted simply from operation of a utilitarian pleasure-pain theory, and if it caused more pain than pleasure, the sensible thing to do would be to abolish it. But the Yankee then observes that though an anvil could be dissolved with acids, he knew no way at all to work off a troublesome conscience—"at least so it will stay worked off." Apparently the pleasure-pain theory (or Lecky's interpretation of it) still did not satisfactorily explain the workings of the conscience to Clemens.

Yet the reduction of Huckleberry Finn's "sound heart" to the Yankee's "one atom" of originality represents another step toward a completely deterministic view. And in the novel the theme of "training" remains a primary one, especially in its continued involvement with the people's "slavery" to Church and State.

For the secular and political side of his attack on man's bondage to "medieval" ideas Clemens relied heavily on the writers who had made France's old régime and its dissolution live again for him. The Frenchmen Taine and St. Simon contributed many elements. But Carlyle's *French Revolution* proved the richest source; and Dickens' *Tale of Two Cities* supplied significant episodes.

It will be remembered that during the summer of 1877, Clemens compared his own mood to that of the fiery Marat. In the novel, that new enthusiasm for the radical revolutionaries first finds explicit voice in the Chapter Thirteen meeting with the freemen. Following the long list (compiled from Carlyle and others) of the harsh feudal duties required of these ostensibly free men,[21] Hank first notes the ironic fact that these citizens who comprised "the actual Nation" were really no better than slaves, and then makes the comparison explicit: "Why, it was like reading about France and the French before the ever memorable and blessed Revolution, which swept a thousand years of such villainy away in one swift tidal wave of blood."

There is little doubt that this passage reflects Clemens' own Marat-like emotions, for again in Chapter Twenty, which he wrote close to the time of the August 22 "sansculotte" letter to Howells, he once more stressed the need for violent action, contending that all successful revolutions "must *begin* in blood, whatever may answer afterward." At this point the Yankee is reacting to the fact that instead of outrage at the treatment of Morgan le Fay's prisoners, their friends and relatives exhibited merely a "dumb, uncomplaining acceptance." Even the writing in the manuscript implies strong feeling, for it is smaller and darker than the immediately preceding lines, as if the author were bearing down hard on his pen. "Goody-goody talk and moral suasion" were of no use, the Yankee says. "What this folk needed . . . was a Reign of Terror and a guillotine." But then to maintain his narrator's point of view, the author has him add, "but I was the wrong man for them." The manuscript further suggests that this was the time Clemens augmented the Chapter Thirteen eulogy of the Revolution by adding the paragraph which cites *two* Reigns of Terror in history—the brief Revolutionary blood-letting and the "older and real Terror" which, over a thousand years, had shed hogsheads of blood for every drop spilled by the Revolution.

The novel's specific debt to Carlyle is more apparent when the Yankee, in the same chapter, launches a diatribe against the sort of loyalty demanded by monarchy and aristocracy. Both imagery and the emphasis on "manhood" (a theme which often recurs later in the book) echo several of Carlyle's comments, and especially a striking passage near the end of *The French Revolution*. Admitting that the Terror had created far less suffering than had the evils of preceding centuries, Carlyle several times confesses himself appalled at the prospect of a nation "rending asunder its Constitution and regulations," even though those institutions may have become "dead cerements for it." Seeing "sansculottism," as only a different, more dangerous sort of "clothes," he rejoices at its death, concluding that to achieve any sort of progress or stability, the wise man must "found on his manhood, not on the garnitures of manhood." For, "he who . . . founds on garnitures, formulas, culottisms of what sort soever, is founding on old cloth and sheepskin, and cannot endure."[22]

Almost as if seeking to refute Carlyle's fear of revolution, Clemens adapted both argument and clothes-imagery to the Yankee's withering attack on irrational loyalty to established political forms. "The country is the real thing, the substantial thing," Hank declares; "institutions are extraneous, they are its mere clothing, and clothing can wear out. . . . To be loyal to rags, to shout for rags—that is the loyalty of unreason, it is pure animal; . . . it was invented by monarchy; let monarchy keep it." But then he emphasizes Carlyle's fundamental premise, when Hank Morgan immediately sends the one *man* who had shown signs of comprehending democratic principles to Clarence so that he may be educated in the "Man-Factory."

Though these specific references to the French Revolution appear relatively late in the chapters written in 1887, earlier episodes were also probably motivated both by Clemens' "sansculottism" and by Carlyle. Most striking of these is the Yankee's destruction of Merlin's Tower in Chapter Seven. Not only does the incident dramatize the effectiveness of drastic action against the forces of superstition and tyranny, but it draws many of its details from Carlyle's chapters on "The Feast of Pikes," which celebrated the first anniversary of the fall of the Bastille.

The connection of this episode with the French Revolution, or even with an assault on political and religious tyranny is perhaps obscured by the fact that Merlin (as antagonist) is not clearly identified with either the monarchy or the Church. Primarily, he is simply another representation of the superstition that dominates men's minds. Yet Clemens was surely relying upon his readers' knowledge (from Tennyson, if not from Malory) of Merlin's role as Arthur's protector and counselor. "The most famous man of all those times," Tennyson calls him,

> . . . who knew the range of all their arts,
> Had built the King his havens, ships, and halls,
> Was also Bard, and knew the starry heavens;
> The people call'd him Wizard. . . .

Sir Edward Strachey, too, in his introduction to the edition of Malory used by Clemens, put Merlin clearly on the side of the king and at the same time suggested a religious note by describing him as "half Christian, half magician, but always with dog-like loyalty to the house of Uther Pendragon."[23] Another bond with the Church appears in the fact that the priests in the Valley of Holiness seek Merlin's aid in restoring their sacred "fountain."

A more significant connection between Merlin and the feudal ideal is the Tower itself. Constructed by the Romans four hundred years before, it stood alone on a hill near Arthur's castle. Massive though "rather ruinous," it was still "handsome after a rude fashion, and clothed with ivy from base to summit, as with a shirt of scale mail." If the ivy-armor makes the Tower an almost too obvious symbol of knighthood, the emphasis on the structure's massiveness, rude beauty, and Roman origin stresses more subtly the strength and endurance of the feudal ideal, despite its "rather ruinous" condition. Therefore, whether or not Clemens consciously intended it, the Tower becomes a symbol of monarchy and aristocracy as they had lasted into his own day—anachronistic, decadent, but still "massive" and still attractive to many.

The relationship of this episode to Clemens' current attitudes and to the course which the novel had taken becomes even more apparent when one explores the specific debt to Carlyle in the action which follows. The Yankee's preparations, his "miracle," and even the time-scheme of the book seem based upon the Scotsman's recreation of events leading up to and including the Feast of Pikes, in Paris July 14, 1790. Clemens obviously knew the passage well; in 1885 he had listed its climactic announcement of the oath-taking by cannon-shot throughout France as one of the items to be included in his proposed collection of "Picturesque Incidents in History and Tradition."[24]

In *A Connecticut Yankee,* the curious crowds begin to assemble from all parts of England "within twenty-four hours" after the Yankee's escape from the stake on June 21. When the Arthurians, who keep coming "for a fortnight" (that is, until July 5 or 6), begin "presently" to demand another miracle, the Yankee announces that in about two weeks he will take a moment from the pressing affairs of state and "blow up Merlin's stone tower with fire from heaven." Granting only the strong probability that the agitation for the new miracle began while the crowds were still assembling, the date set by the Yankee must have been very close to July 14.

Other details both support that conjecture and point to Carlyle's story of the preparations for the Feast of Pikes as the primary source of the episode. In Paris the great amphitheatre on the Champs de Mars was still far from finished only two weeks before the celebration, but "on the 13th of the month" it was finally ready—"trimmed, rammed, and buttressed with firm masonry." So the Yankee, on "the thirteenth night," completed his mining of the Tower's fifteen-foot-thick stone walls and attached his lightning rod. And "on the morning of the fourteenth," he announced that the miracle would occur "at some time during the twenty-four hours."

Even the idea of blowing up the tower very likely came from the same source, though other references to the explosive situation in France before and during the Revolution (in both Carlyle and Taine) could also have influenced Clemens' decision.[25] In speculating that "certain Aristocrats" were secretly bribing the workers to delay construction on the amphitheatre, Carlyle recalled that several months earlier Aristocrats had allegedly stocked the quarries and catacombs of "subterranean Paris" with charges of "gunpowder, which should make us 'leap'."

Moreover, the chief physical details of the Yankee's exhibition— the torch baskets; the wind, rain, and lightning; the lightning-rod; and even a "miracle-worker"—are present in Carlyle's description of the French ceremonies. The cassolettes, or incense pans, hang high over the great amphitheatre as lightning flashes fitfully, and the wind, "moaning cold moisture," finally brings "a very deluge of rain." The lightning-rod appears, though only symbolically, as Carlyle wonders how the blessing of heaven is to be invoked upon the oath-taking and, in his question, all but enunciates the spirit of what the Yankee would ultimately attempt to accomplish in England: "By what thrice-divine Franklin thunder-rod shall miraculous fire be drawn out of Heaven; and descend gently, life-giving, with health to the souls of men?" Then, as Bishop Talleyrand ascends the altar-steps to do "his miracle," the rain pours down. But whereas Carlyle uses the rain as an evil omen, dampening the festivities and promising greater storms to come, in *A Connecticut Yankee* it becomes the means by which the Boss accomplishes *his* miracle. Yet, Hank, too, will face greater storms, will resort to the utmost violence as the French revolutionaries did, and will ultimately fail to establish his utopian republic.

For the actual explosion—the "awful crash" as the "old tower leaped into the sky in chunks, along with a vast volcanic fountain of fire that turned night into noonday"— Carlyle provides two other possible models. During the siege of the Bastille Commandant De-Launey, torch in hand, debates whether or not to touch off the prison's powder magazine, and muses: "But think, ye brawling *canaille*, how will it be when a whole Bastille springs skyward!" In having the Yankee show how it *would* be, however, Clemens perhaps also had in mind the moment during the bombardment of Lyons in 1893 when a "sudden red sunblaze" shatters the August night "with a noise to deafen the world," and the "Powder-tower of Lyons . . . springs into the air, carrying 'a hundred and seventeen houses' after it."[26]

Even in the unlikely event that these close connections with *The French Revolution* were unconscious ones, they suggest that the author himself at this point was thinking of the Yankee's action as more than merely a clever stunt to gain power and prestige (though he was still apparently attempting to maintain the original point of view of his protagonist as opportunist). It is almost, in fact, as if he had in mind Carlyle's remark near the beginning of his discussion of the symbolic import of the Feast of Pikes that in "decisive circumstances" man frequently turns to "Symbolic Representation" in an effort to make visible "the Celestial invisible Force that is in him." Something of an insight into Clemens' characterization of the Yankee seems present also in the further observation that these "representations" are introduced "with sincerity, if possible; failing that with theatricality, which latter also may have its meaning."

Other echoes of Clemens' reading in the literature of the French Revolution, and especially in Dickens' *Tale of Two Cities,* abound in the episode at Morgan le Fay's castle. But in introducing his travelers to that stronghold of corruption, the author drew, perhaps unconsciously, upon a source far-removed from eighteenth-century France, Tennyson's lyric, "The Bugle Song" (from *The Princess,* 1847).

Though Clemens obviously considered Tennyson's *Idylls* one of his targets in *A Connecticut Yankee,*[27] "The Bugle Song" had long been a favorite of his. While courting Olivia, he once had forecast the pleasure they would find in reading it together, hearing "the horns of elfland faintly blowing" as they drifted "dreamily into fairyland with the magician-laureate." Its first two lines—"The splendour falls on castle walls / And snowy summits old in story"— impressed him most, for he quoted them in his notebook and several times adapted them into later works. Once, urging a composer friend to set the whole poem to music, he supplied explicit instructions about the musical effects to be achieved.[28]

Somewhat ironically, the paraphrase of those romantic lines in *A Connecticut Yankee* helps to underscore the novel's attack on monarchy and its attributes. As Hank and Sandy approach the castle (Chapter Five), their first glimpse reveals the "whole majestic mass . . . drenched with splendours flung from the sinking sun." Soon, however, they will see that this beauty is only a façade, for like the beauty of the Queen herself, it masks the evil that lies within. Both castle and queen, in turn, become symbols of the system, whose false values and internal corruption lie concealed beneath glamorous external trappings.

To help dramatize that corruption and the habits of mind which fostered it, Clemens relied heavily on *A Tale of Two Cities*. When the Queen nonchalantly stabs the page, she is surprised that the Boss is shocked, and even more surprised that he does not consider her offer to pay for the boy a truly magnanimous gesture. Here we seem to be in the presence of Dickens' blasé Marquis St. Evrémonde, whose conversation, actions, and attitude provide almost exact models for those of the Queen. When a child is crushed under the wheels of his coach (Book Two, Chapter Seven), the marquis, tossing a coin to the father, rides away "with the air of a gentleman who had accidentally broken some common thing, and had paid for it, and could afford to pay for it."[29] Two chapters later he speaks of a time in the Evrémonde family's past when an indiscreet peasant was "poinarded on the spot for professing some insolent delicacy respecting his [the peasant's] daughter." Very possibly, too, the anguished curse pronounced by the page-boy's grandmother owes something to Dickens' description of the grief-stricken father's howl and of Madame Defarge's knitting "with the steadiness of fate" as the carriage departs. Similarly, the Queen's instinctive command, "To the stake with her!" seems to translate into action the Marquis' comment that if he knew who threw the stone at his coach, "he should be crushed under the wheels."

Here, too, as in *Huckleberry Finn*, Dickens may be credited with helping the author introduce one of the major concerns of the novel. For besides presenting another example of royal callousness, the episode provides the jumping-off place for Hank's discussion of the influence of "training."

Dickens is again called upon for the Yankee's case history of two of the prisoners released from Queen Morgan's dungeons. This unfortunate pair had dared on their wedding night to resist the attempt of Sir Breuse Sance Pité, their feudal lord, to invoke his *droit du seigneur*. Not only had the girl "spilt half a gill of his almost sacred blood" in the struggle, but the young husband had committed a doubly unpardonable sin by laying hands upon the nobleman and then throwing him bodily out into the parlor. Being cramped for dungeon space, Sir Breuse had asked a favor of Morgan le Fay, in whose "bastile" they had remained—in separate cells—ever since.

This incident and its results closely parallel the experiences of Dr. Manette, described in the same journal entry that had furnished Tom Sawyer's instructions to Huck about procuring and paying a physician (Book Three, Chapter Ten). According to Manette's record, he had been abducted by the Marquis St. Evrémonde and his brother and forced to attend a young boy and his sister, victims of the younger Evrémonde's brutality. The noble had ravished the girl, who was the recent wife, and more recent widow, of a tenant-farmer on the Marquis' estate. Her brother, who had dared seek revenge, was dying from the nobleman's sword-thrust. Manette's efforts to save the lives of the pair proved futile. Though sworn to silence and rewarded with the "rouleau of gold," two days later he was again forced into a carriage and driven secretly to imprisonment in the Bastille.

Besides the Yankee's reference to Morgan's "bastile," other details suggest that Manette's story was in the author's mind.[30] The description of the young husband, thirty-four years old though he looks sixty,[31] strongly resembles both in appearance and actions that of the figure whom Lucie Manette and Jarvis Lorry first see in the DeFarges' garret (Book I, Chapter Six). Moreover, just as Manette's jailors refuse to answer his questions about his own young wife, or even to say whether or not she is still alive, Clemens' couple never get an answer to their similar questions about each other. More significantly, their total time in prison matches that of Manette: the doctor is "buried alive" for eighteen years; the Arthurian pair have graced Morgan's vaults for nine. Finally, just as Manette is later restored to his daughter, the Yankee releases these two and sends them to their friends.

One may assume that the attitudes of the friends to whom they are returned is the same "dumb, uncomplaining acceptance" that

the Yankee describes on another occasion. Thus, besides emphasizing once again the cruelty of the aristocracy, the borrowings from
Dickens helped dramatize Clemens' contention that the "superstitions" of monarchy and aristocracy imprisoned not only the bodies
but the spirits of the common people. The reactions of the prisoners, in turn, also formed an important impetus for the Yankee's
declaration that such attitudes could not be rooted out without a
"Reign of Terror and a guillotine."

The adventures of Hank and Sandy in the Valley of Holiness
(Chapters Twenty-one–Twenty-six) further illustrate the twin tyranny embodied in the "holy" alliance between Church and State.
The band of pilgrims and the band of slaves whom they encounter
on the way not only furnish a means of getting to the Valley, but
in themselves symbolize that two-fold tyranny—the mental shackles
of the superstitious pilgrims paralleling the physical bondage of
the pitiful slaves. Moreover, these encounters introduce the next
stage of Hank's development. His adventures, heretofore largely
chance occurrences, now become purposeful when he joins the pilgrims in order to see more of the country and thus better prepare
himself to rule wisely. In the Valley he observes major examples of
religious superstition and of the Church's influence in secular, as
well as religious, matters. The appearance of the slaves symbolically prepares the way for Hank's further observations of secular
"superstitions." Besides provoking comments on the nature of liberty, the band will subsequently provide the Yankee with firsthand
experience, when he and King Arthur inadvertently become members of that very group.

Most of the specific details for the pilgrims and slaves themselves
derive from two sources that deal with historical eras far removed
from the "medieval"—Charles Ball's *Slavery in the United States,*
the alleged autobiography of a Negro slave first published in 1836
and widely reprinted, and George Kennan's articles on Russia and
Siberia in the *Century* magazine.[32] But the spirit is the same as that
propounded by Lecky, thus implying again the identity of "slavery" in any age. The first contact with the slaves graphically underscores the fundamental kinship of the physical and mental bondage
engendered by devotion to the aristocratic ideal, with its insistence
on "reverence." Echoing the notion that human beings could get
used to any sort of cruelty—a point made by both Lecky and Charles

Ball—Clemens used the whipping of a young girl to illustrate the effects of slavery in "ossifying" what one might call "the superior lobe of human feeling."[33] While the slave-master lashed the screaming maiden, the religious pilgrims (who would not have allowed such cruelty to a dumb animal) "looked on and commented—on the expert way the whip was handled."

Many of his other illustrations, the author took directly from Lecky. The story of the "holy fountain," the goal of the pilgrims, he skillfully adapted to Sandy's archaic diction. In borrowing the specific characteristics of St. Simeon Stylites and the other repulsive hermits who inhabited the Valley, he scored an additional satiric point. Omitting some of the more gruesome details, he added a footnote explaining that since this volume was fiction, not history, many of Lecky's frank descriptions were "too strong" for it. For the later ceremony of the Royal Touch (Chapter Twenty-six) he again turned to the historian's discussion of ancient superstitions referred to in connection with the eclipse episode. Here, besides adapting an actual description of the ceremony quoted by Lecky, he updated his materials by suggesting that the English kings would not have had to abandon touching for the "King's Evil" (a practice which, as *European Morals* points out, had continued into the eighteenth century). Faith in the ruler's "divinity" was still so great (the Yankee says) that cures would be effected in forty-nine out of fifty cases. And the same list of superstitions provides two possible models for the allegedly clairvoyant magician discredited by Hank Morgan in Chapter Twenty-four: Appolonius of Tyana, who had "seen in one country events that were occurring in another," and Sospitra, a woman who could "see at once the deeds which were done in every land . . . ."[34]

Beginning with the Valley chapters, Clemens also called upon Lecky's *England in the Eighteenth Century* for supporting details and incidents. Among direct borrowings were the anecdote about the building of the Mansion House by the Sheriffs of London (Chapter Twenty-five); part of the motivation for the episode at the Small-pox hut (Chapter Twenty-nine); the Yankee's "clincher" is his argument with Dowley (Chapter Thirty-three); and the bases for the witch-burning and the hanging of the young mother for her theft of a piece of cloth (Chapter Thirty-five).[35] More indirectly, he found further support for his conviction that ecclesiastical influence had remained strong in England. At numerous points Lecky voices astonishment that the Church had continued to wield such power in an age that had produced thinkers like Newton, Swift, Pope, Addison, and Bolingbroke. Clemens could scarcely have failed to notice the assertion that the Anglican Church had inherited "the scepter of Catholicism" and, as late as the reign of George III, was still inculcating the doctrine of divine right more prominently than any other tenet. He would likewise have been impressed by Lecky's agreement with Edmund Burke that English attachment to the national church was "above all other things, and beyond all other nations."[36]

In addition to the other examples of mental and physical bondage experienced by Hank and King Arthur during their incognito wanderings, Clemens seems once more to have found in *A Tale of Two Cities* inspiration for an episode which evokes one of the Yankee's most specific comments upon the identity of "slavery" regardless of era. In Chapter Thirty, "The Tragedy of the Manor House," many details parallel those in Dickens' account of the murder of "Monseigneur" and the burning of his chateau (Book II, Chapter Twenty-three).

In *A Connecticut Yankee* the Boss and King Arthur come over the brow of a hill to see the distant blackness lit by a fiery glow. Rising winds, rumbling thunder, and faint flashes of lightning signal an approaching storm. Dickens' chapter, "Fire Rises," likewise features a stormy night, beating rain, and watchers on a hilltop. At first the Yankee merely mentions the glow of the fire, but soon the wind that roars through Dickens' chapter finds its fearful counterpart in the roar of men's voices as the mob of villagers pursue and hang all those in any way suspected of involvement in the burning of the manor and murder of its lord. The results of their work provide a grisly obstacle for the Yankee and the King as they push through the "almost solid blackness" to investigate the fire they have seen from the hill. Bumping into a soft object, which gives way slightly when he hits it, Hank is horrified when a lightning flash reveals a corpse hanging from a tree limb. Subsequent flashes illuminate many more such ornaments dangling from other trees.

In describing the action at Abblasoure, Clemens was obviously thinking of the French Revolutionary era, for at one point, to placate Arthur, the Yankee agrees to look for the men who had actually burned the manor and says (again for the King's benefit):

"If they were merely resisters of the gabelle or some kindred absurdity I would try to protect them from capture; but when men murder a person of high degree and likewise burn his house, that is another matter." In referring to the *gabelle*—the salt-tax which the French peasants found so onerous—the author was perhaps thinking specifically of Dickens' symbolic Monsieur Gabelle, village postmaster and tax-collector.

Furthermore, in summarizing the results of the burning, Dickens first notes that with the coming of morning the crowd besieging Gabelle's quarters had dispersed, and then generalizes the scene. Though the tax-collector's life had thus been spared "for that while," he says, "within a hundred miles, and in the light of other fires, there were other functionaries less fortunate . . . whom the rising sun found hanging across once-peaceful streets . . . ; also there were other villagers and towns-people . . . upon whom the functionaries and soldiery turned with success, and whom they strung up in their turn."

Clemens' treatment of the mob and the hangings in Abblasoure seem almost to dramatize that summary comment. But in adapting the situation the humorist introduces a strain of irony not present in the original, for his villagers are not hunting down and executing the "functionaries" of their feudal lord; they are hanging their fellow-townspeople. And for a crime that they are glad has been committed. Ironically, then, almost *all* the citizens of Abblasoure themselves become the "functionaries" of oppression.

Clemens draws on Dickens' largely symbolic picture of the conflagration that was soon to engulf France primarily for the purpose of denouncing once more the subjugation to tradition and a misguided sense of duty which could allow the villagers to hunt down and hang their own neighbors. And he carries that "slavery" forward into later centuries by comparing these villagers to the Southern "poor-whites" in America who subverted their own "freedom" by helping perpetuate the power of the large slaveholders. In terms of the novel's plot, too, the manor-house episode results in the meeting with Marco and Dowley and, subsequently, in Hank Morgan's experiencing the evils of slavery at first hand.

In the book's final chapters, the political and religious "superstitions" once more blend, when the Church's Interdict brings to an end the Yankee's three years of progress. And in Clemens' dramatization of the outcome of Hank Morgan's efforts to educate the Arthurians, both Lecky and Carlyle again figure significantly.

The Church's seizure of complete control, insofar as it reflects antagonism toward the Yankee, is insufficiently motivated. Rather than developing notebook plans for several episodes that would specifically have turned the Church's wrath upon Hank Morgan,[37] the author apparently decided that the mere mention of Hank's many projects was enough to account for the ecclesiastical enmity. But despite that flaw, he provided a vivid symbol of the Church's power in his picture of London blacked out and silent, its inhabitants cowering in abject submission to the Interdict. To the Yankee, just returned from his trip to France, it was a sign that the Church "was going to *keep* the upper hand now, and snuff out my beautiful civilization just like that."

Substantiation of that fear comes with Clarence's news that, save for some fifty youths, the entire populace who had seemed so heartily to favor the Yankee's "improvements," had flocked to the side of Church and King. Here was an almost explicit dramatization of the principle from Lecky that underlay Clemens' abortive Hawaiian novel of 1883–84. The notions inculcated in the Arthurians' formative years indeed "reassumed their sway" and the intellectual habits that had temporarily replaced them swiftly vanished. "Did you think you had educated the superstition out of those people?" Clarence asks.

At this point the Yankee himself finally reaches the position taken by Marat, and decides that nothing but total destruction of the system can bring progress. It was perhaps natural, therefore, that the author should again seek support from writers on the French Revolution. In Lecky's treatment of the event in *England in the Eighteenth Century*, he probably found further justification for emphasizing the Arthurians' irrational eagerness to resume their old ways. One passage, for instance, records a message in which French Ambassador Chauvelin assures his government that revolution in Britain was highly unlikely since most of the people were "profoundly inert" and the whole nation firmly attached to the present system "by old prejudice and habits."

Even more specifically, the Yankee's proclamation of the Republic in Chapter Forty-two all but paraphrases Lecky's description of two similar French decrees issued during the fall of 1792. The first part closely resembles the order from the National Assembly on December 15 that all French commanders in occupied countries "should at once proclaim the sovereignty of the people, the suppression of all existing authorities, the abolition of all existing taxes, of the tithes, of the nobility, and of all privileges" and should arrange for convocations of the people "to create provisional administrations. . . ." And the Yankee's final sentence echoes Lecky's summary of the words and actions of French General Custine, who, during his invasion of Alsace and Germany proclaimed "war to the palaces, but peace to the cottages," confiscated Church and government property, and "invited the conquered towns to reorganize themselves as free democracies."[38] If Clemens used these decrees as models, he could not have missed the National Assembly's conclusion that a people so "enamoured of its chains and . . . its state of brutishness as to refuse the restoration of its rights" was an accomplice of "its own despots" and of "all the crowned usurpers" of the earth. In much the same spirit, after seeing that even the former slaves had joined the other stupid commoners in cheering for the "righteous cause," Hank could only exclaim, "Imagine such human muck as this; conceive of this folly!"

For Clarence's vivid mimicking of the knights' probable reaction to Hank's offer of amnesty, as well as for the action that immediately precedes the Battle of the Sand-Belt, the author once more dug into Carlyle's rich mine.[39] When Clarence strikes the paper from Hank's hand and sneers, "Dismember me this animal, and return him in a basket to the baseborn knave who sent him; other answer have I none," his tone is that implied in Carlyle's cryptic report of Louis XVI's response to a protest against the scarcity of bread in May, 1775. The king appears on a balcony, speaks briefly, and withdraws, and Carlyle comments: "They have seen the King's face; their Petition of Grievances has been, if not read, looked at. For answer, two of them are hanged, on a 'new gallows forty feet high'; and the rest driven back to their dens . . . ."

At some point, too, Clemens drew on Carlyle for help in dramatizing the perilous situation of the Yankee's company of terrified youngsters as they cowered in the cave awaiting the attack. In the Scotsman's account of the famous "Insurrection of Women," the courtiers at Versailles are in somewhat the same position, and the refrain, *"Paris marche sur nous,"* which dominates the episode, finds a close parallel in the boys' repeated awareness that "All England is marching against us." The "prodigious host of England" that follows the mailed knights ("30,000 strong") repeats Carlyle's image of the "thirty-thousand Regulars" and the "whole irregular Saint-Antoine and Saint-Marceau" assembled in the teeming Place de Grève. So, also, the attitudes of the boys echo those of Lafayette's soldiers, some of whom, after urging their leader not to suppress the growing mob, refuse to turn their bayonets "against women crying to us for bread," and even encourage the march on Versailles because "all the people wish it." Since the Arthurian host includes not only the nobility and gentry, but the whole people of England, Hank's troops, too, beg him not to make them use force: "We love them—do not ask us to destroy our nation."

With the recognition of the source for this episode, several other ironic overtones emerge. Whereas Clemens would have considered the mission of the bedraggled Paris mob a noble one, the intent of the glittering Arthurian host, with banners flying and armor "all aflash" is wholly ignoble. An additional bite occurs in the fact that Lafayette's harangue in Carlyle's episode fails to turn the mob from its purpose, whereas the Yankee's speech succeeds in changing the minds of his forces. The very argument which makes them willing to fight again lays human cowardice bare. What convinces the boys that they will not have to attack their friends and relatives is Hank's assurance that once the vanguard of knights is destroyed, the rest of the populace will immediately scatter in terror. Though the episode by no means achieves the vividness and drama of its model, the adaptation of these elements from Carlyle added a depth which it had not originally possessed.

With the battle over and the chivalry of England decimated, the story quickly closes. Merlin (in disguise) succeeds in throwing the Yankee into a sleep that is to last thirteen centuries, and then falls against the electrified fence; Clarence hides the body in a cave[40] before he himself dies of the plague engendered by the piles of decomposing bodies; and the "Final P.S. by M.T." tells of the Yankee's final delirium and death in modern England.

When he finished the novel, Clemens was either in no special hurry to get it out, or had decided to follow his original plans to issue it as a "holiday book" for the Christmas trade.* By mid-April, 1889, two copies of the ms. had been prepared by a publishing company typist. A month later Clemens arranged to send one of them

---

* Notebook 20, TS, p. 33, Mark Twain Papers.

to Edmund Clarence Stedman upon the latter's return from a trip. When Stedman's enthusiastic comments arrived early in July, they included only a few suggestions for changes. In August the author enlisted Howells' aid in reading proof, and from mid-September until November, batches of copy made the rounds between New York, Hartford, and Cambridge. Howells, who found little to criticize and much to praise, on November 10 pronounced his blessing on the final chapter: "As Stedman says of the whole book, it's Titanic."[41] Finally, on December 10—a full five years after the "dream of being a knight-errant" first clothed a modern man in medieval armor—*A Connecticut Yankee* emerged from the portals of Charles L. Webster & Co. to challenge the "superstitions" represented by monarchy, aristocracy, and Established Church, as they had existed in the past and as they had influenced the present.

Because of the numerous confusions in *A Connecticut Yankee,* the question of Clemens' ultimate intention will probably remain a matter of critical controversy. As late as 1906, he himself said, "I think I was purposing to contrast . . . English life, not just the English life of Arthur's day, but the English life of the whole of the Middle Ages, with the life of modern Christendom and modern civilization—to the advantage of the latter, of course."[42] Any number of other comments indicate beyond a doubt that he took for granted the vast superiority of his own century to all that preceded it, and of republican government to any form of monarchy or aristocracy. With the Paige typesetter still promising momentarily to make him one of the world's richest men, his faith in technological progress was also still running high. He firmly believed, along with Lecky, that the chief remedies for the "superstitions" that still lingered as obstacles to progress lay in technological advancement and in education generally.[43]

But his various sources and the uses he made of them clearly indicate that he was not just comparing the backwardness of past centuries with the progress of his own. Much more to the point than the 1906 statement was his tribute a year earlier to Dan Beard, commending the artist's drawings for supplementing the novel's "vast, sardonic laugh at the trivialities, the servilities of our poor human race, and also at the professions and the insolence of priestcraft and kingcraft—those creatures that make slaves of themselves and have not the manliness to shake it off."[44] One of the unfinished manuscripts resulting from the invitation to answer

Matthew Arnold indicates even more forcefully that while writing *A Connecticut Yankee,* Clemens was concerned with the existence of such "slavery" in his own time, for there he defines a "slave" as anyone "owned by another person," anyone, that is, who is subject by law, custom, or tradition, to any requirement "not required of all men in his country," or denied anything "that is privileged to another man."* Hence, stimulated as he was in the late 1880's by an awakened consciousness of abuses in modern England, much of the novel's satire was directed (as Stedman had put it) at "the *still-existing* radical principles or fallacies which made 'chivalry' possible once, and servility and flunkeyism and tyranny possible now." The author surely hoped that his book, through its broad farce, slapstick, serious satire, and direct diatribe, would help to sweep away the nineteenth-century remnants of the "superstitions" that had defeated Hank Morgan.[45]

It could be that his primary concern was the sale of his book in November, 1889, when he cautioned Sylvester Baxter of the Boston *Herald* not to mention that it contained any "slurs at the Church or Protection" because he wished "to catch the reader unwarned and modify his views." Yet his enthusiasm was genuine when he applauded the revolt that had established a republic in Brazil that same month. As he told Howells, he hoped that all who felt as he did would speak up, so as to counteract the many voices that were sure to "deprecate and disenthuse." He wished that he himself could print "some extracts from the Yankee that have in them this new breath of republics," but hastened to add that it was not because he wished to advertise the book, but that he wished the book to "speak now when there's a listening audience. . . . & try to make that audience hear with profit."[46]

In the novel itself, however, under the implicit hope that the nineteenth century would finally achieve the reforms that the Yankee had failed to institute, lies the strong suggestion that the "trivialities and servilities" of the human race were probably too deeply ingrained ever to be educated out of men. One of the book's most striking examples of the juxtaposition of hope and gloom occurs at the ends of Chapter Thirty and the beginning of Thirty-one. When the charcoal-burner, Marco, explains that the citizens of Abblasoure had helped to hang the suspected assassins simply to avoid execution themselves, and then notes his own hatred of the

* Paine 102b, p. 9, Mark Twain Papers.

local lord, Hank once more propounds something like Carlyle's view of "manhood" as the only sound basis for individual action and governmental institutions. "A man *is* a man, at bottom," he says. "Whole ages of abuse and oppression cannot crush the manhood clear out of him. . . ." Then, encouraged by the thought that he need not yet give up his dream of peaceful revolution, he concludes that there is "plenty good enough material for a republic even in the most degraded people that ever existed—even the Russians . . . even in the Germans—if one could but force it out of its timid and suspicious privacy."

But the "if" was a large one. And the next page symbolically emphasizes the difficulty, if not the impossibility, of forcing the good material out of its "timid and suspicious privacy." As Hank walks along with Marco and the King, the charcoal-burner's greetings to passers-by underscore the "nice and exact subdivisions of caste." Toward the fat, sweaty monk, Marco is "deeply reverent"; toward the gentleman, "abject"; with the small farmer and free mechanic, "cordial and gossipy"; but when a slave comes by "with countenance respectfully lowered," Marco's "nose [is] in the air." Thoroughly disgusted, Hank finally says of this man whose basic "manhood" he had so recently praised: "Well, there are times when one would like to hang the whole human race and finish the farce." And the author almost immediately underlines that point by having the group rescue a boy whose playmates have hanged him as part of their game. "It was some more human nature," the Yankee said afterward; "the admiring little folk imitating their elders; they were playing mob . . . ."

Such comments are markedly reminiscent of a notebook entry from the summer of 1888, apparently inspired by recent news stories as Clemens was planning some of the episodes involving the band of slaves. Noting that "every little while" children and "disagreeable relatives" are found "chained in cellars, all sores, welts, worms and vermin," he concluded: "This is to suggest that the thing in man which makes him cruel to a slave is in him permanently and will not be rooted out for a million years."[47]

The novel's ending reveals the same sort of ambivalence as the experience with Marco. Since the author was dealing with past history, the Yankee's failure is inevitable. Yet the fact that Merlin's spell would dissipate after thirteen hundred years might be read as a sign that the nineteenth century had triumphed, or at least *would* triumph, over the forces of superstition and unreason, and would achieve the real civilization that the Yankee had failed to establish in Arthur's England. If so, the Yankee's final delirium and death would have to be considered simply a convenient way for Clemens to end the novel, a partial working out of the original idea to have Hank commit suicide in modern England, yearning for his "lost land" and his medieval sweetheart—a pathetic scene calculated to draw sympathetic tears from sentimental readers.

On the other hand, Hank's conviction that his nineteenth-century life, as well as his attempts to plant modern civilization in the sixth century, had all been merely an illusion might also imply that hope for progress in the battle against superstition and ignorance was also an impractical dream, even in the nineteenth century. Hank's last remarks, in fact, come ironically close to a view once expressed by the author who had inspired some of Clemens' most vehement attacks on rank and caste. For as Hank deliriously begs Sandy to stay by him every moment so that he will not have to endure again "the torture of those hideous dreams" of progress and defeat, and declares that death would be preferable to separation from loved ones—and especially preferable to those wild dreams—he is a cousin, if not a brother, to Matthew Arnold's disillusioned speaker in "Dover Beach," who pleads:

> Ah, love, let us be true
> To one another! for the world, which seems
> To lie before us like a land of dreams,
> So various, so beautiful, so new,
> Hath really neither joy, nor love, nor light,
> Nor certitude, nor peace, nor help for pain;
> And we are here as on a darkling plain
> Swept with confused alarms of struggle and flight,
> Where ignorant armies clash by night.

Though Clemens was to shout for reforms on many occasions during the rest of his life, the view that the basic nature of the human race provided a formidable, if not insurmountable, obstacle to progress was pretty well fixed. It was not so much that he had subconsciously lost faith in the possibilities of technological progress, but that he had become at least partly convinced that "the thing in man which makes him cruel to a slave"—superstition, ignorance, subservience to custom—could not be permanently rooted out by technology nor by any other means.[48]

Chapter Eight

The Road Back

(1890-1894)

DURING THE FIRST FEW MONTHS OF 1890, the breach between Clemens and England gaped its widest. The preceding autumn, fearing that British sales might suffer, Andrew Chatto had requested that the author tone down some of *A Connecticut Yankee's* harsher criticisms. Scornfully replying that he had already taken considerable pains to remove whatever might be offensive in the book's castigation of "monarchy and its several natural props," he refused to make further changes. It was high time, he said, that someone answered the many British efforts to "improve" Americans by "trying to pry up the English nation to a little higher level of manhood in turn." Actually, he did relent slightly in allowing Chatto to omit the final paragraph of his preface, which burlesqued the theory of "divine right." But he persisted in his refusal to alter the text. When his business manager, Fred Hall, was in London to see Henry M. Stanley in January, 1890, he was evidently commissioned to check the accuracy of the English edition, for he wrote back that the book had been printed "just as you wrote it."[1]

Even though Hall also mentioned that the book was doing well, the reception of the novel in England seems to have justified Chatto's fears. One of the first reviews—December 23, 1889—in the usually liberal *Pall Mall Gazette* began by praising Mark Twain's earlier accomplishments. But when it came to *A Connecticut Yan-*

kee, it found almost no virtue, and concluded by deploring the fact that the author had "used his undoubted genius to vulgarize and defile the Arthurian Legend." Some two months later (on February 28) the same paper featured an article entitled "Mark Twain and Tennyson," in which one Reginald Brett again took Mark Twain to task for his blasphemies. Most other critics had followed something of the same line. On January 4 the *Saturday Review* sniffed that the novel was "a triumph of dulness, vulgarity, and ignorance, such as none but a Yankee in the time of Queen Victoria can compass." The *Speaker* of January 11 added the note that Mr. Clemens was "not only dull when he is offensive," but "perhaps even more dull when he is didactic," and regarded the whole performance as "stale." Taking a slightly different tack, the Edinburgh *Scots Observer* declared on January 18 that the book constituted "a 'lecture' in dispraise of monarchical institutions and religious establishments as the roots of all evil, and in praise of Yankee cuteness and Wall Street chicanery as compared to the simple fidelity . . . of the knightly ideal." And a month later the *Academy* pontificated that the book was totally unworthy of Mark Twain, who "had better retire" if he could find "no better raw material for the manufacture of small jokes than the story of the quest of the Sangreal."

The only English notices that can have pleased Clemens at all were W. T. Stead's comments preceding ten pages of excerpts from the novel in the February *Review of Reviews,* and a brief mention on January 2 by Henry Labouchere's Radical weekly paper, *Truth.* The latter cited the attack on king, nobles, and Church as the sort of "admirable preaching" that was "needed still so sorely in England and Ireland." Stead's remarks were more equivocal, for he spoke of "a certain profanation" in the novel's subject and "a certain dulness in its treatment," even while calling it one of the most significant works of the day by virtue of the ideas it embodied. At any rate, his praise outweighed his censure.

As a sort of climax to the initial round of British comments, the *Spectator* for April 5, delivered one of the harshest judgments of all. Charging that Clemens had "surpassed himself as a low comedian in literature," it called the book "a coarse and clumsy burlesque of which America in general, and Mark Twain in particular, ought to be seriously ashamed."

Disturbed, as always, by adverse notices,[2] Clemens this time sought to justify himself through a British friend, the noted author and critic Andrew Lang. In a much meeker letter than the one to Chatto, he all but pleaded with Lang to intercede for him with the British critics. Perhaps taking his cue from Stead's review, which had commended Mark Twain for getting at the heart of the masses more directly "than any of the blue-china set of nimminy-pimminy criticasters," he developed the argument that literature like his, aimed at "the Belly and the Members," demanded different standards of judgment from that with "the Head" as its target. "I have never tried in even one single instance, to help cultivate the cultivated classes," he equivocated. And then, in an almost complete about-face from his earlier statements regarding the purpose of *A Connecticut Yankee,* he asserted that he seldom tried to instruct his readers: "To simply amuse them would have satisfied my dearest ambition at any time; for they could get instruction elsewhere . . . ."[3]

Taken out of context, the letter to Lang summarizes beautifully many of the characteristics of Mark Twain's art. But given the circumstances of its composition, it reveals a man all too willing, in the face of adverse criticism, to renounce his role as reformer in order to protect his book sales.

Lang responded generously to Clemens' request. A long article in the London *Illustrated News* for February 14, 1891, not only heartily seconded Clemens' objections to those obsessed with Culture, but contended that *Huckleberry Finn* entitled Mark Twain to a place "among the greatest contemporary makers of fiction." Lang dodged the main issue, however, confessing that he had chosen not to read *A Connecticut Yankee* because he felt that Clemens lacked sufficient historical knowledge "to be a sound critic of the ideals of the Middle Ages."

Lang's defense did not succeed in removing the stigma which had helped to cause British sales of all Clemens' books to fall off by two-thirds of their usual volume, for they remained at that level for some three years longer.[4] Not only had the new novel failed to "pry up the English nation to a little higher level of manhood," but it had succeeded in reducing the author's income at a time when he badly needed all the money he could get his hands on.

These were the days when the Paige typesetter was taking larger and larger bites of Clemens' finances. In August, 1889, still full of dreams of the vast business enterprise to result from the machine, he had declared to Howells that *A Connecticut Yankee* was his "swan-song"; he was retiring permanently from literature to devote himself exclusively to business.[5] But though his primary concern for the next few years *was* business, the voracious appetite of the typesetter, and diminishing profits of the publishing company, forced him to keep writing. By 1894, besides the first half of *Joan of Arc,* he would complete *The American Claimant* (1892), *Pudd'n-head Wilson* (1894), *Tom Sawyer Abroad* (1894), and a number of stories and articles for various magazines. *Joan of Arc* was a labor of love; the others he wrote chiefly for money.

Business cares were not the only ones that beset Clemens as the 1890's began. Deaths in the family added their burdens. Olivia's brother-in-law Theodore Crane had died in July, 1889, and the autumn of 1890 brought double grief when both Olivia's mother and his own died within little more than a month of each other. With recurrent attacks of rheumatism adding their minor irritations to his major worries, it is small wonder that preparations to take the family abroad again were not very joyous.

As for the concerns which had loomed so large in the creation of *A Connecticut Yankee,* the author's antipathy toward the holders of inherited ranks and titles (though not to the institutions that fostered them), had already significantly lessened before he sailed for Europe in June, 1891. His hatred of England had also passed its peak. But his view of humanity in general continued to darken. If *A Connecticut Yankee* revealed him as hovering between faith in the materialistic and technological progress of democratic institutions and a disillusionment with the "muck" of mankind, the first years of the 1890's saw him leaning farther toward the latter mood. While a slim hope for progress would continue, Clemens was to turn more and more away from a belief that reformation of institutions could improve the lot of man and toward the conviction that the very nature of man himself precluded any real advances.

Two unfinished manuscripts, written by 1891 at the latest, show that disillusionment churning within him.[6] In the first, cumbrously titled "Letters from a Dog to Another Dog Explaining and Accounting for Man," his canine narrator stresses the selfishness and cruelty of men, using much the same arguments that his author would use in later essays. "Give a man freedom of conscience, freedom of speech, freedom of action, and he is a Dog," he declares at one point, "—take them from a Dog and he is a Man."* The second, a "Defence of Royalty and Nobility," seems to indicate Clemens' realization that *A Connecticut Yankee* had taken a wrong tack. Part of its argument is that a hot and bitter presentation of only one side of a controversial issue tends to create a good deal of sympathy for the side under fire. Moreover, in developing that point further, the essay implicitly underlines part of the reason for Hank Morgan's failure to reform Arthur's kingdom. Pretending to quote from a magazine article, Clemens introduces a bitter passage from "Letters from a Dog" and then charges "the author" with having failed to consider two important facets of human nature. In blaming nobles for attempting to retain their privileges, "the writer" had not taken into account the propensity of *any* man to seize privileges that might come his way; in blaming plebians for submitting, he had likewise failed to note a similar tendency to delight in finding objects of reverence to admire and worship.

These same considerations Clemens embodied in *The American Claimant,* which he turned to in February, 1891. Admittedly a potboiler, dashed off in seventy-one days, the novel nevertheless clearly reflects the author's current attitudes. Its weaknesses are obvious, but a consideration of its central "message," is essential to any study of his developing ideas.

For his basic complication, Clemens drew upon the theme which had long fascinated him—the idea of a "claimant" aspiring to high place. In this case he used his own family's legendary claim to the earldom of Durham, which he and Howells had already worked into the play *Colonel Sellers as a Scientist* during the 1880's. According to that legend, as Clemens outlined it in *The American Claimant,* the rightful heir to the Lambton family estates had traveled to America during the eighteenth century, settling in Virginia (and presumably changing the spelling of his name). When no letters came back from him to England, he was presumed dead and his younger brother "softly took possession." After the actual death of the elder brother, his heirs, through successive generations had sought by letter to reclaim their "rightful" title.

Clemens had been aware of the family story since early childhood, for his mother (née Jane Lampton) had delighted in telling it. He had doubtless been reminded of it, too, by the notorious Tichborne case, a *cause célèbre* during his visit to England in 1873.

* DV 344, p. 5, Mark Twain Papers.

He had avidly followed the efforts of Arthur Orton to prove himself Sir Roger Tichborne, long-missing heir to the large fortune. Samuel Webster has even speculated that Clemens considered putting on a "rival show" with his own family claimant. Probably the humorist's major concern was with the literary possibilities of Orton's account, but the Tichborne case no doubt intensified his interest in his own family story.[7]

That interest was further stimulated less than two years later when the first of a series of letters arrived from one Jesse M. Leathers, "a sort of second or third cousin." Identifying himself as the great-grandson of Samuel Lampton (brother of Clemens' great-grandfather William Lampton), and hence the "rightful Earl" of Durham, Leathers sought financial support in establishing his claim to the title. Clemens put him off, denying any prior or present interest in the matter. But the detailed knowledge of the lineage of the English Lambtons in one of his answers to Leathers belies that denial. At one point, too, though he compared the effort of arguing the case before the House of Lords to "tackling Gibraltar with blank cartridges," he admitted that were he himself the "heir," he would probably make a try for the title. He wished Leathers success, he said, but had no doubt that "the present Viscount of Lampton (lucky Youth!)" would in due time "succeed to the honors and the money" of the earldom. Occasional letters from Leathers had continued to arrive. And on being informed of the old man's death in 1887, Clemens again commented on his own interest in "this long, and hopeless, and plucky, and foolish, and majestic fight of a foghorn against a fog," adding on second thought, "Or, reverse that figure perhaps."[8]

This interest in Leathers, too, might be explained in terms of literary potential. Still, there are other indications that Clemens' preoccupation with the earldom went much deeper. Especially significant is an incident that occurred in August, 1877. The author was lying under a tree at Quarry Farm, daydreaming, when a thought struck him. "Suppose I should live to be 92," he said, "and just as I was dying, a messenger should enter and say—" At that point, Olivia interrupted to complete the sentence: "You are become the Earl of Durham"[9]—the very words he was about to speak. Certainly such an incident suggests a large degree of wishful thinking on the humorist's part. It is particularly difficult, too, not to see reflections of his involvement with the family legend in remarks

Lambton Castle, Durham, England, home of the Earls of Durham
Country Life Magazine

Clemens in 1896, age 61

Mark Twain Papers

like the admission that followed a visit with members of the Austrian royal family in February, 1898. Certain princes, he said, "make me regret—again—that I am not a prince myself. It is not a new regret but a very old one. I have never been properly and humbly satisfied with my condition. I am a democrat only on principle, not by instinct—nobody is *that*."[10]

Some such feelings may well have been with him in January, 1891, when he began transforming the play *Colonel Sellers as a Scientist* into the novel *The American Claimant*.[11] With mounting financial problems and the decision to fly to the lower costs of life in Europe, there surely came a sense of defeat, a sense of having fallen from high estate, which made the advantages of social eminence especially attractive.

The changes from play to novel again suggest that possibility. In the play, rather than having developed Sellers' claim to the earldom, the co-authors had concentrated on the Colonel's wild scientific projects—the plan to staff police, armed forces, and legislatures by "materializing" the dead; the use of sewer gas for city lighting; the production of "cursing phonographs" for the convenience of those in positions of command. In the novel, besides adapting these and other such schemes, Clemens expands the Colonel's attentions to his English "claim," heightening the satire of Sellers' aristocratic pretensions with details reminiscent of *Life on the Mississippi, Huckleberry Finn,* and *A Connecticut Yankee.* Both Sir Walter Scott and Southern snobbery again come under fire, for instance, in Sally Sellers' experiences at the properly turreted, towered, and castellated Rowena-Ivanhoe College. Presumably admitted because of her father's tenuous relationship with Simon Lathers, the current American claimant to the Rossmore earldom, Sally there suffers the slights of her more "aristocratic" classmates until the news that Lathers' death had made Sellers himself the "rightful Earl" makes her the darling and envy of all. A specific echo of the "competitive examinations" in *A Connecticut Yankee* recurs in the requirement by Rowena-Ivanhoe College that applicants for admission demonstrate what Sally sneers at as "four generations of American-Colonial-Dutch-Peddler-and-Salt-Cod-McAllister-Nobility."[12] Still, much of this sort of satire is blunted by its excesses.

Where Clemens really embodied his current views of men and institutions was in his expansion of the role of the young English visitor to the United States. In the play, the heir to the earldom of

Dover comes to America simply out of curiosity, wishing to meet the odd American claimant who has been bombarding his uncle with letters. Ultimately, as in the novel, he marries Sellers' daughter; and the Colonel renounces all claims to the earldom. But except for Sellers' brief curtain speeches on the superiority of freedom in America to the titled dignity of an English earldom, the play has few political or social implications.

In the novel, however, the role of the young Englishman is better motivated and far more significant. While still in England, young Viscount Berkeley, son of the Earl of Rossmore, is influenced by his "radical" friends to regard ranks and titles as artificial and undeserved. Learning from Sellers' claims that his father's title is illegitimate in fact, as well as in his new social theory, he resolves to renounce his right of succession, visit the American Claimant, and observe for himself the workings of a democracy. Listed as missing after a hotel fire in Washington, he seizes the opportunity to remain incognito by assuming the name Howard Tracy, and takes a room in a run-down boarding house.

All does not go well with his attempts to win his way in the democratic paradise of America. Efforts to obtain a responsible clerkship, in which his Oxford training might be valuable, prove futile because he lacks political connections. Factory jobs are closed to him because he is not a union member. When he seeks to join a union he is refused on the grounds that he is a foreigner trying to take "honest men's bread out of their mouths" and is bluntly told to go back where he came from.

These and other frustrating experiences clearly reflect Clemens' current disillusionment. As he puts it in one of his preparatory notes, Tracy's "grinding hard luck" finally results in the conclusion that "it is a selfish world and not *worth* lifting up—an Earldom is no bad thing after all, and he will take it."* The turning point comes in Chapter Fourteen, in a conversation with Barrow, a fellow-boarder who is obviously a mouthpiece for Clemens' own views. Tracy's flagging faith in democracy has just been restored by a speaker at the Mechanics Club, who attacked "unearned titles, property, and privileges." But on the way home, Barrow suddenly bursts out: "What an idiotic damned speech that Tompkins made!" Then, using almost exactly the argument Clemens had employed in the unfinished "Defence of Royalty and Nobility," he proceeds

* Paine 41, Mark Twain Papers.

to convince Tracy of the foolishness of his decision to renounce his inheritance. Tompkins had failed to take human nature into account, he says, for any man would jump at the chance to obtain a title, even one who in theory opposes the idea of hereditary nobility. Hence, the nobles are not to blame for retaining their positions. The fault really lies with the masses who allow the system to continue. But though the system is wrong, until the renunciation of a title could contribute to the destruction of the whole, a man would be foolish to give up the honors and privileges that the title provides.

Clemens had already established that emphasis on the faults of human nature two chapters earlier. When Tracy is horrified by the fact that the other occupants of the boarding house persecute one of their fellows who is temporarily unable to pay his bill, Barrow explains the phenomenon in terms of a Darwinian struggle for existence. "Don't you know that the wounded deer is attacked and killed by its companions and friends?" And Tracy, at that time only momentarily disillusioned, exclaims sadly: "In a republic of deer and men, where all are free and equal, misfortune is a crime, and the prosperous gore the unfortunate to death." Shortly thereafter, too, he almost reiterates Huck Finn's "Sometimes I wish there was a country that's out of kings," when he notes in his diary: "It does rather look as if in a republic where all are free and equal, prosperity and position constitute *rank*."

In Howard Tracy's disillusionment and ultimate decision to retain his aristocratic privileges, then, Clemens made explicit the dim view of human nature that had come implicitly, or even unconsciously, to dominate *A Connecticut Yankee*. In addition, the unfavorable English reactions to the *Yankee* must have contributed the pessimistic "message" of the new novel. The proposal to have Tracy decide that the world was a selfish one, "not worth lifting up" and Barrow's arguments in the story itself seem to underscore the author's disappointment that the *Yankee* had not succeeded in "prying up the English nation" to a higher level of manhood. Yet the disillusionment went deeper than that, for *The American Claimant,* despite its many weaknesses, unquestionably reflects the conviction that as long as human nature is what it is, attempts to reform institutions are all but useless. Only if human nature were to change, could real progress be possible. But such a hope seemed slim indeed.

As for Clemens' recent adversary, England, the buffets are nei-ther many nor severe. The author chuckles at the idiosyncrasies of British pronunciations as exemplified in his hero's full name, Kirkcudbright Llanover Marjoribanks Sellers, Viscount Berkeley of Cholmondeley Castle, Warwickshire. He jibes also at other char-acteristics when he shows Tracy immediately succumbing to "that first and last and all-the-time duty of the visiting Englishman, the jotting down in his diary of his 'impressions' to date," and later has him buy "as neat and reasonably well-fitting a suit of clothes as an Englishman could be persuaded to wear." Slightly more acid, but weakened by the fact that it is the hyperbolic Sellers who makes the comment, is the mention of "the traveling Briton's everlast-ing disposition to generalize whole mountain ranges from single sample-grains of sand."[13] A notebook entry of March, 1891, pro-posed also to have Barrow point out to Tracy that American trav-elers in England criticized only trivialities, leaving "your aristo-cratic adulteries unmentioned,"* but Clemens did not ultimately include that remark in the book itself. The most striking feature of the novel, therefore, is that the author now seems to have ab-solved the individual members of the English aristocracy of blame for maintaining their positions, placing the fault in human nature itself.

The conviction that one should make the most of the privileges which came his way was in no way weakened by the treatment Clemens received in Europe that summer. A few explosions like those of the *Yankee* years burst out from time to time, especially in September, 1891, when he proclaimed in his notebook that the "only gospel" of any monarchy should be "Rebellion against Church and State." But soon the notebook assaults on monarchy and aristocracy, as such, ceased almost entirely.[14] When people in high places consistently showered him with attentions, his anti-pathy toward royalty and nobility became more and more theo-retical. Even though as late as March, 1894, he was to write on the flyleaf of one of his books: "I can't find anything durable in the aristocracy of birth and privilege—it turns my stomach," his feel-ing that the attentions he received were not undeserved was seldom so explicitly stated as when he noted in the same comment: "I am an aristocrat (in the aristocracy of mind, of achievement), and from

* Notebook 25, TS, p. 34, Mark Twain Papers.

my Viscountship look reverently up at all earls, marquises, and dukes above me, and superciliously down upon the barons, baronets, and knights below me."[15]

The events of the winter of 1892 in Germany most strikingly illustrate the traveler's change of mood. After a reception for the Prince von Stolberg-Wernigerode in the Hartz mountain village of Ilsenburg, he remarked in his notebook that the Prince had refused to notice the hand offered by the wife of the village doctor (who was not "in society," his father having been a baker). But instead of blasting such insufferable snobbery as one would expect the author of *A Connecticut Yankee* to do, Clemens merely concluded "It was tragic. She had a cry that night," and then characterized the evening as "a pleasant and sociable time." In Berlin, between the efforts of a distant cousin, who had married the distinguished General Von Versen, and those of the American Ambassador to Germany, the Clemenses were treated to a dazzling display of diamond tiaras and titled dignitaries. There was even a command dinner arranged by Frau Von Versen, at the Emperor's request. And Clemens loved Livy's remark that "the way things are going, pretty soon there won't be anybody left for you to get acquainted with but God."[16]

The humorist's emotions during these years must often have been those described by his daughter Clara in 1898. Recalling his reactions to an invitation in Vienna to visit the sister of the German emperor, she said that though he affected indifference, the "little agitated muscles under his eyes" revealed a battle going on "between a largely cultivated inclination toward democratic passions and a largely inborn inclination to worship distinction of position, which supposedly includes distinction of person." Clemens himself would silently attest to that conflict within himself (as well as to the low opinion of human nature that was solidifying during the early 1890's) in notebook entries on successive days in January, 1903. On the twenty-second he would growl: "Why be vain of your lineage? All human beings are despicable—emperors and other slaves alike." But on the twenty-third, presumably for later comment in his autobiography, he would compile a roster of acquaintances that almost shouts for the title "Royalty and Nobility I Have Known": the Marquis of Lorne, the Princess Louise, and the Emperors of Russia, Germany, and Austria.[17]

During the early 1890's, then, Clemens' democratic passions of the "Yankee" years seem increasingly to have reverted to a large respect for rank and position. Albert Bigelow Paine, commenting upon the surprising leniency toward the incident at Ilsenburg, felt obliged to conjecture that if the episode had occurred in England, Clemens would have ransacked the dictionary for adjectives to express his scorn of the Prince. Probably not, for the relatively few anti-British remarks after 1891 indicate that he was mellowing considerably toward his old enemy. He did flare out in support of one of his "heroes" in September, 1891, when he noted cryptically that "history will spit in England's face for her treachery to Napoleon's trust in her." The following year he criticized the irrational reverence of the English toward their Prince of Wales. Yet, at a German resort that summer, when Clemens actually met the man who was to become Edward VII, the Prince's personal charm and intelligence rapidly extinguished the American's theoretical hatred of what he stood for. Indeed, the occasion marked the beginnings of an admiration of Edward that lasted for the rest of Clemens' life.[18]

The three books completed during the first five years of the 1890's provide additional reflections of the author's deepening disillusionment with man, and (the last of them) the lessening antipathy toward England.

Into *Puddn'head Wilson* (1894) he poured some of the hatred of slavery that figures so largely in *Huckleberry Finn* and *A Connecticut Yankee*. Anne Wigger has shown that the "effects of slavery" theme is somewhat obscured because of several passages deleted by the author from the manuscript version preserved in the Morgan Library, one major result being that Tom Driscoll seems more a melodramatic villain than a victim of the system.[19] It is possible, however, that Clemens may not have been so entirely careless in his revision as the deletions seem to indicate. Whereas the final version makes slavery less clearly the antagonist, the emphasis seems to settle more on the base nature of man himself. Underlying Clemens' concern with (in Hank Morgan's words) "the blunting effects of slavery on the slaveholder's moral perceptions," there is again a sense of the baseness in man that would allow slavery to exist in the first place. The novel's shift of emphasis, therefore, seems once more to focus on the impossibility of rooting out "that thing in man that makes him cruel to a slave." From that premise, the confusions of theme and character resulting from the omissions, though annoying, are less significant. Moreover, the scope of the novel broadens to include all men, rather than just those associated (either directly or through heredity) with slavery.

In *Tom Sawyer Abroad* (1894) the humorist's tone is much less biting, as was proper for the children's magazine, *St. Nicholas,* where the novel first appeared. But the view of man is hardly more complimentary. Behind the picture of Tom, Huck, and Jim, floating calmly along in a balloon, able to avoid dangers by a mere touch of the controls, there lurks the author's continuing search for answers to perplexing questions and a less-than-flattering view of human beings. The chief irony of the book, as Albert E. Stone suggests, is that only by being "up in the air" in a balloon may one maintain anything approaching correct perspectives.[20] Down among the foolish muddle of mankind one is overwhelmed by the false views and faulty values of "civilization." Yet the hope of remaining aloof is as futile as the desire of the "erronorts" to ignore Aunt Polly's order that they return home. On delivering the command, Jim says, "Dey's gwyne to be trouble," and Huck concludes the book with: "So then we shoved for home, and not feeling very gay, neither."

From the midst of the financial turmoil of January, 1894, Clemens had completely reversed his announcement to Howells about abandoning literature for business. "When the anchor is down," he wrote to Olivia, "then I shall say, 'Farewell—a long farewell—to *business!* I will *never* touch it again!' I will live in literature, I will wallow in it, revel in it, I will swim in ink!"[21] The project in which he hoped to wallow was his "biography" of Joan of Arc, then about half finished.

At first glance, *Personal Recollections of Joan of Arc* (1896) seems to signal Clemens' return to an optimistic faith in the goodness of man, as personified in Joan herself. There is no doubt that Clemens' worship of Joan and his belief in her absolute goodness was deep and sincere. Yet the book is clearly a pessimistic one. Though Joan's defeat like that of Hank Morgan was dictated by historical fact, the author's treatment of her story carries with it the underlying conviction that such goodness must *always* be defeated or destroyed.

Clemens' narrator, Sieur Louis de Conte, though an actual historical personage (de Contes in Michelet), obviously speaks for his creator in more than his appropriate initials.[22] As an old man reviewing his glorious experiences as Joan's boyhood friend, and later her secretary and page, he reflects not only his author's adoration of Joan, but his general disillusionment with mankind. After the story of Joan's capture by the English in Book Three, Chapter Two (Volume Two), he says that at the time he had believed the rumors that the King or, better yet, a grateful France, would ransom her, but then adds: "I was young and had not yet found out the littleness and meanness of our poor human race, which brags about itself so much, and thinks it is better and higher than the other animals." For the author, Joan herself seems to have been the supreme embodiment of the sort of goodness represented by Huck Finn's "sound heart" or Lecky's "intuitive perception." Considering Joan's skill in battle (Book Two, Chapter Twenty-seven) Louis de Conte concludes that her genius was not from any supernatural source, but from her own inborn powers and capacities, governed by "an intuition which could not err." But this time, that innate goodness was not to achieve even the partial victory of a Huck, for it was completely smothered by the avarice, envy, sloth, and political expediency that surrounded it.

Clemens' original plan to end his story with Joan's execution underscores the novel's pessimistic theme. As Roger Salomon has suggested, the "Conclusion" with its tribute to Joan as "the Genius of Patriotism" was probably added because the author decided that the public demanded some positive meaning. But the real conclusion comes with the "swift tide of flame" that completely swallows the essential goodness of Joan. Recalling those final moments, the narrator remarks: "Yes, she was gone from us: JOAN OF ARC! What little words they are, to tell of a world made empty and poor!" Here indeed is expressed the theme of loss and failure that Salomon correctly sees as central to the meaning of the book.[23]

In this novel the attack focuses less on the institutions of monarchy and the Church than it did in *A Connecticut Yankee,* and more on the meanness and selfishness of individual human beings. The chief villain is not the Church of Rome but those within it who misuse the powers of their holy calling, especially Pierre Cauchon, the Bishop of Beauvais. Cauchon's treachery and outright falsification of evidence does not stem from a desire to protect the Mother Church from heresy; Joan's conviction will help him become Archbishop of Rouen. On the side of monarchy, some of the weakling king's "pet rascals" try to impede Joan's military efforts; others "keep the king idle and in bondage to his sports" so as to further their own personal aims.

The Church itself, by virtue of Joan's faith in it, receives more respect than might be expected from the author. There is no hint of satire in descriptions of the religious trappings—the banners embossed with images of God, angels, and Holy Virgin—nor in the accompanying chivalric ceremonies when Joan's faithful knights swear their fealty. As certain derogatory remarks in the margins of some of his sources indicate, Clemens had not completely changed his attitude toward the Church. Still, during the year in which he completed Joan's story, when his daughter Jean temporarily entered a Catholic convent, he wrote Olivia that he would not object even if Jean were to embrace that "most peace-giving and restful of all the religions," and added: "If I ever change my religion, I shall change to that."[24]

If the Church of Rome was no longer the villain it had been, neither was England. With all the emphasis on the evil of those who sought to destroy Joan, one might expect the English to fare almost worst of all since it was they who insisted that Joan be discredited and executed. But the author caused his narrator to treat them surprisingly well. He does have Louis say that Cauchon and the ecclesiastical court are acting as slaves of the English, but his chief contempt is for the Frenchmen who allow the mockery of justice to take place. Louis abhors the fact that Joan is molested by the half-drunken English guards and vividly describes the harshness and cruelty of the Earl of Warwick. But he seems to understand, if not condone, the political necessity which impels the English to destroy the image of Joan as the rallier of French forces if they wish to retain any of their territories in France. At one point, he actually comments on how "fair and kindly" their administration of those territories had been. He is careful to mention, too, that none of the great English leaders, save the Cardinal of Winchester, knew of Cauchon's ultimate treachery, and remarks that even the Cardinal—"that man with a political heart of stone, but a human heart of flesh"—wept at Joan's last prayer.

The English whom Joan meets in battle are almost invariably kindly drawn. Louis expresses great respect for British pluck in the field and cites the gallantry of an English soldier who saluted Joan at her trial and a little later growled, "By God, if she were but English, she were not in this place another half a second." Joan's chief military foe, the "sturdy old enemy Talbot," he describes as "a fine old lion" with a "tameless spirit," who later passed to his reward "knightly and vigorous." Had the rancor of the late 1880's still burned with anything like its former intensity, Clemens would surely have taken advantage of this excellent vehicle for invective. For one would naturally expect Louis de Conte to be unbendingly bitter toward the enemies of his young patroness, and the author could have drastically increased the vigor of his satire with no risk of violating dramatic propriety.

In most respects, therefore, the years preceding the world lecture tour of 1895–96 saw the bridging of the chasm between Clemens and England well under way.

Chapter Nine

The World Tour and After

(1895-1897)

As early as September, 1893, Clemens had written to Olivia that if worst came to worst with the faltering publishing business, he could clear off his debts by going to Australia and India to lecture.[1] By the time he finished *Joan of Arc* early in 1895, the worst had arrived. The publishing company was bankrupt. Henry H. Rogers, the Standard Oil magnate who assumed the management of Clemens' financial affairs in 1893, had long ago convinced him of the futility of seeking additional finances for the Paige typesetter in a nation staggering in the aftermath of the Panic of 1893. And by mid-April plans were made for a lecture tour which would include stops in the United States, Canada, New Zealand, Ceylon, Mauritius, and England, as well as in Australia and India.

The Clemenses were not exactly paupers during the early 1890's, although they apparently thought they were. Villas, staffs of servants, boarding schools and music lessons for the girls, stays at fashionable spas—all these survived the attempts to pare expenses to the bone. One is reminded of Clemens' alleged comment to Robert Barr, whose *Idler* magazine serialized *The American Claimant* in 1892 and 1893: he and Livy had examined all their accounts and all their needs very thoroughly, he said, and found that "the only things on which they could economize were *Harper's Magazine* and a cheaper closet paper."[2] Nevertheless, the $6000 which continued even after the débacle of 1894 to come in annually from holdings in Livy's name must have seemed infinitesimal to a man accustomed to spending up to $100,000 in a single year. There was also, of course, the huge debt resulting from the failure of the publishing company and the Paige machine. Many friends urged him to negotiate a partial settlement. But Olivia was adamant in her determination that all creditors should receive the full amounts due them, and Henry Rogers agreed with her. Though "business has its laws and customs," he said, "a literary man's reputation is his life. . . ."[3]

With plans for the world tour completed, the Clemenses arrived in New York from England on May 11 and went directly to Elmira for a two-month rest. While there, they decided that Jean and Susy would remain with their aunt.

From its beginning in Cleveland on July 15, the lecture series greatly resembled a royal progress. Once again newspaper columns shouted Mark Twain's praises, but now there was a new note of applause for his gallant effort to reimburse his creditors. At each stop interviewers sought his opinions on matters ranging from humor to race relations, from literature and its makers to international affairs. In Australasia and especially in India he was lavishly entertained. When the exhausting pace of the lecture tour forced a ten-day rest in Jeypore, the attentions of English friends immensely aided his recuperation. Writing to Twichell of this experience, he exclaimed: "All over India the English—well you will never know how good and fine they are till you see them." Even in South Africa, which he liked less well, he concluded a notebook entry listing the charms of his lodgings in "a sincere and genuine old-time English inn," with a contented affirmation: "Life is worth living." And about a week thereafter he wrote Twichell of the "noble good times everywhere and every day" of the trip. If he was exaggerating here, he was also overstating when he wrote to Howells in 1899 that except for "the sea-part & India" he had loathed the entire journey.[4]

Indeed, there had been unpleasantnesses. To the fatigue and other ordinary discomforts of travel, were added the pains of recurrent carbuncles. Though audiences were large and enthusiastic, the concern over finances was ever-present. Among less personal irritations, knowledge of the atrocities visited upon the native populations of some of the lands he toured brought the traveler new evidence of man's essential baseness. But the blow that came with the journey's end no doubt cast an even darker pall over his memories of the trip.

After landing in England on July 31, 1896, the Clemenses took a house in Guildford, Surrey, and anxiously awaited a joyful reunion with Jean and Susy. Instead, there was tragedy—the death of Susy from meningitis. Clemens was alone in England when the news came, for Olivia and Clara had sailed for America three days before, not quite believing the original cable assuring them the illness was not serious. On their return, with Jean, the grief-stricken family went into virtual seclusion. So as to be even more private, at September's end[5] they moved from Guildford to Chelsea's Tedworth Square, informing only a few intimate friends of their whereabouts.

In the dark months that followed, Clemens found solace in burying himself in his writing. Besides long notebook eulogies to Susy, and before plunging into work on *Following the Equator* in October, he completed an essay that he had begun a few days before the stunning news of her death. Inspired by some of his observations during the world tour and by current religious persecutions in Crete, the article (titled "The Lowest Animal" by DeVoto) ridicules man's pretensions by comparing him with the so-called "lower animals" and finding him wanting in every respect—"a British Museum of infirmities and inferiorities."[6]

But though Clemens wrote to Howells in February, 1897, that he was indifferent to everything save his work, he immediately contradicted himself, declaring in the next breath that if he were not in mourning he would visit Parliament every day to hear the members quarrel over Greece's recent efforts to annex the island of Crete and "blether about the brotherhood of the human race."

That letter to Howells is further significant for it reflects two major effects of the world tour. The implication that no amount of "blethering" about human brotherhood could do much good embodies the increased sense of man's worthlessness; the remainder suggests a growing reconciliation with England. Referring to events like the abortive Jameson Raid in South Africa, the French ascendency in Siam, and disputes with Germany and Russia, in all of which British prestige had suffered, Clemens declared: "This has been a bitter year for English pride, & I don't like to see England humbled—that is, not too much." Though a little humbling might do her good, there had been too much that year. Then, sounding much more like his old enemy Matthew Arnold than like Hank Morgan, he described England as basically sound-hearted and sincere, despite some flaws in the "governing-crust," but declared himself "appalled" to see how the "wide extension of the suffrage" had "damaged her manners, & made her rather Americanly uncourteous on the lower levels."[7] Obviously he had come a long way back from the attitudes expressed in *A Connecticut Yankee.*

Not that the turn-about was complete. The American could still raise some of the old objections, as when he entered into his notebook a summary of English "superiorities," with one lone compliment to leaven the sarcasm. The British surpassed Americans he said, in "fun in the Church ('election' of Bishops—clerical rows in graveyards)—cant"; in supporting charities with both money and service; in their "unconscious arrogance," their "adultery in high places," and their "incompetent cooks." In July, 1897, he was moved to defend American manners, albeit somewhat left-handedly, observing that though the United States was considered the worst-mannered nation, her citizens at least did not "elbow women off the walk, nor stare at women as England used to do."* Still, the "used to" removes a good deal of the onus. On the whole, during these years compliments far outnumbered criticisms.

Work on *Following the Equator* had progressed steadily through the winter and spring. By mid-May, 1897, it was ready for final polishing, and by the end of June the manuscript was in the hands of Chatto and Windus.[8] In the book, as in the letter to Howells, the humorist embodied both his bleak view of human nature and his increased respect for England. There is a good deal of humor in the narrative, of course, but since the author far less frequently employed the "poses" of his earlier travel books, *Following the Equator* reflects his current opinions more directly than do any of the others.

Much of what Clemens saw of colonialism had served only to increase his certainty that mankind was despicable. The book's ironic accounts of the "recruiting" of Kanaka laborers, the poisoning of aborigines in Australia, the atrocities that accompanied the settlement of Tasmania, and the methods of Cecil Rhodes and others in South Africa, roundly condemn the carriers of "civilization" to the less privileged races. But almost invariably the author directed his criticisms not at Britain but at human nature generally

* Notebook 32a II, TS, pp. 4, 51, Mark Twain Papers.

—at "the white man's notion that he is less savage than the other savages," as he puts it in one place.[9]

The comprehensiveness of that attack is a little less clear in the published book than in the manuscript, though any careful reading unmistakably reveals human nature as the villain of the piece. Originally the author had spelled out the theme more clearly, particularly in his account of Tasmania, much of which he ultimately omitted at the suggestion of Andrew Chatto.[10] At the end of the passage, after citing example after example of the incredible treatment of the initially friendly natives, he wrote: "This Chapter is an indictment of the Human Race. Not of the English, not of the Spaniards, not of any particular group, tribe or division but of the Race. Apparently Civilization is merely Suppressed Savagery."*

Once he established the basic injustice of the seizure of native lands, however, Clemens' natural tendency toward a paternalistic attitude where other races were concerned seems almost to override his abhorrence of the earlier atrocities. Not only was he generous with his praise when he saw the native populations dealt with fairly, but he often stressed the actual advantages of British rule.

Obviously impressed during his tour of Australia and New Zealand by the size of the British Empire and by Australasia's contributions to it, Clemens marshalled copious statistics in his book to describe them. Lest he appear to be praising too much, perhaps, he did head his Chapter Seventeen with the maxim: "The English are mentioned in the Bible: Blessed are the meek, for they shall inherit the earth"—but upon leaving his account of Australia, he advised his readers against listening to those who cited America's experience as an argument for Australasian independence. Had relations been as pleasant as those between Australasia and England, he said, there would have been no American Revolution.

More strikingly, Clemens developed an admiration which never left him for British colonial policy in India. Slightly skeptical before his arrival, he soon was so impressed by English management of affairs that he forgot his concerns for any hardships the Indian people may have suffered.[11] Typical of some of his on-the-spot reactions which later found their way into the book, a notebook comment in April, 1896, asserted that although patriotism demanded much, it could not require a citizen to prefer the "native-princely government" to "a better form offered by a civilized

* *Following the Equator*, TS, p. 301, Berg Collection, New York Public Library.

foreign conqueror."* He was serious, too, when he told a Calcutta reporter (*The Englishman*, February 8, 1896) that on the basis of progress in industry, education, security, and prosperity one must inevitably judge British rule to be best for India. Moreover, he was sure that England would one day be paramount in the world. She was vigorous, prolific, and enterprising, and, more important, she was composed of merciful people, "the best kind of people for colonizing the globe"—witness the treatment accorded the American Indian in British Canada—far superior to that given him in the United States.[12]

Similar opinions abound in *Following the Equator*. For the author the quiet elegance, quiet colors, and quiet dignity of Government House at Bombay made the building a fitting symbol of "the English power, the English civilization." Shortly thereafter, to illustrate how thankful India should be for the benefits of British rule, he compared the excesses of her former rulers with the achievements of an Indian prince whom Victoria had recently knighted. Elsewhere, the efficiency of the English in exterminating the cult of Thuggee and in suppressing the Great Mutiny of 1857–58 received the traveler's unqualified approval.[13]

As Clemens saw it, bravery, skill, efficiency, and honesty were the keynotes of British rule in India. What allowed the relatively few English officials to govern the Indian myriads "with apparent ease, and without noticeable friction" was their "tact, training, and distinguished administrative ability, reinforced by just and liberal laws" and their "keeping their word to the natives" (Volume Two, Chapter Twenty-eight). Another passage, often erroneously cited to document Mark Twain's sweeping condemnation of imperialism *per se*, makes almost the same point. Though the author here labels imperialism "pilferings from other people's wash" (Chapter Twenty-seven), the burden of his argument is that because *all* history is a succession of "land-grabbings," England would have been entirely justified in seizing Madagascar. If she had lifted Madagascar "from the French clothes-line," he says, she could have saved "those harmless natives" from the "calamity" of French civilization. More generally, he observes that the sooner European nations occupy all the "savage lands," the better it will be, for in many cases "dragging ages of bloodshed and disorder and oppression will give place to peace and order and the reign of law." Again praising

* Notebook 29 II, TS, p. 49, Mark Twain Papers.

England's role in India, he concludes that anyone who compares past and present must inevitably concede that the "establishment of British Supremacy there" was the most fortunate thing that had ever befallen the Indian nation.

Describing British activities in South Africa, however, Clemens was not so complimentary. His travels had brought him there only a few months after the abortive Jameson Raid of December-January, 1895–96. At the time he had been sympathetic with the raiders, thinking that their purpose had been merely to frighten the Boer government into granting much-needed reforms. But during the following year in London, the aftermath of the Jameson Raid apparently caught his interest and caused him to review the accounts of its origins and delve into the history of conflict between the Boers and the British. From his researches he concluded that the Raid had actually been engineered by Cecil Rhodes, who wished to provoke British intervention and ultimate annexation of the Transvaal, not out of patriotism but for personal gain. By virtue of their resistance to the British, then, the Boers had gained a good deal of status in Clemens' mind. Unpleasant as many of their qualities were, they were still not the sort of savages who needed looking after by a benevolent government; hence the author's paternalistic tendency to regard the Indians and other races as children who needed law and order brought into their chaotic lives did not operate here. And in his book he launched a severe attack, though more at the machinations of Cecil Rhodes than at English policies themselves.

There is no question that Clemens violently condemned the oppression of subject peoples which so often accompanied imperialistic expansion. But he likewise felt that the "lesser breeds without the Law" derived many advantages from régimes like that of the British in India. His approval of that régime, in fact, seems never to have wavered even during the years when he publicly espoused the cause of the anti-imperialists. His "foreigner in white linen and sun-helmet" who abuses the Indians in *The Mysterious Stranger* (in Chapter Ten, probably written in August, 1900) is not English, but Portuguese. And when his "Stupendous Procession" passed in symbolic parade late in 1901 to attack American and European imperialism alike, Britain still fared relatively well. Like the other captor nations portrayed in this piece (which the author finally decided was too strong for publication at the time), Britain was accompanied by her conquests, her "Mutilated Figures in Chains." But only the "Transvaal Republic" and "Orange Free State" were in the line. India was nowhere to be seen.[14]

Clemens' favorable reactions to British colonialism, as it operated almost everywhere but in South Africa, resulted from his reading as well as from his own observations. Of particular importance were the opinions of Thomas Babington Macaulay and Rudyard Kipling.

Early intrigued by the "glittering pageantry" of Macaulay's descriptions and by the "march of his stately sentences," Clemens apparently read and reread the *History of England From the Accession of James II* (1849–61). Shortly after Harper's edition of G. O. Trevelyan's *Life and Letters of Lord Macaulay* appeared in 1876, he prepared a paper on Macaulay for the Saturday Morning Club. He likewise read widely in the historian's essays; (and in both *The Innocents Abroad* [1869] and *A Connecticut Yankee* [1889] he alluded to the famous poem "Horatius at the Bridge"). The essay on Bacon would later supply materials for one of his own last literary efforts, *Is Shakespeare Dead?*, written in 1909.[15]

But of all Macaulay's essays, Clemens was fondest of those on Clive and Hastings. Once in 1892, after he read them aloud to his family, the ensuing discussion inspired a poem, "The Derelict," in which he sought to capture the pathos of the fall from greatness that had characterized the careers of both men. While writing *Following the Equator,* however, he was newly impressed by their accomplishments rather than their degradation. "What a romance was Clive's!" he exclaims in a notebook eulogy, and goes on to reveal his own fascination with the thought of sudden elevation to eminence by summarizing the astonishing career of the "no-account boy" who had left England a warehouse clerk, and returned as the hero of Plassey, the founder of an empire, now accustomed to "transacting business exclusively with sovereigns and princes, and dictating the terms himself."* Along with additional praises of Clive in *Following the Equator,* he remarks that in spite of certain corrupt practices, Warren Hastings had been instrumental in saving India for England, and had thus performed the greatest service ever done for the Indians themselves.[16]

Sidney J. Krause's excellent study of possible Macaulay influences

* Notebook 29 II, TS, p. 38, Mark Twain Papers.

on style, structure, and content of the Indian segments of *Following the Equator* clearly shows that the historian exerted a major influence upon Clemens' favorable opinions of British officialdom.[17] But the possible role of Rudyard Kipling should not be overlooked, for the humorist's admiration of Kipling was based on personal friendship as well as literary achievement.

By the time he wrote *Following the Equator* Clemens had known Kipling for almost eight years. They first met one hot August morning in 1889 when Kipling, twenty-three, relatively unknown outside India, knocked on the door of Charles Langdon's house in Elmira. Touring the United States on his way from India to England, the young writer had decided that his trip would be incomplete unless he paid personal homage to the author whose books he had "learned to love and admire fourteen thousand miles away."[18] Too, the report of such a pilgrimage would make excellent copy for his newspaper in Allahabad.

If Clemens was annoyed at the intrusion, he did not show it. "Well," he replied graciously to the mumbled apology, "you think you owe me something, and you've come to tell me so. That's what I call squaring a debt handsomely." From there the conversation, punctuated by puffs from Kipling's cigar and Clemens' "Missouri meerschaum," ranged from copyright laws to Clemens' books and their characters, from autobiography to determinism, and from contemporary novels to the nature of conscience.

Kipling felt abundantly repaid for the difficulties he had encountered in finding his literary idol. When Clemens momentarily rested his hand on the younger man's shoulder it was, Kipling wrote, "an investiture of the Star of India, blue silk, trumpets, and diamond-studded jewel, all complete." But the admiration was not wholly one-sided. The humorist, too, was not only charmed with his guest but profoundly impressed by the range of Kipling's knowledge. He was being only partly facetious when he told Mrs. Langdon that his visitor was a total stranger to him, but was "a most remarkable man," and then added, "Between us, we cover all knowledge; he knows all that can be known, and I know the rest."

Not until the next year, when the English publication of *Departmental Ditties* and *Plain Tales from the Hills* touched off Kipling's meteoric rise to world fame, did Clemens discover that he had entertained someone more than an especially intelligent devotee of Mark Twain. But sometime during the summer or autumn of 1890 he joined the throng of enthusiastic admirers of the Britisher's works, when George Warner left him a copy of *Plain Tales* with the assurance that here was a new talent destined to shake the literary world.

During the years that followed, their friendship flourished. The reprinting of Kipling's Elmira interview in the New York *Herald* for August 17, 1890, could have ended it, for Kipling had included a paragraph of shocked disbelief that Mark Twain had written such a book as *A Connecticut Yankee*. But the glittering encomiums of the rest of the account evidently offset its ending. The humorist must have written his approval, in fact, for Kipling replied from England that he was glad the published interview had not offended. He added, also, that he hoped his business would allow him to revisit America in the near future and "sit at your feet once again." That opportunity came several times during Kipling's four-year residence in the United States following his marriage to Catherine Balestier in 1892. Clemens' notebook and letters record dinners with Kipling and his wife in New York in 1893, an invitation to tea in January, 1894, and a pleasant train trip from Hartford to New York with Kipling that same month.[19]

From his first introduction to *Plain Tales from the Hills,* Clemens read avidly in Kipling's prose and poetry. Early in 1891 he listed several of the poems along with some of Browning's in a program he was shortly to deliver at Bryn Mawr. He consistently added Kipling's books to his library, and ultimately his shelves held two separate sets of the *Works,* as well as a number of individual volumes. "I know them better than I know anybody else's books," he would say in 1906. "They never grow pale to me; they keep their color; they are always fresh." Along with the "incomparable Jungle Books," which "must remain unfellowed permanently," he found *Kim* (1901) a special favorite, probably the more so because of its resemblances to his own *Huckleberry Finn.* It was worth the journey to India to prepare for reading *Kim* understandingly and to "realize how great a book it is," he later said. No other book conveyed so well India's "deep and subtle and fascinating charm," and by reading it every year he could revisit India without fatigue —the only foreign country he ever daydreamed about or deeply longed to see again.[20]

Often when interviewers sought his literary opinions, Clemens expressed his fondness for the "peculiar and satisfying charm" of Kipling's poetry. Most frequently he cited its boldness, dash, daring, and originality. Sometimes he singled out the special appeal of poems like "Mandalay" and "Tommy Atkins," in which humor and pathos skillfully blended, or for others among the Eastern ballads which had the smell of sandalwood about them, and yet "a swing and a go" as well. He stressed the fact also that Kipling's works were "truly human" and full of "genuine feeling."[21]

Particularly attracted by Kipling's skill in adapting materials drawn from actual experience and observation, he had as early as 1891 indirectly welcomed the younger man as a relative of his own in that art. In a letter to an English correspondent, denying any literary influences, he declared that the sources of his fiction lay entirely in his own varied experiences as printer, pilot, soldier, miner, reporter, lecturer, financier, and publisher. To underline his statement he added: "My splendid Kipling himself hasn't a more burnt-in, hard-baked and unforgetable familiarity with that death-on-the-pale-horse-with-hell-following-after which is a raw soldier's first fortnight in the field. . . ." Nevertheless, he also once told Carlyle Smythe that he read Kipling "as much for style as for subject" and doubtless found Kipling's virtuosity as exciting as the stirring action of the poems and stories. No less a critic than T. S. Eliot has praised the amazing variety of form and meter in the ballads and Kipling's genius in uniting both to the mood he wished to convey.[22] As a man keenly sensitive to the rhythms of the spoken and written word, Clemens, too, must have responded to Kipling's gift.

The singular ability of Kipling's poems to intensify personal experience would again come vividly to the humorist's mind in 1903. In thanking Frank Doubleday for a *bon voyage* present of a volume of the poems, Clemens reported his customary delight in reading and rereading several of them. "The Bell Buoy," particularly, evoked memories of trips aboard Henry H. Rogers' yacht *Kanawha*, when the bell buoy had spoken to him nightly, "sometimes in his pathetic and melancholy way, sometimes with his strenuous and urgent note." Then his meaning was clear, Clemens said, but "now I have his words!" and added "No one but Kipling could do this strong and vivid thing." Kipling's picture of "The Old Men," too—self-satisfied, subsisting entirely on their memories, and yet ironically aware of their own shortcomings—Clemens found "delicious" and "so comically true." Whether or not with a sense of relief, he compared them with himself (now sixty-eight): "I haven't arrived there yet, but I suppose I am on the way."[23]

Over the years he often read these and other poems to family and friends. With his own emphasis on the importance of action and experience it was perhaps inevitable that the readings should frequently feature "Tomlinson," the story of a man who had lived only vicariously and hence was refused admission to either heaven or hell until he should accomplish something, be it virtuous or sinful, entirely through his own efforts. Again, a special favorite was "The Mary Gloster," reminiscent in subject, if not in style, of Robert Browning's "The Bishop Orders His Tomb at St. Praxed's Church." Another dramatic monologue, "M'Andrew's Hymn," with its onomatopoetic song of the steam, and its glorification of machinery obedient to a fixed law ("Interdependence absolute, foreseen, ordained, decreed"), appealed to the humorist's fascination with machinery of all kinds and to his own deterministic views as well.

Among other poems that he read and reread were Kipling's tribute to the British Marines, "Soldier an' Sailor Too"; "The Three-Decker," a lament for the passing of the great three-volume Victorian romances; and the swinging "Ballad of the Bolivar." "Chant Pagan" joined "Mandalay,"—that "most fascinating . . . of all Kipling's poems"—to enhance Clemens' own restlessness and love for the lands of the Far East.[24]

The *Jungle Books* also continued to fascinate him. At least two of the unpublished satires from the 1890's or early 1900's probably owed their format to those volumes. "The Jungle Discusses Man" features a Fox, back from extensive travels, who entertains the rest of the beasts with a tale of mankind's strange habits. In "Affeland," the doings of its monkey-tribe and other animal characters satirize the activities of Cecil Rhodes.[25] An 1898 notebook list of characters for a story to be called "The Creatures of Fiction" ends: "Last comes Mowgli on elephant with his menagerie and they all ride away with him."* In that instance, it is almost as if Clemens were returning Kipling's compliments in "The Last of the Stories" (1888), a tale which assembles a somewhat similar cast, including a group of "delightfully mischievous boys, generalled by the irrepressible Tom Sawyer." In June, 1906, after several of the customary

---

* Notebook 32 I, TS, pp. 26–27, Mark Twain Papers.

after-dinner readings in the *Jungle Books,* Clemens borrowed Baloo the Bear and Hathi the Elephant to help people his satire of self-important literary critics in "A Fable" (published in *Harper's* magazine for December, 1909). And in an unpublished piece, "The Refuge of the Derelicts," written in 1905, old Admiral Stormfield, explaining how he had happened to name his cat Bagheera, pulls down "Kipling, Volume VII, Collected Works, Jungle Book," proclaims it "Immortal," and reads to his admiring guest, the sensuous description of the famous black panther.[26]

More generally, Clemens heartily appreciated Kipling's portrait of the monkey-people, the Bandar-log, as a symbol of human stupidity, planlessness, and pretentiousness. During one of his many readings of Saint-Simon's *Memoires,* he borrowed the name for a succinct marginal comment beside the author's reference to the inefficiency of the Duc d'Orleans. Though Kipling used his monkeys chiefly to symbolize the ignorance and incompetence of unrestricted democracy, Clemens once confided to his Bermuda friend Elizabeth Wallace that he considered the Bandar-log one of the best satires ever directed at the human race itself. "We are all Bandar-log," he said, and added that badly as the Almighty had done to create the housefly, mice, rats, and other vermin, the human Bandar-log was His "crowning mistake."[27]

When Clemens had contemplated the trip to India in 1895, it was inevitable that Kipling should come to mind. Shortly before sailing from Vancouver that August, he had announced his plans to his British friend in a letter which sought both to flatter and to amuse. Pretending that his own voyage had been inspired by news of Kipling's intention to be in India, he wrote: "Years ago you came from India to Elmira to visit me, as you said at the time. It has always been my purpose to return that visit and that great compliment, some day." Warning Kipling to be ready for his arrival in January, he played wildly with Indian terms: "I shall come riding my Ayah, with his tusks adorned with silver bells and ribbons, and escorted by a troop of native Howdahs, richly clad and mounted on a herd of wild bungalows, and you must be on hand with a few bottles of ghee, for I shall be thirsty."[28]

All along the route, when reporters sought comments on contemporary men and affairs, Kipling's name repeatedly arose. In India itself, there had been even more reminders. Indeed, as the author was to note in *Following the Equator,* the mere mention of

India automatically suggested "Clive, Hastings, the Mutiny, Kipling, and a number of other great events." At one point, too, he compared his own party to Kipling's "host of tourists who travel up and down India in the cold weather showing how things ought to be managed." While investigating the history of the Thugs, he was grieved to find that one of their chieftains had soiled the "great name" of a better man, "Kipling's deathless 'Gungadin'." Finally, on shipboard once more after the fascinating but fatiguing tour, he found a serenity and contentment that life ashore could not evoke —an aspect of the "bewitching sea" that Kipling had aptly caught in "For to Admire," the song of the "time-expired soldier man" sailing home from long foreign service:

> The Injian Ocean sets an' smiles
>   So sof', so bright, so bloomin' blue;
> There aren't a wave for miles an' miles
>   Excep' the jiggle from the screw.[29]

And since Kipling had become so much a part of Clemens' memories of the trip, it seems particularly fitting that he should have been one of the few people the American had cared to see during the dark days in London following Susy's death.[30]

Interested as he was in Kipling as a writer and as a person, Clemens must certainly have been familiar with his attitudes toward British imperialism which very likely the two had discussed during the early 1890's. Some of these the humorist would have encountered in Kipling's works before, during and immediately after the world tour. If he had not done so before visiting India, he had doubtless read the allegorical *Jungle Books* (1894, 1895) by the time he finished *Following the Equator* in 1897.

Following the Equator shows its author very close to his British friend's paternalistic concern for the "lesser breeds without the Law." With only slight qualifications, C. E. Carrington's summary of Kipling's position could apply equally well to Clemens. "He . . . never lapsed into sentiment over the supposed virtues of savages; but it was the spread of law, literacy, communications, useful arts that he applauded, not the enlargements of frontiers. The Flag of England stood for service and sacrifice, not for racial superiority. The true sanction of Dominion . . . was not national pride but 'a humble and contrite heart.' Civilizing the world was a worthwhile task, and though likely to be thankless, a task in which all might join if they would accept the Law."[31]

Kipling's concept of "the Law" was central to his credo, and Clemens would have disagreed neither with its spirit nor with his friend's view of what was necessary to its implementation. Its purpose was to provide (as one critic has defined it) "that arrangement of life under which the common man is enabled to do the best which is in him for himself, his family, and the rest of the world, including the generations yet to come."[32] Kipling's conviction that the Law's proper operation required a responsible and efficient hierarchy of trained government officials, with enough authority to prevent abuses of power by the ignorant and incompetent, was in many ways a restatement of Clemens' own views during the 1870's and later.

Like the American writer, Kipling was well aware, of course, that perfect administration of the Law could seldom be achieved. Amidst the celebration of Victoria's Diamond Jubilee in 1897, the stern refrain of his "Recessional" would warn against the dangers of allowing a preoccupation with empire for its own sake to overshadow the principles of duty and responsibility. Yet though he often pointed out flaws in the management of South Africa and India,[33] his admiration for the efforts of British civil servants was boundless. He never doubted that England had improved conditions in those lands far more in a few years than their native rulers had done in centuries.

Very likely, Clemens' own observations in India, as well as his rereading of Macaulay convinced him that Kipling was right. Kipling himself might almost have written a number of passages in *Following the Equator*—especially would he have concurred with Clemens' regret that Madagascar's falling to France rather than to England had deprived its inhabitants of the "peace and order and the reign of law" that Britain had brought to India; with the American's conclusion that "if monuments were always given in India for high achievements, duty straitly performed, and smirchless records, the landscape would be monotonous with them"; and with his conviction that "tact, training, and distinguished administrative ability reinforced by just and liberal laws" was the basis for British success.

Clemens' early reactions to the Boer War (1899–1902), also show a closer affinity with Kipling's views than might at first be evident. Though he privately considered the war "sordid & criminal," as he told Howells in January, 1900, he would not say so publicly, for if England were defeated, "an inundation of Russian and German political degradations" would envelop the world in "a sort of Middle-Age night & slavery." Wrong though she is, he concluded "England must be upheld. He is an enemy of the human race who shall speak against her now." To Twichell two days later he repeated much the same thing, emphasizing the fact that though contemporary civilization was "full of cruelties, vanities, arrogances, meannesses and hypocrisies," one must for want of a better "stand by it, extend it, and (in public), praise it. . . . Naturally, then, I am for England; but she is profoundly in the wrong, Joe, and no (instructed) Englishman doubts it."[34] Though there were wrongs involved, the implication that the world was the better for Anglo-American resistance to the less worthy nations took him very close to Kipling's position.

Kipling, of course, never attacked the basic injustice of the Boer War, though he did blast the bungling efforts of the British high command. And when he joined in a call for conscription in 1902 so that the conflict might end more quickly, Clemens could not resist a private jibe. "What! *Kipling* calling for Conscription!" he wrote to Francis Henry Skrine. "Has that immense volunteer-rush of all ranks & conditions of patriots dwindled to such a point . . . since the clarion peal of these great lines in the Absent-Minded Beggar thrilled the world?" And then he proceeded to quote his own version of a stanza from Kipling's poem:

> Duke's son, earl's son, son of the noovo rich,
> Bilk's son, snob's son, bastard son of a bitch,
>   None of 'em whine, they *all* jine,
>   Jine the cavalree,
> And hell they raise for God his praise
> In the Boer his counteree . . .

"Why, why, why! has Kipling gone to satirizing Kipling?"[35]

But for the most part his admiration did not waver. In 1899, just after the Boer War began, he had suggested to T. Douglas Murray that Kipling be asked to contribute an introductory essay on Joan's patriotism for Murray's forthcoming edition of the "Trials and Rehabilitation of Joan of Arc."[36] Given Clemens' near-idolatry where Joan was concerned, his suggestion implies a great deal of respect for Kipling's ideas. Except for the comment to Skrine, his praises of Kipling continued to sound throughout the early 1900's, even after disillusionment with American policies in the Philippines transformed him into an active and vocal anti-imperialist. Very probably, then, the friendship with Kipling not only helped shape Clemens' views of British imperialism, especially as practiced in India, but was also a significant force in the humorist's own reconciliation with England.

Whatever the extent of Kipling's influence, the association between the two writers is a particularly interesting example of nineteenth-century Anglo-American literary relations. On Kipling's side, his acknowledged affection and respect for Clemens suggest a considerable sense of obligation to the older writer. His various comments become even more striking in the light of his biographer's assertion that Kipling seldom remarked upon his contemporaries in his private letters and almost never in his published works.[37] Yet, though the American's influence was noted by reviewers as early as the 1890's, its nature and extent have not really been explored. The consensus has chiefly been that Kipling's robust humor and vigorous, straightforward presentation bear the stamp of Mark Twain. A closer look, however, reveals additional debts to the man whom Kipling once called "the master of us all"[38]: in a number of allusions to books and to characters, in the skillful reproduction of American speech patterns, and, most important, in specific characters, situations, and incidents in Kipling's own stories and novels. The subject is a fruitful one, but unfortunately is beyond the scope of this study. Here we may simply note Kipling's final accolade to Clemens in 1935, when both Britain and America celebrated the Mark Twain Centennial. As chairman of the English committee for the celebration, he wrote the American chairman, Nicholas Murray Butler of Columbia: "To my mind he was the largest man of his time; both in the direct outcome of his work, and, more important still, as an indirect force in an age of iron Philistinism. Later generations do not know their debt, of course, and they would be surprised if they did."[39]

Chapter Ten

Reconciliation and Reminiscence

(1897-1900)

Socially, the stay in London following the world tour was nothing like the earlier visits. During the first several months, the Clemenses seldom left the house in Tedworth Square, and few visitors came to see them. The author sometimes went out alone with business acquaintances, or with friends like Kipling and J. Y. W. MacAlister, editor of *Library* magazine and member of the Savage Club. In October or early November, 1896, he visited Thomas Carlyle's house in nearby Cheyne Row, where he was especially impressed at seeing a scrap of manuscript from *The French Revolution,* the only one to survive the burning of the original first volume.[1]

Had circumstances been different, Clemens might also have wished to visit Oscar Wilde, a long-time resident of Chelsea's Tite Street. He had met the colorful aesthete at Bad Nauheim in 1892 and, according to his daughter's memory of the occasion, had enjoyed a spirited conversation. Clara also recalled that although her father had not introduced Wilde to the family, she and her sisters were charmed by the author's brilliant smile and intrigued by his colored shoes and his carnation "as large as a baby sunflower." But now Wilde was in Reading Gaol, having served almost half of the two-year sentence that followed his sensational trial in 1895, and very likely both Clemens and Livy agreed with their housekeeper

Katy Leary's judgment that "he was a very bad man, Oscar Wilde was, so bad you couldn't talk about what he had done."[2]

One day in February, 1897, another old friend and fellow-author, Poultney Bigelow, persuaded Clemens to take tea with the Bigelows' neighbor, Lady Mary Monkswell. Lady Mary's diary account, besides presenting a brief portrait of the humorist, suggests the sort of occasion he enjoyed during these dark days.

To make "the dear old man" feel at home, the hostess "carelessly" arranged two or three of his books on the table next to where he would sit. Since he had requested that there be no other guests because he was in mourning for "a lost daughter," she warned her brother Henry (who was paying his weekly call) to pretend that he lived there with her. The event proved entirely successful. Clemens stayed more than an hour, regaling them with tales of ghosts, and dwelling upon the appeal of "the old legends." Commenting upon the charm of her guest's manner, Lady Mary further described him as "about 60, very thin & small . . . with a profusion of fair hair turned nearly white, a refined, keen face & glittering eyes," and noted that he spoke slowly and incisively "with a very strong American accent." And she doubted that his "eagle eye" had missed the carefully placed books.[3]

With the approach of spring Clemens began accepting more invitations, but still only to small private gatherings with friends like the Bigelows, the Chattos, the Henry M. Stanleys, and Bram Stoker (author of *Dracula,* and an investor in the Paige machine). Occasionally Olivia accompanied him. In June he gave in to Mac-Alister's urging to spend an evening at the Savage Club. That visit must have helped cheer him up, for the Club Committee voted him an honorary life membership, a tribute paid to only three others before him—Stanley, Arctic explorer Fridtjof Nansen, and the Prince of Wales.[4]

Later the same month, with *Following the Equator* finished and plans made for another visit to the continent, Clemens recorded his impressions of Queen Victoria's Diamond Jubilee. His widely syndicated article treats many of the festivities with characteristic jibes. But under the generally good-natured satire, it once more reveals Clemens' appreciation of British tradition. Always impressed by historical processions as symbols of the "moving history" behind them, he declared this one to be "incomparably the most memorable and most important" that London had ever witnessed.

For the Queen herself, Clemens seems to have shared the respect accorded by most of his contemporaries, his veiled references to her fecundity in *A Connecticut Yankee* notwithstanding. Sometimes he poked fun at her idolaters, as when he pretended in 1895 that Canada could not possibly be British soil since en route to Vancouver his party traveled an entire eighteen miles without passing a town named Victoria. But even in his first serious outburst against England in 1883 he had cited the queen and the boy-king Edward V as the only two British rulers "without blemish." Later he was to make her unique,—the *only* monarch "without reproach in her great office," and one whose consecration "to the virtues and the humanities and to the promotion of lofty ideals," made her a moral force without peer in her time.[5]

In mid-July, the Clemenses were off to the continent. After spending the rest of the summer in Switzerland, they settled in Vienna. Now that their formal period of mourning was over, they went about as they had in the old days in Berlin and earlier, once more mingling with royalty and nobility. Notebook entries during this time clearly reveal that Clemens still held much the same attitudes he had dramatized in *The American Claimant*. In Switzerland he commented again on the tendency of all human beings to worship rank, contending that real democracy could be achieved only by stripping the human race absolutely naked. Even "a rag of tiger skin, or a cowtail" could become a mark of distinction and thus be the beginning of monarchy. In Vienna in September, 1898, he repeated in his notebook almost exactly what he had had Barrow say to Howard Tracy: "Essentially, nobilities are foolishnesses, but if I were a citizen where they prevail I would do my best to get a title, for the consideration it furnishes—that is what we want. In Republics we strive for it with the surest means we have—money."[6]

In May, 1899, the Clemens family once more returned to England, where they would remain (except for a summer in Sweden), until their return to America in October, 1900. This time it was almost the 1870's come again. Private dinners with literary friends and other notables; a round of entertainments and speeches at clubs like the Whitefriars, the New Vagabonds, the Beefsteak, the Authors, and the Savage; participation in the Fourth-of-July Dinner of London's American Society, a benefit banquet for the Royal Literary Fund, and a welcome-home dinner for actor Sir Henry Irving, all did much to brighten the humorist's leisure hours. One

Clemens at Dollis Hill, just outside London, summer, 1900

Mark Twain Papers

wishes that there were a record of the evening he spent in the London home of W. E. H. Lecky, for it is tempting to think that the two authors might have slipped away from the other guests to discuss their differing views of human nature.[7] July, 1900, brought an added pleasure when the family moved to Dollis Hill House, just outside of London and once the country retreat of William Gladstone, where Clemens could enjoy at first hand the beauties of the English countryside that he loved so well.

Many of the social occasions during these years evoked memories of earlier London visits and of the literary men he had known. He mentioned a number of old acquaintances in public speeches and must at times have thought of many others. One of those of whom he spoke was Charles Kingsley, whom he remembered with particular fondness from his earliest trips to England. Not only had Kingsley, newly appointed Canon of Westminster, hosted a luncheon in Mark Twain's honor in 1873, but he had personally guided the tour of Westminster Abbey described in "A Memorable Midnight Experience." When Kingsley and his wife visited the United States in 1874, the American had been delighted at the opportunity to repay that hospitality. What apparently had impressed Clemens most about the clergyman-novelist was a sweetness and gentleness of character, an impression which Olivia obviously shared: "He was a most wonderful man," she wrote to Orion's wife Mollie, shortly after she finished reading the newly published *Charles Kingsley: His Letters and Memories of His Life (1877)*, and added that the depiction of his "perfectly lovely Christian character" had touched her deeply.[8]

Clemens had known some of the clergyman's novels before the English visit (though he had been less than complimentary in 1869 when he called *Hypatia* [1853] "one of Kingsley's most tiresomest books"). It would have been strange, too, if Kingsley had not spoken during their various conversations of his conviction—as expressed in a number of the social novels—that the upper classes must be awakened to a sense of responsibility for the welfare of the masses. Hence Kingsley may well have contributed something to Clemens' political and social views during the 1870's.

Another acquaintance from the 1870's was Charles Reade, whose works attracted Clemens more than Kingsley's *Hypatia*. *The Cloister and the Hearth* (1861), which the humorist read in 1869, was so uniformly "good" that he did not feel (as he did about *Tristram Shandy* and *Gulliver's Travels*) that he had to censor it for Olivia. True, he later included Reade's *Love Me Little, Love Me Long* (1859) among the novels burlesqued in his tale of the ill-fated literary magazine, the *Weekly Occidental* in *Roughing It.* But in 1877, when he read *A Woman Hater* (1874), he reported to Mrs. Fairbanks that the book had "a handful of diamonds scattered over every page."

No doubt his early meeting with Reade in London had stimulated his interest. Tradition has it, too, that the Englishman invited him to collaborate on a novel, but I suspect that Albert Bigelow Paine, who first spoke of the matter, misread two letters of 1876 from Reade to Clemens. The first, dated February 3, does contain an invitation, but it is to join an "Association to Protect the Rights of Authors." The second, on August 6, mentions not a novel but the outline of a play (probably *Cap'n Simon Wheeler, the Amateur Detective*) on which the American had apparently asked Reade to collaborate, at least in getting it produced in London. From that project Reade excused himself, pleading his lack of influence with the "illiterate" London theatrical managers, who were bound to "a small clique of journalists and drinking companions." Since they had never read one of his plays nor one recommended by him, he could not advise Clemens to share his subject with him, no matter how dramatic it might be.[9]

Reade later provided a different sort of assistance, however, for the humorist seems to have borrowed an incident from *The Cloister and the Hearth* to embellish Huckleberry Finn's encounter with the memorable Judith Loftus (Chapter Ten). As one of the ruses which help her penetrate Huck's female disguise, Mrs. Loftus tosses a lump of lead into his lap, and Huck instinctively claps his legs together instead of spreading them to let the skirt do the catching. In Reade's Chapter Sixty-three, as Walter Blair was first to note, one of the girls on a Tiber River boating party reveals the true identity of the "peerless beauty" whom Gerard has introduced to the roistering group as "Marcia." Some nuts tossed into "Marcia's" lap bring the same reflex as that of Huck and the remark: "Aha! you are caught, my lad. . . . 'Tis a man; or a boy. A woman still parteth her knees to catch the nuts the surer in her apron; but a man closeth his for fear they shall fall between his hose."[10]

Here again, as in so many instances when Clemens appropriated materials from other authors, he made them his own and integral with his story. Besides enhancing the shrewd character of Judith Loftus, the incident also points up Huck's shrewdness, for when his deception is revealed, he quickly invents a plausible explanation. The episode as a whole, in turn, becomes an important transitional one, for it is from Mrs. Loftus that Huck learns of the searching parties looking for Jim and realizes that he and Jim must leave Jackson's Island in a hurry.

In looking back on those earlier times in London, Clemens probably also recalled the evening at the Garrick Club in 1873 when he and Joaquin Miller were guests of honor at a dinner given by Anthony Trollope. As he later recorded the event, the other guests were Tom Hughes, Lord Leveson-Gower, and another man whose name he no longer remembered. Besides the fact that Hughes and Trollope appeared over-deferential to Leveson-Gower, Clemens' most vivid recollection was of Trollope and Miller, who had talked all the time and both at the same time—"Trollope pouring forth a smooth and limpid and sparkling stream of faultless English, and Joaquin discharging into it his muddy and tumultuous mountain torrent. . . ."[11]

Perhaps this association inspired Clemens to read some of Trollope's novels, if he had not already done so. He would probably have been more interested in the so-called "parliamentary novels" than the chronicles of Barsetshire, and among them would surely have chosen *Phineas Finn* (1869), and its sequel, *Phineas Redux* (1874), if for no other reason than the surname of their protagonist. One touch in *Phineas Finn* seems to have struck him—Trollope's remark that Aspasia Fitzgerald was so devoted to her brother Lawrence "that there was nothing she would not do for him, short of lending him money." It could, of course, be a coincidence that the maxim which prefaces Chapter Eight of *Puddn'head Wilson* (1894) echoes that comment. But it is also very possible that Clemens' faculty for "unconscious borrowing" was at work when he wrote: "The holy passion of Friendship is of so sweet and steady and loyal and enduring a nature that it will last through a whole lifetime, if not asked to lend money."[12]

Trollope's books had also helped Clemens pass some of the summer hours at Weggis, Switzerland, in 1897. On August 2 of that year he reminded himself of a three-franc deposit at the local circulating library for the two Trollope novels, "two volumes each," which he had borrowed.

In his reminiscing, the humorist would have remembered even more fondly the pleasant hours he, Olivia, and fourteen-month-old Susy had spent with Dr. John Brown, author of "Rab and His Friends," during their vacation trip to Scotland in July of 1873. Besides the warm memories of the doctor's love for Susy, he no doubt recalled his own fascination with Brown's story of the child-prodigy Marjorie Fleming, whom he himself would later eulogize as "The Wonder Child" in the December, 1909, *Harper's Bazaar*. He probably remembered, too, the sting of reproach that had accentuated his grief over "Dr. John's" death in 1882. During the brief stay in England in 1879, Olivia had repeatedly urged that they visit Brown, but her husband, impatient to sail for home, had refused to listen. Later, he would add this memory of his stubbornness to the other instances of self-recrimination listed in his autobiography.[13]

Other recollections of literary friends long dead would surely have included memories of Robert Louis Stevenson, whom Clemens had met in New York one April day in 1888. Stevenson, visiting the city after his long residence at a Saranac Lake tuberculosis sanatorium, had invited Clemens to call at his rooms in St. Stephen's Hotel on East Eleventh Street. Taking advantage of the warm spring afternoon, they strolled to Washington Square, where they sat on a bench "among the nursemaids, like a couple of characters out of a story by Henry James," and talked of books and authors, troubles with publishers, and the vagaries of literary reputation.[14]

Unfortunately, all that remains of their opinions of fellow-writers is the humorist's comment in his *Autobiography* that Stevenson was right in what he said "about the others," but that he should never class Bret Harte's pleasant but thin conversation with real brilliance like that of Thomas Bailey Aldrich, whose talk was "a fire opal set around with rose diamonds." No doubt they spoke of their own books also, with Stevenson confessing—as he had done to others —his admiration and envy of Mark Twain's "adventure stories." One of Stevenson's biographers says, in fact, that they specifically discussed *Huckleberry Finn* and "the art of comic adventure."

As they chatted, Clemens was struck by the way Stevenson's clothes hung on his gaunt figure and how the lank hair and dark complexion suited his long face with its "musing and melancholy expression." Yet all of these features, he later said, seemed especially planned to focus one's attention on the Scotsman's splendid eyes, which "burned with a smoldering rich fire under the penthouse of his brows and . . . made him beautiful."[15]

After Stevenson established his residence in Samoa (in 1889), the pair corresponded occasionally. In 1893 it appeared that they might become business associates as well as friends. Difficulties with Charles Scribner, his American publisher, led the Scotsman in April of that year to explore the possibility of placing *David Balfour* and his subsequent books with Charles L. Webster & Co. By August, however, when Clemens' answer that he would be most happy to see Stevenson join the "clean and intelligent" finally completed the long voyage to Samoa, the problems with Scribner had been resolved. News of that reconciliation no doubt proved a great disappointment to Clemens, for the acquisition of so popular an author as Stevenson could have gone far toward reviving the moribund publishing firm.

In his own letter the humorist had apparently included a characteristic comment on the attractions of the peaceful life in a South Sea Island paradise, and the reply probably added a prop to Clemens' conviction that where man was, peace could not be. "I wish you could see my 'simple and sunny heaven' now," Stevenson wrote; "war has broken out . . . with its concomitants of blackened faces, severed heads and men dying in hospital. Also, I am sorry to say, the government troops have started a horrible novelty—taking women's heads." If that practice inspires reprisals, he concluded, "we shall be a fine part of the world."[16]

Stevenson was a great admirer of Mark Twain's books. On one occasion, while discussing the art and techniques of story-telling with Brander Matthews, he praised *Huckleberry Finn* especially and commented that it was indeed a greater and richer book than *Tom Sawyer*. To John Addington Symonds he mentioned how amazingly well the author had portrayed "a healthy boy's struggle with his conscience." Among the compliments perhaps the most heart-warming to Clemens himself was the Scotsman's report that *Tom Sawyer* and *Huck Finn* (along with *Treasure Island*—from "family partiality") were his son's favorite books. In fact, on the momentous occasion of his first sea voyage without his parents, the boy had insisted, in almost his last words to them, that *Tom Sawyer* be left unpacked so he could carry it with him. Then, Stevenson said, "he faced the universe alone for the first time with that bracing volume in his hand."[17]

Clemens, in turn, had high regard for Stevenson's works. At one point he considered using an episode from *Travels with a Donkey* (1879) to bolster the story of his visit to the South African Trappist monastery in *Following the Equator*. In 1898 one of his birthday gifts to his beloved Livy was the volume of Scottish poems entitled *A Lowden Sabbath Morn*. When he had read *Prince Otto* (1885) during the voyage from Australia to India, however, he had not cared much for it. Though the novel, as would be expected, was "full of brilliancies," its characters did not inspire sufficient sympathy to make the reader care "whether any of them prospered or not." Yet even then the humorist evidently could not bring himself to denigrate Stevenson's works, for he immediately added that the fault may have been in his own lack of insight rather than the novelist's presentation.[18]

The book that appealed most was *Dr. Jekyll and Mr. Hyde* (1866). Having attempted to present the problem of man's duality in his own "Recent Carnival of Crime in Connecticut" (1875), Clemens was intrigued by Stevenson's efforts in the same direction. The novel had also furnished an important step along the way to the theory of "multiple selves" that Clemens would later seek to dramatize in the "Print-Shop" version of *The Mysterious Stranger*. In a notebook entry which outlined that theory in 1898, he observed that Stevenson's creation of two separate entities, each with its individual conscience, represented man's condition more accurately than his own "Carnival of Crime" had done in making the conscience the "other" self. More than likely, then, until he derived his "new notion" from the French psychologists that the two "selves" were in no way cognizant of each other, Clemens had accepted the underlying assumptions in *Dr. Jekyll and Mr. Hyde*. And in 1904 a notebook allusion to the novel would help him enhance the bitterness of one of his many attacks on the inconsistencies of Scripture. Describing God, "so atrocious in the Old Testament, so attractive in the New," as "the Jekyll and Hyde of sacred fiction," he further stressed the anomaly with the ironic question: "Stevenson plagiarized it?"[19]

During the world tour in 1895, it was natural that Clemens should think of his Scottish friend when the ship reached the vicinity of Samoa. If he remembered Stevenson's sudden death there in December, 1894, however, he made no reference. Instead, while describing that part of the trip in *Following the Equator,* he injected a light note by recalling directions for reaching Samoa that the novelist had once allegedly given to James M. Barrie and Conan Doyle: "You go to America, cross the continent to San Francisco, and then it's the second turning to the left." Still, it is difficult to believe that the news of his friend's passing had left Clemens unmoved.

Stevenson's travel instructions may have again come to Clemens' mind during these last years in England when he met one of the recipients. The humorist had known some of J. M. Barrie's works at least since an 1892 business trip to New York during which he spent most of one night reading *The Little Minister* (1891), and liked it so well that he began on *A Window in Thrums* (1889) the first thing next morning. After meeting Barrie himself, he was as much impressed with the man as he had been with the writer. But the friendship proved to be a frustrating one, for on two occasions in England during that visit and again in New York several years later, Barrie was seated at the opposite side of a banquet table, just out of conversational range. When the two finally got together at these affairs, each time some interruption seemed to spirit Barrie mysteriously away after no more than five minutes. The same thing having happened again at the Garrick Club in 1907, Clemens sighed to his secretary that he wished it were possible to have "one good unbroken talk with that gifted Scot some day before I die." But if the opportunities for personal conversation had not been sufficient, Barrie apparently had done a good deal of listening, for he later paid tribute to the charm of Clemens' "witching talk."[20]

The author whom Clemens most frequently mentioned in his London speeches was Rudyard Kipling. At the Savage Club, reviewing some of the changes that had occurred since his first visit, he noted that Kipling, unknown in those days, now "fills the world." At the Authors Club he stressed his friend's contributions to Anglo-American unity and mutual understanding by virtue of his wide popularity, his residence in both countries, and, particularly, the mutual concern of Americans and Englishmen when Kipling and his daughter fell seriously ill in New York in February, 1899. As evidence of his own desire for continued progress toward mutual understanding, he proposed a toast he pretended to have labored over for eight days: "Since England and America may be joined together in Kipling, may they not be severed in 'Twain'."[21]

Those remarks, besides tacitly underscoring Kipling's influence on Clemens' attitudes, represented a kind of culmination of the American's renewed affection for England. The world tour had obviously all but wiped out any lingering animosity, replacing it with a new conviction of the importance of Anglo-American solidarity. In South Africa, in May, 1896, he had dismissed as "not worthy of serious discussion" a reporter's query about the possibility of war between England and the United States over the Venezuelan boundary dispute: "They were made to help and stand by each other."[22] Nor was he being ironic in Chapter Sixteen of *Following the Equator,* when he applauded the moderation of Australian and Indian newspapers in reporting Anglo-American negotiations and once more revealed his general approval of British colonialism. "The outlook is that the English-speaking race will dominate the earth a hundred years from now, if its sections do not get to fighting each other," he said. *"It would be a pity to spoil that prospect* [my italics] by . . . wars when arbitration would settle their differences so much better and also so much more definitely." In January, 1897, news of the signing of the Olney-Pauncefote "General Arbitration Treaty" of 1896 brought a jubilant notebook entry hailing the event as one of the three or four most important in history—"perhaps the greatest"—in its promises for eventual achievement of universal peace.*

During 1898–99 in Vienna he had continued the same theme. Writing to his friend, Theodore Stanton, to regretfully decline an invitation to speak at a Decoration Day ceremony in Paris, he added that he would have liked to hear the proposed tribute to the friendship of England and America—those "two kindred nations," who were "competent sureties for the peace of the world" when they stood together. On another occasion he remarked to an Austrian acquaintance that the Spanish-American War had paid "the biggest dividend" of any war in the world, for it had helped bring England and America together in a friendship that he hoped would never again grow cold.[23]

At a London party given by Sir Gilbert Parker in 1899, Clemens met another Englishman whom he came to regard as a link between the two countries. Winston Churchill, then twenty-five and not yet

* Notebook 32a I, TS, p. 4, Mark Twain Papers.

active in politics, had made a considerable reputation as a soldier-
correspondent, and had already published books about his experiences with the Malakand Land Force in India in 1897 and Kitch-
ener's Nile expedition of 1898. As the two writers strolled off for a
few moments of private conversation, one of the other guests con-
jectured that whichever one of the inveterate monologists got the
floor first would keep it, betting on Clemens as the older and more
experienced hand at such matters. When the pair returned, the
wagerer asked Churchill if he had enjoyed himself. The eager "Yes"
suggested who had won the bet, and when Clemens answered the
same question with a less-than-joyous "I have had a smoke," the
verdict was sure.[24] Nevertheless, when a fund-raising lecture tour
brought the budding politician to New York in December, 1900,
the humorist gladly consented to provide the speech of introduction
for Churchill's appearance at the Waldorf-Astoria.

By this time Clemens had begun to voice publicly some of the
views that he had heretofore restricted to communications with
friends. Shortly after his return to America, an interview published
in the New York *Herald,* October 16, 1900, reviewed his change of
attitude toward the Spanish-American War. Admitting that he had
earlier favored American expansion—a position that may well have
stemmed from admiration and a little envy of England's far-flung
empire—he told how he had left Vancouver in 1895 a "red-hot
imperialist," anxious to see the American eagle "go screaming into
the Pacific." But upon further thought, and after reading the terms
of the peace treaty, he had become convinced that America had not
intended to free the Filipinos, but to subjugate them. Even then,
however, he did not directly criticize England's role in South
Africa, though he praised the Boer leader, Paul Kruger, as "a great
rugged character."

On the evening of December 12, 1900, the ballroom of the
Waldorf-Astoria was filled, despite the fact that American sympathy
for the Boers had sparked a number of protests against Churchill's
appearance. To begin his introduction, Clemens once more stressed
the mutual interests of England and America, pronouncing himself
a self-appointed missionary, dedicated to fostering permanent and
beneficent relations between them. Then, in a partly ironic resumé
of the "virtues" of both countries, he sincerely admitted the superiority of the British and American brand of imperialism to that of
other nations, but condemned their respective excesses (their "sin")

in South Africa and the Philippines. Coming finally to introduce the speaker of the evening, he capped his theme by declaring that Churchill, as the son of an English father and an American mother, enjoyed a "blend which makes the perfect man." The two nations were now at their friendliest—mainly through his own missionary efforts, he supposed—and he was glad. Then he sprang his ironic "snapper." The two nations had always been kin—in blood, in religion, in representative government, in "just and lofty purposes"— and "now" he said "we are kin in sin, the harmony is complete, the blend is perfect, like Mr. Churchill himself. I have the honor to present him to you."[25]

Following the speech, Clemens and Churchill had continued discussing the Boer War, Clemens arguing that his visitor's retreat to the last defense of the patriot, "My country right or wrong," could be accepted as a valid position only if one's country were fighting for her life.[26] It is unlikely, however, that there was any personal animosity either in the speech or the ensuing conversation. The humorist obviously admired the younger man's accomplishments. Whether before the speech or later, he was moved at one point to note on the typescript of his introduction: "What a career Winston Churchill is making over there!"* No doubt he would have been further amazed and gratified if he could have known how much greater a symbol of Anglo-American unity Churchill would become during World War II.

As for the humorist's relations with England generally, cordiality prevailed during the years that followed. At least once the "kinship" theme recurred, though in another context, when he identified England's worship of her king and America's worship of money as the offspring of a common human trait—the tendency to worship power and those who wield it.[27] But never again did England herself become the sole target of his satire.

* DV 101, Mark Twain Papers.

Chapter Eleven

Literary Efforts: The Later Years
(1895-1906)

ESPITE THE MANY BRIGHT SPOTS during the last years of Clemens'
European sojourn, joy was not the prevailing mood. It was
almost as if the saddened American were seizing upon the social
occasions as his own kind of "clean well-lighted place" where he
could momentarily forget his continuing grief for Susy and the keen
sense of encroaching age that made him rail more than ever against
man's frailty, pettiness, and hypocrisy. During this period, too, he
came to a complete acceptance—at least intellectually—of the deterministic philosophy that had fascinated him for so long. The
major works of these years, therefore, merit further consideration,
especially insofar as they reflect the continued influence of some of
Clemens' favorite British authors.

The disillusionment with man reached its nadir in him during
the years from 1895–1898. One of his most succinct comments occurs
in the 1895 essay describing the pre-Darwinian evolutionary theory
of his alleged friend "Macfarlane." Whether or not there was an
actual model for Macfarlane, the opinions in the essay were
Clemens' own. Though animal life had evolved in "an ascending
scale," over millions of years from "a few microscopic seed germs,
or perhaps *one* microscopic seed germ deposited upon the globe by
the Creator in the dawn of time," with mankind the scheme broke

down. As the only animal "capable of feeling malice, envy, vindictiveness, revengefulness, hatred, selfishness, . . . the only animal that loved drunkenness, almost the only animal that could endure personal uncleanliness and a filthy habitation," man belonged not at the pinnacle of evolutionary development but "far below the plane of the other animals." His highly touted intellect he used consistently and continually "all his life to advantage himself at other people's expense."[1]

As already suggested, these views had been developing over a number of years and should not be attributed solely to the personal and financial tragedies of the 1890's. "The Character of Man," written about 1885 but not published until 1923, discusses many of the same qualities listed in the "Macfarlane" piece and concludes that "the mainspring of man's nature is . . . selfishness." In "Letters from a Dog, etc." (circa 1891), the canine narrator says substantially the same things. So does "The Lowest Animal," the essay that Clemens began in England shortly before Susy's death in August, 1896. In addition, each of these pieces names man's possession of the Moral Sense as his primary defect.[2]

Whereas most of the venom in these essays is directed at man himself, subsequent letters and notebook entries beginning in 1898 and 1899 suggest that the author was more and more tending to blame man's shortcomings on the God that created him. Often the two targets blended as in the comment to Howells in 1899 that man seemed to be "an April-fool joke, played by a malicious Creator with nothing better to waste his time upon." As late as May or June, 1898, however, the author was still trying to argue that the sublime and immense Deity who could fashion such an infinitely complicated universe must have *some* plan that man's limited mind could not comprehend. A God of such immensity certainly could not be expected to be concerned about the sufferings of mankind. But neither should the various tragedies be attributed to His malice any more than a scientist should be blamed for the deaths of millions of microbes boiled in a test tube during a scientific experiment. But by 1899, in a section of *What is Man?* that he later deleted, Clemens seems to have reached the conclusion that in establishing man's basic temperament, hence his reaction to all "circumstances" he might meet, God was fundamentally to blame for all the sufferings, shams, hypocrisies and pretenses of the human

Clemens in London, 1899

Mark Twain Papers

race. This view he would later amplify in several chapters dictated for his autobiography in June, 1906, and in "Letters from the Earth" which he wrote in 1909.[3]

The scientific concepts in the writings of these later years no doubt derived chiefly from Darwin and other works already mentioned (see Chapter Five, *ante*).[4] But for other underlying ideas, several of Clemens' favorite British authors are even more relevant. The "philosophic" bases still appear to be rooted in the continuing "discussion with Lecky," with recurrent echoes from FitzGerald's *Rubaiyat* providing significant underscoring. Moreover, in *The Mysterious Stranger,* the author's favorite passage from Shakespeare and Carlyle's *Sartor Resartus* both supply essential elements.

The *Rubaiyat,* beloved by Clemens since 1879, had often come to his mind during the 1890's. On a trip to Italy in April, 1892, he entered four of FitzGerald's stanzas into his notebook, from memory. His mood at the time could not have been very cheerful. Though the publishing company had not yet failed, the outlook was hardly encouraging. More immediately, recurrent attacks of rheumatism made writing extremely painful for the author. Two of FitzGerald's stanzas perhaps also reflected for him some of his disappointment at the reception of *A Connecticut Yankee,* published little more than a year before, for stanza 65 proclaims that the "revelations of devout and learned" are "but Stories, which, awoke from sleep, / They told their fellows and to sleep return'd"; and stanza 26 tells how the "saints and sages" who discussed "the Two Worlds" so learnedly are thrust "like foolish prophets forth," their words "scorned," and their mouths "stopt with rust."[5]

The other two stanzas (80 and 81), which Clemens wrote down first, are even more significant. Not only do they indicate that he was currently pondering the question of moral responsibility, but along with stanza 79 they present an idea that underlies numerous later comments on the injustice of man's being held accountable by his Creator for sins that his very nature requires him to commit. More about these in a moment.

Omar again came to Clemens' attention during the spring of 1894, when his artist friend, Frank D. Millet, gave him a copy of the 1888 Houghton-Mifflin edition of the *Rubaiyat.* We know also that he was thinking of FitzGerald's poem during the summer of 1897, when the ideas for *The Mysterious Stranger* were taking shape, for he reminded himself on July 10 to "inform Sir Douglas

Straight or J. M. Barrie that I am the Omar Khayam [*sic*] Club of America."[6]

The following year Clemens tried his hand at composing some *rubaiyat* of his own. Of these, three stanzas and several fragments present in verse the same picture of man's infirmities that appears so graphically in "The Lowest Animal" (written two years earlier) and in a part of the "Eseldorf" version of *The Mysterious Stranger* that was written in 1898. (Perhaps it was at this time, too, that he composed a pair of bawdy quatrains lamenting the effect of age on sexual prowess). Shortly thereafter he considered grouping a number of FitzGerald's stanzas with several of his own under the title of "AGE—A Rubaiyat."[7] That latter project, too, came to nothing. But the following summer in Sanna, Sweden, where the family had gone for treatment by the famous osteopath Henrick Kellgren, the humorist once more attempted an imitation of Omar. This time he completed twenty stanzas, which he entitled "To the Above Old People" and included in a farcical essay called "My Boyhood Dreams."[8]

The essay, a mock-serious discourse on the failure of most men to achieve the dreams of their youth, teases a number of the author's friends—Howells, John Hay, Brander Matthews and others—by describing how the progress of their careers had thwarted their real ambitions to be auctioneers, steamboat mates, horse doctors, and the like. But though both essay and poem seem to joke about the advance of old age and the "indignity of its infirmities," an underlying bitterness and pathos is there, reflecting some of Clemens' most serious, and even savage, moods.

Reflecting the author's increasing fascination during these years with investigations in microbiology,[9] "To the Above Old People" depicts man's infirmities, his helplessness in the face of disease and decay, more vividly than do the 1898 stanzas. Four of its quatrains present a picture that is especially similar to the descriptions of man in "The Lowest Animal" and *The Mysterious Stranger*. The first two are revisions of two of the 1898 stanzas (which in turn had echoed FitzGerald's stanzas 55 and 17). The third derives its final line from stanza 26, one of those quoted in 1892.

> From Cradle unto Grave I keep a House
> Of Entertainment where may drowse
>   Bacilli and kindred Germs—or feed—or breed
> Their festering Species in a deep Carouse.

> Think—in this battered Caravanserai,
> Whose Portals open stand all Night and Day,
>   How Microbe after Microbe with his Pomp
> Arrives unasked, and comes to stay.
>
> Our ivory Teeth, confessing to the Lust
> Of masticating, once, now own Disgust
>   of Clay-plug'd Cavities—full soon our Snags
> Are emptied, and our Mouths are filled with Dust.

The fourth stanza was all his own, and its description of a specific disease, the more disgusting for its prosaic and commonplace name, helps to reduce man's condition to ultimate absurdity:

> Our Gums forsake the Teeth and tender grow,
> And fat, like over-ripened Figs—we know
>   The Sign—the Riggs Disease is ours, and we
> Must list this Sorrow, add another Woe.

Here and elsewhere in this poem flat language and sordid imagery replace the luxuriance and beauty which grace even the most graphic of Omar's considerations of man's inevitable return to the dust from which he came. In "To the Above Old People," therefore, man's ultimate demise becomes revolting instead of merely pathetic or tragic.

Another stanza suggests Clemens' continued interest in Omar's discussion of man's relationship with his Maker, which is climaxed in FitzGerald's stanzas 80 and 81, the two most significant of the stanzas quoted in 1892. In this part of the *Rubaiyat* Omar ponders the fact that man is merely a helpless piece, moved about "this Checker board of Nights and Days," by a mysterious "Master of the Show" (stanzas 68 and 69). Concluding that all is predestined (73), he cites "the Vine" as his one protection against whatever may befall him. But his rage seems to mount as he notes with increasing irony the paradox that man, created "out of senseless Nothing," should have been so made as to chafe at "the yoke of unpermitted Pleasure" (i.e. that he would by his very nature tend to *seek* that unpermitted pleasure), but at the same time be subject to "Everlasting Penalties" if he should break the "yoke" (78). In stanza 79 the sense of injustice increases still more as Omar sees "the Master" not only holding man responsible for "a Debt he never did contract and cannot answer" but requiring payment of "Pure Gold for what he lent him dross-allayed." To Omar, this stipulation that man was expected to behave as if he were perfect even though created imperfect, seemed indeed a "sorry trade!" And then, in the two stanzas that Clemens put into his notebook, Omar expands that point and takes "the Master" severely to task:

> Oh Thou! who didst with pitfall and with gin
> Beset the Road I was to wander in,
> Thou wilt not with Predestined Evil round
> Enmesh, and then impute my fall to sin!

> Oh Thou who man of baser earth didst make
> And even with Paradise devise the Snake,
> For all the Sin wherewith the face of Man
> Is blacken'd—Man's forgiveness give—and take!

Besides making substantially the same point as the section of the *Rubaiyat*, the stanza in "To the Above Old People" seems particularly to borrow its "financial" imagery from FitzGerald's stanza 79:

> For every nickeled Joy, marred and brief,
> We pay some day its Weight in golden Grief
>   Mined from our Hearts. Ah, murmur not—
> From this one-sided Bargain dream of no Relief!

This passage, in turn, points to similar treatment of Omar's thesis in *The Mysterious Stranger* and to materials Clemens dictated for his autobiography in 1906. In Chapter Seven of *The Mysterious Stranger* (a passage written in 1900) Satan describes man as a machine—a suffering-machine and a happiness-machine combined—and further explains that "for every happiness turned out in the one department the other stands ready to modify it with a sorrow or a pain—maybe a dozen." Sometimes they were equally balanced, but if not, pain always predominated. But Omar's attack on the injustice of enmeshing man's life with "predestined Evil," and then holding him responsible for sinning, and the point that God rather than man ought to ask forgiveness was to find its most direct expression in the June, 1906, dictations. There, in defining his concept of God and assigning the blame to the Creator, the author considers man's ridiculous pride in declaring himself the "noblest work of God." But then he notes that man should be pitied for his thoughts and actions, not blamed or condemned: "All the control is vested in his temperament—which he did not create—

and in the circumstances which hedge him round from the cradle to the grave and which he did not devise and cannot change by any act of his will, for the reason that he has no will." A few pages earlier, Clemens had borrowed both idea and language from Fitz-Gerald to argue that God had made it an unavoidable and unchanging law that every one of His creatures "should suffer wanton and unnecessary pains and miseries every day of its life . . . , that its way, *from birth to death should be beset by traps, pitfalls, and gins,* ingeniously planned and ingeniously concealed." Under this "ten-thousandfold law of punishment," he goes on to say, *"the debt, whether made innocently or guiltily,* is promptly collected by Nature—and in this world, without waiting for the ten-billionfold additional penalty appointed—in the case of man—for collection in the next." Then, after enlarging upon man's case in particular, Clemens sums up by reiterating substantially the same point, i.e., that God so contrived man as to make him a slave to his passions, appetites, and other undesirable qualities—a slave whose "goings out" and "comings in" [another echo of the *Rubaiyat,* stanza 27] "are beset by traps which he cannot possibly avoid and which compel him to commit what are called sins." And yet God punishes man for "doing these very things which from the beginning of time He had always intended that he should do." As a final outburst, the humorist expands Omar's "Man's forgiveness give—and take!" into the contention that any man must inevitably admit "in his secret heart" the ridiculousness of believing that one could commit a sin against such a God, or that he owes Him any obligations, thanks, reverence, or worship.[10]

The subject of determinism, so strong in the autobiographical dictation, does not appear in the poem "To the Above Old People," but FitzGerald's phrasing of Omar's deterministic views seems to have come to mind some years earlier, in 1895, when Clemens was writing the "Macfarlane" essay. The image of man's development from "a few microscopic seed germs . . . deposited upon the Globe by the Creator in the dawn of time,"[11] is much like Omar's more vivid expression near the beginning of the poet's description of man's place in an entirely predestined universe (73):

> With Earth's first Clay They did the Last Man knead,
> And there of the Last Harvest sowed the Seed;
>   And the first morning of Creation wrote
> What the Last Dawn of Reckoning shall read.

In view of these various relationships between the works of these years—and of Clemens' enthusiasm for the *Rubaiyat* as early as 1879 when his deterministic philosophy was in its formative stages, there is little doubt that the poem provided an important impetus for his later concepts. If it did not actually help to inspire his view of man as helpless in the grip of external forces, it provided a fundamental picture of man's relationship with the Deity and, in several instances, the imagery with which to express it.

What is Man? was Clemens' most systematic attempt to deal with the same sort of questions which Omar poses. The answers which Clemens found to the psalmist's query "What is man that thou art mindful of him?" (Psalms 8:4) are much closer to Omar's resignation than to the psalmist's wonder at the power and dominion granted to man by a generous God. Still, in its final version, Clemens' "Bible" does offer a possibility for man's improvement beyond that afforded by Omar's paean to "the Grape." More of that later.

The writing of *What Is Man?* extended over some eight years from its beginnings in 1898.[12] As the author himself said, the Monday Evening Club essay of 1883, "What is Happiness?" had consisted "partly of a skeleton sketch, but mainly of talk." Now anxious to develop his arguments more fully, he chose one of the oldest devices for philosophical disquisition, the dialogue, and for his participants he introduced a variant of his "old-timer"— "tenderfoot" relationship—an Old Man and a Young Man.

Whatever other sources contributed, it is not at all far-fetched to see this dialogue as Clemens' formal summing up of the "discussion with Lecky."[13] Most of the Old Man's arguments embody those of the utilitarian philosophers, especially the theory of "associations" propounded by David Hartley and popularized by James and John Stuart Mill and Adam Bain. When Clemens later denied having read the works of such authors, he was probably telling the truth.[14] But firsthand knowledge was not necessary, for their arguments lay readily available in the long first chapter of the *History of European Morals*. That Lecky was his source is further suggested by the fact that whenever variations from the "associationist" point of view appear in the Old Man's discourse, they seem designed to counter some of the historian's own objections to the utilitarian argument.

When one sifts through the obscurities thrown up by the confused and confusing terminology in *What Is Man?* the answer to the title's question is substantially as follows: Man's essential nature—compare Hank Morgan's "one atom in me that is truly me"— becomes the basic "make" or "temperament" with which God endows each individual at birth. This essential element, however, consists only of "possibilities," which may be developed or trained in any of several directions, within the limits set by the basic nature, or "make" of that element [e.g. iron can be "trained" into steel (by refining and processing), but not into gold]. "Whatsoever a man is," the Old Man says, "is due to his *make,* and to the *influences* brought to bear by his heredities, his habitat, his associations." Since all "training" of a man thus results from outside forces only, man is actually an impersonal machine, originating nothing, "not even a thought."[15]

In both content and language, the Old Man's explanation of the "training" process closely parallels Lecky's summary of the "associationist" position.[16] As the historian puts it, the "associationists" deny the existence of such qualities as innate "benevolent feelings." But, though individuals are at first motivated solely by self-interest to seek pleasure and shun pain, the infant soon "learns to associate its pleasures with the idea of its mother, the boy with the idea of his family, the man with those of his class, his church, his country, and last of all mankind, and in each case, an independent affection is at length formed." Development of specific character traits follow the same pattern. Man is first attracted to attributes like benevolence or justice because they become associated in his mind with the esteem of his fellow-men or the possibility of future rewards. But finally, because of these pleasurable associations, man comes to love the attributes themselves rather than merely the advantages they can bring. In the same way, too, "opposite trains of association produce opposite feelings toward malevolence and injustice." Ultimately, since more pleasures are derived from acts which are termed virtuous than from any other source, "virtue, considered as a whole, becomes the supreme object of our affections."

The thing called Conscience develops from this same "train of associations." After having arrived at the point where virtue has become "peculiarly associated with the idea of pleasurable things," we feel "a glow of pleasure" when we practice it; "an intense pain," when we do not. These emotions constitute the Conscience, which

[219

becomes "the ruling principle of our lives," and we learn "to sacrifice all earthly things rather than disobey it." On this argument, then, the associationists based their contention that it was possible for man to progress from pure selfishness into "the loftiest region of heroism."

The "message" of *What is Man?* is strikingly similar. Early in the discussion of how the Conscience might be trained, the author all but paraphrases Lecky when he has the Old Man say that "all training is one form or another of *outside influence,* and *association* is the largest part of it." And, elaborating: "It is his human environment which influences his mind and his feelings, furnishes him his ideals, and sets him on his road and keeps him in it. If he leaves that road he will find himself shunned by the people whom he most loves and esteems, and whose approval he most values. . . . The influences about him create his preferences, his aversions, his politics, his tastes, his morals, his religion."[17]

According to Lecky's summary, the utilitarians also stressed the importance of education and training as the means by which what began as pure selfishness might evolve into a love of virtue for its own sake. If one's early associations indicated that he would derive more pleasure from vice than from virtue, he would readily yield to vice; if he associated pleasure and praise with virtue, then virtue would irresistibly attract him. That "readiness to yield to one or other set of motives," constituted "disposition," and was "altogether an artificial thing, the product of education, and effected by the association of ideas." Through education, also, an early tendency to find pleasure in vice and hence "to gravitate toward evil," could actually be remedied, since the education could provide a change in the "train of associations."

As noted in earlier chapters, it was the nature of the Conscience itself that constituted perhaps the chief bone of contention between the intuitionists and the utilitarians. Both agreed that the Conscience was the master of man. But for Lecky and the intuitionists, the "associationist" theory failed adequately to account for the sense of obligation (Duty), which could keep a man from doing wrong, even though that deed might bring him a good deal of pleasure. A deeper motivation (such as an innate moral sense or intuitive perception of good and evil) must be necessary to make a man avoid such an action.

Though agreeing with the utilitarians on the primary importance of "training," Clemens may have thought that Lecky had scored an important point in thus refusing to accept the Conscience as an *entirely* artificial product of one's "associations." For the Old Man, too, declares that the Conscience is an *inborn* element of the "make" or "temperament," which *does* impose a rigid sense of obligation on man. But he then defines that sense of obligation in such a way as to bring his argument back into agreement with the associationists. Rather than being "a *guide* or *incentive* to any authoritatively prescribed line of morals or conduct," as the "other moralists" maintained, it was merely a basic *need*—a *"necessity* for self-approval." As such, the obligation it imposed was not the sense of *moral* duty posited by Lecky, but (as the Old Man puts it) merely one that causes man to seek those things—good *or* evil—that contribute to his "self-approval" (or "self-contentment"). By so defining the Conscience, then, Clemens could return to the associationist view with the Old Man's assertion that only when affected by "training," does the Conscience become a guide to morality, and even then it prefers good to evil "for spirit contenting reasons only."

Once he establishes that point, the Old Man repeatedly stresses the fact that an individual's attraction toward good or evil results solely from the "outside influences" acting upon his Conscience. Again like Lecky's summary, he asserts that man's associations can "train him upward or . . . train him downward." Even if a man chanced to be "evilly placed," however, he still might not necessarily be "trained downward," for all that was needed was "to change his habitat, his *associations*." Lest that statement seem to contradict his contention that man was merely a machine, reacting to outside impulses, the Old Man hastens to add that the "initiatory impulses" for such a change must of course come from outside the person himself, possibly by pure chance. A sweetheart, for instance, might call a timid man a coward, and he in turn, to win her approval (and hence his own) might be set on a course that, by degrees (and always through the pleasure-pain motivation), could lead to exploits of the utmost bravery. Or perhaps a chance thought derived from his reading might cause a man to seek new associations "that are in sympathy with his new ideal," and thus eventually change his way of life entirely.

At this point, too, the Old Man emphasizes the importance of education, asserting that the improvement of mankind need not be left to pure chance, but could be directed by laying "traps" for people, "baited with *Initiatory Impulses toward high ideals*." Then, after a lengthy "proof" of the proposition that man lacks intuitive perceptions of any sort (including the "intuitive perception of good and evil" urged by those "other moralists") and a discussion of the role of the "temperament" in man's training, he complies with the Young Man's request to put the plan for improving the human race into the form of an "Admonition." "Diligently train your ideals *upward* and *still upward* toward a summit where you will find your chiefest pleasure in conduct which, while contenting you, will be sure to confer benefits upon your neighbor and the community."

This advice from one who has been arguing that man is a machine, reacting only to external impulses, has disturbed many critics who have not looked closely enough at *What is Man?* If one stops with the literal statement of the "Admonition," Clemens' argument does fall apart, for the idea of a *self*-training machine is patently absurd. In the context of the dialogue, however, it becomes plain that the Old Man's advice has to be addressed to those individuals (like himself or the Young Man; i.e., the world's would-be moralists) whose own particular "make" causes them to derive pleasure or "spiritual contentment" from attempting to improve mankind. That pleasure, in turn, would outweigh any "pain" resulting from the self-sacrifices that might be involved in their efforts. These persons, then, once the idea came to them from an outside source (such as the "Admonition" itself, perhaps), would be motivated to lay before others the "traps baited with Initiatory Impulses toward high ideals."

Shortly thereafter, Clemens again suggests the function of the moralist in such a process. Almost certainly with Lecky in mind, he has the Old Man attack one of the apparent fallacies in the intuitionist point of view—the requirement that man "do good for *others'* sake chiefly; and . . . duty for duty's sake chiefly; and to do acts of *self-sacrifice*." This is inconsistent, the Old Man says, for by offering "bribes" to encourage virtue (i.e. religion's promises of future rewards and punishments), these "others" are really conceding the necessity to conciliate and content "the Interior Master" (the Conscience). To be logical, therefore, they should stick to their admission that the individual's Conscience is the supreme master, but should not hedge that position about with requirements of duty to *others*. This sort of moralist (he says somewhat later) should "teach unreservedly what he already teaches with one side of his mouth and takes back with the other: Do right *for your own sake,* and be happy in knowing that your *neighbor* will certainly share in the benefits resulting." Then, after the Young Man requests him to repeat the "Admonition," the Old Man sets out to provide additional evidence that "one's *every* act proceeds from *exterior* influences."

That renewed emphasis again suggests that Clemens conceived of the "Admonition" as a procedure by which the moralists could assist in the improvement of mankind, and not an appeal to individuals to train *themselves.* Hence, though he may well be criticized for not making his point more clearly, Clemens' argument is by no means so contradictory as has been charged.

In a number of other instances, the Old Man's discussions seem designed not so much to answer as to eliminate some of Lecky's objections to the associationist philosophy. At several points the historian scoffs at the utilitarians' notion that their theory was not really a selfish one, since it could (by the process already outlined) ultimately result in altruism. He likewise rejects the view that individual efforts to obtain happiness could result in the general happiness of mankind. *What is Man?* invalidates both of these objections simply by eliminating any pretense of altruism. The Old Man not only admits, but insists, that *all* motivation is selfish, the product of the individual's inborn "necessity for self-approval." Though "training" might result in a coinciding of "individual pleasure" and "community pleasure," the basic motivation still would be a selfish one.[18]

Another of the Old Man's illustrative examples seems aimed especially at Lecky's fundamental premise that the existence of a "common voice of mankind"—the "universal sentiment" which considers selfishness reprehensible and self-sacrifice noble—constitutes "proof" of the existence of an innate moral sense.[19] Admitting that "the eye of the mind, like the eye of the body may be closed," and that moral and rational faculties may be dormant, particularly when men are "wholly immersed in the gratification of their senses," the historian maintains that the moral sense "when quickened into action," will *inevitably* "discharge its appointed function."

Using almost exactly the same terms, the Young Man contends that when one's moral sense seems to go wrong, his Conscience is merely lazy or drowsy and needs to be awakened. This opinion elicits a double-barreled assault which condemns both the concept of self-sacrifice and the belief in the infallibility of the Conscience as a moral guide. The Old Man tells of an Infidel who, following what he considers his duty, converts to paganism a sick lad for whom he is caring, but then is filled with remorse when the mother reproaches him for destroying the boy's faith. "So his Conscience was awakened," the Young Man exclaims, and therefore he would never experience that sort of trouble again. Not so, says the Old Man. Because of the grief of the boy and his mother (outside influences), and his own remorse at having wronged them, the Infidel was himself converted to Christianity and became a missionary, hoping to save other imperilled souls. But as a missionary he repeated his experience, this time destroying another boy's faith in the pagan gods, and again his supposed good deed brought sorrow to others and remorse to himself.[20]

When the Young Man then declares that the man's Conscience must have been a fool, the Old Man clinches his argument. Such an admission, he says, pulls down "the whole doctrine of infallibility of judgment in conscience," for if one conscience can be wrong, so can others. The fact that both acts brought the Infidel pleasure until he was distressed by the sorrow of those he had "helped" shows that the Consciences are "absolutely indifferent," until something external becomes a source of pain to oneself. Love, hate, charity, compassion, avarice and the like, therefore, are merely forms of "self-contentment, self-gratification," and the *only* motivating force for human beings is "self-approval." Though there are sacrifices and men do perform duties, the individual must always feel better for making the sacrifice or doing the duty than he would for shirking it.[21]

That objection to Lecky's insistence upon man's universal approval of "disinterestedness" and abhorrence of selfishness arises in another context almost at the end of *What is Man?*. As one last argument, the Young Man contends that if a man were to realize that he is actually a slave to his own "self-contentment," he would lose all pride, confidence, ambition, happiness—in fact, all that makes life worth living. Here it is as if Clemens were echoing the historian's assertion that because men are naturally repelled by the thought of a good act resulting solely from a desire for personal pleasure, no one could deliberately make happiness his sole objective without his character becoming "despicable and degraded."[22]

In denying that his philosophy would disillusion or degrade, the

Old Man suggests a different, more cynical concept of a "common voice of mankind." Nations do not think, he says; they only feel. And since "they get their feelings at second hand through their temperaments, not their brains," any nation can be brought through "force of circumstances" to accept *"any kind of government or religion that can be devised."* Though Clemens perhaps did not fully understand what Lecky meant by the "common voice," it is almost as if he were asking, "How can anyone—the world being as it is—suggest that there is a 'common voice of mankind' crying out for the pursuit of virtue, condemning selfishness, exalting self-sacrifice?" For him, as he had declared in "The Character of Man," human characteristics and actions rendered entirely illogical any such concept as an innate moral sense that had been "put into man ready charged with the right and only true and authentic correctives of conduct, with the self-same correctives, unchanged, unmodified, distributed to all nations and all epochs." And in concluding *What is Man?* his spokesman ironically assures his young friend that he need have no fear of possible "degrading" effects of this "selfish" philosophy. Considering what man has endured through the ages and still remained generally contented, it would do him too much honor to suppose that this system of "plain, cold facts" could take the cheerfulness out of human beings.

Clemens probably thought that his system effectively refuted the contentions of Lecky and the intuitionists. There is no denying, however, that his arguments at a number of points are confused or superficial, or both. One of the chief flaws in terms of his own theories is that there *is* an "upward" toward which the individual may be trained. One might also ask who decides what that "up" actually is. Nevertheless, in the light of Lecky's summary of the "associationist" philosophy and Clemens' apparent effort to avoid some of the inconsistencies observed by the historian, *What is Man?* is itself more consistent than many have thought.

Moreover, despite its sneers at man's pretenses and pride, the dialogue embodies a brighter outlook than had dominated the earlier essays like "The Character of Man" and "The Lowest Animal." Rather than stressing the implication that the nature of man all but precluded any progress, the work suggests that hope for man lies simply in the realization that he is directed solely by outside forces, and his own "make." Once he is rid of his false pride and ridiculous posturing—and with the help of the moralists whose own

[225

"make" causes them to supply proper "initiatory impulses" for others—many faults could be eliminated, or at least drastically cut down in number.[23]

That Clemens attempted to put his philosophy into practice, there is little doubt. Most of his speeches and published writings of the early 1900's suggest that he was consciously adopting the role defined by the Old Man. In listing his occupation on a questionnaire circulated by one of the many reform groups that sought his support during these years, he was not entirely facetious when he wrote "Professional Moralist."[24]

The most successful fictional expression of the principles set forth in the humorist's "Bible" is the bitter short story, "The Man that Corrupted Hadleyburg." Written in Austria between August and October, 1898, almost immediately after the first draft of *What is Man?*,[25] the tale effectively projects the author's withering scorn for man's pretensions. Yet it, too, concludes on a somewhat positive note.

Reading this story as an additional phase of the "discussion with Lecky" is further justified by the fact that Clemens took the text for his sardonic sermon from that same encyclopedic first chapter of *European Morals.* As far as its central point is concerned, the author was agreeing with Lecky, for the passage in question points out the absurdity of the theological notion that one must avoid any sin, however trivial. As the historian puts it, such a tenet would require the suppression of all desires, the avoiding of all temptations. One would have to ignore the fact that temptations can serve to elevate moral character and that "a torpid sinlessness is not a high moral condition." Hence, such a notion is not only absurd, but could actually serve to "paralyze our moral being."[26]

In the story, the "moral being" of the Hadleyburgers is indeed paralyzed. Proud of their town's reputation for incorruptibility, they had trained their children in "principles of honesty" from the cradle onward. To allow that honesty to "solidify," they removed all temptations from the experiences of their young people. Secure in their own convictions, with "Lead Us Not Into Temptation" as their town's motto, they remained totally unaware that this "torpid sinlessness" was actually corrupt.

When temptation finally does appear in the form of an alleged fortune in gold coins, greed rapidly supplants the heretofore untested honesty, and the town's demise is swift. Paradoxically (and just as Lecky indicates), the temptation to sin later results in the beginnings of a "moral elevation" for Hadleyburg. Even more ironically, the very temptation itself originates in a sin—a desire for revenge harbored by the "passing stranger" whom the town had chanced to offend some years earlier. Though acting from an evil motive in devising the fraud that tempts all the "best" people of Hadleyburg, he actually becomes an agent of good in opening the villagers' eyes to the absurdity of their pious pretensions.

Though Clemens here agrees with Lecky on the theological position involved, his story does not contradict the argument of *What is Man?*. If questioned, he would probably have explained that the "passing stranger's" scheme, undertaken solely for the "spiritual contentment" he would receive from its success, served at the same time as one of the "initiatory impulses" toward virtue described by the Old Man. For, with the falsity of its earlier self-approval exposed, the chastened town could drop the "Not" from its motto and find its own *greater* self-approval in real honesty rather than in the former "torpid sinlessness."

Nor does the author's satiric treatment of his chief character, Edward Richard's attempt to rationalize his guilt by asserting that all is ordered imply a reversal of Clemens' deterministic philosophy. Selfishness, or the desire for "spiritual contentment," rules all. Like the other eighteen of Hadleyburg's leading citizens, Richards takes the stranger's bait and writes the letter that he expects will win him the sack of gold. When the Reverend Mr. Burgess, because of a supposed favor, refrains from reading Richards' letter at the town hall meeting, Richards yields to a second temptation, allowing his integrity to be publicly praised. Conscience then torments him, and doubly so when he and his wife receive the money from the sale of the gilded lead discs in the alleged bag of gold. Soon, fear of discovery replaces pangs of conscience, and finally, wrongly convinced that Burgess has revealed their deception, both Richards and his wife fall ill. The ultimate irony occurs when the dying Richards confesses all, so that he may *forgive* Burgess for betraying his secret.

Throughout the story, therefore, the Richardses are at the mercy of *their* desire for "spiritual contentment" or "self-approval." The contentment in preserving their reputation for honesty—not to mention that provided by the money—overrides their shame for what they have done. Their moral sense (as Lecky would define it) was certainly not strong enough to make them do what they knew to be their duty. Even the confession results not from any inner sense of moral compulsion, but merely from Richards' desire to set the record straight *after* he is sure his dishonesty had been exposed. Moreover, he gained additional contentment and self-approval from the fact that he was magnanimously forgiving Burgess (for an injury that had never occurred).

Besides the debt to Lecky, "The Man that Corrupted Hadleyburg" reveals Clemens' continued interest in the comic operas of Gilbert and Sullivan. During the world tour he had remarked to an Australian reporter that Gilbert's talent not only for saying "the wittiest of things," but for saying them in verse was truly astonishing. Speaking of the fundamental seriousness of humor—the "grinning skull" that lurks behind the broadest smile or most ludicrous situation—he found no better example than Gilbert's Jack Point.[27] Actually, few statements about the role of the humorist in general correspond more closely to Clemens' own concepts than those which Gilbert puts into the mouth of his jester in *The Yeoman of the Guard.*

In "Hadleyburg," as in *Connecticut Yankee,* the borrowings from Gilbert and Sullivan provide the basis for a satire more biting than that of the originators. During the exposure of the leading citizens at the fateful town-hall meeting, the audience spontaneously composes a song for the occasion and delivers it like a typical Gilbert and Sullivan chorus:

> Hooray! Hooray! it's a symbolical day
> And don't you this forget—
> Corruptibles far from Hadleyburg are—
> But the Symbols are here, you bet!

The satire gains additional force by comparison with the model: "the lovely 'Mikado' tune of 'When a man's afraid, a beautiful maid—.'" In *The Mikado,* Act II, Pitti-Sing (one of the "three little maids from school")[28] interjects that song into the Lord High Executioner's false account of his recent beheading of Nanki-Poo. Ko-Ko claims exceptional efficiency in discharging his duty, but even if true, his claims would pale beside the efficiency with which the "passing stranger" had symbolically beheaded the paragons of Hadleyburg. And the memory of the fervent support of Ko-Ko's veracity by the Mikado chorus—

> We know him well,
> He cannot tell
> Untrue—or groundless tales—
> He always tries
> To utter lies,
> And every time he fails.

ironically underscores the more serious deception—Hadleyburg's erstwhile pride in its own honesty.

A final enrichment of the irony of the whole comes with the realization that just before Ko-Ko's song, the Mikado delivers his own famous admonition to "let the punishment fit the crime"—

> And make each prisoner pent
> Unwillingly represent
> A source of innocent merriment!
> Of innocent merriment!

There is merriment in Hadleyburg, to be sure, and it is almost as grisly in its way as that which the Mikado terms so "innocent." Whereas Ko-Ko's execution of Nanki-Poo never actually takes place, the stranger's symbolic execution not only of the leading citizens but of the whole town of Hadleyburg, is fully accomplished. The audience at the town hall roars with laughter at the exposure of the criminal gullibility of their leaders, but ultimately all feel their implication in the same hypocrisy and deceit.

Still, though it focuses a merciless spotlight on human hypocrisy, "The Man that Corrupted Hadleyburg" reveals the underlying hope that all of Clemens' ponderings on man's worthlessness seemed unable to kill. For besides substantiating the premise that temptation can result in moral elevation—as implied by dropping the "not" from the town's motto—the story makes explicit the "message" implied by *What is Man?*: if human beings could come to understand their essential nature, *some* progress might be possible.

The other most important fictional representation of Clemens' views during these later years was *The Mysterious Stranger,* or rather, the three versions of the story which John Tuckey has labeled "Eseldorf," "Hannibal," and "Print Shop." The composition of these efforts extended over roughly the same years as *What is Man?,* with the author several times changing both plot and setting in an effort to find the right fictional form for his current ideas.[29]

A complete analysis of the several manuscripts is beyond the scope of the present study, which will concentrate upon the chief British sources for the tale and draw some conclusions about the place of *The Mysterious Stranger* as a final episode in Clemens' "discussion with Lecky."

The "Eseldorf" story (published in 1916 with alterations and deletions by Paine) more obviously reflects that "discussion" than does the longer "Print-Shop" version, though the latter contains many of the same elements. In "Eseldorf" Satan's denunciations of human claims of superiority over the so-called "lower" animals are simply more vehement expressions of the Old Man's comments on the ridiculousness of man's pride in his innate Moral Sense. (This Satan is not the Devil, but an unfallen nephew of the great archangel, who assumes the name Philip Traum when he comes to Eseldorf.) The portrait of man as totally controlled by forces outside himself recurs in the explanation that each individual's first act, itself caused by his "circumstances and environment," sets off a sort of chain reaction. "Circumstances" here doubtless was intended to include both the basic "temperament" and the "heredities," as defined in *What is Man?*. More particularly, the villagers' treatment of alleged witches (Chapters Six and Ten) involves specific details from Lecky's *England in the Eighteenth Century* and a vivid illustration of how the principal of "self-approval" affects the action of mobs. Like the witch-burning in *A Connecticut Yankee,* the stoning and hanging in Chapter Ten was adapted from the case of Jane Corphar. Here Clemens turned Lecky's largely factual account into a savage indictment of man's cowardly conformity to public opinion.[30] But under the implied anger that this should be so, there lies the principal expressed in *What is Man?* and even more explicitly in "The United States of Lyncherdom," that the villagers' "self-approval" depends so much upon the approval of others that they have no choice but to conform. It was Lecky's brief comment—immediately preceding his account of the Corphar case—that in 1678 ten women had been "confined to the flames" in a single day for "having had carnal intercourse with the devil" which no doubt furnished the idea for the less explicit but more vivid story in Chapter Six of the experiences of the eleven convent girls ultimately burned at the stake. Additional implications for the continuing "discussion with Lecky" which occur in the final chapter will be considered after further discussion of the literary backgrounds of that episode.

In that last chapter, intended for the "Print-Shop" story but appended to "Eseldorf" by Paine, Satan reveals to the astonished narrator that all life, and even the universe itself is "only a vision, a dream" in which nothing exists but Theodore himself. "And you are but a *thought*—a vagrant thought, a useless thought . . . wandering forlorn among the empty eternities." What the single immediate source of the author's dream-imagery may have been is impossible to say. Clemens' current interest in the literature of hypnotism and other psychic phenomena, his fascination with Adolf Wilbrandt's *Master of Palmyra*, or his studies of the writings of Mary Baker Eddy each could have contributed something.[31] But whether or not one of these provided the immediate stimulus, there were other, more "literary" expressions of the idea that "life is a dream" in works with which Clemens had been acquainted for a much longer time.

Three works of British authors stand out as particularly important. As Coleman O. Parsons has noted, a central role must be accorded the speech in Shakespeare's *The Tempest* (IV, i) in which Prospero announces the end of his magic "revels." I also believe that Carlyle's *Sartor Resartus* furnished a powerful assist, and that FitzGerald's *Rubaiyat* contributed its share.

Of all the passages in Shakespeare, Clemens' favorite seems to have been that which follows Prospero's declaration that his "spirit-players" have vanished "into thin air":

> And like the baseless fabric of this vision,
> The cloud-capped towers, the gorgeous palaces,
> The solemn temples, the great globe itself,
> Yea, all which it inherit, shall dissolve
> And like this insubstantial pageant faded,
> Leave not a rack behind. We are such stuff
> As dreams are made on, and our little life
> Is rounded with a sleep.

The humorist may well have first heard the speech read by his pilot friend George Ealer during the long night watches on the river. In any case, it came vividly to his attention during his tour of Westminster Abbey with Kingsley in 1873, for among the most vivid memories of his "Memorable Midnight Experience" was the statue of Shakespeare with his finger pointing to a carved scroll bearing five of the lines. Early in 1876 he was asking Howells where the passage occurred in Shakespeare's plays; and sometime the same year he cited it as a touchstone of literary perfection against which one might measure the excessive verbiage of writers like Scott and Dickens.[32] In his own fiction an obvious echo sounds in Chapter Seventeen of *A Connecticut Yankee* when Sandy, in the name of the Boss, orders Queen Morgan to rescind her decision to burn an old lady at the stake. "Recall the commandment," she says, "or he will dissolve the castle and it shall vanish away like the instable fabric of a dream," whereupon the courtiers scramble for the door lest this Prospero of Arthur's kingdom change his mind and "puff the castle into the measureless dim vacancies of space."[33] Finally, in 1909, while striving to prove that Shakespeare was not the author of the plays attributed to him, Clemens would argue that Prospero's perfect lines could not have been penned by the same hand as the "authentic" doggerel epitaph, "Good friend for Jesus sake forbeare. . . ."[34] Very probably then, this image of a world dissolving like "the baseless fabric of a vision" became so firmly fixed in his memory that it came forth each time he encountered similar ideas in the works of others.

The first chapter of "Eseldorf" reflects the author's long-time fascination with this passage. Though he modelled the story's setting primarily on the view from Weggis, Switzerland (where he and the family spent July and August of 1897), he borrowed much of his imagery from the *Tempest* lines. A notebook entry from that July comments upon the strange exactness with which Mount Pilatus and the other crags and peaks counterfeited "towers, castles, temples, fortresses, and the human face." A few days later he again saw Pilatus as a castle fortress and noted the "spiritualizing" effect of the faint and delicate haze that invested the "imposing mass" with a "softness and unreality which makes it seem rather *the perishable fabric of a dream* than a passionless pile of grass and indestructible rocks" [italics mine].*

Having decided in November or December, 1897, to shift his story to an Austrian setting, the author apparently looked back to that summer's notes and worked the "enchantments" of the Swiss

* Notebook 32b I, pp. 12, 19–20, Mark Twain Papers.

scene into a description that parallels Prospero's speech even more closely:

> Yes, Austria was far from the world and asleep, and our village was *in the middle of that sleep.* . . . It drowsed in peace in the deep privacy of a hilly and woodsy solitude where news from the world hardly ever came to disturb its dreams, and was infinitely content. At its front flowed the tranquil river, its surface painted with *cloud-forms* . . . ; behind it rose the woody steeps to the base of the lofty precipice; from the top of the precipice frowned a vast castle, its long stretch of *towers and bastions* mailed in vines. . . .
>
> The whole region for leagues around was the hereditary property of a prince, whose servants kept the castle always in perfect condition for occupancy, but neither he nor his family came there oftener than once in five years. When they came it was as if the lord of the world had arrived, and had brought *all the glories of its kingdoms along;* and when they went they left a calm behind which was *like the deep sleep which follows an orgy* [all italics mine].

Besides establishing the sleepy quality of life in the Austrian setting, that first chapter (which Clemens later adapted for the "Print-Shop" story) prepares the way for Satan's final Prospero-like revelation. His declaration that life, the universe, and even himself were all a dream signals the end of the particular kind of "revels" (or "orgy"?) experienced by Theodore. And then Satan, too, ultimately vanishes into the nothingness out of which Theodore's mind had created the "players" in this "insubstantial pageant." (For the sake of familiarity, I continue to refer to the Satan and Theodore of the version published in 1916, though the final scene as Clemens wrote it for the "Print-Shop" story involves a "stranger" called "44" and a narrator named August Feldner.)

There is also evidence that Carlyle's *Sartor Resartus* helped to supplement the image derived from *The Tempest*. Clemens wrote the "dream-ending" in 1904, before he had finished parts of the "Print-Shop" story that led up to it. That same year, consciously or unconsciously, he borrowed Carlyle's "clothes-philosophy" for the beginning of "The Czar's Soliloquy," in which the Russian monarch explains at length how all his power depended upon the people's worship of external appearances—the "clothes" he wore. Originally, Clemens had begun the second paragraph of that discussion with: "But upon consideration . . . what would *any* man be without his clothes." When David Munro, editor of the *North American Review,* called to his attention how closely the passage echoed some of those in *Sartor,* he replaced the initial phrase by "As Teufelsdröckh suggested." He also told Munro that he had never read *Sartor* and at first had thought of suppressing the article. But upon reflecting that *any* "new" idea was only an old one newly phrased, and that most readers would not know Carlyle's book any better than he, he had decided to go ahead with the plans for publication.[35]

In denying that he had ever read *Sartor Resartus,* Clemens was stretching the truth far beyond the breaking-point. Given his lasting affection for *The French Revolution,* it is inconceivable that he would have bought the volume containing *Sartor* (as he did in 1888) and then not have read it. Clemens' correspondent friend, Henry Fischer, also remembered Clemens' mentioning Teufelsdröckh several times in their conversations during the late 1890's, and recalled the humorist once attributing to Heine a quatrain that he almost certainly had concocted himself:

> Life's a yawning Nitchevo,
> The Shadow of a single nought,
> The Dream of a Flea,
> A Drama by Teufelsdroeckh.[36]

Though Fischer's reminiscences are not the most reliable, the juxtaposition of elements in the quatrain further suggests that *Sartor* was on Clemens' mind during the time he was working on *The Mysterious Stranger.* If Clemens honestly had forgotten that he had read Carlyle's book, some of Teufelsdröckh's speculations almost certainly had slipped into the reservoir from which his "unconscious borrowing" so often came.[37]

What is especially pertinent, perhaps, is that at a number of points in *Sartor,* the "clothes-philosophy," the idea that life is an illusion created by man's mind, and Carlyle's specific echoes of Prospero's speech all touch one another. In Carlyle's Book One, Chapter Eight, for instance, occur the musings out of which emerges Professor Teufelsdröckh's "philosophy of clothes." Save for the fact that in *Sartor,* God is the creator of the Dream, Satan's final speech strongly resembles in its imagery the passage in which the Professor tries to answer the questions, "Who am I; what is this ME?": "We sit as in a boundless Phantasmagoria and Dream-grotto . . . sounds

and many-coloured visions flit round our sense. . . . This Dreaming,
. . . is what we on Earth call Life; wherein the most indeed un-
doubtingly wander, as if they knew right hand from left; yet they
only are wise who know they know nothing." Then, dismissing
Time and Space as nonexistent save as "modes of our human Sense,"
he borrows some of the *Tempest* imagery to conclude that the "so
solid-seeming World," after all was "but an air-image, our ME the
only reality: and Nature, with its thousand-fold production and
destruction, but the . . . 'phantasy of our Dream' . . . ."

Moreover, Carlyle quotes directly from Prospero's speech in a
later discussion of the world as dream. Earlier (in Book Two, Chapter Ten), in his own role as "Editor," he had described his "philosophy of clothes" as the means by which Teufelsdröckh could look
"through the Shows of things into Things themselves." Now (in
Book Three, Chapter Eight) the Professor has actually achieved this
ability, having "looked fixedly on Existence, till, one after the other,
its earthly hulls and garnitures . . . all melted away," and has come
to the Transcendental conclusion that all is an emanation from the
Deity. As for human beings, Teufelsdröckh announces, not as metaphor but as "scientific *fact*," that "we start out of Nothingness, take
figure, and are Apparitions; round us, as round the veriest specue,
is Eternity." Though we do leave some mark in our passage, the
only other thing we can know about our origin or destruction is that
the journey is "through Mystery to Mystery. . . ." For " 'We *are*
such stuff / as Dreams are made of [*sic*], and our little Life / Is
rounded with a sleep!' "[38]

Relevant to the "dream-ending" of *The Mysterious Stranger* is
another passage that Clemens wrote in 1908, probably to link the
final chapter to what had preceded it in the "Print-Shop" story.
There "44" conjures up for the narrator a shadowy procession of
skeletons—the illustrious dead of past ages in world history—which
he then dispels, leaving himself and the narrator alone in an
"empty and soundless world." Carlyle may well have been at least
partly responsible for inspiring that image, for in several passages
Teufelsdröckh speaks of ghosts of the past in similar terms. In one,
imagining that the suits in Monmouth Street's old-clothes shops are
ghosts whose silence expresses "all the fathomless tumult of Good
and Evil in 'the Prison men call Life,' " he describes Monmouth
Street as "a Mirza's Hill, where in motley vision, the whole Pageant
of Existence passes awfully before us; with its wail and jubilee, mad

loves and mad hatreds, church-bells and gallows-ropes, farce-tragedy, beast-godhead,—the Bedlam of Creation!" (Book Three, Chapter Six). Again in Chapter Eight of the same book, Teufelsdröckh, speaking of the illusion of Time, and of transporting the reader from "the Beginnings to the Endings," refers to a number of famous characters from history, and then asks: "Was it all other than the veriest Spectre-hunt; which has now . . . flitted away?" In the next chapter, Carlyle voices the hope that the Professor's experiences may have helped lead the reader through the "Clothes-Screen" into "the true land of Dreams . . ." so that he might enjoy, if only for a moment, a glimpse into "the region of the Wonderful. . . ." And at the end of the book, he concludes by observing that Teufelsdröckh seems to have vanished from the earth.

If these were indeed among the inspirations for Clemens' historical pageant and "dream-ending," the author probably intended his conclusion to be a direct contrast to Teufelsdröckh's glances into the "region of the Wonderful." His procession of skeletons (rather than suits of clothes) suggests a complete stripping away of illusions. In the final episode, too, Theodore is led (by the Prospero-like Satan rather than by his own deductions) to look through "the Shows of things into Things themselves," and to see existence as so "frankly and hysterically insane" that it *must* be a dream. But behind this parallel to Carlyle's "Bedlam of Creation," there is no comforting concept of the "star-domed City of God," and Theodore's realization that all is illusion gains ironic force by the implication that he is well rid of such an insane dream, even though behind "the Shows of things" there seems to be only emptiness.

Clemens very likely found an additional stimulus for the solipsism of his final chapter in Omar Khayyam's search for answers to some of the same questions that had baffled Teufelsdröckh. After noting in stanza 64 that no one had ever discovered what lay behind "the Door of Darkness," and in 65 (one of those Clemens quoted in 1892) that so-called "revelations" were merely "stories" dreamed by alleged prophets, Omar sends his own Soul "through the Invisible" to learn for itself about the after-life. His Soul's discovery that "I myself am Heav'n and Hell" is very much like what Theodore learns from Satan's revelations.[39]

It is unlikely, however, that Clemens accepted the solipsism of his conclusion as a serious philosophical position. As John Tuckey observes, the humorist once scribbled a note describing a man apparently sane and intelligent, whose "foible" was believing existence to be a dream and himself only a thought wandering in an empty universe.[40] Yet he was obviously fascinated by the idea, and the recurrence of the image in letters and elsewhere indicates a large measure of wishful thinking.

Clemens probably wrote the "dream-ending" chapter during the intense period of worry and depression preceding his wife's death on June 5, 1904. Obviously finding some solace in the very act of writing, he spoke significantly on May 9 of its power to sweep away the cares of life and put him in a world which no one but himself had visited.[41] Or he might possibly have written the chapter in the sad weeks following the return to the United States, for a letter of July 28 to Twichell reports his current state of mind in almost the exact words of his story. Life, he said, looked as it had for some years: "That is, that there is *nothing*. That there is no God, no universe; that there is only empty space, and in it a lost and homeless and wandering and companionless and indestructible Thought. And that I am that thought. And God, and the Universe, and Time, and Life, and Death, and Joy and Sorrow and Pain only a grotesque and brutal *dream,* evolved from the frantic imagination of that insane Thought." Just as in the novel, too, he explained that the many contradictions of life could be accounted for only as "the drunken dream of an idiot thought drifting solitary and forlorn through the horizonless eternities of empty Space. . . ." This idea, he said, had become part of him because he had been living it for seven years and had written a long story to embody and develop it—"a book which is not finished and is not intended for print." For part of each day, then, Livy was "a dream and never existed," but the rest of the time was filled with painful memories: a "long procession of remorses . . . filing by uncountable, and both ends dimming away and vanishing under the horizons."*

Whether the letter antedated the writing of the "dream-ending" or was based on it, the author closely identified the concept with his own experiences.[42] This fact allows a further speculation upon the one ray of hope that the novel seems to emanate. Though Theodore is left "appalled" by Satan's revelations, he nevertheless notes a "vague, dim, but blessed and hopeful feeling" created by

* SLC to Joseph Twichell, 7/28/04, Clemens-Twichell Collection, Yale University.

the knowledge that the irrational nightmare of human existence *was* only a dream from which he could awake. Once aware of the truth of things, then, he could perhaps realize the implications of Satan's additional pronouncement that "I, your poor servant, have revealed you to yourself and set you free. Dream other dreams, and better!"

A somewhat similar development occurs in the *Rubaiyat* passages that had been so intriguing. Following Omar's discussion of determinism and the irony of blaming man for sins his fundamental nature makes inevitable (Stanzas 62–98), the poet's address to his "Love" in stanza 99 closely parallels elements of the "dream-ending":

> Ah, Love! could you and I with Him conspire
> To grasp this sorry Scheme of Things entire,
> Would we not shatter it to bits—and then
> Remold it nearer to the Heart's Desire!

For Omar, that total "grasp" is impossible; his only recourse is "the Grape," which aids him in making the best of this "sorry Scheme of Things." But even if Clemens actually believed the idea of a dream-universe to be a "foible," Satan's shattering of Theodore's earlier views by revealing the actual nature of things seems almost to contain a plea: "If only it *were* possible to remold the sorry scheme of things nearer to our heart's desire!" The narrator's "relief" at Satan's revelation and also the fact that he is presumably telling this story years after the events have occurred, suggests he has been able to accept his lonely condition and perhaps even dream some "other dreams and better," so as actually to accomplish some of the "remolding."

It is in this regard that the ending of *The Mysterious Stranger* seems most closely related to the author's final position in the "discussion with Lecky." In most of the writings that followed, he continued to preach the deterministic philosophy of *What is Man?* Yet, as some have noted, the very vehemence of his denial of free will and moral responsibility suggests a lack of total conviction. In *The Mysterious Stranger,* particularly, he seems to cling, perhaps even unconsciously, to a belief in man's ability to direct his own destiny. Both in Satan's rhapsody on the powers of the creative imagination and in the concept of Theodore as "creator" of the universe there lies the suggestion that the human mind does possess the ability to originate thoughts and ideas.

Here again it seems that some of Carlyle's preachments may have rubbed off, for other parallels between the experiences of Theodore and Teufelsdröckh stress the significance of human creativity. Very much like Satan's "freeing" of Theodore to dream "better" dreams is Teufelsdröckh's statement at the end of his long climb to the "Everlasting Yea" (Book Two, Chapter Nine). Arguing that the "Ideal" is to be found in the "Actual," miserable as the latter may be, the Professor urges the reader to work, believe, live and be free: "The Ideal is in thyself . . . thy Condition is but the stuff thou art to shape that same Ideal out of. . . ." The next chapter, describing the beginnings of Teufelsdröckh's "spiritual majority," stresses the importance of the creative writer, the "miracles performed by Pens." Almost as if he were illustrating the Old Man's concept of the operation of "initiatory impulses," the Professor suggests that perhaps some of his writings may yet have fallen "not altogether void, into the mighty seedfield of opinion." Finally, in Book Three, Chapter Nine (which contains still another quotation from Prospero's speech), Carlyle, in his role as "Editor," concludes that an understanding of the "clothes-philosophy" can provide an insight into "the far region of Poetic Creation and Palingenesia, where that Phoenix Death-Birth of Human Society, and of all Human Things appears possible. . . ."[43]

Clemens' view of the possibilities for man's progress was of course less optimistic than Carlyle's. Yet his grasping at the thought that one might "dream other dreams and better" suggests that he could not completely win his argument with Lecky. The "sound heart" of Huck Finn may have evolved into Hank Morgan's "one atom in me that is truly me," and thence into the "vagrant thought" of Theodore Fischer, but there remains the hope that through the process of creative thought, man might still be, in some small measure, the master of his own fate.

In terms of his own career, however, Clemens' failure to finish *The Mysterious Stranger* may be read as the failure of his own ability to "dream other dreams and better." After giving up work on the "Print-Shop" manuscript in July, 1905, he pretty much bade farewell to fiction. During the rest of that summer and much of the following year he labored primarily on his autobiography, dictating his reminiscences for several hours a day. By 1906 he had abandoned work on the various manuscripts later published in *Which Was the Dream, Etc.* (1967).

Several comments during these years suggest that he had at least unconsciously assumed the role of a Prospero. In a letter of August 3, 1905, to his daughter Clara, he spoke fancifully of the prospect of her arriving in moccasins, feathers, and war-paint to help with the management of his New York home that autumn. And then he mentioned that he himself had burned his bow and broken his arrows. That sentiment, as John Tuckey has suggested, is close to Prospero's vow to abjure his "rough magic," to break his staff and drown his book "deeper than ever plummet sound." (Or was he echoing the passage in Act IV, scene i, where Ceres says of Cupid that "Venus' waspish-headed son has broke his arrows," and has sworn to "shoot no more, but play with sparrows / And be a boy right out"?) In any case, the following summer, while continuing work on his autobiographical dictations, Clemens several times mentioned that a number of books [including *The Mysterious Stranger*] remained unfinished because he was "tired of the pen," and felt that after "forty years of slavery" to his writing he had earned his freedom. In July, 1907, complimenting Clara on her career in music, he once more revealed how thoroughly the image of Shakespeare's artist-magician had permeated his thought. Recalling the joys of his own literary efforts "long ago," he emphasized the uniqueness of the artist's life and declared that "only genius could live splendidly, regally, in the towered and pinnacled palaces, gilt and bejeweled, which were provided by those 'splendid hellions,' the genie-slaves of the master-artist."[44] If there was a sense of relief at freedom from slavery to the pen, there was a good deal of regret as well for that "life lived long ago," for he must have been keenly aware of the diminution of his own creative powers.

Still, there continued to be bright moments among the black. Besides rejoicing in the many honors heaped upon him, he reveled in his role as a sage whose comments on current affairs were avidly sought and widely quoted. But of all the acclaim, the most gratifying came from England. There, in June, 1907, only a month before the July 25th letter to Clara, the accomplishments of his own "genie-slaves" received one of the greatest compliments ever paid them.

The Final Honor

(1907)

THOUGH MEN AND EVENTS FREQUENTLY INCURRED CLEMENS' wrath during the early years of the twentieth century, his relations with England remained cordial. In 1905 he once more felt a special affection when his seventieth birthday celebration brought a cablegram from twenty-eight of Britain's leading writers and artists, including Kipling, J. M. Barrie, A. Conan Doyle, W. S. Gilbert, Thomas Hardy, George Meredith, and Mrs. Humphrey Ward. And if Clemens really did feel abandoned by his own "genie slaves" at the time of his letter to Clara in July, 1907, the events of the preceding month had at least shown him that their earlier efforts on his behalf were widely appreciated.

The final trip to England was set in motion by a cable on May 3, 1907, from Whitelaw Reed, Clemens' old friend and former editor of the New York *Tribune,* now Ambassador to Great Britain. In 1900 Clemens had vowed never to cross the ocean again. But when Reid's cable announced that Oxford's new Chancellor, Lord Curzon, requested his presence on June 23 to receive an honorary degree, he could hardly wait to pack his bags.[1] Honorary degrees were no new things for Samuel L. Clemens, A.M., Yale, 1888; Litt. D., Yale, 1901; LL.D., Missouri, 1902, but recognition by Oxford was something else again! "I am quite well aware—and so is America, and so is the rest of Christendom—" he said, "that an Oxford decoration is a loftier distinction than is conferrable by any other university on either side of the ocean, and is worth twenty-five of any other, whether foreign or domestic." The fact that he considered the award no more than was really due him by no means minimized the thrill.[2]

Cabling his acceptance immediately, he set about making plans for this last and most triumphal English tour. His follow-up letter of thanks to Reid requested that there be no formal engagements except the two already set up—the Ambassador's own banquet on June 21, and the Pilgrims Club luncheon on the twenty-fifth. He wanted to leave plenty of time, he said, for "private dissipation and last goodbyeing" with old friends whom he would not be meeting again "without their haloes."[3]

Once in England, however, Clemens found that his time was seldom his own. During the entire three and a half weeks invitations poured in, and he found it difficult to resist any of them. Soon he was engaged for luncheon and dinner almost every day, and often for breakfast. But even the formal affairs gave him a good chance to mingle with old cronies. Many of the forty guests at the Embassy party were good friends or at least old acquaintances. Those guests whom he did not already know, he was delighted to meet.

A garden party at Windsor Castle on the twenty-second brought an opportunity for reminiscences with Edward VII about their meeting in Germany fifteen years earlier. Reporting the affair in a letter to Jean the next day, he stressed the cordiality of all—that of the king and queen being "as hearty as the heartiest." He also assured Jean that he had behaved well, except for yielding to the temptation of shaking hands with one "phenomenally beautiful" young lady, who in turn, had graciously excused his effrontery by admitting that she had been trying to find courage enough to "make the first advances herself."*

Most of the speeches for which he was called upon in the days that followed, he professed not to enjoy. Except for the one at the Pilgrims Club on the twenty-fifth and another at a dinner for American Rhodes Scholars on the twenty-eighth, they were all "cases of *had to*," he told Jean on the thirtieth, adding: "I don't like that kind."** The Pilgrims dinner, however, was a huge success. Augustine Birrell, Chief Secretary for Ireland, himself a humorist of note,

* SLC to Jean Clemens, 6/23/07, TS, Mark Twain Papers.
** SLC to Jean Clemens, 6/30/07, TS, Mark Twain Papers.

Clemens in his Oxford Robes, 1907
Mark Twain Papers

Form No. 2; 9

The Anglo-American Telegraph Company,
LIMITED
INCORPORATED, 1866.

FOUR DIRECT CABLE ROUTES
BETWEEN
THE UNITED STATES OF AMERICA AND EUROPE.

CABLEGRAM RECEIVED AT 445 BROOME ST. (Silk Exchange Building),   MAY 3 1907   190

| PLACE FROM | | No. Message | No. of Words | Received by | Time Received | |
| Q GOVT | LONDON | 28 | 33 | SU | 240PM | M |

To   S L CLEMENS CARE HARPER BROTHERS

I will come with greatest pleasure

                                                                NY

OXFORD UNIVERSITY   WOULD   CONFER   DEGREE

OF DOCTOR   OF   LETTERS   ON   YOU   ON

JUNE   26TH   BUT   PERSONAL   PRESENCE   NECESSARY

CABLE   ME   WHETHER   YOU   CAN   COME

WHITELAW   REID

Cablegram from Whitelaw Reid, forwarding
Lord Curzon's invitation to Clemens to accept
honorary degree from Oxford
Barrett Collection

The Lord Chamberlain is
commanded by Their Majesties to invite

Mr Samuel Clemens
to an Afternoon Party on Saturday
the 22nd June, 1907, from 4.30 to 7 o'clock.

Windsor Castle.   Morning Dress
                                    See other side.

Invitation to garden party at Windsor Castle
Barrett Collection

Special Trains will leave Paddington as follows:—

| Paddington | 2.45 | 2.50 | 2.57 | 3.5 | 3.10 | 3.17 | 3.25 | 3.33 | 3.37 | 3.43. |
| Windsor | 3.13 | 3.18 | 3.25 | 3.33 | 3.38 | 3.45 | 3.53 | 4.0 | 4.5 | 4.41 |

Special trains will leave Windsor from 6.30 p.m on return.

Their Majesties' Guests are requested to take advantage
as far as possible, of the early special trains in order to
prevent any over-crowding
The Pass accompanying this card must be given up to
the Officials on duty at the entrance at Windsor Castle.

introduced the speaker, applauding Clemens as a "true consolidator of nations," whose humor served to "dissipate and destroy national prejudices."

Clemens' response began in the humorous vein that was expected of him, but then he grew serious. Even when allowances are made for the exaggerations natural to such an occasion, and especially in the light of his comment to Jean, the sincerity of his emotion shows through the rhetorical flourishes. What meant most to him, he said, and what helped most to relieve his own grief and cares, were the expressions of affection in the many letters from the English people. Such warm messages made him feel that wherever he might stand under an English flag, he was "not a stranger, not an alien, but at home." Bowing amid the rousing cheers, he called forth another burst of applause with the studiedly prosaic exit-line, "I have to catch a train for Oxford."[4]

That evening he spoke again at Jesus College's "gaudeamus" dinner for old graduates. The next day came the long-awaited Convocation. The group of thirty-five who assembled at All Souls College the memorable morning of June 26 was a brilliant one. First in the line processing double-file to the Sheldonian Theater were the twenty-two candidates for the Doctorate of Civil Law, whose ranks included Prince Arthur of Connaught, Whitelaw Reid, Prime Minister Sir Henry Campbell-Bannerman, Field Marshall Sir Evelyn Wood, Lords Loreburn and Alverstone (Lord High Chancellor and Lord Chief Justice of England, respectively), Foreign Secretary Sir Edward Gray, sculptor Auguste Rodin, and General William Booth of the Salvation Army. Next came the prospective Doctors of Science, Sir Richard Powell, astronomer Sir Norman Lockyer, Sir William Ramsay, Sir William Perkin, and Professor William W. Cheyne of the Royal College of Surgeons. Following them were the Doctors of Letters: The Archbishop of Armaugh; Canon Henry Scott Holland of St. Paul's Cathedral; Henry Sayce, Fellow of Queen's College and Professor of Assyriology; Sidney Colvin, biographer, and Keeper of Prints and Drawings at the British Museum; Sidney Lee, Shakespearean scholar, and editor of the *Dictionary of National Biography;* and finally Clemens, Kipling, and the lone nominee for Doctor of Music, Camille Saint-Saëns.[5]

At the theater, while waiting in "a fine old hall" near the auditorium for ceremonies to begin, Clemens asked if smoking were permitted. It was not, but Sir William Ramsay offered to show him a place where they might be safe for a time. Joined by Kipling and Sir Norman Lockyer, they crossed an adjoining quadrangle to one of the massive arches that formed its exit, where they smoked and chatted until summoned for the ceremony.

Clemens and Kipling had not seen each other for almost ten years. But that decade had seen the bond between them strengthened by mutual sympathy in times of sorrow. In 1899 when Kipling and his daughter Josephine were critically ill in New York, Clemens eagerly watched for news of their progress, railing at the time it took for London papers to reach Vienna. With the news that Josephine had succumbed to pneumonia, memories of his visit with Kipling in the dark days after Susy's death must have flooded back to add a special poignancy to his heartfelt note of sympathy. When Olivia died in 1904, it was again Kipling's turn to supply much-appreciated condolences. A few months thereafter, hearing of Frank Doubleday's recent return from Europe, Clemens wrote to him that had he known of the trip, he would have sent Kipling "such messages of homage and affection" and would have "pressed his hand, through you, for his sympathy with me in my crushing loss," adding "You know my feeling for Kipling and that it antedates that expression."[6]

The American had been understandably puffed up in October, 1903, when Doubleday quoted a recent letter in which Kipling had said: "I love to think of the great and God-like Clemens. He is the biggest man you have on your side of the water by a damn sight, and don't you forget it. Cervantes was a relation of his." And on August 11, 1906, prompted by a news item quoting the British author, Clemens returned the compliment in much the same vein. Asserting that Kipling's name and words always stirred him more than those of any other living man, he went on to cite his friend's unique position as the only person not a head of state "whose voice is heard around the world the moment it drops a remark, the only such voice in existence that does not go by slow ship and rail but always travels first-class by cable."

Small wonder, then, that both men had eagerly anticipated their meeting at the Oxford festivities. They had, in fact, written each other, hoping to spend some time together either at Clemens' hotel or Kipling's home in Sussex, but the press of affairs had interfered. Now, however, they made the most of their opportunity and talked for more than an hour before they were called to the theater.[7]

The Convocation was a long one. From shortly after 11:00 A.M. until well past 1:00 P.M., the list of citations droned on. According to the London *Times* for June 27, if Clemens and Kipling had not been kept until near the end of the procession, many of the audience would have left long before. But the long wait had not dampened audience enthusiasm; when Clemens advanced to receive the academic accolade, the warm applause which had greeted most of the others swelled to a roar. Kipling himself was to remember a few months before his death in 1936 that "even those dignified old Oxford dons stood up and yelled."[8] Kipling, too, was fondly hailed, and then Saint-Saëns, and with the closing orations, the ceremony ended.

As the wave of well-wishers rushed at the group emerging from the auditorium, Clemens showed himself, as always, to be entirely human. He graciously consented to an interview by the young editor of Oxford's undergraduate paper, the *Varsity*. But before the excited student could begin his questioning, the new Doctor of Letters startled him with: "Young man, I want first to ask *you* a question; where is the nearest urinal?"[9]

For the two weeks following the academic ceremonies, the round of public appearances and private visits continued to occupy almost every minute. Clemens and Kipling were able to be together twice more: at a dinner in the Great Hall of Christ Church, Oxford, on the night of the *Encaenia,* and as guests of Lord Curzon at the famous Oxford historical pageant the next day. At the pageant they were both delighted by the implied tribute to their friendship when someone in the crowd thrust a folded paper at them with the words "Not true" written on the outside. Inside was the opening line from Kipling's "Ballad of East and West"—"East is East and West is West and never the *Twain* shall meet."

The pageant itself could not have been better calculated to appeal to Clemens. His love of spectacle and his feeling for the personal side of history—for the people who made it—found ample satisfaction in seeing some 3,500 citizens of Oxford in authentic costumes recreating many of the famous events of Britain's past. "It was far and away the most superb spectacle of massed and mighty and rhythmical movement and splendid costumes I have ever seen," he wrote to Jean a few days later; next to it the most spectacular efforts of grand opera seemed "poor and small and cheap and fictitious."* To Clara, the same day, he went on at length about the sense of living history afforded by the great event. The costumed townspeople wandering through Oxford's streets on their way to the meadow where the pageant itself was held, harmonized perfectly "with the quaint and mouldy old buildings." At one corner, he continued, "I . . . came suddenly upon an ecclesiastic of A.D. 710 and up went his two fingers in prelatic blessing, as he called me by name and made me welcome to his long-vanished day; and I met Charles I in the same way—oh, Charles to the life! . . . and no end of others, . . . and always it was a charming and thrilling surprise."[10]

Clemens had not often been in London without attending one of the Lord Mayor's dinners, and on June 29 he was again at the Mansion House with other members of the Savage Club as a guest of the present Lord Mayor, Sir William Purdie Treloar. On this evening he shared the limelight with the explorer Fridtjof Nansen, then Minister from Norway. Coming just the evening before his comment to Jean, his speech that night must have been one of the cases of *had-to*. But though he may not have enjoyed it himself, his host did, and took the trouble to note in his diary that "Mark Twain amused us with a humorous speech."[11]

On the Fourth of July, as in 1899, he attended the annual banquet of the American Society of London and responded to the toast "The Day We Celebrate." But if this speech also was a chore, its repetition of his hopes for Anglo-American unity and its list of America's many debts to the Motherland nevertheless re-emphasized his current affection for England. Two days later he was with the Savages again, this time at the Club itself, for a testimonial dinner in his honor, where the burden of speech-making may have been lightened somewhat by gratitude for the honorary membership bestowed during those dark days of 1897.

But a truly unique honor was yet to come. On July 9 Henry Lucy, the editor of *Punch,* invited the humorist to one of the traditional "round table" dinner meetings at the magazine's offices in Bouverie Street, Whitefriars. Almost from its beginnings in 1841, *Punch* has maintained the famous "round table," at which the editor, art editor, the regular cartoonist and perhaps five or six artists, and literary contributors of long standing, meet once a week. There, amid abundant good food and drink, they achieve their

* SLC to Jean Clemens, 6/30/07, TS, Mark Twain Papers.

primary purpose of choosing the editorial cartoon for the forth-coming issue of the magazine and their subsidiary goals of good conversation and good fellowship. The proprietors and editor of *Punch* choose the members of the group, and mere presence on the magazine's staff by no means guarantees an invitation. In fact, as a recent history of *Punch* puts it, "To be 'on the Table' is a little like being given one's colours at school." In inviting Clemens, Lucy broke a precedent of better than sixty years. For (as he later said in his diary) never before had *Punch* seen "the admission of a stranger within the sanctum."

Touched as he was by the honor, Clemens was even more touched by the climax of the evening when eight-year-old Joy Agnew, the owner's daughter, entered the room to present him with Bernard Partridge's original drawing for the editorial cartoon of June 26. In the drawing "Mr. Punch" raises a glass to Mark Twain, with the words, "Sir, I honor myself by drinking your health. Long life to you —and happiness—and perpetual youth." Always susceptible to praise, and especially to the sweet innocence of little girls, Clemens could not keep his voice from breaking when he acknowledged the presentation.[12]

Not all of his speeches were unqualified successes, however. Whitelaw Reid later remembered that his effort at the Christ Church "gaudeamus," the night of the *Encaenia* (obviously one of the *had-to's*) was long, rambling, and a little thin in its straining for humor.[13] Nor were all pleased by the attentions showered on Mark Twain. The August issue of *Blackwood's* protested violently against the adulation accorded him by public and papers alike. Raising the old cries of "flippant impertinence," "irreverence" and "lack of taste," author Charles Whibley found it impossible to grant a place on the Parnassus of true humorists to this "bull in the china shop of ideas." He did see fit to contrast what he deplored as "studied antics" (the demeaning of wonderful old Merlin to the role of a carnival charlatan, for instance) with the "genuine talent" exhibited in *Life on the Mississippi, Tom Sawyer,* and *Huckleberry Finn.* But the attack was a harsh one. Max Beerbohm let fly a brickbat with a cartoon protesting the choice of candidates for honorary degrees. In the picture, Lord Curzon, surrounded by assorted odd-looking persons in academic regalia, is shaking hands with one of them who looks like a professional wrestler. And the caption reads: "The Encaenia of 1908: Being a humble hint to the Chancellor based on

Mr. Punch toasts Mark Twain, from the original drawing
by Bernard Partridge

Mark Twain Papers

the Encaenia of 1907, whereby so many idols of the market-place were cheerily set in the groves of the Benign Mother." Yet, if Beerbohm was consciously including Mark Twain among those "idols," he was charmed when he met Clemens in person at George Bernard Shaw's luncheon for the humorist on July 3.[14]

For Clemens that luncheon with Shaw, Beerbohm, and Archibald Henderson, the playwright's biographer, was one of the trip's unexpected pleasures. He had not known Shaw before this time, except by reputation. Whether he had read any of the plays is questionable. But when Henderson, a fellow-passenger on the *Minneapolis,* introduced the two authors at the London station (the playwright had come to meet his biographer) the attraction was immediate and mutual.

Both Clemens and Shaw immensely enjoyed the gathering at Shaw's flat in Adelphi Terrace. The playwright was delighted with the flood of anecdotes which resulted when he mentioned a long-time fascination with his guest's experiences on the Mississippi. What particularly impressed him was the American's "complete gift of intimacy," which allowed the two of them to act as if they had known each other—"as indeed I had known him through his early books which I read and reveled in before I was 12 years old." Most of Shaw's own conversation, Clemens remembered, was of William Morris, "whose close friend he had been and whose memory he deeply reveres." Shaw evidently reported Morris' fondness for Mark Twain's writing and his own appreciation of the humorist's style, for Clemens' note of thanks the next day fairly bubbled over: "Between you and William Morris, I find myself richer this morning than I have ever been before. For I have my vanities, and my English has been one of them, this long time, though for many a year I had my admiration of it all to myself. But you know good English, for you are a master of it, and Morris was a competent judge, too. . . ."[15]

Summing up his impressions in an autobiographical dictation about a month later, the humorist, though less effusive, was no less complimentary. Probably with a twinkle in his eye, he noted that this mere lad of fifty-two had accomplished much as a writer. The "vague and far-off rumble which he began to make five or six years ago" had now turned to thunder, and the editorial world, which had laughed at him for four or five of those years, was obliged to reckon with him as a serious literary force. Characterizing Shaw as "pleasant . . . simple, direct, sincere, animated; but self-possessed, sane, and evenly poised, acute, engaging, companionable and quite destitute of affectations," Clemens concluded his reminiscence with a simple and direct accolade, "I liked him."[16]

Shaw, in turn, left no doubt that besides the American's personality, he appreciated the latter's efforts to point up the faults and flaws in society. A note, written the same day as the luncheon, assured Clemens that the future historians of America would find his works as "indispensable" as the French historian finds the political works of Voltaire. "I tell you so," he continued, "because I am the author of a play in which a priest says, 'Telling the truth is the funniest joke in the world,' a piece of wisdom which you helped to teach me." Few compliments could have been better calculated to please.[17]

The one serious unpleasantness of the visit itself came when Clemens gave in to the urgings of the novelist Marie Corelli to call at her home in Stratford-on-Avon. Having reluctantly agreed, on condition that there be no large gathering nor expectation of a speech, he was appalled to find not only a crowd of admirers but the student body of a nearby military school drawn up in an adjoining field, eagerly awaiting words of wisdom from the famous American. He did not let them down, but Marie Corelli thenceforth found a permanent place on his list of pet aversions.[18]

The dissenting voices and the irritations, however, were few. When the time came for him once again to sail for America, the old reluctance to leave engulfed him just as it had thirty-five years earlier. But now it was heightened by the knowledge that he would probably never return to England.

All his joy and gratitude for the attention paid him, and his sadness over leaving, he poured into a farewell speech at the banquet given for him by the Lord Mayor of Liverpool on July 10. For his climax he built upon an incident which he had stored away in his notebook as early as 1888 and had noted again in 1890 and 1903, as if waiting for just the right occasion to use it. Now the proper time was here. Vividly and dramatically Clemens sketched the portrait of a pompous skipper of a small coastal steamer who, though he carried only commonplace goods, habitually hailed all passing ships, as if to show off his own small grandeur. When, one day, a "majestic Indiaman" with towering canvas and a rich cargo of Oriental luxuries crossed his course, the skipper followed his usual practice of demanding its name, origin, and destination. Loud and clear its answer boomed out: "The *Begum of Bengal,* one-hundred and forty-two days out from Canton, homeward bound! What ship is that?" His vanity soundly crushed, the skipper managed a weak "Only the *Mary Ann,* fourteen miles out from Boston, bound for Kittery Point—with nothing to speak of."

Stressing the abject humility hanging upon that word "only," Clemens described his own position. During the one hour of the twenty-four in which he paused to reflect, he was humble—"only the *Mary Ann,* fourteen hours out, cargoed with vegetables and tinware." But during the other twenty-three, he said "my vain self-complacency rides high on the white crest of your approval, and then I am a stately Indiaman, ploughing the great seas under a cloud of canvas and laden with the kindest words that have ever been vouchsafed to any wandering alien in this world, I think; then my twenty-six fortunate days on this old mother soil seem to be multiplied by six, and *I* am the *Begum of Bengal,* one hundred and forty-two days out from Canton, homeward bound."[19]

Given the real emotion which lay behind the rhetoric and the consummate artistry of Clemens' delivery, it is likely that few eyes were dry when he finished.

Three days later, after a final round of goodbyes in London, Clemens was in fact homeward bound. True to his many predictions he did not see England again. He planned to recapture some of the thrills of the Oxford visit by attending the even more lavish historical pageant to be presented in London during the summer of 1910. But his hopes of rejoicing at the sight of 15,000 historical personages "dug from the misty books of all the vanished ages and marching in the light of the sun—all alive."[20] were cancelled by his death on April 21 of that year.

If Clemens felt any animosity toward England during the two and one-half years between his departure and his death, it did not show. Some of his happiest times were those spent in Bermuda, the place he had described in 1877 as "grovelling in contentment" under the efficient British rule. With his renewed appreciation of the kinship between England and America in the late 1890's crowned by the honor of the Oxford degree, he had come almost full circle to the affection of the 'seventies. Whatever the other cares and griefs and discouragements of his last years, Clemens and England were at peace.

Clemens in his library, 1908 or 1909

Mark Twain Papers

MARK TWAIN & BRITISH AUTHORS

IN THE MAIN BODY OF THIS BOOK I have suggested the important roles
played by some British authors in the development of Clemens' ideas.
Additional insights into his relationships with Britain and his debts to
her writers may be gained through a consideration of his knowledge of
other authors who do not fit easily into the chronology of the foregoing
discussion. Hence these postscript pages.

As indicated in the Foreword, I have made no attempt to produce
here a definitive list of all British writers whose works Clemens may have
read. Rather, I have again emphasized his actual use of specific elements
derived from his readings. I have not dealt, however, with the humorist's
extensive knowledge of historical and scientific works beyond those already treated; nor have I attempted to analyze his debt to the King
James Version of the Bible, a subject that could fill a small volume of its
own. Except in a few instances which supplement material introduced
in earlier chapters, I have concentrated chiefly on *belles lettres*.

I

The Eighteenth Century and Earlier

EXCEPT FOR MALORY's *Le Morte Darthur* and some of the volumes
available in Bohn's Antiquarian Library Series, like the *Chronicles
of Henry of Huntington* and Ingulph's *Chronicle of the Abbey of Croyland,* Clemens' first-hand reading of English literature before Shake-

speare seems to have been slight. The works and authors he does mention, he perhaps knew chiefly from secondary sources like Taine's *History of English Literature,* a book that he prized. Possibly the angel Sandy, in *Captain Stormfield's Visit to Heaven,* spoke for the author when he told Stormfield (in Chapter Four) that talking with inhabitants of the English district of heaven became extremely difficult "the minute you get back of Elizabeth's time." He had tried, he said, to talk with "one Langland and a man by the name of Chaucer—old-time poets—but it was no use, I couldn't quite understand them, and they couldn't quite understand me."[1]

Clemens knew the *Canterbury Tales,* however, and liked them well enough to jot down some notes early in 1897 for an operetta or fantasy to be titled, "The Pilgrimage to Canterbury," with Chaucer himself in a featured role. Before that he had bestowed many of the characteristics of Chaucer's pilgrims on his own group in Chapter Twenty-one of *A Connecticut Yankee,* specifically citing their variety of occupations and attitudes. Though his greatest emphasis was on their slavery to superstition, he used the allusion to Chaucer chiefly to stress the coarseness and indelicacy of some of the "merry tales" which they told. And to sharpen his jabs at England generally, he added that the members received those tales "with no more embarrassment than [they] would have caused in the best English society twelve centuries later."

The plays of Shakespeare early attracted Clemens. Long before he and George Ealer enlivened the long hours in the pilothouse with readings and literary discussions, the young writer had already developed interest in the theater. He had seen a number of Shakespearean performances of varying excellence—the river-town rendition of *Richard III* which he would later resurrect in the ludicrous sword-fight in *Huckleberry Finn;* an amateur *Merchant of Venice* and a professional *Julius Caesar* in St. Louis, and in Washington, D.C., Edwin Forrest's *Othello.*[2] But it was probably Ealer who sparked the real development of his affection for Shakespeare's works.

The fact that Clemens ultimately adopted a version of the "Baconian heresy" (which he claimed to have championed at first simply for the sake of argument with Ealer) by no means diminished his admiration for the plays nor for the talent which produced them. He was fascinated by the "Gobelin loom" of Shakespeare's mind, which could produce "that pictured and gorgeous fabric which still compels the astonishment of the world." In January, 1889, when the Paige typesetter was temporarily in operation, Clemens himself tapped out "William Shakspeare" as the first proper name to be set on the machine. A walk through Chelsea one February morning in 1897 inspired a notebook comment concerning the pleasant sight of "Shakespeare's people all on hand, as usual." At least twice during the early 1900's he recorded the fact that April 23 marked the birth date of the great poet.[3]

In his own writings Clemens levied frequently on Shakespeare to make a point or to enhance a description. His many allusions show that he knew most, if not all, of the plays, and at least *Venus and Adonis* among the poems. His first significant use occurred in 1864, when he drew heavily on one of his favorites for a burlesque sketch, "The Killing of Julius Caesar 'Localized.' "[4]

The piece, published in the San Francisco *Californian* on November 12, is a more skillful burlesque than has generally been noted. At first glance it seems aimed simply at getting a laugh from the sometimes ludicrous clash of the narrator's modern idiom with the readers' memories of the eloquence of Shakespeare. But the sketch also satirizes contemporary journalistic practices. It begins with the narrator's comment on how violence and especially murder inspires the efforts of newspaper reporters. He mourns losing the "scoop" that might have been his had he lived in Caesar's Rome, for the famous assassination had "all the characteristics of an 'item' of the present day, magnified into grandeur and sublimity" by the rank and fame of the participants. But then to soothe his grief he presents his "translation" of an account which had appeared in *The Roman Daily Evening Fasces* shortly after the event. With all journalistic clichés flying, he records the incidents leading up to the assassination, the "killing" itself, and a warning that riots are likely to result from the funeral speeches of Antony and Brutus. So little has the treatment of such "items" as murders (and even the language in which they are reported) changed since the sketch was written, the satire is almost as appropriate for our own day as for the mid-nineteenth century.

Much of Clemens' use of Shakespeare continued the burlesque vein of the early references. *Hamlet,* particularly, furnished a real source of fun. In 1857, Thomas Jefferson Snodgrass denied to readers of the Keokuk *Daily Post* that his long silence meant he had "shuffled off this mortal quile." In the Sandwich Island letters of 1866, Mark Twain's companion Mr. Brown regurgitates over "Mr. Twain's" pious paraphrase of Polonius' advice to Laertes.[5] But Clemens' real study of the play probably began in 1873. One evening in London, during a backstage chat with Edwin Booth, the humorist introduced the notion that the play might be revised so as to insert a contemporary character. Booth allegedly greeted the suggestion with "immoderate laughter"—one wonders whether *with* or *at* the idea.

Whichever it was, Clemens briefly attempted a revision at the time, dropped it, and then picked it up again in 1881. Into that version he introduced one Basil Stockmar, "a book agent with a canvassing copy," and foster brother to Hamlet, by virtue of their having had the same wet-nurse. Basil first sets the situation—his hope to achieve status by presenting his spiel to Denmark's royal family—and then Shakespeare's play begins, with Basil's country vernacular providing "smart" commentary on the characters and incidents. When the ghost of Hamlet's father appears, for instance, Basil overcomes his first fright by concluding that what the ghost really wanted was to subscribe to his book.

Enthusiasm for this project lasted only long enough to carry Stockmar to the end of the second scene in Act II. But though Basil died there, he continued to be attractive to his author. As late as 1897, Clemens again reminded himself to write a piece involving Hamlet's "country cousin," but this time to make him a character in the drama itself rather than just a commentator on the action. At this point, too, Clemens recalled, probably incorrectly, that Booth had urged him to try such a scheme and, more accurately, that the attempt had been a failure.[6] The effort was not a total loss, perhaps, for the practice which Stockmar provided may have helped his author take the brash Connecticut Yankee to Camelot.

Specific echoes from *Hamlet* were also to appear in *A Connecticut Yankee*. In Chapter Fifteen a line from the famous "advice to the players" creeps in to add a fillip to Sandy's musings over the intricacies of Hank Morgan's slang. Asked where the ogres "hang out," she plays with the phrase: "Hang they out . . . where hang—where do they hang out. . . . the phrase hath a fair and winsome grace. . . . Even so! already it falleth trippingly from my tongue." In Chapter Thirty-nine, Sir Sagramor le Desirous clad in an all-enveloping "web of gossamer threads," provided by Merlin's "magic" and designed to befuddle the Boss, is likened to "Hamlet's ghost."[7]

By far the most skillful use of the play, however, had come several years earlier in *Huckleberry Finn* (Chapter Twenty-one) where the bogus Duke summons "from recollection's vaults" his version of the great "To be or not to be" soliloquy (Act III, Scene i). Sixteen garbled and rearranged lines from that piece form the basis of the Duke's oration. But the author also borrowed, for good measure, all or part of three lines from Act I (i, iv) and two from Act III (ii) of *Hamlet,* five lines from four scenes in *Macbeth* (IV, i; II, i, iii; I, vii), and one from the first scene of *Richard III*. A draft of the passage on the back of an envelope presumably jotted down on March 19, 1883, suggests that Clemens set down the piece from memory, and so accurately that he made only minor changes when he transferred it to the novel.[8]

Burlesques of Shakespeare were fairly common among the thespians who "worked" the river towns during Clemens' youth. Henry B. Fearon, one of the British travelers consulted for *Life on the Mississippi,* mentions a burlesque of *Hamlet* itself. In his *Reminiscences* (1854) the famous theatrical agent and actor, Sol Smith, records the unintentional burlesque provided when an elocutionist, annoyed by the inattentiveness of his audience, interspersed the "seven ages of man" speech from *As You Like It* with exasperated comments to his listeners. That same device Clemens himself was to use in *Is Shakespeare Dead?* (1909), where he portrays George Ealer declaiming the passage from *Macbeth* (III, iv) which begins, "What man dare I dare," while barking salty commands at the steamboat deckhands between the lines.[9]

Whatever its immediate inspiration, the Duke's garbled soliloquy, with its wild *non sequiturs* that just miss being meaningful, is a more unified piece of burlesque than those already mentioned. More important, as Walter Blair notes, this farcical treatment of Hamlet's musings on the nature of death is significant dramatically and thematically in *Huckleberry Finn*. Not only does it add another facet to the Duke's fraudulent character, but it also introduces succeeding episodes which are themselves fundamentally farcical, but which end in violence and murder.[10]

Note should be made also of the parallel to *Romeo and Juliet* in *Huckleberry Finn*. The travesty of the balcony scene by the King and Duke may be read as a comic underscoring of the more tragic travesty of the chivalric code of honor in the feud between the Grangerfords and the Shepherdsons, which forces the runaway marriage of Sophia Grangerford and Harney Shepherdson.

Next to *Hamlet,* the chronicle plays *Henry IV* and *Henry V* yielded most grist for Mark Twain's mill. In one of his letters to the Sacramento *Union* in 1866, the young correspondent relied on his readers' knowledge of the plays when he noted that the Hawaiian King Kamehameha had caroused wildly during his youth but then had "renounced his bad habits and rejected his Falstaffs" to become a thoroughly responsible ruler. When the humorist gathered his ribald group at Queen Elizabeth's fireside some ten years later, he had "Shakspur" read them parts of *Henry IV,* presumably those dealing with Falstaff's amorous exploits. About the same time, many of the insults hurled at Falstaff by his fellows, along with other bits of dialogue from *Henry IV,* found their way into the list of "Middle Age phrases" for the "historical story" that ultimately became *The Prince and the Pauper.* Describing the great London parade in "Queen Victoria's Jubilee" (1897), the humorist, for purposes of comparison, introduces an "eyewitness" account of the procession that had honored Henry V's triumph at Agincourt, in which Falstaff appears as his own progenitor, Sir John Oldcastle. Nodding to the obvious anachronism of his appearance *after* Agincourt (Falstaff's death is described in Act II of *Henry V*), the "spirit-correspondent" notes that Sir John is "now risen from the dead for the third time." Followed by his "infamous lieutenants" and his "paladins"—the "mangiest lot of starvelings and cowards that was ever littered," he marches along "fat-faced, purple with the spirit of bygone and lamented drink," smiling a "hospitable, wide smile upon all the world," and "leering at the women." Characteristically "taking the whole glory of Agincourt to his single self," he measures off "the miles of his slain . . . multiplying them by 5, 7, 10, 15, as inspiration after inspiration came to his help. . . ."[11]

Probably it was the "spirit-correspondent" rather than Clemens who considered Sir John "a living, breathing outrage" and "a slander upon the human race." But even if the author shared his narrator's opinion, a part of him reveled in the braggart side of Falstaff's nature. For only a few years earlier he had revived Sir John in *Joan of Arc* (1896) as the boastful standard-bearer, Edmund Aubrey, who was "called the Paladin because of the armies he was always going to eat up some day."

Aubrey's boasts of prowess, it is true, were limited to the field of battle rather than those of bed or bottle, but from the very first, his parentage is plain. Wherever he roams, his vast gift for story-telling makes him the center of attraction. With his appearance, something of the atmosphere of Dame Quickly's tavern descends upon the inns of the villages near where Joan's army encamps. At one of these (Chapter Seven, Book Two), an episode from *II Henry IV* (II, iv) recurs as Sieur Louis de Conte and Noel Rainguesson bribe the hostess of the inn to admit them to a private parlor so that they may eavesdrop upon the pompous Paladin and later deflate him, much as Prince Hal and Poins had disguised themselves as drawers in order to spy on and later discomfit their friend Falstaff.

On the several occasions when Louis analyzes Aubrey's character, he makes explicit what is implicit in Shakespeare's portrait of Falstaff. Speaking of the incident at the inn, Louis explains that the Paladin's boasting was not really aimed at deceiving his listeners; the tales merely burgeoned and bloomed under the enthusiasm of their narrator, who continued wholeheartedly to believe them himself. And just as Falstaff's libelling of Prince Hal and Poins sprang not from malice, but from the same sort of self-aggrandizement as the tales, so the Paladin's aspersions upon the courage of Noel Rainguesson at the time of their impressment (Book Two, Chapter Three) were likewise untouched by malice.

Noel Rainguesson's relationship to Aubrey is much like that of Prince Hal's to Falstaff. Both encourage the excesses of their companions for the entertainment that results. Louis de Conte might well have been describing Prince Hal when he says that Noel's "careless light heart had to have somebody to nag and chaff and make fun of," and since the Paladin had "only needed development in order to meet its requirements," that development "was taken in hand and diligently attended to and looked after, gnat-and-bull fashion, for years, to the neglect and damage of far more important concerns."

Other episodes from Book II of *Joan of Arc* also echo those in Shakespeare's play. The "recruitment" of Noel, the Paladin, and four others in Chapter Three parallels Falstaff's impressment of Mouldy, Bullcalf, and four others (*II Henry IV*, III, ii). In Chapter Five Noel discusses Aubrey's "discretion," expanding upon Falstaff's famous comment about "the better part of valor." And Noel's remark that the Paladin had emerged from his hiding place in the bushes to "attack a dead man single-handed" recalls Falstaff's feigning death and subsequent stabbing of Hotspur's corpse (*I Henry IV*, V, iv). Falstaff's triumphant exit with the dead body flung over his shoulder is magnified in the Paladin's story of how, at Patay, he and his followers had slaughtered all of the English but the leaders Talbot and Fastolfe, whom he himself had saved "and brought away, one under each arm" (Chapter Thirty-nine). Finally, Falstaff's ironic disquisition on "honor" (V, i) finds its counterpart in the Paladin's praise of the "merit" which had elevated him to his lofty position as Joan's standard-bearer (Chapter Twenty-four).

More generally, the comic incidents involving the Paladin and his cronies, like the Falstaff episodes, fill the time between scenes at court or on the battlefield. Even though the Paladin is only a shadow of his great forebear, many of the scenes of his boasting and discomfiture provide a high order of comedy. Like Shakespeare, too, the author uses his boaster to help reveal the true character of his protagonist. Prince Hal, fond of Falstaff and amused by his extravagances, encourages his profligacy and buffoonery. But later, under the stress of his new responsibilities as king, he rightly (though some have argued the point) rejects

Sir John, and with him all youthful folly. Joan, too, is fond of the Paladin and greatly amused by him. In her case, however, the giving up of youthful folly is not involved. Rather, her assigning the Paladin to a position of responsibility and through the force of her own noble character making a truly brave hero of him, serves to point up her essential goodness. Hence, unlike the pathetic death of the lonely Falstaff, the Paladin's death occurs at Joan's side in the fateful battle for Compiègne, where he has fought valiantly to the last. Sentimental as the braggart's reformation is, it is true to the spirit of Clemens' story as yet another illustration of Joan's all-but-miraculous goodness.

Clemens drew copiously upon Shakespeare for assistance in emphasizing a point or expressing an emotion. To mention only a few instances (see Note 12 for others), in August, 1880, he jotted down part of Portia's "quality of mercy speech" from *The Merchant of Venice* (IV, i) to be used as an epigraph for *The Prince and the Pauper*.[12] At the time of Susy's death, he perhaps derived some solace from Macbeth's description of the dead King Duncan (III, ii), for he wrote to Livy (with appropriate change of gender): "After life's fitful fever, she sleeps well." When Jean died in 1909, he made that line her epitaph. One of his most eloquent borrowings, in a much happier mood, was his message in 1906 to Ellen Terry, then celebrating her fiftieth year on the stage. Pleased to honor the famous actress, whom he had known since his first visit to England in 1872, he called upon Enobarbus' tribute to Cleopatra—"Age cannot wither her, nor custom stale her infinite variety" (II, ii). No doubt also thinking of Antony's comment that Augustus wore "the rose of youth upon him" (III, xiii) he cabled: "Age has not withered, nor custom staled, the admiration and affection I have felt for you so many many years. I lay them at your honored feet with the strength and freshness of their youth upon them undiminished."[13]

More generally, the humorist several times praised Shakespeare for his contributions to the betterment of man. In 1871, incensed by the Reverend Mr. Sabine's refusal to conduct funeral services in his church for actor George Holland, Mark Twain blasted the minister's notion that the stage taught no moral lessons. "Where was ever a sermon preached that could make filial ingratitude so hateful to men as the sinful play of 'King Lear'?" he queried his *Galaxy* readers. "Or where was there ever a sermon that could so convince men of the wrong and cruelty of harboring a pampered and unanalyzed jealousy as the sinful play of 'Othello'?" A quarter-century later he was advocating establishment of a New York theater devoted exclusively to tragedy, where patrons could enjoy the refreshment of mind and heart provided by a climb among "the intellectual snow-summits" built by Shakespeare and the other great tragedians.[14] Though Clemens may have accepted the argument that the Shakespeare of Stratford-on-Avon did not write the works attributed to him, he obviously loved the works themselves.

Of Clemens' acquaintance with and use of works by Shakespeare's contemporaries and immediate successors, specific evidence is scanty. In 1893 he reminded himself to return "Sir Philip Sidney" to a friend. He owned and marked a copy of the *Diary and Correspondence of John Evelyn* (ed. William Bray, London, 1872). The cup-bearer in *1601* speaks of the ladies being pupils of that "poor ass, Lille [Lyly]" and of Shakespeare's and Jonson's unwillingness to vent their scorn since the queen was "ye very flower of ye Euphuists herself." Of those others present at the fireside, Clemens knew Beaumont's (and Fletcher's) *A King and No King* well enough to compare the careers of certain Civil War generals notable for their retreats with the exploits of the cowardly braggart, Bessus. Perkin Warbeck, whom he mentions in "Is Shakespeare Dead?" he probably knew from his reading of history rather than from John Ford's play. What he knew of Sir Francis Bacon's work and what he used in "Is Shakespeare Dead? doubtless derived chiefly from Macaulay's essay on Bacon and from the writings of the Baconian "heretics."[15]

The two giants of English Puritanism, John Milton and John Bunyan, Clemens knew better.[16] If not before, he doubtless encountered *Paradise Lost* among the volumes on Ealer's pilothouse shelves, for in 1858 he was writing to Orion that he considered "the Arch-Fiend's terrible energy" the "grandest thing" in Milton's poem. His reaction to Milton was a mixed one, however. In 1869 he said he looked forward to sharing with Olivia "the drum-beats of Milton's stately sentences." But in 1877 he included *Paradise Lost* among several works which he would have burnt had their authors submitted them to him as a publisher; and in 1900 he named it a "classic"—"a work that everybody wants to have read and nobody wants to read."[17]

How much of Clemens' fascination with Satan and with the Adam and Eve story stemmed from *Paradise Lost* cannot be estimated with any accuracy, but certainly there was some influence. The strong appeal of the "Arch-Fiend's terrible energy" unquestionably was among the elements which ultimately created *The Mysterious Stranger* and "Letters from the Earth." In 1904, moreover, the author presented a peculiarly prophetic embodiment of that "terrible energy" in a sketch which combined his interest both in Satan and in science.

Though basically a burlesque, "Sold to Satan" has unusually serious implications. As the narrator haggles with the Devil over the price of his soul, the Arch-Fiend reveals that he is made of radium. Here, only six years after Pierre and Marie Curie discovered the element, Mark Twain and Satan discuss in some detail the great power latent in even small amounts of the substance. Shades of our present dilemma arise when the author has Satan say: "I can release from my body the radium force in any measure I please, great or small; at my will, I can set in motion the works of a lady's watch or destroy a world." And the fear that was born when the mushroom cloud rose over Hiroshima in August, 1945, finds one of its earliest forecasts in Satan's assertion that if he peeled off the "skin" which controlled the forces raging within him, "the world would vanish away in a flash of flame and a puff of smoke, and the remnants of the extinguished moon would sift down through space a mere snow-shower of gray ashes!"[18]

Another prognosis of "things to come" in Chapter Eight of *The Mysterious Stranger* seems to point directly back to *Paradise Lost*. As Coleman O. Parsons has suggested, the visions which Satan calls up for the boys, to show them "the progress of the human race," probably owes much to Michael's projection for Adam (in Book Eleven) of that same history—from the first murder to the Flood.[19] Michael's various examples of "The whole Earth fill'd with violence, and all flesh corrupting," find a parallel in Satan's "entertainment." Beginning also with Cain's murder of Abel, the latter goes well beyond the Flood to foresee slaughters of the future, "more terrible in their destruction of life, more devastating in their engines of war, than any we had seen." But rather than the hope which Adam finds in Michael's continuing account of the eventual salvation of man through Christ (in Book Twelve), the underlying despair of *The Mysterious Stranger* is reinforced by Satan's conclusion that since the Christian era had so greatly improved deadly weapons, all men would some day confess that "without Christian civilization, war must have remained a poor and trifling thing to the end of time."

Some years earlier, in the essay he appended to *A Tramp Abroad* (1880), Clemens called in a specific echo of *Paradise Lost* to help express his humorous exasperation with the intricacies of "The Awful German Language." The difficulties of distinguishing among the complex variations of gender, case, and auxiliary verb forms must have suggested a comic parallel to the problems facing Adam and Eve as they wandered from Eden to make a new life for themselves—"The world was all before them, where to choose / Their place of rest. . . ." With the world of German syntax before him, Mark Twain all but throws up his hands and comments, "Well, take your choice . . . as Goethe says in his Paradise Lost."

Milton and Bunyan almost merged for Clemens at one point. In September, 1887, inspired by a fresh reminder of the Shakespeare-Bacon controversy, he filled a number of notebook pages with suggestions for an elaborate analysis designed to "prove" that it was actually Milton who wrote *The Pilgrim's Progress.* Clemens had either done, or proposed to do a good deal of research into the subject, for he also listed the names of four noted Milton scholars: John Toland, Henry J. Todd, Charles Symmons, and Thomas Keightly, as well as a reference to "Southey's Bunyan." The project may have been an interesting one, but it is probably fortunate that it went no farther than the planning stage.

Shortly thereafter, the humorist outlined another scheme which might prove profitable when he got around to it "someday." He would dress a group of models as characters from *The Pilgrim's Progress* and photograph them in appropriate spots throughout the world—in a wild gorge for the "Valley of the Shadow of Death," for instance, and in the "Vanity Fair" of Paris. The resulting "stereoptical panorama" could then be exhibited to admiring audiences in many countries. But again the project died a-borning.[20]

Though Clemens obviously knew the book well, specific allusions to *The Pilgrim's Progress* are rare in his fiction. He several times toyed with the idea of incorporating parts of Bunyan's vision of Paradise into *Captain Stormfield's Visit to Heaven.* He once filled some seven manuscript pages with the Puritan's description of the Celestial City; and as late as 1897 he proposed that Stormfield should visit "several old abandoned heavens," among which Bunyan's would be of interest as "a historical-theological Tower of London."* Certainly the antipathy toward the orthodox conception of heaven as filled with psalm-singing, palm-waving, harp-playing holy ones, which the author attacked so humorously in *Captain Stormfield* and so harshly in "Letters from the Earth," must have found some of its first stirrings in the early readings of *The Pilgrim's Progress.*[21]

He did adopt *The New Pilgrims' Progress* as a subtitle for *The Innocents Abroad,* and the adventures and misadventures of this group

* Notebook 32a II, TS, p. 40, Mark Twain Papers.

en route to the Holy Land doubtless gain some comic force by association with the serious struggles of Christian to reach the Celestial City. But the most important reference found its way into Chapter Seventeen of *Huckleberry Finn* to add a touch to the description of the Grangerford parlor and, at the same time, to the character of Huck himself. Huck's comment that *Pilgrim's Progress* was "about a man that left his family, it didn't say why," points up his realistic approach to life. The fact that he "read considerable in it," finding that "the statements was interesting, but tough," suggests his instinctive appreciation of human problems. The allusion likewise foreshadows the many obstacles he will continue to encounter during his pilgrimage down the Mississippi; and his own moral decisions become "interesting but tough." Finally, the thought that what awaits him at the end of his journey is not the triumph of a Celestial City but the travesty at Phelpses' farm strengthens the dark undercurrent of the book.

Mark Twain's works in a number of respects look back to the eighteenth century. Much of what he inherited from the Southwestern Humorists had its origin in the theories and practice of the English humorists of the Enlightenment. His several assertions that his own humor sought fundamentally to "preach" place him squarely in the neo-classical tradition. As Miss Brashear has noted, he employed many of the literary forms favored by eighteenth-century English authors: "the character, the informal essay, the apologue, the maxim, and the picaresque-like narrative."22 Certainly the deistic philosophy of such writers as Tom Paine contributed important groundwork for Clemens' view of God and the universe. Nevertheless, one must not over-emphasize the eighteenth-century provenience. Though the author's roots may have been deep in the Enlightenment, most of the elements of his literary practice and the philosophical and scientific ideas that attracted him came largely through the writers of his own century. Once that fact is recognized, however, some of his specific debts to the eighteenth-century authors are well worth noting.

The wondrous adventures of Lemuel Gulliver early attracted young Sam. After one of his excursions into Swift's masterpiece, he decreed that one of his Hannibal gang, Norval Brady, should thenceforth be called "Gull." In the Hannibal *Journal* for September 23, 1852, Clemens' early *alter ego*, W. Epaminondas Adrastus Blab, sounds much like Gulliver himself when he informs the editor of his projected "furrin' tour" to Glascock's Island, and promises to gratify such readers "as have never been so far from home, with an account of this great island, and my voyage thither." Two years later Swift helped Sam picture for the readers of another *Journal* in Muscatine, Iowa, the confusion of dwellings in Washington, D.C., which looked as though "some Brobdignagian [*sic*] gentleman" had emptied them out of a sack.[23]

The same sort of astonishment which greets many adults who reread *Gulliver* hit Clemens during a lecture tour in 1869. He had always been intrigued by the book's "prodigies" and its "marvels," but now he saw what a "scathing satire" of Britain's government the book really was. Secure in his love for Olivia—he was writing these comments to her during their courtship—Clemens even ventured a somewhat patronizing pity for "Poor Swift," whose "simply-worded" book concealed under its placid surface the "full tide of his venom—the turbid sea of his matchless hate." Despite his own enthusiasm, however, Clemens did not think the book proper fare for young ladies. If Olivia wished to read it, he would censor it for her, lest her pure mind be contaminated by some of the coarser passages.[24]

When he came to read Thackeray's *English Humorists of the Eighteenth Century,* Clemens found support for that characteristic Victorian disapproval. In the margins he jotted bitter notes about Swift's "prurient taste" and his trifling with the affections of Stella and Vanessa. He agreed, too, with Thackeray's general criticism of Swift's tendency to truckle to superiors and to bully those whom he considered inferior. Nevertheless, the character of the great Dean fascinated him in its "startling contrasts—of goodness & badness, of worth & unworthiness, of greatness & littleness, of towering pride & cringing baseness, of feeble love & fickle hate, of imperial genius & groveling vulgarity & obscenity." He concurred heartily with Thackeray's judgment that Swift and his career represented "an immense genius; an awful downfall and ruin," to consider which "is like thinking of an empire falling." Underlining the last seven words, he pronounced the whole passage "an able summing up."[25]

Besides its probable influence on Clemens' satirical report of a journey to "The Curious Republic of Gondour" (1875), *Gulliver's Travels* left its mark in a number of other specific instances. The humorist was obviously intrigued with the concepts of Lilliput and Brobdingnag. In Chapter Three of *Roughing It* (1872), the narrator enlivens a siesta in the sagebrush with the notion that he is "some vast loafer from Brobdingnag," peering out from under a bush and imagining that "the gnats among its foliage were lilliputian birds, and that the ants marching and countermarching about its base were lilliputian flocks and herds." In this case, the allusion does more than merely add a descriptive touch. The narrator has been brought to his reverie by recalling his first long-awaited glimpse of Western sagebrush, which looked to him like "a gnarled and venerable live oak tree reduced to a little shrub two feet high." Hence the "lilliputian flocks and herds" continue a miniaturization of the scene. The whole episode, in turn, becomes an element in the theme of the novel—the initiation of the romantic tenderfoot to the realities of life in the "wide, open spaces." A portion of the "grandeur" which he had expected in the West lies before him in the "little shrub two feet high" and its Lilliputian inhabitants.

On the occasion of Henry Ward Beecher's death some fifteen years later, Lilliput again came to Clemens' mind, this time with a more Swiftian sting. Remembering the Beecher-Tilton adultery trial of 1874, he exclaimed to Joe Twichell about the irony of a situation in which "so insignificant a matter as the chastity or unchastity of an Elizabeth Tilton could clip the locks of this Samson & make him as other men, in the estimation of a nation of Lilliputians creeping & climbing about his shoe-soles."[26] He called again on Lilliput's opposite number for a vivid detail when he wrote to Olivia in 1902 that the wreck of the battleship *Maine* in Havana Harbor looked like "a brobdignagian [*sic*] tarantula in its death squirm."*

Other reductions of man and his pretensions almost surely owe their inspirations to Swift. The learned bugs, reptiles, and rodents of "Some Fables for Good Old Boys and Girls" (first published in 1875 in *Sketches New and Old*), with their proclivities for building "a mountain of facts out of a spoonful of supposition" reflect the various attacks on "projectors" in *Gulliver* as well as the emphasis on the pettiness and pomposity of man in general. *Tom Sawyer Abroad* (1894) also furnishes numerous pictures of the tininess of man as the "erronorts" float high above the insect-like beings below. At one point, too, Clemens has Tom refer to Jim and Huck as "Yahoos" when they fail to understand an explanation, and Huck uses the same term to describe a desert robber trying to kidnap a child. In the unfinished "3000 Years Among the Microbes," the author reduces the pretensions of man even farther by bestowing them on microscopic organisms, two of whom he names Lem Gulliver and Lurbrulgrud. And perhaps even the time-travels of the Connecticut Yankee and his thoughts of himself as a giant among the

* SLC to Olivia L. Clemens, 3/4/02, Mark Twain Papers.

"pigmies" of Arthurian England derive partly from his creator's memories of Gulliver's adventures in Lilliput.[27]

Clemens apparently found Swift lacking in humanity, a quality which was for him essential in a writer. His summary at the end of Thackeray's essay, for instance, proclaims the satirist "a bare glittering iceberg" of "mere intellectual greatness," devoid of "every tender grace, every kindly humanizing element." He was probably not conscious—at least at that time—of how closely his own attitudes toward man approached those of Swift. Yet in a letter to Olivia in July, 1889, he all but repeated Swift's famous comment to Alexander Pope about loving individuals but hating man in the mass. As if trying to reach out for hope, Clemens was arguing for the preponderance of good over evil in the world; for evidence he cited the fact that among "the various Tom-Dick & Harry's" whom he knew, he found "goodness the rule & ungoodness the exception." And then: "I detest Man, but nevertheless this is true of him."[28]

Even more strikingly Swiftian are some of Clemens' descriptions of "the damned human race" in the late 1890's. In Chapter Three of *The Mysterious Stranger*, Satan, though much interested in mankind, pronounces men "dull and ignorant and trivial and conceited, . . . a shabby, poor, worthless lot all around." In a note for the story, not subsequently used, the author also speaks of the earth as a living animal and describes "the stinking little human race" as "the vermin that infest it."[29] Given Clemens' fascination with Lilliput and Brobdingnag, it is difficult not to hear in Satan's comments specific echoes of the famous judgment of the King of Brobdingnag (Part Two, Chapter Six) that Gulliver's countrymen must be "the most pernicious race of little odious vermin that nature ever suffered to crawl upon the surface of the earth."

Whether consciously or unconsciously, Clemens came to share Swift's view of man, and consciously or unconsciously made good use of *Gulliver's Travels*.

The great fathers of the English novel, Defoe, Fielding, Richardson, Smollett, and Sterne also found places on Clemens' library shelves. But except for *Robinson Crusoe,* their works seem to have become important to him primarily as symbols of the coarseness of eighteenth-century England. When he wrote to Olivia about *Gulliver* in 1869, Clemens had recently finished *Tristram Shandy* as well, but though he praised the "Recording Angel" passage, he could recommend none of that novel as fit for her to read. His several references to Fielding and Smollett in *A Tramp Abroad* (1880), a speech "On Foreign Critics" (1888), and *A Con-*

necticut Yankee (1889) stress the indelicacy of language and situation in
their novels. About 1880, too, he included *Tom Jones, Joseph Andrews,*
"Smollet's [sic] Works," and Defoe's *Moll Flanders* in a list of books from
his library which could be used to exemplify the "indecent literature"
of the past.[30]

He did compliment *Tom Jones* on one occasion, noting that its characters were "mighty well drawn." But he almost immediately took back
what he had grudgingly given with the qualification that all except one
were "prigs, or humbugs, or sentimental gas-bags. . . ." That sole exception was Squire Western who would always be welcome, "especially if he
is particularly drunk profane and obscene . . . —he is the only man whose
violent death one does not hunger for."*

Generally, then, these novelists became representatives for Clemens of
an age which had fortunately passed away. Yet before seizing upon such
opinions as evidence of excessive or obsessive prudery, one must always
keep in mind his separate notions of what was proper for mixed company
and what was permissible for private consumption. As suggested earlier,
Clemens' own excursions into bawdry testify to that compartmentaliz-
ing. In the private sector may be noted his interest in another classic of
the eighteenth century, John Cleland's *Memoirs of the Life of Fanny
Hill* (1749). Writing to James Osgood in March, 1881, about the possibility of publishing the autobiography of the "rightful earl" of Durham,
Jesse Leathers, Clemens jokingly said of Howells, who had not liked the
manuscript: "Howells don't seem to have no taste. The Earl's literary
excrement charmed me like Fanny Hill. I just wallowed in it."[31]

The humorist's disapproval of the Fielding and Smollett novels did
not extend to Defoe's *Robinson Crusoe,* for the story of the famous
castaways does not, of course, include any of the elements which made
the others objectionable. In Chapter Eight of *Huckleberry Finn,* Huck's
stumbling upon the ashes of Jim's campfire on Jackson's Island parallels
Crusoe's discovery of Friday's footprint. In *A Connecticut Yankee,*
Crusoe's situation furnished the author an effective point of departure
for the adventures of Hank Morgan. Surveying his bare quarters just
after his escape from the stake, the Yankee sees himself as another
Crusoe, on an island inhabited only by "some more or less tame animals."
He then decides that if life is to be bearable he must emulate Crusoe and
"invent, contrive, create, reorganize things; set brain and hand to work,
and keep them busy." Somewhat more cocky than Crusoe, he concludes:
"Well, that was in my line."[32]

* Notebook 14, TS, p. 4, Mark Twain Papers.

The allusion to Defoe's masterpiece, therefore, helps set up the subsequent progress of the novel's plot: the ten-year attempt by the practical Yankee, aided by Clarence as his man Friday, to civilize the desert island of Arthurian England. Just as the Yankee's self-assurance exceeds that of Crusoe, however, so does his ambition. Where Crusoe is content merely to provide himself with some of the comforts of a civilized life, Hank Morgan's goal becomes no less than the reformation of an entire political and social system.

If the humorist read *Roxana, or The Fortunate Mistress* when Howells recommended it to him in August, 1885, he perhaps classed its heroine's adventures among the other examples of eighteenth-century coarseness. But Howells' recommending the book not merely for its insight into the "lying, suffering, sinning, well-meaning human soul," but for "the best and most natural English that a book was ever written in," would also have appealed strongly to him.[33] Though proof is lacking, it is quite possible that Defoe's novel furnished Clemens with the name for his own Roxy in *Puddn'head Wilson*.

Clemens obviously admired the "naturalness" of Defoe's writing. In New Zealand, during the world tour he was holding forth to a reporter on the proposition that personal experience presented a writer with elements that could not be achieved through artificial means. When the reporter cited Defoe's *Journal of the Plague Year* as a notable exception, Clemens had an answer. Defoe could write well about the plague because he knew London thoroughly, "every spot and corner of it." Besides learning details of the plague at first hand from those who had experienced it, he studied cases of illness by visiting hospitals and sick friends. Then, by merely adapting his own observations to accounts of the plague itself, he produced his "wonderful study." But, the humorist concluded, to do a book of travel that way, "one would have to know every city in the world as well as Defoe knew his London."[34]

In his 1887 list of novels which illustrated the "indelicacies" of the English past, Clemens included those of Fanny Burney, and "even the Vicar of Wakefield."[35] This is one of a very few scattered references to Miss Burney. But the works of Oliver Goldsmith, Clemens knew very well. Perhaps his first acquaintance came during the river days, for Goldsmith's books apparently shared a place with Shakespeare's plays among George Ealer's "Bibles." Though the *Vicar* was later to become a pet target for ridicule, young Sam Clemens came to share at least Ealer's love for *The Citizen of the World*. In 1860, in fact, he confided to Orion that Lien Chi Altangi's letters ranked with *Don Quixote* as one of his own *"beau ideals* of fine writing." Some twelve years later that interest paid off in literary coin when he borrowed Goldsmith's format in order to give readers of *The Galaxy* a look at contemporary society through the eyes of an Oriental visitor. In a series of seven letters entitled "Goldsmith's Friend Abroad Again," one Ah Song Hi, describes to a countryman, Ching Foo, his experiences in America, "that noble realm where all are free and all equal. . . ."[36] The specific allusion to Goldsmith in the title serves to give the author's satire an added bite, for the reader familiar with Lien Chi Altangi's genial tone and generally kindly satire would doubtless be struck by the harsher implications of Ah Song Hi's misadventures among unscrupulous labor exploiters, ignorant Irish policemen, and the dregs of humanity whom he joins in the San Francisco jail.

The Citizen of the World may also have helped Clemens create one of his most colorful characters: the expansive Colonel Sellers of *The Gilded Age* and *The American Claimant*. Though Clemens himself insisted that he had drawn the Colonel from life, with his mother's cousin James Lampton as model, other elements doubtless crept in. Besides the traits common to both Orion Clemens and Samuel himself, and those contributed by the author's memories of Jesse M. Leathers (in *The American Claimant*), Charles Dickens' Wilkins Micawber probably contributed additional details (to be discussed in Section Three, *post*). As for *The Citizen of the World,* certain very close parallels in Letters LIII and LIV suggest that Sellers likewise owes something to Goldsmith's raffish poseur, Beau Tibbs.

As E. H. Weatherly has pointed out in greater detail, the most striking similarities occur in Sellers' various attempts to deal with the disparity between his grandiose statements and his obvious poverty. In Chapter Eleven of *The Gilded Age,* for instance, he expounds to the embarrassed Washington Hawkins upon the benefits to be derived from their "simple family dinner" of raw turnips and cold water. He particularly urges Washington to try mustard on the turnips, praising it as a favorite condiment of his good Russian friend, the Baron Poniatowski.[37] Similarly (in Letter LIV), Beau Tibbs, after grandly suggesting that his wife prepare an elegant turbot or ortolan, agrees that perhaps their guest might enjoy a "bit of ox-cheek" more, but urges her to be sure to add "the sauce that his Grace was so fond of."

Both Tibbs and Sellers also glibly describe their wretched living quarters as if they were models of good taste and elegance. Weatherly points out the resemblance between Tibbs' references to several pitiful oils that he claimed to have painted himself and Sellers' description of the erratic clock on his mantelpiece (*Gilded Age,* Chapter Seven). Both pretend to have refused large sums for their treasures—Tibbs from a countess who had wanted him to make a copy of one of his pictures (which would have been simply a "mechanical" operation and thus unworthy of his great artistry), and the Colonel from "old Gov. Hager," because the clock was his grandmother's and unique: "There ain't another clock like that in Christendom." An almost closer parallel, however, occurs in *The American Claimant,* where Sellers several times calls attention to the virtues of the garish "chromos" in his "art gallery." Some, which were actually portraits of famous Americans, he represents as his ancestors, the former "Earls of Rossmore"; others he proclaims the only extant pieces by various old masters.

Another quality shared by both men is their emphasis upon friendships with those in high station. Inveterate name-droppers, they consistently pretend to be "in" on numerous great schemes, the nature of which they must, of course, keep secret. Both are dextrous, too, in extricating themselves when others call attention to the obvious contradictions that their wild stories inevitably create. But just as Sellers is more fully drawn than Tibbs, so his skill and his schemes far surpass those of "the little beau," whose hopes for five hundred pounds a year "to start," hardly stack up against the Colonel's dreams of millions.

One might argue that this sort of person is fairly common in real life and, more particularly, that James Lampton probably possessed all of these characteristics. Clemens himself once said that he had actually eaten the turnips-and-water dinner at Cousin James' house. On the other hand, the humorist's memory was often faulty (or convenient). Moreover, his niece Annie Moffett Webster, who was almost like a younger sister, has said that she doubted the story about the turnips, for though Cousin Jim was always "temporarily hard-up," he still managed to set a good table when she and Sam visited his family.[38] Given Clemens' fondness for *The Citizen of the World,* therefore, it is not unlikely that Goldsmith's brief but vivid sketch of Beau Tibbs fixed itself in his memory and helped him, perhaps unconsciously, present the full-blown portrait of Sellers. The Colonel's monumental financial schemes were probably based on the dreams of James Lampton, but his attitude toward his dilapidated surroundings were so much like those of Tibbs both in spirit and in detail that it is difficult to attribute them solely to coincidence. Here again, as so often happened in his work, Clemens seems to have combined life and literature to create something richer than would have resulted had he relied on one or the other alone.

Memories of Goldsmith's works apparently were useful to the humorist in at least two other instances. What was long considered a substantially factual account of his premiere platform appearance in San Francisco bears a striking resemblance to an anecdote in Washington Irving's biography of the good Doctor. As Paul Fatout has shown, Clemens' story of that first lecture (in *Roughing It*) and of the claque he arranged to insure its favorable reception closely parallels Irving's account of a similar claque led by Dr. Johnson at the opening of *She Stoops to Conquer* in 1773. In Chapter Twenty-five of *Huckleberry Finn*, too, the author seems to have swallowed his distaste for *The Vicar of Wakefield* enough to borrow one particular bit of pomposity. Speaking of the forthcoming funeral services for Peter Wilks, the King refers to the ceremonial observances as "orgies" rather than as "obsequies" and then, to cover up, embarks on an elaborate derivation of the word "orgies." Here he becomes a close relative of Goldsmith's rascally Ephraim Jenkinson, whose similar etymological extravagances are likewise aimed at bamboozling his audience. As Walter Blair suggests, this piece of foolery, which the author probably remembered from *The Vicar*, not only spotlights the ignorance and the brazenness of the King, but also throws a bright glare on the gullibility of his audience and their delight in emotional excess. In respect to the latter characteristic, the word "orgy" becomes all too appropriate.[39]

Goldsmith may also have contributed something to various other character sketches and anecdotes, and perhaps his emphasis in the preface to *The Citizen of the World* on "colloquial ease" as a prime characteristic of good prose had its effect on Clemens' literary development.[40] But such influence cannot be assessed accurately.

Much the same thing must be said for the contributions of one of Goldsmith's contemporaries, Horace Walpole, another early favorite. Yet the humorist seldom described an important facet of his own literary practice more accurately than when he commented on his admiration for Walpole in a speech at the Authors Club of London in 1899. In one of his relatively rare public admissions of debt to the past, he cited his boyhood reading of Walpole's letters to illustrate the influence of literary "heredities" on the works of later authors. "I absorbed them," he said, "gathered in their grace, wit, and humor, and put them away to be used by-and-by." And then he added, "One does that so unconsciously with things one really likes."[41]

Exactly when that boyhood reading of the letters occurred cannot be precisely determined. Clemens' own set was an 1861–66 reprint of Peter Cunningham's nine-volume edition (1857–59). He had those volumes during the 1870's at the latest, but very likely he had read Walpole a good deal earlier, perhaps during his days as a pilot.

Certainly Walpole's sprightly style, sophisticated wit, vivid anecdotes, and gossip about peccadilloes in high places attracted Clemens and perhaps strengthened his own flair for the vivid phrase and effective use of illustrative anecdotes. At one point in Volume Nine he underlines—delightedly, one would imagine—a comment by Walpole that the opinion of an acquaintance was "hogwash."[42] He also marked, as if for future reference, a number of the anecdotes themselves, some serious, some racy. Most of his concern in this extant volume, however, seems to have been with Walpole's unfavorable assessment of the French character. But again, specific influence is difficult to assign.

Clemens' claim that he detested poetry is as patently misleading as his assuring an English correspondent in 1890 that he knew nothing whatever about books. Far from disliking it, he was obviously intrigued by the poets' ability to capture in a few words the essence of a scene, an emotion, an incident, an idea. As he once said to Howells, "Prose wanders around with a lantern & laboriously schedules & verifies the details & particulars of a valley & its frame of crags & peaks, then Poetry comes, & lays bare the whole landscape with a single splendid flash."[43]

Yet, except for Robert Burns, he did not much like the poets of the eighteenth century. He apparently knew Pope's translation of Homer, for he listed it among the several volumes he would have burned if their authors had submitted the manuscripts to him for possible publication.[44] Nor did he concur with one of the famous maxims from the *Essay on Man*. Doubtless thinking principally of the recently defunct Paige type-setter and the ruined publishing company, he proposed in a notebook entry of February, 1894, to have Puddn'head Wilson declare that "Whatever is is wrong."* In an interview in Australia (September 17, 1895) he referred to Pope as "one of the wittiest writers who ever put pen to paper," but then went on to differentiate that wit from real humor. "Most of us agree that he was 'artificial'," Clemens said to the reporter for the Sydney *Morning Herald,* and "humour is never artificial."

The humorist had indirectly satirized that "artificiality" early in his career. In one of his letters to the Keokuk *Gate City* (March 20, 1862),

---

* Notebook 27, TS, p. 55, Mark Twain Papers. Two pages later he offered another version: "Whatever is wrong is right."

he borrowed another line from the *Essay on Man,* and added three of
his own:

> Lo! the poor Indian, whose untutored mind,
> Impels him, in order to raise the wind,
> To double the pot and go it blind,
>   Until he's busted, you know.

One of his purposes in these early letters, which may be read as preparatory sketches for *Roughing It* (1872), was to satirize the traditional
image of the "noble savage," as well as to disabuse his fictive "Mother"
of some of her notions about the Great West. What could be more appropriate for such burlesque, then, than Pope's famous idealization of
the Red Man who "sees God in clouds, or hears him in the wind." The
author could doubtless count on considerable familiarity with Pope's
lines, and hence his further explanation adds another jab at Pope's
"artificiality." His narrator explains to his mother that the last three
lines of the quatrain were his but that Daniel Webster had written the
first—"which was really very good for Daniel, considering he wasn't a
natural poet. He used to say himself, that unabridged dictionaries was
his strong suit."[45]

Clemens' one favorite among eighteenth-century poets was Robert
Burns, who probably appealed because he seemed more concerned than
most of the others with man as a human being rather than as a generalized abstraction. Details from the Burns' poems often popped into
Clemens' mind to add zest to a description. The frolicking at a Carson
City wedding in February, 1863, took on a sparkle for Burns-loving
readers of the *Territorial Enterprise* when the humorist reported that
the dance Tam O'Shanter saw was "slow in comparison to it." The same
dance helped the ostensibly shocked narrator of *The Innocents Abroad*
describe the naughty Paris can-can. Though he hid his eyes, as was
proper, he allowed his fingers to part often enough to conclude that the
activity of the dancers was like nothing seen on earth "since trembling
Tam O'Shanter saw the devil and the witches at their orgies that stormy
night in 'Alloway's auld haunted kirk.'" Later in *The Innocents,* an
anecdote from Burns' biography furnished a barbed illustration of the
ironic truth that merit often is rewarded either inappropriately or too
late. The statue in Odessa to the memory of the Duc de Richelieu (the
famous cardinal's nephew), who had died poor after a lifetime of service,
reminded the traveler of the comment of Burns' mother concerning a
memorial to her son: "Ah, Robbie, ye asked them for bread, and they
hae gi'en ye a stane." Late in life, remembering a time when eight-and-
a-half-year-old Susy had misbehaved, Clemens commented that Burns'

spirit would have approved her defense when she said, "Well, mamma, you know I didn't see myself, and so I couldn't know how it looked."[46]

The author's most effective use of Burns' poetry, however, occurs in *Letters From the Earth*. In 1880, considering a speech for a Chicago Burns festival to which he was invited, he had contemplated taking issue with the point of "Man Was Made to Mourn" by introducing an emphatic "not" into the title. But when he came to create Satan's reports to his heavenly friends, he gave that poem's most-quoted lines a twist that transforms them into ironic satire on traditional concepts of God. Describing the horrors of diseases like sleeping-sickness, Satan observes (in Letter VII) that he "whom Church and people call Our Father in Heaven" invented insects as a means of spreading this "misery and melancholy and wretchedness." Arguing that any human being on earth would, if possible, help a sufferer from sleeping-sickness, he charges that God on His part is wholly pitiless, the only father who could be so cruel as to afflict his child with that horrible disease and refuse to heal him. To underscore his point for those readers who might appreciate true poetic indignation "warmly expressed," he quotes two lines "hot from the heart of a slave":

> *Man's* inhumanity to man
> Makes countless thousands mourn![47]

By thus italicizing the initial word, the author transformed the poet's condemnation of man's cruelty to his fellows to an indictment of God—or rather, the kind of God whom man has conceived. At the same time the lines implicitly satirize man's stupidity in worshipping such a God: having the emotion proceed from the heart of a "slave" ironically attests to man's bondage to such notions of God. Given the concept of God as omnipotent father, having the "slave" blame *man* for "inhumanity" becomes doubly ironic.

I I

Nineteenth-Century Poetry

AS MIGHT BE EXPECTED, especially in the case of a self-educated man, Clemens liked the poets of his own century more than those of earlier eras. More frequently than is usually realized he drew on them for ideas, situations, or specific lines.

On several occasions the poems of the two greatest of the first-generation Romantics provided notable assistance. *The Rime of the Ancient Mariner* must have been a favorite, for after buying a copy for himself in 1875, the following year he presented Livy with a new edition illustrated by Gustave Doré. He was particularly fascinated by Coleridge's description of the old sailor's hypnotic gaze and insistence on telling his tale. At least three times he invoked that image—to describe the penetrating stare of a waiter on the 1877 Bermuda trip, to enliven an anecdote, allegedly told by his friend Riley, in *A Tramp Abroad* (Chapter Twenty-six), and to indicate the name-dropping proclivities of Andrew Carnegie. In "The Enchanted Sea Wilderness," a fragment omitted from *Following the Equator,* there appear a mysterious "great white albatross," frost-coated rigging, and a derelict ship crewed by corpses.[1]

The humorist's most elaborate use of the *Ancient Mariner* however, took the form of a burlesque ballad in *Roughing It* (Volume Two, Chapter Ten), where "The Aged Pilot Man," sings of a fierce storm on the Erie Canal and lauds the efforts of the intrepid pilot Dollinger to guide the vessel through her perils. Perhaps to cover the author's tracks somewhat, the narrator observes that the poem—"(not the chief idea, but the vehicle that bears it)"—was "probably suggested by the old song called 'The Raging Canal' but I cannot remember now." As Roger Brooks has pointed out, the idea of the stormy voyage may indeed have come from the "old song," but its real "vehicle" was the *Ancient Mariner*. Besides the obvious similarity of title, "The Aged Pilot Man" employs the meter and stanzaic pattern (even including one variation in that pattern) of Coleridge's ballad. More significantly, some eleven lines echo similar ones in the *Ancient Mariner*.[2] One resemblance (not noted by Brooks) occurs when the narrator, hearing "words of hope and faith" from only one person on board, says, "And I worshipped as they came" (line 119). Here his reaction closely parallels that of the ancient mariner to the beauty of the water-snakes: "And I blessed them unaware" (line 285).

Despite the reference to "The Raging Canal," the author almost surely expected his readers to see through his (or his narrator's) dodge. Recognition of the kinship with Coleridge's famous poem would, in turn, enhance the ridiculousness of Mark Twain's tempest on a canal—an adventure that reaches a suitable climax when a "mysteriously inspired" farmer lays a plank across the short distance separating the grounded ship from the canal-bank, whereupon the "amazed" passengers step quickly ashore.

Though this burlesque was doubtless aimed partly at some of the "romantic" elements in the *Ancient Mariner* itself, the "Pilot Man" serves a more direct purpose in helping develop the theme of *Roughing It*. It comes at the end of a discussion of the abortive attempt to establish a literary paper, the *Weekly Occidental* in Virginia City, then a rough mining town. Besides the poem, the episode introduces a series of plot summaries for a "composite novel" which is to appear in the paper. Both the plot summaries and poem, in satirizing various romantic conventions, represent additional aspects of the "mellow moonshine of romance" which the "tenderfoot" must slough off on his way to becoming an "old-timer." In introducing the poem, in fact, Clemens specifically underlines the change by having his narrator say, "I do remember . . . that at that time I thought my doggerel was one of the ablest poems of the age."

The poems of Wordsworth, Clemens treated more seriously. Especially receptive to poetry after Susy's death in 1896, he found a vivid parallel to his own emotions in "The Wanderer" (from *The Excursion*, Book One). As he read (or remembered) the poem on June 20, 1897, the old Wanderer's sad tale of the now long-dead Margaret probably brought memories of Susy flooding into his mind. When he came to the old man's declaration of his love for Margaret, he copied three of the lines into his notebook to express his own anguish: "The good die first, / And those [Wordsworth wrote "they"] whose hearts are dry as summer dust, / Burn to the socket!"[3]

Obviously attracted to this poem, Clemens very likely had it in mind that same summer when he wrote his own lament for a lost girl on August 18, the first anniversary of Susy's death. In *The Excursion*, a few lines after those just quoted, the Wanderer mentions that Margaret had lived in the house where they stopped to rest, and that with her death, "the light . . . of her lonely hut" had been extinguished and the cottage itself "abandoned to decay." Some lines earlier, too, he had commented more generally that with a person's death, everything he loves and prizes also perishes, or at least is so changed that "even of the good is no memorial left." Yet the Wanderer dedicates himself to keeping the memory of Margaret alive and bright.

Clemens' "In Memoriam: Olivia Susan Clemens" (though the title echoes Tennyson) describes a similar situation. In a peaceful rural valley there once had stood a Temple, the dwelling-place of a "Light" which served as both an inspiration and an object of worship for the villagers.

But suddenly a "vast disaster" fell. The villagers awoke one morning to find the Temple gone and only "vacant desert" where it had stood the night before. In the "ages" since the tragedy, the "hamlet-folk" had all but forgotten the Temple and the Light which inhabited it (just as Margaret and her hut were forgotten by many). But even as the Wanderer's father-like love for Margaret lives on, so the "stricken ones" who were most closely associated with the Light still remember and revere it.

Though similar in many respects, Clemens' poem is much more emotional than *The Excursion*. Whereas Wordsworth's narrator finds consolation in the thought of Margaret's strong religious faith, Clemens' mourners are left only with a vague despair (compounded with self-pity). Unwilling to accept the fact that their Light is gone, they stand and murmur that it will surely return, for "It knows our pain—it knows—it knows—." This contrast, therefore, provides a clearer insight into the nature of the author's grief. He apparently was never able to accept the death of a loved one with any consolation of philosophy.

Wordsworth's "Lucy" poems also attracted Clemens, again probably because of their memories of a dead girl. The last lines of "She Dwelt Among the Untrodden Ways": "But she is in her grave, and, oh, / The difference to me!"—would have held a special poignancy. Yet the exquisite picture of young girlhood also must have appealed, for in 1907 he called upon that same poem to cite his affection for young Joy Agnew, whose presence at the *Punch* dinner in London had so touched him. Answering a letter from her shortly after his return to America, he recalled her presence at that dinner, where she sat beaming among "those somber swallow-tails, 'Fair as a star when only one / Is shining in the sky'." Then, as if he were also remembering Wordsworth's comment at the beginning of "Three Years She Grew in Sun and Shower" that "A lovelier flower / On earth was never sown," he teased her about being so beautiful as to discourage the flowers in her own garden.[4]

He had not always been so appreciative of young children, or at least pretended not to be in such pieces as "Those Blasted Children," which first appeared in the New York *Sunday Mercury* for February 21, 1864. Here, however, as in "Story of the Good Little Boy" (1870) he was the realist attacking both the romantic idea of the divine innocence of unspoiled childhood and the fatuous moralism of the Sunday school tale. And though it is pure conjecture, the arrival "trailing clouds of glory" of Wordsworth's child in the "Intimations" ode seems to find an ironic counterpart in the sad fate of the good little boy, Jacob Bliven. Though he follows to the letter all of the precepts taught him in Sunday school,

Jacob always comes to grief, until finally, blown through a factory roof by a nitroglycerine explosion, he soars away toward the sun "with the fragments of . . . fifteen dogs stringing after him like the tail of a kite."[5] That echo, intentional or not, does add an additional fillip to Mark Twain's satiric touch.

Of all the Romantic poets, Byron was the one whose works the humorist knew best. In 1867 Mark Twain told his *Alta* readers that Byron's "The Destruction of Sennacherib" was the only poem he had ever learned by heart; its rhythmic lines had been impressed upon his mind at school "by the usual process, a trifle emphasized."[6] If so, it is not surprising that he should later find a place for that piece among the "Examination Evening" declamations in *Tom Sawyer* (1876).

By 1867, he had already made "The Destruction of Sennacherib" serve his humorous purposes well. He had kidded the readers of the San Francisco *Californian* in 1865 by presenting it in his "Answers to Correspondents" column as an anonymous specimen of "Dutch Flat" poetry. Cries of outrage from some of the country papers, denouncing author and editor for their ignorance, showed that the hoax had succeeded. From the Sandwich Islands in 1866 he decorated one of his letters to the Sacramento *Union* by alternating the opening lines from Byron's same poem with some from Charles Wolfe's widely popular "The Burial of Sir John Moore."[7]

On the *Quaker City* tour, several spots evoked other allusions to the poet. In writing of Venice, the author mentions Byron's residence there and the group's visit to the house where the poet had lived. He must also have remembered some of the exploits of Byron's "Beppo," for his description of a gondola as "an inky, rusty old canoe with a sable hearse-body clapped on to the middle of it," is simply a vernacular rendering of Byron's description of a similar craft gliding "along the water looking blackly, / Just like a coffin clapt in a canoe."[8] By thus picking up and amplifying the anti-romanticism of Byron's poems, Clemens enhances a major theme of *The Innocents Abroad* in its realistic look at the traditionally romantic mode of travel in Venice.

The Roman portion of the tour provided another opportunity to use Byron for an additional overtone to the dominant chord of *The Innocents*. Ever since Childe Harold had meditated upon the gory history of Rome's great Coliseum, travelers who followed him had quoted Byron. But Clemens' narrator refuses to follow suit, and proudly pronounces himself the only "man of mature age" to recall the storied processions of gladiators, martyrs, and lions without including the poet's famous phrase, "butchered to make a Roman holiday." Even more flippantly, during the voyage through the Hellespont, he remembers Byron's (and perhaps Don Juan's) emulating Leander "merely for a flyer."[9]

After *The Innocents Abroad* Clemens continued to call upon the poet occasionally, usually for humorous purposes. The Mark Twain of *A Tramp Abroad* (1880) claims to have lost much of his "deep and reverent compassion for . . . the 'Prisoner of Chillon' whose story Byron has told in such moving verse" when he saw what a comfortable cell the prisoner had occupied in the famous Swiss castle. In a sketch of 1892, entitled "About All Kinds of Ships," the author pretends to lament the passing of the public's taste for sentimental songs of the sea and offers a number of excerpts to illustrate their excellence. Including among the selections a stanza from Byron's tribute to Tom Moore—"My Boat is on the Shore"—he further satirizes such sentimentality by declaring the poem to be a former "favorite in the West with the passengers on stern-wheel steamboats."[10]

The humorist's most extensive discussion of the poet resulted from the so-called "Byron Scandal," set off by the appearance in the September, 1869, *Atlantic Monthly* of Harriet Beecher Stowe's "True Story of Lady Byron's Life." Like a gallant knight Mark Twain rushed to the defense of not one, but two fair damsels Lady Byron and her defender, Mrs. Stowe. He fully accepted the latter's account of Byron's incestuous relations with his half-sister, Augusta, and in articles written for the Buffalo *Express* he attacked the "sentimentalists" who so worshipped the colorful Byron that they refused even to listen to the "foul slander" which Mrs. Stowe had heaped upon their idol.

Yet on several occasions he also satirized the attackers of Byron for raising such a furor. On September 18 his essay described a meeting with a "Wild Man," whose name turned out to be "Sensation." This creature, after recounting several exploits undertaken merely "to gratify the whims of a bedlam of crazy newspaper scribblers," shoulders a spade and sets off on another "mission," bemoaning his inability to find peace and rest. Asked the nature of his new assignment, he replies "TO DIG UP THE BYRON FAMILY." A week earlier (in his "People and Things" column) Mark Twain had presented some "Last Words of Great Men" and included those of Byron, slightly revised from the dying request which Tom Moore had reported (and which Mrs. Stowe had quoted). Instead of "Go to my sister; tell her—Go to Lady Byron,—you will see her and say—," the author had Byron muttering: "Augusta—sister—Lady Byron —tell Harriet Beecher Stowe,—etc., etc." The next day, too, brought a brief note that "Another Byron, the nephew of his own father, has transpired."

Much more flippant than those published comments, however, was a manuscript "letter" to Mark Twain from Byron's ghost. In it Byron freely admits the guilt charged against him by Mrs. Stowe and many other critics. But then the author makes humorous capital of the Byron Scandal by having the poet declare his fascination with such controversies and remind his listener that his poem "The Vision of Judgment" had involved the question of the character of George III. As Heaven and Hell contended for George's soul, Byron says, Satan committed an "amazing blunder" by calling witnesses to affirm the wickedness of the English monarch. But his witnesses surprised him: "that little vicious viper, John Wilkes, who never lost a chance to traduce and revile the king while he lived," and even "implacable Junius," refused to speak against the dead. "And so did your Washington and your Franklin. But not so Bob Southey. Didn't I show up Bob Southey handsomely? And I was right. To this day that fellow steals my brimstone and borrows my shovel, and then blackguards me behind my back."[11] So much for those who try to blacken the reputation of the dead.

As Paul Baender has indicated, such comic treatment of the Byron Scandal bespeaks an ambiguity in the humorist's position. In his deprecation of Byron's immorality, he is a writer of "respectable literature," whereas particularly in the "letter" from Byron, he is the literary jester, free "to laugh at the violation of sexual mores."[12] Which attitude reflected his "real" feelings probably cannot be ascertained. Certainly his current position as the fiancé of Olivia Langdon and defender of one of the Beechers (close friends of the Langdon family) influenced his views. A desire to appear well in their eyes would have been sufficient cause for him to suppress the burlesque letter.

A comment in *The Galaxy* the following summer (July, 1870) also argues a moral pose, if not moral conviction. There the author asserts that any attempts to burlesque the Byron Scandal were doomed to failure because the central feature of the controversy—incest—was "a 'situation' so tremendous and imposing that the happiest resources of burlesque seemed tame and cheap in its presence." If this *was* a pose, it was one which Clemens consistently assumed when it came to public morality.

Byron's own satiric writing may well have fathered the vivid comparison of the respective influences of *Don Quixote* and *Ivanhoe,* which concludes the attack on "Scottism" in *Life on the Mississippi* (Chapter

Forty-six). In *Don Juan* (Canto Thirteen, stanza ten), discussing Cervantes' efforts at reform, Byron declares that when Cervantes "smiled Spain's chivalry away," he created a masterpiece, but at the same time caused the decline of his own country by removing the elements of romance that had inspired her heroes to great deeds. Clemens, though seeming to adapt Byron's phrase to his own more forceful image, reverses the sentiment expressed in *Don Juan*. He applauds Cervantes' having "swept the world's admiration for mediaeval chivalry-silliness out of existence" and bemoans the fact that Scott had restored the romantic spirit which in turn, had stifled progress in the American South.

Whatever Clemens may have thought of Byron's personal life, he must have admired the poet's works, including *Don Juan,* for he not only reminded himself in 1891 to get a copy of that poem, but the following year he included a volume of Byron's poetry among his Christmas gifts to his daughter Susy.[13]

Mention of Byron's friend and biographer, Tom Moore, recalls the fact that Clemens had also parodied Moore's "Those Evening Bells" in *Sketches New and Old* (1875). The title of his piteous piece, "Those Annual Bills," more than implies the nature of his sad lament in the lines that follow. In his story of the 1877 Bermuda trip, the author also remembered that Tom Moore had once held the post of registrar of the island's admiralty, and then joked about the poet's alleged capacity for strong drink. Near the beginning of that account, he borrowed a line from Moore's moralistic "This world is all a fleeting show" to point up the hypocrisy of two brothers who haggle over who gets which cemetery lot in a parcel of ground that one of them has bought for the family. William, the original purchaser, piously comments: "Life's on'y a fleetin' show, John, as the sayin' is. We've all got to go, sooner or later. To go with a clean record's the main thing. Fact is, it's the on'y thing worth strivin' for, John." He then proceeds to make a "mistake" in describing the lots, so that his brother winds up owning the least desirable one.

Thirty years later, among extensive plans for a eulogy of Susy, Clemens turned to another of Moore's popular poems, "Oft in the Stilly Night," for a stanza lamenting the vanished smiles and tears "of childhood's years" and the "happy hearts now broken" [Moore says "boyhood's years" and "cheerful hearts"].[14]

The humorist's most vivid allusion to Moore appears, however, in Chapter Thirty-two of *Huckleberry Finn,* where mention of the famous oriental romance, *Lalla Rookh,* becomes a subtle missile in Clemens' war on overdone romanticism and man's dependence on outworn codes. When Huck fabricates the story of a steamboat explosion in order to explain his arrival on foot at the Phelps farm, Aunt Sally is reminded of the time her husband "was coming up from Newrleans on the old Lally Rook, and she blowed out a cylinder-head and crippled a man." This is the point, too, at which the kind old lady asks if anyone had been hurt in Huck's explosion. Her reaction to his reply, "No'm. Killed a nigger," climaxes the irony of the author's attack on the crippling effects of the old codes. "Well, it's lucky," she says, "because sometimes people do get hurt."

For Byron's friend and sometime fellow traveler, Percy Bysshe Shelley, Clemens had considerably less sympathy than for Byron. On two separate occasions he mounted his white charger to challenge those who sought to excuse Shelley's treatment of his wife Harriet. The first attack (which he never published) he launched at the Shelley described by Matthew Arnold in the *Nineteenth Century* for January, 1888. The second aimed its barbs at Edward Dowden's *Life of Shelley* (1886), to which Arnold had frequently referred. This time he published the results as "In Defence of Harriet Shelley" in the *North American Review* (July, August, September, 1894).

Both essays deplore the efforts of biographers to gloss over the poet's callous desertion of Harriet, and both have their moments of superb ironic invective. In the earlier one, for instance, discussing Arnold's description of Shelley as "a perfect gentleman"—modest, enthusiastic, generous, and delicate—the author pretends to be reminded of a boyhood acquaintance named Injun Aleck, who likewise possessed all the attributes of "a winning and beautiful and elegant Christian." "He was all that," the author says, "but one day he hanged his mother."

What seems to have disturbed Clemens most about Arnold's article was that even though the author claimed to be sickened by the "irregular relations" of the poet with Mary Godwin (and others), he had concluded that he must still stand on his portrait of Shelley as a man "of marvelous gentleness, of feminine refinement, with gracious and considerate manners, a perfect gentleman." For, in concluding his own case Clemens, too, stood on an earlier description. As if delivering a razor-cut that is hardly noticeable until the blood begins to gush, he quoted Arnold's statement and then commented simply: "It is the very picture of Aleck."[15]

This exercise probably led him to look at Dowden's biography itself, which in turn inspired the much longer and more detailed "In Defence of Harriet Shelley." Though Harriet was not so lily-white as Clemens painted her, his demolition of Dowden's "literary cake-walk" otherwise remains basically sound. Newman Ivey White makes many of the same points in his 1940 biography of Shelley and is said to have commented in 1948 that he considered Clemens' conclusions to be valid ones.[16]

The humorist's chief interest in Shelley was obviously in the man rather than in the poet. Yet he doubtless knew some of the poetry, for Shelley was one of Susy's favorites. Besides the volume belonging to her, the family library contained a copy of the Tauchnitz edition of Shelley's poems. By 1909, too, Clemens had mellowed enough to grant the poet some measure of admiration. Thanking his Bermuda friend, Elizabeth Wallace, for a copy of "Thompson's beautiful appreciation of Shelley," which he found as "rich in sumptuous imagery" as Shelley's poetry, he further remarked that the book had inspired him to read some of the poems.[17]

Another of Byron's friends, Leigh Hunt, also provided the humorist with material for satire, though of a far less personal sort. Hunt's "Abou Ben Adhem" was probably Clemens' favorite poem among the works of the Romantics—one of the few literary works, in fact, that he once listed as "perfect" examples of effective expression. Nevertheless, as he often did with things he admired, he several times turned it to purposes of humor or parody. In Chapter Nine of *The Innocents Abroad*, for instance—and probably with tongue in cheek—he bestowed Hunt's famous blessing "May his tribe increase!" on "the stately, the princely, the magnificent Hadji Mohammed Lamarty," who guided the group through exotic Tangier. Much more elaborate, however, was a notebook draft of a satiric adaptation of Hunt's poem—"Abou Ben Butler." Dedicated to the Civil War general and Congressional demagogue of the 1870's and eighties, the poem by changing a few significant words of the original and adding a flatly prosaic last line, presents Ben Butler as a hypocrite posing as a paragon, the complete antithesis of the saintly Ben Adhem.[18]

Of the nineteenth-century poets, Tennyson fares better than most as far as respectful treatment is concerned. According to friends, the humorist often quoted from the laureate's poems and then proceeded to deliver competent discourses on the ideas contained therein. He enjoyed more than just the "standard" ones, for in 1875 he bought the newly published drama *Queen Mary* and in 1893 went with Howells to see Tennyson's *Becket* at New York's Abbey Theater. In one of his darkest moments following Susy's death in 1896, "Break, Break, Break!" helped him express his sense of loss. As he told Olivia, the lines "O for the touch of a vanished hand / And the sound of a voice that is still," described his bereavement more eloquently than he himself could do. Both he and Livy also found solace during those dark days in Tennyson's "noble" poem, "In Memoriam." Four years later, in happier times at Dollis Hill, he usurped a line from "Locksley Hall" to note "Better sixty days of Dollis than a cycle of Cathay." In America again in 1901, the echo of the plaintive refrain from "Mariana," helped make graphic his reaction to a Player's Club bill shortly after the turmoil of the family's move to Riverdale-on-the-Hudson: "I was aweary, aweary, and I put it in the wastebasket."[19]

What Clemens apparently found most attractive in Tennyson was an almost magical blend of music and sentiment which evoked for him a dreamworld, far removed from the ordinary cares of life. Some of the Pacific Islands visited during the world tour of 1895–96 reminded him of such a world—"the very home of dreams and romance and mystery" he said in *Following the Equator* (1897). Proposing to show that no one could create such an atmosphere as well as Tennyson, he had orginally quoted some twenty-one lines from *Enoch Arden* (1864) describing the island on which the shipwrecked Enoch lived for twelve years. The "enduring magic" of such verses, the author said, preserved them "fresh and fragrant of the woods and the sea and eloquent of the loneliness and remoteness of the island world." But because he perhaps feared to sound too sentimental, especially since the preceding chapter had treated the islands humorously, he deleted the long reference to Tennyson some-time during the proof stage of the book.[20]

Yet that affection for the passage in *Enoch Arden,* as well as for Tennyson's poems generally, permits a conjecture that the "magician laureate" may have helped inspire one of the memorable scenes in *Tom Sawyer* (1876)—the "drowned" Tom's nocturnal visit to his family in Chapter Fifteen. If so, the humorist here subjected *Enoch Arden* to burlesque if not to satire.

In that episode, Tom's actions both parallel and implicitly ridicule those of Tennyson's protagonist. Back in his home village after his twelve-year absence, Enoch peers in through a window to observe his happy wife (now remarried) and his nearly grown children. Tom, back from hiding-out on Jackson's Island, looks in through the window at his mourning family, and then ducks into the house and under the bed. Just as Tennyson's "dead man come to life" laments his sad lot, Tom "welters" in tears, "more in pity of himself than anybody else." Enoch has to resist a "shrill and terrible cry" which would shatter all the happiness of the hearth; Tom longs to rush into the room to bring joy to the mourners. But both restrain themselves. Enoch prays for strength "never to let her know"—until he is dead, that is. Tom, standing over Aunt Polly's bed, remorseful over his trick, starts to leave a message explaining that he and the others had not drowned, but then hits on a happy solution to his dilemma and leaves.

The solution is to have the "drowned" boys appear at their own funeral. Ironically, then, whereas Enoch is meant to be considered heroic for not destroying his wife's happiness by revealing his presence, the boys become "heroes" despite their deception. The funeral ceremonies, pretty elaborate for the small town, which Tom, Huck, and Joe Rogers watch from the church gallery, also tacitly satirize the unfortunate last lines of Tennyson's poem: "And when they buried him, the little port / Had seldom seen a costlier funeral."

Though he admired the description of the island and doubtless was moved by some of the domestic scenes, the humorist certainly must have objected to much of the poem's sentimentality. And so he may have transmuted Enoch's sentimental self-sacrifice into Tom's mischievous, but basically cruel, deception of his family, and his triumphal return from the escapade on Jackson's Island. Enoch's funeral may have been grand, but that of the boys was more so—for they were alive to enjoy it.

Clemens had once considered carrying Tom through "the Battle of Life in many lands" and having him return at age thirty-seven or forty (Enoch was about forty-two) to find all changed. If he had done so, the resemblance to *Enoch Arden* would have been even stronger. Again there would have been an ironic reversal of situation, for whereas Enoch found his Annie blooming in the bliss of a new marriage, Tom was to find "the Adored Unknown" a "faded old maid & full of rasping, puritanical vinegar piety."[21]

Thus it may even be that *Enoch Arden* was instrumental in stimulating, if not actually creating, the humorist's fascination with the idea of bringing a character back to his home after a long absence. In several notebook entries, including the variation which involves the Connecticut Yankee's return to modern England, he was to jot down plans for stories based on that situation. Similarly, the "man at his own funeral" idea, which recurred in at least three unfinished pieces within a few years of *Tom Sawyer*, perhaps sprang from the same "return" theme.[22]

As Hamlin Hill has shown, marginal notations in the *Tom Sawyer* manuscript indicate that the novel hit a snag in September, 1874, just at the point where Tom stood over Aunt Polly deciding whether or not to leave the message which he had written on a piece of sycamore bark. The implication of that situation is clear; the message was to involve much more than the information that the boys were merely off playing pirate on Jackson's Island. Probably the author had intended to say that Tom was leaving St. Petersburg to begin "the Battle of Life in many lands" as mentioned in the planning note. But he apparently could not decide where to have Tom go, and the story remained snagged until the following spring when the "funeral" idea helped solve the problem of Tom's future actions.[23]

In the light of Clemens' affection for the *Rubaiyat's* somber strains (as discussed in Chapter Eleven, *ante*), one might not expect to find the fundamentally optimistic poems of Robert Browning sharing a high place among his literary preferences. Nevertheless, in 1886 when Olivia and some of her friends talked him into preparing weekly readings for their newly formed study group, Browning gained a fervent admirer.

William Lyon Phelps once observed that Clemens was bucking a serious critical trend by taking on this club at a time when "ridicule of the Browning Societies was almost universal." Actually, though there was some sneering at the organized worship of the poet, the revolt was hardly that widespread in 1886. The Browning Society of Boston had been founded less than a year earlier (in December, 1885); the one in Chicago began meeting in 1886, and the Philadelphia Browning Club was not organized until 1888.[24]

Clemens had not read a great deal of Browning up to this point even though he had met the poet himself during his first visits to England in 1872–73. Once the new project was under way, however, he was all enthusiasm. "Think of it!" he wrote to Mrs. Fairbanks that November. "I've been elected Reader to a Browning class." Then, as if he felt he had overstepped his characteristic role, he added—"I who have never of my own inclination, read a poem in my life." He took his duties seriously, often spending several days preparing materials for the one-hour sessions. He even familiarized himself with some of the current Browning scholarship and arranged for Professor Hiram Corson, one of the pioneer Browning scholars in America, to come from Cornell to address the Hartford Club.[25]

The meetings continued through the winter and into the spring of 1887 and were so successful that the reader agreed to resume them the following season. From time to time additional members and guests joined the group, and at one point Clemens' interest became so absorbing that he wanted to read Browning even at the dinner table. That proposal drew an immediate veto, for Livy did not fancy the clatter of dinner dishes and the chatter of children as background music for the poet's verse.[26]

As a result of all this, Clemens knew Browning's works better than those of any other poet except Kipling. He probably began with Livy's copy of *Men and Women* (Boston, 1856), but then bought the six-volume Riverside Edition of 1887, which included all of the poet's earlier books and *Parleyings with Certain People of Importance in Their Day*, first published that same year. Later, his library would contain a copy of *Asolando* (1889), a gift from Browning's daughter-in-law, who inscribed the book "for Mr. Clemens with Mrs. Browning's affectionate regards" shortly after she and her husband had met the Clemenses in Italy in 1892.[27]

The humorist's first letter to Mrs. Fairbanks had expressed doubts about his ability to handle any but the "easy" poems. But soon he was regaling his audience with such pieces as "Clive," and the various *Parleying* (with Daniel Bartoli, Christopher Smart, Charles Avison, and others), as well as *The Ring and the Book, Christmas Eve, Easter Day, Sordello,* and *Strafford.* Only *Sordello* gave him much trouble, and he abandoned it after two attempts.[28]

When the class complained that Browning became obscure only when Clemens attempted to explain the poems (or so he told a correspondent during the second winter of readings), he gave up the brief lectures and let the reading itself impart the meaning. He was not just being facetious when he said that he could read the poetry so that Browning himself could understand it. Several members of his audience have vouched for his effectiveness. Grace King, a young novelist and protégée of Charles Dudley Warner, was later to remark that his understanding of Browning was greater than that of anyone she had ever known: "To him there were no obscure passages to be argued over, no guessing at meaning. His slow deliberate speech and full voice gave each sentence its quota of sound, and sense followed naturally and easily." Another guest who came to the group as a skeptic remained as a convert both to Browning and to Clemens as his interpreter. As she later admitted to Howells, she had long known and appreciated Mark Twain as a clever humorist, but now saw him as "a man of the highest quality responsive to the imaginative suggestions of a poet." At her first session the class was studying *The Ring and the Book,* and even though they had dealt with the opening cantos at earlier meetings, Clemens' skill made it possible for the new-comer to follow the poem's meaning with no difficulty whatsoever. One fact which especially surprised her was that the famous drawl disap-peared as soon as the reading began. Avoiding the "swelling voice and tragic emphasis" with which so many performers tended to obscure rather than to clarify their subject, he let the sentences speak for them-selves, skillfully keeping the thread of thought free of entanglements as he easily mastered "the parenthetical style so habitual with Browning."[29]

The interest in Browning which the humorist had helped create was sufficient to carry the Hartford group along for several years after he relinquished its direction. Not that he himself abandoned Browning when he gave up the class, for visitors and friends often requested read-ings and were seldom refused.[30]

Obviously the process of puzzling out Browning's meaning and the pleasure of helping others to understand the poems was one of the chief sources of satisfaction for Clemens. At the club meeting of February 23, 1887, when the members requested him to write down the comment he had made after finishing "Easter Day," he wrote on the flyleaf of his copy of *Dramatis Personae:* "One's glimpses & confusions, as one reads Browning, remind me of looking through a telescope (the small sort which you must move with your hand, not clock-work). You toil across dark spaces which are (to *your* lens) empty; but every now & then a splendor of stars & suns bursts upon you and fills the whole field with flame." The following August, in a letter to Howells, he used much the same image, though with deeper implications, to touch upon some of the compensations in life which helped one bear the loss of certain illusions. Commenting that formerly impressive things, like a childhood home or the Bible, tend to shrink to commonplace proportions as one matures, he noted that sometimes one could "tilt the tube skyward & bring planets & comets & corona-flames a hundred & fifty thousand miles high into the field" as Howells had done in finding Tolstoi. "I can't get *him* in focus yet," the humorist concluded, "but I've got Browning."[31] Obviously, such rewards were ample payments for any difficulties in-volved in interpreting the poems.

Browning's poems doubtless appealed both to the bright and to the dark sides of Clemens' shifting moods during these years. The joys of life in "Up at a Villa, Down in the City," the accomplishments of Abt Vogler, Rabbi Ben Ezra's gratitude for doubt even while proclaiming that "the best is yet to be," and David's rescue of Saul from black de-pression—these and other attributes of Browning's "positive" poems may well have helped offset the deeping strain of the humorist's darker thoughts in the late 1880's. Yet there is also a great deal in Browning to attract one who might not share some of his more sanguine views. In many of the poems that appeared frequently in the readings, man's aspirations and strivings meet with frustration. Fra Lippo Lippi chafes under the restrictions of his monastic life and the demand that he paint "religiously" rather than realistically. Andrea Del Sarto, having prostituted his artistic integrity to mere technical skill, bids his wife a sad farewell as she hurries to an assignation with her "cousin." At both the beginning and at the end of "Evelyn Hope," Browning's tribute to a lost love who had died at sixteen, Clemens wrote "Setebos."[32] Probably here he had pondered the question of why one so young and so beautiful should die, and was reminded of "Caliban upon Setebos," in which the deformed monster of Shakespeare's *Tempest* describes the arbitrary and cruel god whom he has created in his own image. Especially in "Mr. Sludge, 'The Medium'" do human greed, gullibility, and hypocrisy stand revealed under a merciless spotlight.

Much more attractive than any "message" they might contain, however, were the dramatic qualities of the poems. The humorist's love of history found great satisfaction in Browning's vivid recreations of the past and its personages. He responded vigorously, also, to the excitement of such incidents as the horse-race in "Muleykeh" and to the psychological drama which unfolded in pieces like "In a Balcony." No doubt Browning's genius at assuming the guises of his various narrators and the colloquialism of some of their language struck a responsive chord in the author whose own art depended so much on the *persona* or pose. And the actor in Clemens certainly thrilled at the opportunity to bring these narrators to life in his readings.

Browning came to mind a number of times in subsequent years. As already noted, the Clemenses met Browning's son Barrett and his wife in Italy in 1892. They were very much pleased, also, to renew that acquaintance in Florence in 1904. Barrett Browning apparently was most complimentary, for he is said to have remarked that the humorist's appreciation of his father's poetry was keener than that of almost anyone he had ever met. While pondering his prospective book during the sea voyage from India to South Africa in April, 1896, Clemens had considered quoting the whole of Browning's "Clive" when he dealt with the hero of Plassey's career in India, but he later gave up the idea. In view of the difficulties with *Sordello* during his "readership," one may also infer a certain satisfaction in a notebook entry shortly after the comment on "Clive" which reported an anecdote about the poet told by Carlyle Smythe. Asked the meaning of one of the passages in *Sordello,* Browning puzzled over it for a time and then said: " 'Once there were two who knew'—glancing skyward, then touching his own breast—'Now there is only One'—glancing again skyward."[33]

In 1903 Clemens turned to Browning's poem about the heroic dog "Tray" for a part of the central argument of his short story, "A Dog's Tale." Both works attack human callousness in general and vivisection in particular. In the poem, Browning's Tray (not to be confused with Stephen Foster's "Old Dog Tray" of 1853), dramatically rescues a drowning child and then, to the amazement of the observers, dives a second time to retrieve the child's doll. Some of the watchers seize this action as evidence that the dog acted from "mere instinct" rather than from reason. As Tray trots off, they all laugh at the stupidity of risking a life for a worthless doll—

> Till somebody, prerogatived
> With reason, reasoned: "Why he dived,
> His brain would show us, I should say."

And the poem ends with bitter understatement as the speaker proposes to buy Tray so that

> "By vivisection, at expense
> Of half an hour and eighteenpence,
> How brain secretes dog's soul, we'll see!"

Since the piece was one of those included most often in notebook lists for readings in 1886 and 1887, it may well have been a major source of inspiration for Clemens' own antipathy toward vivisection.[34]

"A Dog's Tale" expands "Tray's" attack considerably. After a number of satiric thrusts at various human foibles, the canine narrator describes how she had once dragged her master's baby from a burning room, only to be beaten because he thought that she was attacking the child. The author then sets the stage for even greater irony than in Browning's poem by having the master, when he realizes the truth, *oppose* the contentions of his scientifically-minded friends that the dog's action must have been purely instinctive. "It's far above instinct," he says; "it's *reason,* and many a man, privileged to be saved and go with you and me to a better world by right of its possession, has less of it than this poor silly quadruped that's foreordained to perish." But then, after thus arguing for the heroic dog's superiority to many men, he callously subjects her puppy to an operation designed to settle an argument about whether a certain injury to the brain would cause blindness. The operation proves that it would, and as the blind and bloody pup staggers about the laboratory and finally dies, the group exults at the boon to "suffering humanity" which the experiment represents.

Potentially, "A Dog's Tale" is a moving story, and a powerful indictment of cruelty to animals. Unfortunately, however, Clemens did not maintain Browning's detachment. As was so often the case when he dealt with family relations and the inflicting of pain, he allowed his own emotions to intrude too blatantly. The unabashed sentimentality at times approaches the maudlin. His choice of a dog as his narrator also offers difficulties that hinder the effectiveness of his tale. Nevertheless, the story received wide notice. Shortly after its appearance in *Harper's* for December, 1903, Harper and Brothers reprinted it as a book, and in England both the National Anti-Vivisection Society and the London and Provincial Anti-Vivisection Society issued it as a pamphlet.[35]

During the preceding summer, the approaching sixth anniversary of Susy's death had once again inspired Clemens to attempt a poem of his own.[36] This time in seeking to express his sense of bereavement, he turned to Browning rather than to Wordsworth. Borrowing the poet's favorite device, the dramatic monologue, he assumed the role of "a bereft and demented mother," who laments the loss of the past and its joys, as well as the loss of her daughter. Besides the monologue form, the piece also employs the sudden exclamations and interior questions characteristic of many of Browning's poems. When Clemens made the dead daughter sixteen, he was perhaps remembering Browning's "Evelyn Hope," for Susy was twenty-four when she died.

Excessively sentimental, Clemens' poem by no means reflects Browning's genius at capturing the psychological states of the characters he creates. But stilted as its diction at times became, the emotions were ones which the author felt very deeply. And the fact that he took Browning as the model for this, his last poem, may be read as a final sign of his longtime affection for the English poet and his works.

III

Nineteenth-Century Fiction

ONE OF CLEMENS' MOST CHARACTERISTIC COMMENTS on his knowledge of fiction, and of literature in general came in June, 1909. He and Albert Bigelow Paine were returning to Redding from St. Timothy's School, Baltimore, where the humorist had just delivered the commencement address. As they talked of literary matters, Clemens once again noted that he had never been able to appreciate such authors as Jane Austen, Thackeray, or George Meredith. Possibly because the academic ceremonies of the day before had reminded him of his own lack of formal education, he added: "I don't know anything about anything, and never did," and then he cited one other example: "My brother used to try to get me to read Dickens, long ago, I couldn't do it—I was ashamed; but I couldn't do it."[1]

If such remarks were not wholly inspired by the author's characteristic tendency to dramatize himself as an "original," they at least suggest a considerable feeling of inadequacy on his part. As a consequence, possibly even in his most violent criticisms there appears a guilty sense that he perhaps really *ought* to like certain works. As for the comment on Dickens, though he did except *A Tale of Two Cities* from the rest of the canon, it could not have been farther from the truth.

Many of Clemens' early reactions to nineteenth-century fiction appear indirectly in the form of burlesque, and, particularly, in his use of the so-called "condensed novel" in his own works. He may not have cared much for Thackeray's serious novels, but he did learn a good deal from the Englishman's pioneer efforts in the use of the "condensed novel" as a vehicle for parody and satire. He studied the device, also, as it was practiced by Thackeray's imitators in British and American humor magazines, like *Punch, Fun,* and *Vanity Fair,* receiving special help from his San Francisco friends, Charles H. Webb and Bret Harte. His own experiments with the form, as Franklin Rogers has shown, had an important influence on many of his subsequent writings.[2]

On a number of occasions during the Western years and after, Clemens used the "condensed novel" not only to burlesque specific authors or particular literary types, but also to enhance certain themes in his longer works. In Chapter Twenty-one of *The Innocents Abroad* (1869), for instance, he turned to Thackeray's *The Legend of the Rhine* (itself a burlesque of Dumas' *Othon, l'archer*) for a part of his "Legend of Count Luigi." But whereas Thackeray's burlesque was directed primarily at Dumas, Clemens does more than merely poke fun at chivalric derring-do and peculiarities of literary style. His "legend," told to the group by the driver of their barouche, implicitly satirizes the practice of foisting such tales on unsuspecting tourists, as well as the gullibility of those who believe them. "Splendid legend—splendid lie—drive on," the narrator says at the end of the story.

Postscript III

In *Roughing It* (1872), the humorist employs the "condensed novel" form several times, burlesquing not only the romantic notions of his "tenderfoot," but also the books the youth had read in the days of his fondness for the "mellow moonshine" of romance. Most of these were books of western travel and adventure, but in the passage which also includes "The Aged Pilot Man," the author focuses his satire more directly upon currently popular romances of a more "literary" sort.

That episode involves the publication of a serialized "composite" novel in the newly established "literary" paper, the *Weekly Occidental*, and the resultant controversy which helps cause the *Occidental's* downfall. In presenting summaries of four of the chapters, each of which was to be contributed by a different author, Clemens doubtless drew on his memory of similar "composite" novels in British magazines. It was *Fun* which had introduced this refinement on the "condensed novel," when it announced on August 29, 1863, the appearance in future issues of *Philip Dombey, The Scalp Hunter's Roundabout Secret Legacy,* to be written by "every eminent writer of the day." That opus finally began in the issue of September 19, after several numbers of the magazine had discussed "future plans" and described some of the wrangling among the supposed authors over how to proceed.[3]

Two of Clemens' targets in the *Occidental* episode are highly conjectural. The first chapter of the composite novel, which is contributed by Mrs. F ("an able romanticist of the ineffable school") who introduces the traditional blonde heroine and a French Duke in love with her, could be aimed at either Mrs. M. E. Braddon or Mrs. Henry Wood, both frequent subjects for literary burlesquers. Mr. F's providing a lawyer "who set about getting the Duke's estates into trouble" could also be poking fun at Anthony Trollope's fondness for lawyers. But with the further complications which accompany the entrance of a "mysterious Rosicrucian" in the chapter furnished by Mr. D (the "dark and bloody editor of one of the dailies"), the identifications become more specific. As Rogers observes, Thackeray had used the Rosicrucian in his burlesque of Bulwer-Lytton in *Punch's Prize Novelists* (1847), and by the 1870's so many writers (including Bret Harte) followed his lead that the presence of a Rosicrucian in a literary burlesque immediately pointed to Bulwer-Lytton as its victim. Finally, one version of the chapter contributed by "a dissolute stranger with a literary turn of mind" was based partly on Charles Reade's *Love Me Little, Love Me Long* (1859).

In this latter instance, however, the burlesque becomes a double one. Not only does the stranger's chapter thrust at some of the absurdities of the target novel (or novels), but by the utter ridiculousness of its several

versions also satirizes the ostensibly serious chapters of the other contributors. Their objections, in turn, result in the controversy that
contributes to the death of the *Weekly Occidental.*

The burlesque of romantic stereotypes at this point in *Roughing It*
does more, however, than merely spotlight the foibles of the nineteenth-
century novel. Along with "The Aged Pilot Man," the account of the
Occidental novel, coming as it does at the conclusion of the narrator's
report of "flush times" in Virginia City, helps to show that the tenderfoot has now obtained much of the wisdom of the "old-timer." As Rogers
says, the fact that the author placed his tale of the *Weekly Occidental*
and its failure just after a number of episodes which show "flush times"
to be at their height, emphasizes the naiveté of the novelists in assuming
that their romantic balderdash would find a favorable reception in these
surroundings. A further implication may also be drawn from the narrator's own failure as a novelist and as a poet, for he has now moved
beyond his love for books bathed in the "mellow moonshine of romance,"
and cannot himself write that sort of literature. In effect, "the episode
becomes an implicit commentary upon the work which contains it—that
is, upon *Roughing It,* which becomes by contrast the antithesis of
romance."[4]

Besides the works of Reade mentioned in Chapter Ten, Clemens knew
well a number of Bulwer-Lytton's efforts. While in the West he had
quoted from the play *Richelieu* in an 1862 letter from Nevada and had
reviewed a performance for his San Francisco paper. Writing his description of the Lake Como region for *The Innocents Abroad* (Chapter
Twenty), he "suspected" that "this was the same place the gardener's
son deceived the lady of Lyons with" and included the appropriate
quotation from *The Lady of Lyons* itself. Though he complained to
Livy in 1871 that he found *Eugene Aram* "tedious," he later found a
place in his own library for *Kenelm Chillingly; Harold, or The Last of
the Saxon Kings; Rienzi, or The Last of the Tribunes; The Last of the
Barons;* and *The Last Days of Pompeii.*[5]

Clemens' direct criticisms of specific novels and novelists follow a
fairly consistent pattern and repeat many of the objections implied in
his burlesques. What he complained of most often were their absurdly
romantic (or at least unrealistic) situations, their excessive sentimentality, their dearth of "interest," and most of all their lack of believable or
likable characters.

Some of his harshest blows were directed at the works of Jane Austen,
though perhaps on occasion some of his vehemence was designed to tease

his friend Howells, who was one of Jane's ardent admirers. Writing to Howells in 1909, for instance, he termed Austen's novels "impossible" and remarked upon the gross injustice which had been perpetrated when the author had been allowed to die a natural death rather than being executed for her literary crimes. Somewhat earlier, in an unfinished manuscript, he had said that although he could see the sharpness of character drawing and sureness of touch so often praised by the critics, he could not fully appreciate them since they became apparent only when Austen dealt with "odious characters." Yet in the same passage he again seemed willing to admit that the fault might lie in himself. Excursions into *Pride and Prejudice* (1813) and *Sense and Sensibility* (1811), made him feel, he said, "like a barkeeper entering the Kingdom of Heaven," secretly ashamed to find that there were "fine things, great things, admirable things" that others could perceive but he could not.[6]

Clemens had a few more favorable words for the novels of George Eliot, but not many. *Middlemarch* (1871–72) brought "frequent blinding flashes of single-sentence poetry, philosophy, wit & what-not." For the most part, however, he found the analyses of motives and feelings "labored & tedious," the characters "paltry & tiresome," and the story "unexciting & uninteresting." He tried to read *Daniel Deronda* (1876) at about the same time, but gave up after he had "dragged through three chapters, losing flesh all the time." Some years earlier he had found Eliot's treatment of Tito's struggle with his conscience (in *Romola*, 1863) and his resolving "to do, not a bad thing, but not the *best* thing," an impressive piece of characterization. Nevertheless, adverse reactions outweighed favorable ones.[7]

What he saw as faulty characterization and excessive verbiage also prevented Clemens from sharing the enthusiasm of Livy and her friends for the novels of George Meredith. He dutifully attended some of the readings of the "Meredith cult" in Hartford during the 1880's, but failed to be impressed. He did jot down the title of *The Egoist* (1879) in April, 1888, as if to remind himself to read it. But as his daughter Clara remembered, when Olivia read Meredith to the family, Clemens usually played cards, interrupting from time to time with humorous comments on the prolixity of Meredith's style.[8]

Clemens' aversion to Jane Austen and George Eliot should not suggest a special antipathy toward women writers, though his taste in some of those he liked might well be questioned. Besides his fascination with Mrs. Humphrey Ward's *Robert Elsmere* (1888), he confessed to Olivia in 1893 that he had come to appreciate Mrs. Gaskell's widely popular

Cranford (1853), which until then he had never managed to read. This time, however, perseverance had brought its reward; he had blasted through "the obstructing granite, slate and clay walls" to the "vein," and from then on extracted "pay ore right along."*

During the last two decades of his life, the humorist became interested in a number of British women novelists of his own day. In *Following the Equator,* he several times mentioned Olive Schreiner, whose *Story of an African Farm* (1883) had helped him understand conditions in South Africa. He also praised Flora Annie Steel's study of the Indian Mutiny, *The Face of the Waters* (1896) as "the finest novel ever written by a woman" and in 1899 wrote to Elizabeth Robbins that her *Open Question* had "enriched" him more than any book he had read in recent years. Elinor Glyn's *Three Weeks* (1907) intrigued him, too, both because of its frank treatment of sex and because of its underlying assumption that human beings were wholly governed by the basic law of their natures. When the attractive authoress called on him early in 1908, he told her that he considered her literary workmanship excellent and that he "quite agreed" with her view that man's statutory regulations of sexual matters were a distinct interference with the "higher law" of Nature. When she wished to publish his opinions, however, he drew back into his usual position regarding public expression of matters relating to sex: It would damn me before my time," he said "and I don't wish to be useful to the world on such expensive conditions."[9]

The following year, Clemens' attention was newly drawn to the British physician-novelist, Sir Arthur Conan Doyle, whom he had met in England in 1907, and who in 1908 began his active role in the Congo Reform Association. As Clemens had done in 1905 with *King Leopold's Soliloquy,* Doyle turned the profits from his pamphlet *The Crime of the Congo* (1909) to the work of the Association. When he sent Clemens a copy, the American congratulated him for his efforts, offering to help in the campaign against the Belgian king if he could so do.[10]

Before their meeting and mutual interest in the Congo, however, Clemens' regard for Sir Arthur, or at least for his Sherlock Holmes stories, had been considerably less warm. The humorist evidently looked upon detectives and detective fiction with mixed emotions. In the mid-seventies, he satirized the operations of Allan Pinkerton and his agents with the bumbling adventures of his own amateur detective, Simon

* SLC to Olivia L. Clemens, 4/18/93, Mark Twain Papers.

Wheeler. In 1879, the sensational theft of the body of Alexander T. Stewart, a wealthy New York merchant, inspired "The Stolen White Elephant" (1882). For that piece the author adapted some of the actual newspaper accounts of the New York case, burlesquing especially the private detectives' absurdly detailed reports (again à la Pinkerton) of commonplace observations and their submitting of huge expense accounts as they vainly struggle to locate the missing pachyderm. In describing the story to Howells shortly after finishing it, he commented that he had burlesqued the detective business "very extravagantly," but then added a final jab: "—if it *is* possible to burlesque that business extravagantly."[11] Yet he was obviously fascinated by the dramatic possibilities of crime detection, and put the device of court-room revelation of the facts of a crime to serious use in *Tom Sawyer* (1876), *Puddn'head Wilson* (1894), *Tom Sawyer, Detective* (1896), and *The Mysterious Stranger* (1916).

It may even have been, as Albert Stone suggests, that the swift rise of Doyle's stories to best-sellerdom in America in the early 1890's had some influence on the humorist's use of that device in the latter three works. There is no doubt that a large market for detective fiction resulted when *The Sign of the Four* appeared in *Lippincott's Magazine* during the winter and spring of 1890, followed in rapid succession by a reprinting of *A Study in Scarlet* (1887) and S. S. McClure's serial publication of the stories later to be collected in *The Adventures of Sherlock Holmes* (1892) and *The Memoirs of Sherlock Holmes* (1894). Yet in June, 1896, only two months before *Harper's* published the first installment of *Tom Sawyer, Detective,* Clemens wrote in his notebook: "What a curious thing a 'detective' story is. And was there ever one that the author needn't be ashamed of, except 'The Murders in the Rue Morgue' "?[12]

What especially irked him from the beginnings of his acquaintance with Sherlock Holmes was Doyle's insistence on the almost supernatural intellectuality of his detective. And in August, 1901, inspired by the first installment of *The Hound of the Baskervilles* in that month's *Strand* magazine, the humorist returned to a modified form of the "condensed novel" and aimed "A Double-Barrelled Detective Story" at the "cheap and ineffectual ingenuities of Doyle's "pompous sentimental 'extraordinary man'."[13]

As he told Joe Twichell early that September, the seed for the story had been planted many years before when the minister had loaned him one of Doyle's books for bedtime reading. But though he had several times attempted to write the story, until 1901 he had been unable to do so.

The bedtime "seed"-book was almost certainly *A Study in Scarlet* (1887). Like Clemens' tale it, too, is "double-barrelled." Part One, set in London dramatizes Sherlock Holmes' identification of Jefferson Hope as the murderer of his fellow-Americans Enoch Drebber and Joseph Stangerson; Part Two is a flashback to the events in Utah that had led, years before, to Hope's vow of vengeance. In Part Two, Drebber, Stangerson, and their Mormon "Avenging Angels" cause the death of John Ferrier and force Ferrier's daughter Lucy (Hope's sweetheart) to become one of Drebber's wives. With Lucy's death shortly thereafter, Hope haunts the mountains around Salt Lake City until Drebber and Stangerson fear to leave their homes. When Hope becomes ill, however, the pair flee from Utah. Several years pass before Hope finds their trail again and tracks them through the United States and most of the capitals of Europe. "Year passed into year . . . but still he wandered on, a human bloodhound, with his mind wholly set upon the one object to which he had devoted his life." Finally catching up with them in London, he dispatches them so skillfully that only through the aid of the great Holmes does Scotland Yard manage to apprehend him. Before he can be brought to trial, however, he dies of an aneurism brought on by the rigors of his long search.

Swinging wildly between melodrama and farce, "A Double-Barrelled Detective Story" likewise records a life devoted to revenge. Its protagonist, Archy Stillman, pursues one Jacob Fuller through the western states, Mexico, and ultimately through Australasia and India. Archy, too, is a human bloodhound, but Clemens goes Doyle one better by actually bestowing upon his human bloodhound a bloodhound's exceptional sense of smell.[14]

As in *A Study in Scarlet,* the revenger's quest is inspired by a mistreated bride. But to endow his hero with the unusual "gift," the humorist invented an even more melodramatic crime than that in Doyle's novel. Here the first installment of *The Hound of the Baskervilles* perhaps helped, for therein Holmes learns the Baskerville family legend of Hugo Baskerville's abduction of a yeoman's daughter, setting his hounds on her trail when she escapes him, and finally dying himself under the fangs of the huge "hound of hell."

Clemens' story begins with the wedding of Jacob Fuller and the proud daughter of an aristocratic Virginia planter. On the morning after the ceremony, the bride, who had married against her father's wishes, learns that Fuller's one aim is to use her as a means of punishing her father for his many insults. As his climactic act after three months of cruelty and humiliation, Fuller ties his pregnant wife to a tree near a public road at midnight, lashes her across the face with a cowhide whip, and sets his bloodhounds on her. When they have ripped off her clothes, he abandons her to the shame of being discovered there the next morning. From this pre-natal experience, then, her son Archy receives "the gift of the bloodhound."

After her father's death, which swiftly followed this degradation, the young mother moves to New England, adopts the name Stillman, and discovering Archy's talent, plots her revenge. When Archy reaches sixteen, she sets him on the trail of Fuller, who she has learned is a successful miner in Denver. The youth is not to kill the villain, but merely to hound him from place to place with notes threatening exposure (much like the successive notes left by the Mormon "Avenging Angels" warning John Ferrier of the number of days left for him to consent to the marriage of his daughter to Drebber or Stangerson).

Though Archy's quest does not continue so long as that of Jefferson Hope, it does go on for three-and-a-half years. To the ridiculousness of Archy's "gift," the author adds the irony that the man whom he pursues from Denver to Mexico is not the brutal husband at all, but a cousin with the same name. Seeking to rectify his terrible error, Archy then follows his quarry to Australia, India, and back without being able to catch up with him. In California again, he loses his trail completely near the silver-mining area of Hope[!] Canyon. ("Someone gave him a lift in a wagon, I suppose," Archy says, implicitly satirizing a device which frequently threw Sherlock Holmes momentarily off the scent.)

At that point, just as Doyle's flashback in Part Two of *A Study in Scarlet* begins as if he were writing an entirely new story, so Clemens' Chapter Four introduces a whole new series of events, whose many absurd coincidences were doubtless designed to burlesque what he saw as similar faults in the Sherlock Holmes stories. In the mining camp, Fetlock Jones (an English youth whose presence there remains wholly unexplained and who turns out to be a nephew of Sherlock Holmes) plans the murder of Flint Buckner, a brutal miner to whom he is apprenticed. Just as he is about to execute his scheme, the great Holmes himself arrives in Hope Canyon, again with no explanation of why he has come there. From then on the author subjects this "Extraordinary Man" (as Dr. Watson, too, so often calls him) to all manner of abuse.

Much of Clemens' direct attack is too bald for effective humor, and the piece as a whole is too farcical for wholly effective satire. But among the many characteristic descriptions and devices which the author laughs at, several are worthy of special note. One in particular provides the best expression of the humorist's annoyance with Holmes' almost supernatural intellectuality. Shortly after the detective's arrival, three of Hope Canyon's rough miners worshipfully observe him through the hotel window. Though the men are entirely serious, their vernacular comments effectively parody Doyle's generally overdone references to Holmes' appearance and abilities, and at the same time satirize the fact that Doyle had, in effect, brought Holmes back from the dead in *The Hound of The Baskervilles*. "By gracious! *That's* a head!" Ferguson exclaims, and Jake Parker, the blacksmith, adds: "Look at his nose! look at his eyes! Intellect? Just a battery of it!" Ham Sandwich adds a subtle barb by echoing Hamlet's "sicklied o'er with the pale cast of thought" in his remarks on Holmes' characteristic pallor: "Comes from thought—that's what it comes from. Hell! duffers like us don't know what real thought *is*." Then they decide that the "awful gravity" and "pallid solemness" which make the detective's countenance so impressive have resulted from the fact that Holmes has "been dead four times a'ready. . . ."[15]

The best burlesque in Clemens' story—the beginning of Chapter Four —is of another order altogether. Yet, though the passage has often been cited as an example of his distaste for overblown nature description so common in Victorian novels, its position in the tale as well as its tone suggests that his specific target was the more than six-hundred-word effusion in *A Study in Scarlet,* which describes Utah's "great alkali plain."

Part Two of Doyle's novel opens with no reference whatever to preceding events: "In the central portion of the great North American Continent there lies an arid and repulsive desert. . . ." Then follows a description of its "snow-capped and lofty mountains . . . dark and gloomy valleys . . . swift-flowing rivers which dash through jagged cañons; and . . . enormous plains, which in winter are white with snow, and in summer are gray with the saline alkali dust." In this wilderness, "the coyote skulks among the scrub, the buzzard flaps heavily through the air, and the clumsy grizzly bear lumbers through the dark ravines, and picks up such sustenance as it can amongst the rocks." North of the Sierra Blanco Mountains "stretches the great flat plain-land, all dusted over with patches of alkali, and intersected by clumps of the dwarfish chapparal bushes. . . . There is no sign of life, nor of anything appertaining to life. There is no bird in the steel-blue heaven, no movement upon the dull, gray earth—above all, there is absolute silence." Then, after inviting the reader to approach and examine the skeletons of men and animals which mark a "ghastly caravan route," the author introduces John Ferrier, and his small daughter, the sole survivors of an Indian attack on their wagon train, who stand "looking down on this very scene . . . upon the fourth of May, eighteen hundred and forty-seven. . . ."

Chapter Four of "A Double-Barrelled Detective Story" begins in almost exactly the same way as Doyle's Part Two. Just after Archy has lost Fuller's trail near Hope Canyon, Clemens introduces a description of a morning in Hope Canyon itself:

It was a crisp and spicy morning in early October. The lilacs and laburnums, lit with the glory-fires of autumn, hung burning and flashing in the upper air, a fairy bridge provided by kind Nature for the wingless wild things that have their homes in the tree-tops and would visit together; the larch and the pomegranate flung their purple and yellow flames in brilliant broad splashes among the slanting sweep of the woodland; the sensuous fragrance of innumerable deciduous flowers rose upon the swooning atmosphere; far in the empty sky a solitary œsophagus slept upon motionless wing; everywhere brooded stillness, serenity, and the peace of God.

"October is the time 1900; Hope Canyon is the place, a silver-mining camp away down in the Esmeralda region. . . ."[16]

After publication of his story, the author received a number of letters from readers showing that the double-talk, flowery non-sequiturs, and sentimental gush had indeed fooled many who were schooled in the sort of nature descriptions so aptly illustrated by the quotation from *A Study in Scarlet*. Some were startled by the sudden appearance of the "solitary œsophagus" but failed to notice the earlier idiocies in the passage. An additional fillip is added also by the fact that even if Clemens had been playing it straight, the description is wholly inappropriate to the actual Esmeralda region.

To complete his tale, Clemens introduced further wild coincidences. After Archy's discrediting of Holmes, a ragged stranger limps into town and reveals himself to be the "wrong" Jacob Fuller whom Archy had sought for so long. Even here the satire on Sherlock Holmes continues when the now insane Fuller addresses Archy as the great detective. In the old man's mutterings, the humorist seems also to snipe at Conan Doyle's interest in spiritualism. While hiding in the mountains, Fuller relates, he had heard spirit voices saying that they must call for Sherlock Holmes to track him down. Heartbroken, for he knew what it would be to have Holmes on his trail "with his superhuman penetration and tireless energies," Fuller had thenceforth imagined that the great sleuth was always just behind him.

Enraged by Holmes' alleged persecution of the old man, the miners form a lynch mob, but one of them, remembering the detective's propensity for rising from the dead, urges burning rather than hanging or shooting. The sheriff rides in to quell the mob and the tale ends with the escape of Fetlock Jones and Archie's final note to his mother explaining that his quest had ended with the discovery that the murdered Flint Buckner was the real Jacob Fuller. In the sheriff's final speech the author implicitly satirizes even the probable reaction to his own audacity in trifling with Doyle's popular hero. In the name of the whole nation, and "with feeling," the lawman apologizes to Sherlock Holmes, declaring it "a blot on the country that a man whose marvelous exploits had filled the world with their fame and their ingenuity . . . whose histories of them had won every reader's heart by the brilliancy and charm of their literary setting, should be visited under the Stars and Stripes by an outrage like this." The reference to "their literary setting" also provides further support for the assumption that the "lilacs and laburnums" passage was directed specifically at overwritten passages like that in *A Study in Scarlet*.

It is indeed unfortunate that the humorist was unwilling to work over this story sufficiently to weed out the elements that detract from its otherwise superb burlesque of Conan Doyle's style and characterization.

When Clemens told Paine in 1909 that except for *A Tale of Two Cities*, he had never been able to read Charles Dickens' books, he was merely giving way to his mood of the moment. For he had read most of them, if not all, and had often incorporated allusions, ideas, and even specific incidents into his own writings.

Some of the novels he obviously read as they appeared. In November, 1856, when *Little Dorrit* was still running in monthly installments, Thomas Jefferson Snodgrass alluded to the book's chief symbol of governmental red tape in his summary of Shakespeare's *Julius Caesar*. "Missus Brutus come out when the other fellers was gone," he says, "and like Mr. Clennam at the Circumlocution Office, she 'wanted to know'." The author may well have had the Circumlocution Office in mind again in Snodgrass' third letter, which describes the difficulties of "an indigent Irish woman," who is shunted from official to official in her efforts to obtain coal from the public supply. He was to do a much more thorough job with the concept in 1870, however, when his *Galaxy* story, "Facts in the Case of the Great Beef Contract," traced the struggles of its protagonist in "the Circumlocution Office of Washington."[17]

During the 1860's Clemens alluded to Dickens in a number of letters, both private and professional.[18] Writing to Orion about six months prior to their Nevada trip, he told of a fortune teller's recent prediction that no matter how many times he might fall in love in the future, he would always think of Laura Wright, his newly estranged love, immediately before falling asleep at night. She had unfortunately been correct so far, he said, and then summoned a comment from the world of *Martin Chuzzlewit* (1843–4) to bewail his sad state: That "will be devilish comfortable, won't it, when both she and I (like one of Dickens' characters) are Another's?"[19]

Such spontaneous recollection of Augustus Moddle's habitual reference to the loss of Mercy Pecksniff argues that Clemens was fond of *Martin Chuzzlewit,* as does his including its delightful malaprop Sairey Gamp, among the "sublime women" of history whom he saluted a decade later in a London speech.[20] And if Mark Twain's traveling companion in *A Tramp Abroad* received the name Harris because of the author's interest in Sairey's imaginary crony, "Mrs. 'arris," the association provides an additional humorous touch when one considers that his actual companion on the German tour was the minister Joseph Twichell.

One of the highlights of the 1863–64 social season in Carson City was a benefit for the First Presbyterian Church, featuring the Shakespearean actor James Stark in a reading from the *Pickwick Papers* (1836–7). Reporting the event in the *Territorial Enterprise,* Clemens especially praised Stark's handling of the speech of Sergeant Buzfuz at the Bardell vs. Pickwick breach-of-promise suit. Up to that time, he said, he had considered the episode "the tamest of Mr. Dickens' performances," but now he was certain that such renditions would insure the piece's continued existence as a classic.[21]

References to *Dombey and Son* (1846–8), a favorite during the Western years if not earlier, found their way into at least two professional letters and one personal one. A piece in the Keokuk *Gate City* early in 1862 mentioned the volume's presence among the "luxuries" taken to the Humboldt mining region. A few weeks later he was quoting from the novel and entertaining his friend Bill Claggett with enthusiastic descriptions of some of its characters. Warmed by his recollections of the pleasure of their company, he exclaimed exasperatedly, "Oh, d--n it,

I wish I had the book." He particularly liked the old salt, Captain Ed'ard Cuttle, whose name he borrowed in one of the Sandwich Island letters of 1866 for a passenger on the steamer *Ajax*—a member of the jolly group of three who found nineteen gallons of whiskey insufficient for their ten-day voyage.[22]

During the Hawaiian tour, also, *David Copperfield* (1849–50) helped the humorist describe what he meant when he said that the unscrupulous Minister of Finance and Attorney General (an American) was *"hoopi-limeai"* to the king. The word means, he said, "well, it means Uriah Heep boiled down—it means the soul and spirit of obsequiousness."[23] On the same trip and several other times during the next few years, *Our Mutual Friend* (1864–5) provided a bright touch when the humorist recalled the incongruous tendency of Dickens' villainous "man of low cunning," Silas Wegg, to "drop into poetry" upon the slightest provocation. The first instance occurred during the episode involving Mr. Brown's seasickness when Mark Twain says that in order to entertain the sufferer, he "dropped into poetry" and recited his version of Polonius' advice to Laertes, whereupon Brown regurgitated. In 1868 the phrase helped enliven a Chicago *Republican* item dealing with the author's professed horror at the reported efforts of certain Congressmen to write verse. Ironically granting that Congress had no equal among legislatures for solemn stupidity, he called upon Dickens, to add: "But I did hope it would not 'drop into poetry.' I *did* hope it would confine its dullness to prose." The following January he used the phrase again to tease Mrs. Fairbanks, this time identifying its source. His Cleveland friend had written that the perfume of his cigars still lingered in the guest room to remind her of his recent visit and then quoted a purposely banal couplet apropos of the sentiment. Replying in kind, Clemens urged her to go up to his room and take another whiff of that fragrance which had so inspired her to " 'drop into poetry' like Silas Wegg."[24]

As Clemens implied in his review of James Stark's Carson City reading, the *Pickwick Papers* was not one of his favorites. By 1885, in fact, he was saying ironically (in notes for a speech on humor) that his inability to enjoy the book must prove that he lacked a sense of humor. More specifically, he complained that the actions of Pickwick and his friends were too much like those of the circus clown, with every line of the book saying, "Look at me—ain't I funny." But he did soften his criticism somewhat by praising others among Dickens' people: "Capt. Cuttle is good anywhere and so also are all of Dickens' humorous characters except those in Pickw[ick] Papers, and the body-snatcher—Tale of 2 Cities."[25]

If he did not like Pickwick and his cronies as characters, Clemens was at least intrigued by the comic overtones of the name Augustus Snodgrass. From his very early writings onward, the surname of Pickwick's poetic friend recurs with some frequency, and the given name at least once. After his *alter ego* of 1856, Thomas Jefferson Snodgrass, came Arthur Augustus, one of the "correspondents" to Mark Twain's column in the San Francisco *Morning Call,* and then another Snodgrass, who appeared briefly in a sketch for the *Californian* (11/4/64). Some years later, Clemens introduced a more "literary" counterpart of the poetic Pickwickian in "About Magnanimous Incident Literature" (1878). There, in one of the incidents, a young writer named Snagsby climbs to fame by exploiting an already famous author, "the renowned Snodgrass." (Snagsby, incidentally, shares his name with the kindly law-stationer in *Bleak House.*)[26] Finally, in Chapter Twenty-four of *The American Claimant* (1892) Washington Hawkins tries to lessen Sally Sellers' interest in Howard Tracy by telling her that Tracy is really S. M. (for Spinal Meningitis) Snodgrass, the horse-thief son of a Cherokee Strip doctor. Moreover, Washington claims to know Dr. Snodgrass personally, and also S. M.'s brother, Zylobalsamum Snodgrass.

Upon occasion, Clemens did react strongly against Dickens' indulgence in sentimentalism. As he remembered it many years later, he had been disgusted with his fellow-writers in San Francisco for their slavish imitation of Dickens' "pathetics." At least one newspaper sketch (in the *Californian,* 12/2/65) reflects that reaction. Though the author himself announced that his immediate target was a novelette by his friend Dan de Quille, he was obviously thinking also of the sort of sentimental relationships epitomized by that of Little Nell and her grandfather in *The Old Curiosity Shop* (1840–41). Turning again to the "condensed novel" form, he wove a touching story of the devotion of fair-haired, sweet-faced, little eight-year-old "Addie" to her "poor, blind-drunk Uncle Lige," who (in Addie's words) was just "the best uncle and tells me such stories." Uncle Lige, in turn, like Little Nell's grandfather, is profuse in his protestations of affection and gratitude (drunkenly slobbered out over his shirt front) to "l'il (hic!) Addie." Not for Clemens was that brand of sentimentalism, at least at this stage of his career.[27]

The humorist's interest in Dickens was stimulated anew during the Christmas holidays of 1867, by a chance to see the novelist himself.

Clemens was in New York for a reunion with some of his *Quaker City* shipmates, including Charles Langdon, who had come from Elmira with his parents and sister Olivia. Dickens was appearing nightly (and at some matinées) in Steinway Hall for the duration of the New York run of his famous reading tour of 1867–68.

As Clemens later remembered it, he first met Olivia and her family at the St. Nicholas Hotel on December 27 and went with them the same evening to hear Dickens read from *David Copperfield* and other works. Actually, his memories of his "first date" with Olivia were slightly confused, for though they may have met on the 27th, they could have heard selections from *David Copperfield* only on the evening of the 31st. Even so, the charm of the performance was hardly lessened by the presence of the girl whom Clemens had wished to meet ever since he had seen the portrait her brother had carried on the Mediterranean excursion.[28]

Of the reading itself, there are two accounts, significant in their differences. As roving reporter for the *Alta California* the humorist could hardly let this occasion pass without treating his Western readers to a firsthand impression of the great English novelist. The report which he wrote early in January mingled his own personal reactions with some which doubtless reflected his current literary "pose."

"Promptly at 8 p.m. . . . a tall, 'spry' (if I may say it), thin-legged old gentleman, gotten up regardless of expense, especially as to shirt-front and diamonds, with a bright red flower in his buttonhole, gray beard and mustache, bald head with side hair and beard brushed fiercely and tempestuously forward, as if its owner were sweeping down before a gale of wind, the very Dickens came!" He did not merely emerge from the wings but strode across the broad stage "in the most English way and exhibiting the most English general style and appearance . . . heedless of everything . . . as if he had seen a girl he knew turn the next corner."

After that appeal to the typical American tendency to belittle those in high places, and foreign visitors especially, Mark Twain continued:

> But that queer old head took on a sort of beauty bye and bye, and a fascinating interest, as I thought of the wonderful mechanism within it, the complex but exquisitely adjusted machinery that could create men and women, and put the breathe of life into them and alter all their ways and actions, elevate them, degrade them, murder them, marry them, conduct them through good and evil, through joy and sorrow, on their long march from the cradle to the grave, and never lose its godship over them, never make a mistake.

The stage setting for Dickens' performance also impressed the *Alta* correspondent. Like the novelist himself, it reflected flawless showmanship and "style" with its specially designed reading table, backed by a huge red screen, and its series of overhead lights "which threw down a glory upon the gentleman, after the fashion in use in the picture galleries for bringing out the best effects of great paintings."

Both the man himself and the actual performance, however, were allegedly disappointing. Mark Twain took issue with the "extravagant praises" bestowed by the New York *Herald* and *Tribune,* citing the disturbing huskiness of Dickens' voice and the monotony of the reading in general. He professed to be disturbed, too, by the reader's seeming inability to enliven his pathetic passages with genuine emotion, a fault which made the "beautiful pathos of his language" seem mere "glittering frostwork." More specifically, he found Dickens "a little Englishy in his speech"; the rendition of Peggoty's search for "Em'ly" was "bad"; and the episodes featuring "Dora the child-wife," and the storm at Yarmouth in which Steerforth drowned, "not as good as they might have been." He did like "Mrs. Micawber's inspired suggestions as to the negotiations of her husband's bills," but concluded that the whole performance was far inferior to what Dickens' reputation had led him to expect.

A number of factors were at work here. Anxiety to impress his Western readers doubtless contributed to the jibes at the New York critics. Those critics, by the way, had also mentioned the huskiness of Dickens' voice, the result of a current cold, but they had invariably noted that the distraction quickly disappeared as the performance proceeded. Clemens' "superior" attitude and his role of brash humorist, too, probably accounts for much of the flippancy of his review—especially in such remarks as the parenthetical reference to "the beautiful young lady with me—a highly respectable white woman." Finally, both the pose and his own natural feelings combined to play up the traditional condescension of the American toward the "invading" foreigner and the "Englishy" way that Dickens spoke and walked.

The report of the occasion which Clemens dictated for his autobiography in 1907 bears out some of these contentions. The approval of the stage setting and Dickens' "striking and picturesque appearance" remains, but the flippancy is gone. Moreover, the earlier estimate of the performance itself is almost completely reversed. Now Clemens declares that Dickens read "with great force and animation, in the lively passages, and with stirring effect." And the storm scene, rather than lacking force is now remembered as "so vivid, and so full of energetic action, that the house was carried off its feet, so to speak."[29]

Perhaps the glow induced by the recollection of his meeting with Olivia helped to soften the earlier appraisal. By 1907, also, whatever earlier animosity the author may have felt toward Britain had largely vanished. More important, Clemens no longer felt the necessity either to impress his readers with an appeal to American and Western superiority or to "be funny." Hence, the 1907 account may well represent a truer picture of his reaction to the performance than does the contemporary one.

Clemens had also paid a somewhat oblique tribute to Dickens following the novelist's death in June, 1870. "The Approaching Epidemic" in the September *Galaxy* ridicules the sort of literary leech who seeks to capitalize on even the slightest acquaintance with famous men. Listing the probable titles of lectures which would now engulf the public, he included such gems as " 'Remembrances of Charles Dickens' A Lecture. By John Jones, who saw him once in a streetcar and twice in a barbershop." Conversely, he was pleased and impressed in 1872 to find that admirers still brought fresh flowers daily to Dickens' grave in Westminster Abbey.[30] And in 1887 (as noted in Chapter Seven) when the novelist's son and namesake came to lecture in Boston, the Clemenses entertained him and his daughter in Hartford.

But in 1868 perhaps it had been the new interest stimulated by seeing Dickens in person which led the American to turn to the Englishman's works for an inspiration when he was revising the *Alta* letters for *The Innocents Abroad*. Whether the borrowing was conscious or unconscious, his description of Leonardo's *The Last Supper* in Chapter Nineteen bears a striking similarity to Dickens' reactions in *Pictures from Italy* (1846), a resemblance which the original *Alta* letter shares only slightly.

Dickens, in his chapter on Milan, introduces his readers to the great painting by noting that "in the old refectory of the dilapidated Convent of Santa Maria della Grazie is the work of art, perhaps better known than any other in the world: The Last Supper, by Leonardo da Vinci— with a door cut through it by the intelligent Dominican friars, to facilitate their operation at dinner time." Disclaiming any technical knowledge of the art of painting, he apologizes for his ignorance of "the 'touch' of this or that master," and then proceeds to describe the painting itself: "I would simply observe that in its beautiful composition and arrangement, there it is at Milan, a wonderful picture; and that, in its original colouring, or in its original expression of any single face or feature, there it is not."

Citing both the damage from dampness, decay, and neglect, and the clumsy efforts to retouch and patch which have utterly distorted the expressions, he remarks that any remnants of the original artist's genius, "which almost in a line or touch separated him from meaner painters and made him what he was," have been completely "blotched and spoiled." So obvious is that fact, Dickens says, that he would not have mentioned it "but for having observed an English gentleman before the picture, who was at great pains to fall into . . . mild convulsions, at certain minute details of expression which are not left in it." But, though it would be rational to conclude that the painting must once have been "a work of extraordinary merit," now since "few of its original beauties remain," tourists should be content to perceive the skill in design and should not praise excellences which have long ceased to exist.

The parallels in *The Innocents Abroad* are immediately apparent. "Here, in Milan, in an ancient tumbledown ruin of a church," Mark Twain begins, "is the mournful wreck of the most celebrated painting in the world—'The Last Supper,' by Leonardo da Vinci. We are not infallible judges of pictures, but, of course, we went there to see this wonderful painting, . . . always so worshiped by masters in art. . . ." Of the picture itself: " 'The Last Supper' is painted on the dilapidated wall of what was a little chapel attached to the main church in ancient times, I suppose. It is battered and scarred in every direction, and stained and discolored by time, and Napoleon's horses kicked the legs off most the disciples [*sic*] when they (the horses, not the disciples) were stabled there more than half a century ago. . . . The colors are dimmed with age; the countenances are scaled and marred, and nearly all expression is gone from them; the hair is a dead blur upon the wall, and there is no life in the eyes. Only the attitudes are certain."

Seizing on Dickens' brief mention of tourist enchantment with the painting, Clemens expands it into a biting criticism of the hypocritical pose. At great length his narrator describes the travelers standing before the picture "with bated breath and parted lips," speaking "only in the catchy ejaculations of rapture." If such reactions were honest, he says, they would be worthy of envy, or, at the least, would reveal "an astonishing talent for seeing things that had already passed away." But whereas a practiced artist could perhaps restore in his own mind, the former glories of the painting, the narrator himself could not, nor, in his opinion, could "those other uninspired visitors." And then in a first-person vernacular version of Dickens' final comment he concludes: "After reading so much about it, I am satisfied that the Last Supper was a very miracle of art once. But it was three hundred years ago."

In his borrowing and explaining the material, however, the author made it eminently his own, heightening both the comic and the satiric effect by his juxtaposition of the vernacular idiom of narrator and tourist and the highflown rhetoric of guidebook art criticism. Nevertheless, in the very order of the description, the denial of aesthetic expertness, the details noted, and the conclusion drawn therefrom, the debt to Dickens stands revealed. What is most ironic is that this passage has been cited perhaps more often than any other in *The Innocents Abroad* as evidence of the brash Westerner's reprehensible lack of appreciation for the culture of Europe. At the same time, however, that very criticism constitutes something of a tribute to the skill of the adaptation.

Some of the same sort of borrowing may lie behind the American humorist's treatment of the "Noble Red Man" in his letter of March 22, 1862, to the Keokuk *Gate City,* in a *Galaxy* article (September, 1870), and in Chapter Nineteen of *Roughing It*. Though it could be entirely coincidental, the tone of these passages (especially the first and last) is almost identical with that of Dickens' "The Noble Savage," which first appeared in *Household Words* on June 11, 1852 (reissued in *Reprinted Pieces,* 1858). Both authors mock the sentimentality responsible for the apotheosis of the primitive life; both emphasize the dirt, smell, and generally repellant nature of the savages. Both mention Pope's line, "Lo! the poor Indian," and both refer to the "Bosjesmans (Bushmen) of South Africa" (Clemens' phrase) as examples of primitive repulsiveness. (Dickens, for instance, depicts the Bushman "in his festering bundle of hides, with his filth, his antipathy to water, and his cry of 'qu-u-u-u-aaa!' [Bosjesman for something desperately unworthy, I have no doubt].") If these parallels *are* merely coincidental, they nevertheless suggest a strong kinship of response in the two authors.

It is even more likely that in 1870 Clemens again drew on Dickens for some of the details in his "Boy's Manuscript," another experiment in the "condensed novel" tradition. This burlesque, from which one of the major themes of *Tom Sawyer* ultimately evolved, seems directed at the type of adult courtship portrayed in David Copperfield's wooing of Dora Spenlow. It makes its point, as Franklin Rogers suggests, not only by reducing the actions of adults to those of children (Billy Rogers and his "Darling Amy") but also by paralleling Billy's actions with those of the "tall young man" enamored of nineteen-year-old Laura Miller. Much of the story's action, of course, derives from the author's own memories of his Hannibal boyhood, with perhaps some assistance from T. B. Aldrich's *Story of a Bad Boy* (1869). But Dickens, too, seems to have contributed his share.[31]

Among minor elements which point to the English novelist, Amy shares her name with the heroine in *Little Dorrit;* and Bob Sawyer (the boy who "licks" Billy), with the medical student in *Pickwick Papers*. Indeed, the use of Bob Sawyer's name here and its later inclusion in the aforementioned notebook plan for the "Creatures of Fiction" story suggests not only a considerable interest in Dickens' medical student, but also the most likely source for Tom Sawyer's surname.[32]

The closest parallels to *David Copperfield* exist in the characteristics and the actions shared by Billy and David and the respective objects of their affections.[33] Like David, Billy moons about the house of his love, hopefully watching the windows for even a glimpse of her dress. Both walk for miles on the chance that they might see or be seen—David in excruciating pain from shoes too small for him, Billy braving punishment for playing hookey in order to walk on Amy's street, and also persuading a torchlight procession in which he marches to pass her house, not once but four times. Present in the "Boy's Manuscript," too, are echoes of the frequently broken engagement; the rival lover, Red Whiskers; and David's attempt to arouse Dora's jealousy by flirting with the lady in pink. A geranium leaf dropped by the beautiful Laura Miller, which Billy and "the tall young man" both stoop to retrieve, recalls the importance of geraniums to David and Dora—in the greenhouse where they are first alone, in the bouquet for her birthday, in the memories of "a straw hat and blue ribbons, and a quantity of curls, and a little black dog being held up, in two slender arms, against a bank of blossoms and bright leaves," which the "scent of a geranium leaf" conjures up for David. Amy, too, wore a blue ribbon and a white frock

More specifically, David's habitual reference to Dora as "my little wife" and "dear little wife" is several times repeated in Billy's calling Amy, "my little wife" (which in turn recalls Clemens' own mention of "Dora, the child-wife" in his *Alta* review of the Dickens' reading). The heroines themselves are remarkably similar, also, since Dora never does grow out of her childish fancies. Amy envisions "a little cosy cottage with vines running over the windows and a four-story brick attached where she could receive company and give parties." Dora and David hope for exactly the same sort of cottage, and while not specifying a four-story addition, would require at least that much extra room if Dora's elaborate plans for entertaining were to materialize. Such suggestions, though not conclusive, point to *David Copperfield* as an important source.

The "Boy's Manuscript," in turn, becomes a significant document in American literature for several reasons. Not only does it represent its author's first attempt to put the material of his Hannibal boyhood to literary use, but it also contains one of the main elements in the plot of *Tom Sawyer.* Though parallels to *David Copperfield* itself become less clear when the names are changed and additional episodes and plot-strands are added, the events of the "courtship" do serve as a central element which helps to bind the whole work together.

As for surface resemblances, the most "Dickensian" of all Clemens' novels is *The Gilded Age* (1873). Yet, as Delancey Ferguson has aptly observed, the multiple plot, the beautiful maiden of unknown parentage, the youth of upright life who finally wins fame and fortune, were staple devices of the Victorian "Three-Decker" novel and hence should not really be emphasized.[34]

On the other hand, additional similarities might well be noted. One of the earliest English reviews (*Spectator,* March, 1874) found the description of Colonel Sellers' astounding clock in Chapter Seven particularly reminiscent of Dickens. Edward Wagenknecht, who shares that opinion, also sees in Senator Dilworthy's hypocritical oration to his Cattleville constituents an echo of the Reverend Mr. Chadband's oily exhortations in Chapter Nineteen of *Bleak House.*[35]

If Wilkins Micawber was not a parent of Colonel Beriah Sellers, he, like Goldsmith's Beau Tibbs, was certainly some other close relative. The same *Spectator* article comments on the resemblance between Micawber and Sellers, but also notes a significant difference. Instead of merely waiting for something to turn up, Sellers (the reviewer says) "turned up the most surprising Kohinoors by merely delving into the inexhaustible mine of his own inventive fancy." Probably it was this quality that the Colonel had inherited from Clemens' cousin James Lampton, unquestionably the principal model for Sellers. But in view of the author's favorable comment on one of the scenes involving the Micawbers in his *Alta* report of the Dickens' reading, it is tempting to assume that he also drew on *David Copperfield* for some of the characteristics of his comic visionary.

Numerous examples of the proclivities of both men for enlarging upon the commonplace and minimizing the usual could be cited. For instance, though there also may be an echo from Goldsmith in Sellers' transformation of the lowly turnips into a sumptuous feast (in Chapter

Eleven), the same magic is present when Micawber, in his sordid quarters, concocts a batch of rum punch (Chapter Twenty-eight). "It was wonderful," David says at that point, "to see his face shining at us out of a thin cloud of these delicate fumes, as he stirred, and mixed, and tasted, and looked as if he were making, instead of punch, a fortune for his family down to the latest posterity." The Colonel's family also resembles that of Micawber more than that of James Lampton. Lampton had five children, four daughters and a son. Micawber has a set of twins and two others, a boy and a girl. Sellers' family, as perhaps fits his grander dreams, simply doubles the number of Micawbers, with two sets of twins and four other children. Such parallels, of course, could be stressed too much, but a total denial of indebtedness would be equally ill-advised.

In 1882 Clemens made brief use of another of Dickens' books in *Life on the Mississippi* when he consulted *American Notes* along with other British accounts of travels through the United States. As with Mrs. Trollope and Captain Marryat, he implied his agreement with a number of the author's criticisms. He cited without objection, for instance, Dickens' less-than-glowing description of Mississippi steamboats and his unfavorable portrait of Cairo, Illinois (later used as the model for Martin Chuzzlewit's "Eden").[36]

It is uncertain when Clemens first read *A Tale of Two Cities* (1859), the one among Dickens' novels which he did not abjure in 1909. He had doubtless been familiar with it for a long time before he pressed it into use in 1879 as one of his guides to Revolutionary landmarks in Paris. By 1898 he was telling his friend Henry Fischer in Vienna that he read the book "at least every two years," and had recently finished it "for the 'steenth time."[37] How fully he absorbed it has already been suggested in the foregoing discussions of *Huckleberry Finn* and *A Connecticut Yankee.*

One other instance deserves mention. Just as *David Copperfield* may have supplied details for the "courtship" episodes of *Tom Sawyer,* so *A Tale of Two Cities* very probably helped the author introduce a second major plot-strand, which begins in the village graveyard and culminates in the trial of Muff Potter for the murder of Dr. Robinson. Neither Clemens' own recollections of boyhood nor Dixon Wecter's detailed study of the Hannibal years indicate that graverobbers had ever plied their trade in Hannibal. However, in Dickens' novel (Book Two, Chapter Fourteen) young Jerry Cruncher peers fearfully through a cemetery gate to watch his father and two companions at their "honest" nocturnal toil. Similarly, in Chapter Nine, Tom Sawyer steals from bed, goes to the graveyard with Huck, and there watches Dr. Robinson, Muff Potter, and Injun Joe at the grave of the recently-buried Hoss Williams.

It is not strange that Clemens should have been attracted to Dickens' novels. The two authors shared remarkably similar backgrounds, which, in turn, doubtless contributed to similarities of outlook and of method. Both were largely self-educated, Dickens having gone from school to the blacking-warehouse at twelve and Clemens to Ament's print-shop at about the same age. Each had subsequently become a newspaper reporter and later, for a time, had covered the proceedings of legislative bodies—Clemens in Nevada and Washington, Dickens in the House of Commons. While in their twenties, both were jilted by sweethearts, though Dickens' loss of Maria Beadnell probably left deeper wounds than Clemens' loss of Laura Wright. Yet, the American author's experience must have given him a considerable jolt, too. (Not only did he note down in 1885 the anniversary of his parting from Laura—fully twenty-seven years after the event—but he also spoke at some length about their relationship in an autobiographical dictation in 1906. This sort of interest lends support to Samuel Webster's conjecture that in the "icy Laura Hawkins" of *The Gilded Age,* Clemens was endeavoring to get Laura Wright out of his system.)[38] Both writers had gusto, robustness, and closeness of observation; and, with humor, sentimentality, and social criticism as stocks in trade, both went on to achieve wide popularity as public personalities as well as authors. More important, both drew heavily on personal experience to create novels that brought the vernacular idiom and the use of the first-person boy narrator to new levels of artistry.

Why then was Clemens' rejection in 1909 so sweeping? Much of the reason perhaps lies in a comment reported in the Sydney *Morning Herald* on September 17, 1895. Citing Dickens among those authors who were keenly aware of the pathos and tragedy behind every humorous situation, he qualified his praise by confessing that over the years he had lost much of his youthful admiration for the British humorist: "I seem to see all the machinery of the business too clearly, the effort is too patent. The true and lasting genius of humour does not drag you thus to boxes labelled 'pathos,' 'humour,' and show you all the mechanism of the inimitable puppets that are going to perform. How I used to laugh at Simon Tapperwit [*sic*], and the Wellers, and a host more! But I can't do it now somehow; and time, it seems to me, is the true test of humour. . . ."

Whether the confusion of Simon Tappertit (the bombastic apprentice of *Barnaby Rudge*) with Martin Chuzzlewit was Clemens' error or the reporter's cannot be determined. But the statement itself is fairly consistent with the "Look at me—ain't I funny" complaint of 1885. Hence, Clemens may have extended this disenchantment into a complete rejection during his conversation with Paine in 1909. Still, the American's desire to be known as one who had risen to literary eminence almost solely through his own efforts doubtless also contributed its share. Even in the Australian interview he had traded to some extent on his role as an "original" by remarking that he did not read contemporary writers for fear that he might unconsciously pick up their literary styles or techniques.

If Clemens actually had lost interest over the years in all of Dickens' books except *A Tale of Two Cities,* at least his early enthusiasm had been a real one—and one that he put to good use. When it is considered that Mark Twain and Charles Dickens share the distinction of being probably the most widely popular humorous writers of their respective countries, the record of Clemens' interest in the older author forms both a notable chapter in Anglo-American literary relations and a fitting conclusion to this Postscript.

Afterword

W HEN SAMUEL L. CLEMENS DIED IN APRIL, 1910, messages of con-
dolence arrived from all over the world. Seldom has the death
of a celebrity evoked a greater sense of personal loss. His own love of
spectacle would have found great satisfaction in the scene at New York's
Brick Church on the day of his funeral: masses of flowers banked the
casket where he lay in state; the street outside was jammed with the
crowds of mourners waiting to file by to pay their last respects. His
sentimental nature would have been touched especially by the wreath
woven from laurels that grew at Stormfield, which Dan Beard and his
wife placed on the casket. These last expressions of homage climaxed
the popular acclaim that marked his later years.

With all of the tributes during these years, however, the undercurrent
of gloom had remained strong, deepened by the failures and tragedies
of the 1890's and early 1900's. But pessimism never entirely won out.
Until the very end idealism battled despair. Like his much-admired
Cromwell (as described by Carlyle) Samuel Clemens was "a kind of
chaotic man" struggling to see the light amid a dark pessimism. What is
more, his gloom doubtless derived from the same source as Cromwell's—
from "the depth and tenderness of his wild affections: the quantity of
sympathy he had with things—the quantity of insight he would [i.e.
wished to] yet get into the heart of things, the mastery he would yet get
over things."[1] His failure to achieve these last two qualities was especially frustrating. It was almost as if he were summing up his own search
for answers when in *Tom Sawyer Abroad* (Chapter Nine), after an
argument over whether the Sahara Desert was made or just happened,
he had Tom say that the trouble with arguments is that they are merely
theories—and theories prove nothing: "They only give you a place to
rest on, a spell, when you are tuckered out butting around and around
trying to find out something there ain't no way *to* find out." And another
trouble with theories is that "there's always a hole in them somewheres,
sure, if you look close enough."

Yet in spite of all his frustrations and all his railings, sympathy *was* still there. To borrow from another of Carlyle's books, mankind might have said of Clemens what Teufelsdröckh said of mankind: "Thy very Hatred . . . those foolish lies thou tellest of me in thy splenetic humour: what is all this but an inverted Sympathy? Were I a Steam-engine, wouldst thou take the trouble to tell lies of me? Not thou! I should grind all unheeded, whether badly or well."[2] If Clemens had been an absolute determinist, he, too, would not have bothered to rail.

Clemens' faults as a writer and thinker are obvious ones. He did not see life steadily nor see it whole, but fitfully, through flashes of affection, indignation, or scorn. Many of his inconsistencies resulted from opportunism, others from the fact that he reacted violently to specific political, social, or ethical situations and almost entirely in terms of the individuals involved. At the same time, he often generalized too broadly from these individual instances. Yet from his own experiences and from his reading he created a body of literature that subjects human foibles to a searching scrutiny. What he borrowed from books, he often adapted so skillfully that we have been a long time discovering his debts and are still a long way from identifying all of them. His moulding the American vernacular into a powerful literary tool and his re-creation of an entire era in American civilization helped to produce a truly American literature. Few subsequent American writers have not been touched by his example. Many, like Hemingway and Faulkner, have freely admitted their kinship. But Mark Twain's works, like theirs, transcend national boundaries, for his major concern was not with frontier man, nor even with American man, but with mankind. Despite Clemens' scorn for human pretensions, he never stopped trying—*in his own way*—to pry man up to a little higher level of manhood.

Bibliographical Note

S PACE LIMITATIONS DO NOT PERMIT listing of all the books and periodicals consulted in the course of this study. I have tried to acknowledge specific debts in the notes. I wish, however, to make special mention of those un-published works that come closest to my subject. Except for one Master's thesis, all are doctoral dissertations. Those which treat some of the more general concerns of my discussion are Paul J. Carter, Jr. "The Social and Political Ideas of Mark Twain," Cincinnati, 1939, and Arthur L. Scott, "Mark Twain as a Critic of Europe," Michigan, 1948. Robert M. Rodney, "Mark Twain in England: A Study of the English Criticism of . . . Mark Twain," Wisconsin, 1946, considers the reception of Clemens' works in England, as well as his relations with England generally. Those studies that emphasize the humorist's reading are Harold Aspiz, "Mark Twain's Reading: A Critical Study," California (Los Angeles), 1950 [the fullest treatment, which attempts to list all the books known or referred to by Clemens, and to which I am indebted for a number of references that I might otherwise have missed]; George W. Feinstein, "Mark Twain's Literary Opinions," Iowa, 1945; Edgar H. Goold, "Mark Twain's Literary Theories and Opinions," North Carolina, 1950; and Henry A. Pochmann, "The Mind of Mark Twain," M.A. thesis, Texas, 1924 (the pioneer study).

TO CONSERVE SPACE IN THE NOTES, I have used the following abbreviations for frequently cited persons, libraries, books, and periodicals. The abbreviations are, for the most part, those used in the definitive Iowa-California edition of the writings of Mark Twain.

[I.] PERSONS

MT	Mark Twain	SLC	Samuel L. Clemens
OLC	Olivia L. Clemens	WDH	William Dean Howells
Orion	Orion Clemens (brother)	JHT	Joseph H. Twichell
Pamela	Pamela Clemens Moffett (sister)	CLW	Charles L. Webster

[II.] LIBRARIES AND SPECIAL COLLECTIONS:

MTP — The Mark Twain Papers, University of California, Berkeley. (In references to MTP, "DV" or "Paine" labels preceding num-bered items—e.g. DV 250; Paine 79—refer to classification of

manuscript materials by Bernard DeVoto and Albert Bigelow
Paine respectively. "Nbk" citations are to typescripts of SLC's
notebooks in MTP.

Berg   The Henry W. and Albert A. Berg Collection, Astor, Lenox, and
Tilden Foundations, New York Public Library

Brownell   The George Hiram Brownell Collection, University of Wisconsin, Madison

Huntington The Henry E. Huntington Library and Art Gallery, San Marino,
California

Redding   The Mark Twain Library, W. Redding, Connecticut

Yale   The Willard S. Morse-W. F. Frear or the Clemens-Twichell Collection, Yale Collection of American Literature, Beinecke
Library, Yale University, New Haven

[III.] COLLECTED EDITION

EXCEPT WHERE OTHERWISE NOTED, page numbers of MT's works cited in notes
refer to the Author's National Edition of *The Writings of MT*, 25 vols. (New
York and London: Harper and Bros., 1907–1918). Often references (both in
text and notes) are merely to the chapter of the work discussed, since pagination
differs greatly in the many editions. Titles of the volumes from which I have
quoted are included in the general list of abbreviations below.

[IV.] WORKS BY AND ABOUT MT:

A1911   Anderson Auction Company, catalogue no. 892–11 ("The Library and Manuscripts of Samuel Clemens . . . to be Sold
February 7 and 8, 1911")

AMCL   *The American Claimant and Other Stories and Sketches*

AMT(N)   *The Autobiography of Mark Twain*, ed. Charles Neider (New
York, 1959)

BAL   Jacob Blanck, Bibliography of American Literature, Vol. II
(New Haven, 1957)

C1951   Catalogue of Mark Twain Auction, April 10, 1951. (In this
catalogue items are listed by title and author only, no places,
publishers, or dates are given)

CY   *A Connecticut Yankee in King Arthur's Court*

E&E   *Europe and Elsewhere*, ed. A. B. Paine (New York, 1923)

FEQ   *Following the Equator* (2 vols.)

GA   *The Gilded Age* (2 vols.)

HADLEYBURG *The Man that Corrupted Hadleyburg and Other Stories and
Essays*

HF   *Adventures of Huckleberry Finn*

IA   *The Innocents Abroad* (2 vols.)

IE   Albert E. Stone, *The Innocent Eye* (New Haven, 1961)

LAMT   Edgar M. Branch, *The Literary Apprenticeship of Mark Twain*
(Urbana, 1950)

LE	*Letters from the Earth,* ed. Bernard DeVoto (New York, 1962)
LitE	*Literary Essays* (cover title); on title page, *How to Tell a Story and Other Essays*
LLMT	*The Love Letters of Mark Twain,* ed. Dixon Wecter (New York, 1949)
LOM	*Life on the Mississippi*
LSI	Letters from the Sandwich Islands, ed. G. Ezra Dane (San Francisco, 1937)
LWMT	Mary Lawton, *A Lifetime with Mark Twain* (New York, 1925)
MFMT	Clara Clemens, *My Father, Mark Twain* (New York, 1931)
MMT	William Dean Howells, *My Mark Twain* (New York, 1910)
MTA(P)	*Mark Twain's Autobiography,* ed. Albert Bigelow Paine, 2 vols. (New York, 1924)
MTAm	Bernard DeVoto, *Mark Twain's America* (New York, 1932)
MTB	Albert Bigelow Paine, *Mark Twain: A Biography* (New York, 1912)
MTBur	Franklin R. Rogers, *Mark Twain's Burlesque Patterns* (Dallas, 1960)
MTBus	*Mark Twain, Business Man,* ed. Samuel C. Webster (Boston, 1946)
MTE	*Mark Twain in Eruption,* ed. Bernard DeVoto (New York, 1940)
MT&EB	Hamlin Hill, *Mark Twain and Elisha Bliss* (Columbia, Mo., 1964)
MT&EF	Henry W. Fis[c]her, *Abroad with Mark Twain and Eugene Field* (New York, 1922)
MTEnt	*Mark Twain of the Enterprise,* ed. Henry Nash Smith, with the Assistance of Frederick Anderson (Berkeley, 1957)
MTF	*Mark Twain to Mrs. Fairbanks,* ed. Dixon Wecter (San Marino, 1949)
MTFP	Henry Nash Smith, *Mark Twain's Fable of Progress* (New Brunswick, 1964)
MT&GWC	Arlin Turner, *Mark Twain and G. W. Cable* (East Lansing, 1960)
MTH	Walter Francis Frear, *Mark Twain and Hawaii* (Chicago, 1947)
MT&HF	Walter Blair, *Mark Twain and Huck Finn* (Berkeley, 1960)
MTHI	Elizabeth Wallace, *Mark Twain and the Happy Island* (Chicago, 1913)
MTHL	*Mark Twain-Howells Letters,* ed. Henry Nash Smith and William M. Gibson, with the Assistance of Frederick Anderson (Cambridge, 1960)
MTL	*Mark Twain's Letters,* ed. Albert Bigelow Paine (New York, 1917)
MTLBowen	*Mark Twain's Letters to Will Bowen,* ed. Theodore Hornberger (Austin, 1941)
MTLec	Paul Fatout, *Mark Twain on the Lecture Circuit* (Bloomington, 1960)
MTLit	Gladys C. Bellamy, *Mark Twain as a Literary Artist* (Norman, 1950)

MTLMARY *Mark Twain's Letters to Mary,* ed. Lewis Leary (New York, 1961)

MTLMUSC *Mark Twain's Letters in the Muscatine Journal,* ed. Edgar M. Branch (Chicago, 1942)

MTLP *Mark Twain's Letters to His Publishers,* ed. Hamlin Hill (Berkeley, 1967)

MTML DeLancey Ferguson, *Mark Twain: Man and Legend* (Indianapolis and New York, 1943)

MTMW1 Edward P. Wagenknecht, *Mark Twain: The Man and His Work* (New Haven, 1935)

MTN *Mark Twain's Notebook,* ed. Albert Bigelow Paine (New York, 1935)

MTS&B *Mark Twain's Satires & Burlesques,* ed. Franklin R. Rogers (Berkeley, 1967)

MTS(H) *Mark Twain's Speeches,* ed. William Dean Howells (New York, 1910)

MTS(P) *Mark Twain's Speeches,* ed. Albert Bigelow Paine (New York, 1923)

MTSATAN John S. Tuckey, *Mark Twain and Little Satan* (West Lafayette, Ind., 1963)

MTSC Philip Foner, *Mark Twain: Social Critic* (New York, 1958)

MTSM Minnie M. Brashear, *Mark Twain: Son of Missouri* (Chapel Hill, 1934)

MTSP Louis J. Budd, *Mark Twain: Social Philosopher* (Bloomington, 1962)

MTTB *Mark Twain's Travels with Mr. Brown,* ed. Franklin Walker and G. Ezra Dane (New York, 1940)

MTW Bernard DeVoto, *Mark Twain at Work* (Cambridge, 1942)

MTWWD *Mark Twain's "Which Was the Dream?" and Other Symbolic Writings of the Later Years,* ed. John S. Tuckey (Berkeley, 1967)

NF Kenneth R. Andrews, *Nook Farm: Mark Twain's Hartford Circle* (Cambridge, 1950)

P&P *The Prince and the Pauper*

PRI *The Pattern for Mark Twain's Roughing It,* ed. Franklin R. Rogers (Berkeley, 1960)

PW *Puddn'head Wilson* and *Those Extraordinary Twins*

RI *Roughing It* (2 vols.)

RL *Republican Letters,* ed. Cyril Clemens (Webster Groves, Mo., 1941)

RP *Report from Paradise,* ed. Dixon Wecter (New York, 1952)

SCH Dixon Wecter, *Sam Clemens of Hannibal* (Boston, 1952)

SN&O *Sketches New and Old*

SSIX *Sketches of the Sixties* (San Francisco, 1927)

TA *A Tramp Abroad* (2 vols.)

TIA *Traveling with the Innocents Abroad,* ed. D. M. McKeithan (Norman, 1958)

TIH Roger B. Salomon, *Twain and the Image of History* (New Haven, 1961)

TJS   *The Adventures of Thomas Jefferson Snodgrass,* ed. Charles Honce (Chicago, 1928)

TS   *The Adventures of Tom Sawyer*

TSABR   *Tom Sawyer Abroad, Tom Sawyer Detective, and Other Stories*

W1868   *Washington* in 1868, ed. Cyril Clemens (Webster Groves, Mo., 1943)

WIM   *What is Man? and Other Essays,* ed. Albert Bigelow Paine (New York, 1917)

[V.] PERIODICALS

AL	*American Literature*	N&Q	*Notes & Queries*
AQ	*American Quarterly*		*(England)*
MLN	*Modern Language Notes*	NEQ	*New England Quarterly*
MP	*Modern Philology*	PMLA	Publications of the Modern Language Assn. of America
MTJ	*Mark Twain Journal*		
MTQ	*Mark Twain Quarterly*		
NAMREV	*North American Review*	SAQ	*South Atlantic Quarterly*
		UTSE	*University of Texas Studies in English*

[VI.] OTHER REFERENCES OFTEN CITED:

EURMOR   W. E. H. Lecky, *The History of European Morals from Augustus to Charlemagne,* 2 vols. (New York, 1870). This edition has the same pagination as Clemens' edition of 1874.

FRREV   Thomas Carlyle, *The French Revolution: A History,* 3 vols. (New York, 1890). In references, capital Roman numerals indicate the Volume number; arabic numerals, the Book; and lower case Roman, the Chapter; e.g. III, 4, iv.

TTC   Charles Dickens, *A Tale of Two Cities* (New York, n. d.). References are to Book and Chapter; e.g. I, iii.

Notes

IN THESE NOTES *all quotations from previously unpublished works (i.e., from manuscripts or letters labeled Barrett, Berg, Huntington, MTP or Yale; or from notebook entries labeled Nbk) are copyright © 1970 by the Mark Twain Company. Nbk citations are to typescripts of the originals in MTP.*

FOREWORD

1. *MTL*, II, 543; *MTB*, iii, 1500.
2. *MTLec*, p. 65.
3. SLC to WDH, 11/23/75, *MTHL*, I, 112; SLC to Robert J Burdette, in *Robert J. Burdette, His Message* (Pasadena, 1922), p. 136; SLC to WDH, 9/14/76, *MTHL*, I, 152–153.
4. Quoted in *MT&HF*, p. 60.

Chapter One, THE VOYAGE OUT

1. Joseph Blamire to SLC, 7/26/72, 8/6/72, 8/9/72, 8/15/72, MTP; SLC to Bliss, 8/7/72, Yale.
2. For documentation of all discussion of British publication of Mark Twain's works, see *BAL*.
3. Quoted in Hingston's preface to *The Innocents Abroad . . . The Voyage Out* (London: J. C. Hotten, 1872), p. 8. Many writers on Mark Twain have said that among his reasons for the London visit was a desire to protect *Roughing It* from literary pirates. The English edition, however, was issued in February, 1872, some six months before he started for England, and other publishers had respected the Routledge copyright.
4. For a more detailed discussion of English critical reaction, see Robert M. Rodney, "MT in England: A Study of the English Criticism of . . . MT, 1867–1940," unpublished Ph.D. dissertation (Wisconsin, 1945).
5. For a fuller discussion of these revisions, see Arthur L. Scott, "MT's Revisions of *The Innocents Abroad* for the British Edition of 1872," *AL*, XXV (Mar. 1953), 43–61.

6. Nbk 30 I, p. 1 (1896); "My Platonic Sweetheart," *Harper's* CXXVI (Dec., 1912), 20.

7. SLC to OLC, 11/9/72, *LLMT*, pp. 181–182.

8. *MTB,* I, 464.

9. *Spectator,* XLV (Sept. 21, 1872), 1201–1202. For a fuller account of Clemens' relations with Hotten, see Dewey Ganzel, "Samuel Clemens and John Camden Hotten," *Library,* XX (1965), 230–242.

10. Stephen Gwynn, *Life of Sir Charles W. Dilke* (London, 1917), I, 160.

11. *MTF,* pp. 166–169, 11/2/72.

12. *MTL,* I, 200–201.

Chapter Two, THE COMPLEAT ANGLOPHILE

1. London *Times,* 11/7/72, p. 8, col. 1.

2. *GA,* II, 24.

3. For a full account of Pomeroy's activities and Clemens' use of them, see Albert R. Kitzhaber, "*Götterdamerung* in Topeka: The Downfall of Senator Pomeroy," *Kansas Historical Quarterly,* XVIII (Aug., 1950), 243–278, and "MT's Use of the Pomeroy Case in *The Gilded Age,*" *Modern Language Quarterly,* XV (Mar., 1954), 42–56. For the most complete study of *GA,* see Bryant M. French, *MT and "The Gilded Age"* (Dallas, 1965), which appeared after this chapter was written. Mr. French's book further emphasizes the scope of the satire of *GA* and also identifies many additional persons and incidents, showing that the novel was indeed a *roman à clef* as well as a burlesque of current sentimental fiction.

4. *GA,* II, 298–299.

5. See *MTB,* III, 1601, and *MTH,* passim.

6. "Clippings, 1873," MTP.

7. *MTS(P),* pp. 46–52.

8. *MTF,* 7/6/73, pp. 174–175. For Shah's visit, see *E&E,* pp. 31–86.

9. SLC to Mrs. Jervis Langdon, *MTL,* I, 207–208.

10. London *Daily News,* 10/19/73, quoted in *MTB,* I, 493–494.

11. *Punch,* LXV (Dec. 20, 1873), 248.

12. SLC to JHT, 1/5/74, *MTL,* I, 211.

13. Tennyson's comments: Tennyson to SLC, 12/16/73, MTP; Archibald Henderson, *Mark Twain* (New York, 1912), p. 170.

14. Charles W. Stoddard, *Exits and Entrances* (Boston, 1903), p. 64. New acquaintances included Wilkie Collins, George Meredith, Arthur Pinero, George DuMaurier, Herbert Spencer, Thomas Hughes, and Anthony Trollope.

15. London Scrapbook, 1873, MTP.

16. SLC to Fitzgibbon [Dec. 1873], MTP, quoted in *MTSP,* p. 57. First meeting with Finlay described in OLC to "Mother Livy," 8/31/73, MTP.

17. Stoddard, p. 73.

18. June 25, n.d. Quoted in catalogue of the American Art Assn., Anderson Galleries (New York, 1931), p. 27; New York *World,* reprinted in Hartford *Courant,* 5/14/79, p. 1, col. 8.

19. *LE,* pp. 172, 173.

20. Paine 176, MTP.

21. Routledge to SLC, 6/20/74, MTP.

22. *Morning Post,* 12/10/73, quoted *MTLec,* p. 187. Clemens speaks of having written the piece as a publicity stunt in a letter to Shirley Brooks, editor of *Punch,* 12/12/73, MTP.

23. "Clippings, 1869–78," MTP.

24. St. Louis *Missouri Democrat,* Mar. 12, 13, 15, 1867. "Universal Suffrage," delivered 2/15/75, in advocating votes for women also emphasized the ridiculous situation in which the vote of a "consummate scoundrel" equalled that of "a president, a bishop, a college professor, a merchant prince." Cf. also his scorn for the mass of voters in his letter to J. H. Burrough on 11/1/76, the eve of the Hayes-Tilden election (*MTL,* I, 289).

25. WDH to SLC, 8/16/75, *MTHL,* I, 97.

26. The Disraeli forces, after several revisions, had favored allowing two, three, or four votes for persons who had savings bank deposits, paid direct taxes, or possessed certain educational qualifications. (O.F. Christy, *The Transition to Democracy,* London, 1934, pp. 18–19).

27. *Memories of A Hostess* (Boston, 1922), pp. 251–253.

28. In a letter to Orion (3/27/75, MTP), for instance, he deplored the moral decay symbolized by such men as Boss Tweed, the Congressional demagogue Benjamin Butler, and the famous minister Henry Ward Beecher, then involved in a sensational adultery suit. Their careers suggested, he said, that "the present era of incredible rottenness is not democratic, it is not republican, it is *national.* . . . *Politics* are not going to cure moral ulcers like these, nor the decaying body they fester on." But this was not the dominant mood during these years.

29. Summarized in Appendix, *MTHL,* II, 865.

30. WDH to SLC, 10/8/76, *MTHL,* I, 156.

31. The first real progress came some seven years later with the Pendleton Act of 1883 which reestablished the Civil Service Commission (first authorized in 1871). The early commission, almost wholly ineffectual, had lasted only a few years and had been totally inactive for nine years preceding its reestablishment.

32. SLC to Mollie Fairbanks, 9/6/77, *MTF,* p. 207.

33. SLC to WDH, 8/22/87, *MTHL,* II, 595. There is a delightful irony in what may have been Clemens' first published reference to Carlyle. A Buffalo *Express* column, August 27, 1869, bristles with patriotic righteousness in attacking Carlyle for some of the same opinions that Clemens himself was soon to preach. Pretending (sarcastically) to sympathize with "old Tom Carlyle" over the "awful Democracy" of the United States, he has the Scot comment to an American visitor: " 'As sure as the Lord reigns you are rushing down to hell with a desperate velocity. The scum of the world has got possession of your country, and nothing can save you from the devil's clutches. Not perhaps,' cried he, raising his voice to its shrillest notes, 'a hell burning with material fire and brimstone, but the wide, weltering chaos of corruption in high places, and the misrule of the people. A fine republic that!' "

34. *FrRev,* Vol. I, Bk 6, Chs i, ii. Future references will indicate the volume

by capital Roman numeral, the book by Arabic numeral, and the chapter by lower case Roman numeral.

35. Ibid., I, 6, v; see also II, 1, iv.

36. Ibid., III, 7, i.

37. Marginalia is from Clemens' copy (at Yale) of Volume IX, pp. 386, 398, *The Letters of Horace Walpole*, 9 vols., ed. by Peter Cunningham, 1861–66.

38. *MTB*, II, 644.

39. Books listed in SLC to Mollie Fairbanks, 8/6/77, *MTF*, p. 207.

40. See *The Ancient Regime* (New York, Henry Holt, 1876), pp. 242, 235, 278, 324; and passim for quotations from Arthur Young.

41. SLC to Mollie Fairbanks, 8/6/77, *MTF*, p. 208.

42. *TSAbr*, pp. 292, 294. "Some Rambling Notes of an Idle Excursion" originally appeared in the *Atlantic Monthly* from Oct. 1877–Jan. 1878.

43. SLC to WDH, 9/19/77, *MTHL*, I, 203–204. Clemens even went so far as to telegraph President Hayes, who referred him to Treasury Secretary John Sherman (See ibid., p. 204, n. 3). Sherman's reply that the *Colfax's* investigation had revealed nothing unusual aboard the *Jonas Smith* probably did not placate Clemens much, for he stored up the incident to be used as a glaring example of governmental ineptitude in a proposed history of civilization which he planned to cast in the form of a diary of Methuselah (See *LE*, p. 68).

44. SLC to Mollie Fairbanks, 8/6/77, *MTF*, p. 208.

Chapter Three, EUROPE ONCE MORE

1. For a full account see Henry Nash Smith, " 'That Hideous Mistake of Poor Clemens's'," *Harvard Library Bulletin*, IX (Spring, 1955), 145–180. Interestingly enough, two years earlier, Clemens himself had referred (in another context) to Longfellow, Whittier, and Holmes as "men whom the country cannot venture to laugh at" (SLC to WDH, 9/18/75, *MTHL*, I, 99).

2. Scrapbook, 1869–78, MTP.

3. SLC to Jane Clemens, 2/17/78, *MTL*, I, 319.

4. *MTN*, p. 133; SLC to Bayard Taylor, quoted by John R. Schultz, "New Letters of MT," *AL*, VIII (Mar., 1936), 49.

5. SLC to WDH, 5/4/78, 6/27/78, 1/30/79, *MTHL*, I, 227, 236, 248–249.

6. *MTN*, p. 153.

7. Nbk 13, p. 48; 14, list at beginning.

8. *MTB*, II, 647, 646; SLC to Chatto, 9/19/79, Berg.

9. *MTA(P)*, II, 232; Sydney *Morning Herald*, 9/17/95; R. L. Green, *The Diaries of Lewis Carroll* (New York, 1959), II, 382, entry for 7/28/79.

10. *MTN*, p. 155.

11. *MT&HF*, p. 177.

12. Nbk 14, p. 23, quoted in *MTSP*, p. 75.

13. *TA*, II, 229 (Ch. XVIII)

14. *MTN*, p. 150.

15. *MTN*, pp. 156–157.

16. Scrapbook, 1878–79, MTP.

17. DV 16, MTP.

18. Interview, New York *World,* reprinted in Hartford *Courant,* 5/14/79, p. 1, col. 8.

19. This is the period, too, when Clemens several times considered the ideas and aims of Communism, declaring at one point that "Communism is idiocy" (*MTB,* II, 644), and another time planning a story to illustrate the fallacy of "community of 'start' where there isn't community (equality) of brains" (Nbk 14, p. 38). It is not strange that such items have been neglected by those critics who seek to impose a Marxist orientation on MT's ideas. (See also *MTHL,* I, 237).

20. *FrRev,* III, 1, i; III, 5, iii; *LE,* pp. 184, 188.

21. *FrRev,* II, 1, i.

22. Carlyle, too, makes special mention of Thorwaldsen's impressive statue to conclude his account of the massacre (II, 6, vii); Clemens uses the statue as the starting point of his discussion. Elsewhere Clemens many times expressed his admiration of Napoleon. One note, from June, 1879, reads: "Never been but one great era in F and that was under the great foreigner, Nap" (Nbk 14, p. 27).

23. *FrRev,* II, 3, iv.

24. *MT&HF,* p. 184.

25. *LE,* p. 186.

26. While still in Germany, Clemens outlined his scheme for the book to Howells on January 30, 1879 (*MTHL,* I, 248–49). Three themes were to guide the adventures of his wandering narrator. The old travel device would feature hiking tours and mountain-climbing, with the humor being buttressed by the hiker's continually boarding "the first conveyance that offers" and yet always pretending to be "unconscious that this is not legitimate pedestrianizing." A fictional raft trip down the Neckar to Heidelberg would provide for picking up "useful passengers" who could relate the various local legends, some of which Clemens would invent himself. The traveler's two other objectives—"to become a German scholar" and "to study Art, & learn to paint"—would furnish opportunities to satirize devotees of foreign study and "appreciators" of art. No amount of pruning, of course, could have made *TA* really sustain those three themes, and yet Clemens was correct that much of the deleted material would have seriously impeded the narrative.

27. Quoted in *MTB,* II, 650.

28. SLC to WDH, 11/28/79, 1/8/80 *MTHL,* I, 283, 287.

Chapter Four, THE PRINCE AND THE PAUPER

1. *MTE,* p. 206.

2. SLC to WDH, 3/5/80. *MTHL,* I, 290; SLC to E. H. House, 8/31/80, *Twainian* (Mar.–Apr., 1963), p. 2.

3. SLC to F. V. Christ, "Aug. '08," *MTL,* II, 814. For further discussion and documentation of Clemens' debt to *The Little Duke,* see my "MT's 'The Prince and the Pauper,' " *N&Q,* I, n.s. (Sept., 1954), 401–403. In addition,

Franklin R. Rogers conjectures convincingly that the description and career of Gwynplaine in Victor Hugo's *L'homme qui rit* inspired both the Edward-Tom Canty switch and the general structure of the novel (*MTBur*, pp. 114–126).

4. SLC to WDH, 8/9/76, 8/23/76, *MTHL*, I, 144, 148; *MT&HF*, p. 398, n. 1.

5. SLC to OLC, 1/10/70, MTP. It should be noted, however, that as late as 1866 he was praising the "simple and touching eloquence" of Jeannie Deans' plea to Queen Caroline on behalf of her sister Effie in *The Heart of Midlothian* (Nbk 4, p.25.)

6. Jervis Langdon, *Samuel L. Clemens, Some Reminiscences and Some Excerpts from Letters and Unpublished Manuscripts*, pamphlet, n.p., n.d. (Dedication dated 10/7/38). Langdon dates this ms. about 1870, but since many of Clemens' comments are based on H. H. Breen's *Modern English Literature: Its Blemishes and Defects* (London, 1857), the 1876 date is a more accurate one, for on the flyleaf of his personal copy of Breen (MTP), Clemens dates his acquisition of the book "1876," noting that a bookseller had "ransacked England" to find it for him that same year.

7. DV114, 115, MTP. Of several references to *Quentin Durward*, only the description of the Count de Crèvecoeur at his audience with Louis XI (Ch. VIII) seems to have provided specific details ultimately used in *P&P*. In Ch. VII Clemens mentions that "Madame Parr, the Queen" has given Tom Canty a "suit of shining armor, covered all over with beautiful designs exquisitely inlaid in gold," and in Ch. XXXI a suit of "Milan armor" is named as the hiding place of the Great Seal. Crèvecoeur wears "a gorgeous suit of the most superb Milan armor . . . inlaid and embossed with gold . . . in the fantastic taste called arabesque." As for *The Fortunes of Nigel*, Clemens doubtless remembered Scott's extensive treatment of the low-life in Whitefriars when planning some of his own scenes. Perhaps the "councils of state" of "Duke Hildebrod," Alsatia's "ruler," furnished some of the inspiration for the organization of Hugo's beggar-band. Even more likely, Clemens perhaps decided to include the Chapter XIV passage about the whipping-boy, Humphrey Marlow, as a result of Scott's vivid description (Chapter VI) of how the ridiculous old cynic, Sir Mungo Malagrowther, had got "an early footing at court" by serving as whipping-boy for James I. That *Nigel* made a considerable impression on Clemens is further suggested by the possibility that some twenty years later he borrowed the names of Marget and her devoted servant Ursula in the "Eseldorf" version of *MysStr*. One of *Nigel's* most vivid minor characters is Ursula Suddlechop, the barber's wife, whose "infinite desire" is "to be of service to her fellow creatures," and who often aids Margaret Ramsay, whom she habitually calls Marget. Clemens may well have remembered the names and possibly the relationship—perhaps without recalling the source—and borrowed them as appropriate to his Austrian setting.

8. DV 114, MTP.

9. *MTN*, p. 129.

10. *MTF*, p. 218. The ms. of *P&P* in the Huntington library shows that Clemens broke off a session of writing at ms. 215 (final numbering), i.e. at the end of Ch. XI. He had completed two long paragraphs of what was to be a

continuation of Tom's adventures into Ch. XII, but when he returned to the manuscript (in 1880) he decided to go on with Edward's story and so postponed using the two paragraphs (and some fragments of dialogue) until the beginning of Ch. XIV ("Toward daylight" to "Leave me to my sorrows"). My thanks to Roger Salomon for checking this detail for me.

11. DV 115, MTP.

12. SLC to Orion, 2/29/80, 3/5/80, *MTBus*, pp. 143, 145; SLC to WDH, 3/5/80, *MTHL*, I, 290. The manuscript of *P&P* shows that ms. pages 327–414 completed the portion of the novel finished by mid-June, 1880 (letter to me from Walter Blair, 1/20/59); SLC to Aldrich, 9/15/80, *MTL*, I, 386; SLC to Osgood, 1/21/81, quoted by Blair ("When was HF Written?" *AL*, XXX, Mar. 1958, 9) from Parke-Bernet Galleries Catalogue, Sale No. 325, Dec. 10, 11, 1941.

13. SLC to WDH, 3/5/80, *MTHL*, I, 291–292.

14. For a somewhat fuller discussion, see Leon T. Dickinson, "The Sources of *The Prince and the Pauper*," *MLN*, LXIV (Feb., 1949), 103–106. Clemens' copy of *A Classical Dictionary of the Vulgar Tongue* (London, 1785) is inscribed "Saml. L. Clemens, Hartford, 1875" (listed in *C1951*). My thanks to Mr. Justin Turner for allowing me to examine this book from his MT collection. The pig-stealing scene in *P&P* is drawn from *The English Rogue*, I, 63–65.

15. See discussion and notes re: Pepys, Chapter Five, *post*.

16. All references to Clemens' marginalia and underscorings in *EurMor* (in both this and later chapters) are from Chester L. Davis, "MT's Religious Beliefs as Indicated by Notations in His Books," *Twainian* (May-June, July-Aug., Sept. Oct., Nov. Dec., 1956). Davis describes an 1874 edition of Lecky—*EurMor* was first published in 1869—the flyleaf of which is inscribed "T. W. Crane, 1874" and "S. L. Clemens, 1906." As Walter Blair points out (*MT&HF*, p. 401n.), many of Clemens' notes were obviously made much earlier than 1906. Clemens may also have had another copy. All of my references are to the 1870 ed. (D. Appleton & Co.), which has the same pagination as the 1874 edition used by Clemens.

17. *MT&HF*, pp. 132–145 and passim.

18. *EurMor*, I, 3 ff.

19. *EurMor*, II, 20, 21, 22.

20. He would hardly have failed to notice the Autocrat's assertion that both mind and body function "not *by*, but *according to* laws, such as we observe in the larger universe." He was probably struck, too, by Holmes' use of mechanical imagery to describe the workings of man's mind, as well as by the various arguments that hereditary and environmental influences made free will all but nonexistent (*Autocrat*, Boston, 1892, pp. 71, 85, 86, 89). See Sherwood Cummings' discussion of the influence of Holmes and Darwin, *"What is Man?: The Scientific Sources,"* in *Essays on Determinism in American Literature* (Kent, Ohio, 1965), pp. 108–116.

21. *MTA(P)*, I, 146. See Paul Baender, "Alias Macfarlane": A Revision of MT Biography," *AL*, XXXVIII (May, 1966), 187–197.

22. *Descent of Man* (1871), I, 78, in MTP, quoted by Cummings, op. cit., in n. 20.

23. Nbk 19, p. 25; *MTB*, II, 614. Clemens had heard of "old Omar-Khéyam"

(as he called him in a letter to Howells) as early as 1876 (*MTHL*, I, 164). In 1878 James Osgood had published the first American edition of the *Rubaiyat*, a reprint of the third English edition of 1872. But the *Courant* article (clipping in MTP) shows that the stimulus for Clemens' enthusiasm was Bernard Quaritch's fourth English edition, which had gone on sale in England in August, 1879 (A. M. Terhune, *Life of Edward FitzGerald*, New Haven, 1947, pp. 329–330). Besides a number of references to the poem over the years (e.g. SLC to CLW, 5/19/84, *MTBus*, p. 254; Nbk 19, p. 11, Apr., 1885, MTP; SLC to Clara Spaulding Stanchfield, Sept., 1886, TS, MTP; *MTLMary*, 8/26/06, p. 54; SLC to "Mr. Logan," 2/2/07, TS, MTP; see also notes to Chapter Eleven, *post*), Clemens remarked in an autobiographical dictation of 11/7/07 how strange it seemed to think that there was a time when he had never heard of Omar Khayyam, and then went on to say that the *Rubaiyat* was the only poem he had ever carried about with him—that it had not been "from under [his] hand for twenty-eight years" (TS, pp. 2317–2318, MTP; last part quoted in slightly different form, *MTB*, III, 1295). *A1911*, pp. 55–56, lists two editions of Fitz-Gerald's *Rubaiyat:* Boston, n.d. (almost certainly the Osgood edition) and Philadelphia, n.d., inscribed "S. L. Clemens, 1900" and another translation by E. F. Thompson, privately printed, 1901, inscribed "S. L. Clemens, 1907," a presentation copy from one James Logan of Worcester, Mass., obviously the "Mr. Logan," above.

24. For Lecky's discussion of the role of the conscience, see *EurMor*, I, 64–67.

25. Quoted in *MT&HF*, p. 143.

26. *EurMor*, I, 137–144.

27. *MTBur*, p. 125.

28. Hume, *History of England* (New York, 1880), III, 301, 278, quoted in *TIH*, pp. 151–152.

29. Clemens underlined the beginning sentence of Lecky's discussion, which also includes a consideration of religious insanity (*EurMor*, II, 90–107).

30. *EurMor*, II, 103. Though Clemens' knowledge of penalties for begging could have come from several sources, two indications point to Lecky. First, "Note 10" in which Clemens observes that Yokel suffered from this law *"by anticipation"* is the only one dealing with ancient law that is not attributed to a specific source; the others cite either Hume or Trumbull. More significantly, in the cases of most of the beggars, Clemens usually shifts Lecky's emphasis on the theological causes of begging—i.e. the "superstition" that alms-giving would benefit the giver—to political and social ones. In Yokel's case, however, the misfortunes *do* occur as a result of religious superstition. Whereas several of the husbandmen had turned to begging when their farms were seized for sheep ranges, Yokel had done so after his lands were confiscated as a result of his mother's being convicted of witchcraft.

31. *EurMor*, II, 124, 92–93.

32. *MTAm*, p. 269.

33. According to Paine (*MTB*, II, 597) Clemens had originally considered a plan to use a contemporary setting and hero (the then Prince of Wales, who

became Edward VII) and to accomplish the reversal of positions by the "changeling-in-the-cradle" device. If Paine is correct, Clemens' decision to abandon the idea because of the impropriety of losing "a prince among the slums of modern London" and "having his proud estate jeered at by a modern mob" also argues against any conjectures that the novel was designed to attack either England or monarchy in general.

Chapter Five, THE BRIGHT AND THE DARK

1. See SLC to OLC, 11/27/71, *LLMT*, p. 166. In 1875, too, Will Bowen, congratulating Clemens on the *Atlantic* articles, advised him to write a book about his river life and expressed regret that his friend had not been able to take a proposed river trip that February (Bowen to SLC, 3/29/75, MTP).

2. This was the invention of one James W. Paige, in which Clemens began investing in 1881, and which cost him some two hundred thousand dollars before its final failure in 1894. Several prototype machines were built, but proved too delicate and temperamental. It remained for the Mergenthaler Linotype (patented in 1885, produced in 1886, and operating on an entirely different principle) to provide the kind of success that Clemens envisioned for the Paige typesetter.

3. *MTB*, II, 831.

4. *MTB*, II, 744.

5. Cf. Roger Salomon, *TIH*, pp. 136–139. Quotations in this paragraph: SLC to OLC, 5/17/82, *MTL*, I, 419; *MTN*, p. 165; *LOM*, p. 394.

6. In *LOM*, these incidents occur in Chs. Fifty-three, Fifty-four, Fifty-six. Besides using the gift-of-matches incident in Chapter Twenty-three of *TS* (though without the tragic consequences), Clemens mentioned the calaboose fire in a letter to Will Bowen on 2/6/70 (*MTBowen*, p. 19), and in *MTA(P)*, I, 130–131, he dwelt at some length on the torments of conscience he had suffered.

7. See *MT&HF*, p. 337, and note.

8. *MTE*, pp. 240–241, dated 2/19/83 in *MT&HF*, pp. 337; 415 n. 8.

9. This had been a long-time concern with Clemens. In July, 1870, for instance, he devoted a column in the *Galaxy* to derisive comment about the announcement of a mock tournament to be held in (of all places) Brooklyn, New York. Confidently predicting that the North would not permit further appearances of such an anachronism, he concluded that the custom should "retire permanently to the rural districts of Virginia, where, it is said, the fine mailed and plumed, noble-natured, maiden-rescuing, wrong-redressing, adventure-seeking knight of romance is accepted and believed in by the peasantry. . . ." Some of Clemens' praise of modernity in *LOM*, however, carries interesting sidelights. While commenting that the existence of the telegraph in 1812 would have prevented the Battle of New Orleans (fought after peace had been declared), he again showed that he was not the robust Jacksonian so often portrayed. Not only would lives have been saved, he said, but "better still," Jackson would probably not have become president. "We have gotten over

the harms done us by the war of 1812, but not over some of those done us by Jackson's presidency" (p. 354). See also the comment on worship of money by "go-getter" salesmen (p. 304).

10. Clemens would again dramatize this unfortunate influence in *AmCl* (1892), where the students at the towered and castellated Rowena-Ivanhoe College exhibit all of the characteristics of "Scottism" illustrated in *LOM*.

11. See the Heritage edition of *LOM* (New York, 1944), ed. Willis Wager, pp. 385–418. Quotations and summaries in the following discussion are from pp. 391–392; 402; 407–411; 412–414.

12. This would have followed Chapter Forty-seven, a short but complimentary discussion of the works of G. W. Cable and Joel Chandler Harris as evidence of the excellence the South might achieve in literature if it would throw off its devotion to flowery romanticism.

13. Riverside Editions *HF* (Boston: Houghton Mifflin, 1958), p. xii.

14. *MT&HF*, pp. 293; 411, n. 13, 18. Clemens agreed to the cuts partly because he was heartily sick of the project as indicated in a penciled note to CLW on letter from Osgood (1/3/83), who had requested information: "I will not interest myself in *any*thing connected with this wretched God-damned book." *MTBus*, p. 207.

15. *LOM*, p. 346 (Ch. Forty-six).

16. All marginal comments are quoted from Caroline Ticknor, "MT's Missing Chapter," *Bookman*, XXXIX (May, 1914), 298–309.

17. *MTSP*, p. 118.

18. *Blackwood's*, CXXXIII (Jan., 1883), 136–161.

19. Hartford *Courant*, 5/14/79, p. 1, col. 8. The same sort of ambivalence during these years reveals itself in another unpublished fragment from 1883 or 1884, presumably the draft of a reply to an English correspondent who had asked if Clemens had ever considered adopting British citizenship. There Clemens said that even if he were not too old to pull up his roots, his love for the United States would preclude his being happy in another country. But when he began to enumerate the "advantages" of life in America, satire superseded sentiment. In England, he said, an obscure man could perform great actions with no one being aware of them; in America any action, large or small, immediately produced the interviewer. Whereas English political preferment was restricted solely to those "born to it," in America "*any*body can go to Congress,—and as a general thing that's just the kind that *do* go." Finally, in America both burdens and labor are divided for the common good: "the minority are required to furnish the taxes, and the majority are required to say how the money shall be spent" (Ms. fragment, MTP).

20. The *Athenaeum* (June 2, 1883) called the passages concerning the "mournful influence" of Scott—"monuments of misplaced and unhappy ambition."

21. WDH to SLC, 7/10/83, *MTHL*, I, 434. Clemens had read Hardy's *Far From the Madding Crowd* (1874) during the year following its publication (*A1911*, p. 36) and Paine notes that Clemens highly approved of Hardy's point of view in *Jude the Obscure* (1895), a volume that was among his last continu-

ous reading in 1910 (*MTB*, III, 1567). His library also contained a copy of Hardy' *Poems Past and Present* (1901).

22. SLC to OLC, 5/24/83, *LLMT*, pp. 215–216; SLC to WDH, 8/22/83, *MTHL*, I, 439.

23. *MTHL*, I, 441.

24. D. M. McKeithan, "More About MT's War with English Critics of America," *MLN*, LXIII (Apr., 1948), 221–228.

25. Robert Hunting has discussed this point in "MT's Arkansas Yahoos," *MLN*, LXXIII (Apr., 1958), 264–268.

26. SLC to JHT, 6/9/73, *MTL*, I, 207. As for his lifelong fondness, note Isabel Lyon's comment that on the way to Bermuda, late in 1906, Clemens spent most of his time reading Vols. V and VI of Pepys (Secretarial notebook, "Feb. 2 '06–07," MTP).

27. *MTF*, pp. 117–118n. As Wecter notes, he had perhaps been planning "Shem's Diary" as early as 1870 in Buffalo. Besides other indications of his interest yet to be discussed, Clemens was reading Pepys again in January, 1884 (SLC to E. H. House, 1/14/84, Barrett). In 1885 he proposed to copy Pepys' vivid accounts of the Plague (1665) and Fire (1666) for a projected compilation of "Picturesque Incidents in History and Tradition" (Nbk 19, p. 37), and in January, 1894, he included Pepys' name on a list of favorite autobiographical works (Nbk 27, p. 46). Paine says, also, that the *Diary* was one of the books that Clemens read often during the last years of his life (*MTB*, III, 1540).

28. *MTE*, p. 206. Pepys' name is also listed in later planning notes for *P&P*, (DV 115, MTP) and in a late August, 1879, notebook entry (Nbk 14, p. 43). All of Clemens' references to genesis of *1601* are also to *MTE*, pp. 206–207.

29. All references to Pepy's *Diary* will be to the dates of Pepy's entries. My quotations are from *Diary and Correspondence of Samuel Pepys, F.R.S.*, with a Life and Notes by Richard Lord Braybrooke, 3rd ed., 5 vols. (London, 1848). Other links between Pepys and *1601:* The fact that the cupbearer mentions Shakespeare's reading from *Henry IV* and that Clemens' list of "Middle Age phrases for a historical story" (DV 114) draws heavily on the same play helps substantiate Clemens' memory that *1601* was born of his search for "authentic language" to be used in *P&P*.

In another instance, Pepys (12/11/63) repeats a coffee-house tall story by a Mr. Harrington concerning "the country above Quinsborough" (presumably a fictitious region). Harrington's tale of how the Duke of Corland had the villagers drive "bears, wolves, foxes, swine, and stags, and roes" into a compound where the nobles and gentry "have their stands . . . and shoot at what they have a mind to, and that is their hunting"—doubtless also provided the idea for one of Clemens' proposals (not ultimately carried out) for a similar hunting-party in *CY*, but with the satire on such noble sport intensified by having the quarry consist of "cats and other tame game" of which the nobility would " 'bag' 2,000 'pieces'—tame fawns, kids, lambs, &c" (Nbk 23 II, p. 34). The link with *1601* occurs in the added comment that the region was not a populous one because the women there seldom married until they were "towards or above thirty," and the men until thirty or forty, or more. Therein seems to lie the inspiration for Sir Walter Raleigh's information that there was "a people in ye uttermost parts of America, yt capulate not until they be five and thirty yeres of age, ye women being eight and twenty." Raleigh "tops" Mr. Harrington, however, by adding that even then they "do it . . . but once in seven yeres."

30. His copy was published in London: Bohn, 1864, tr. W. K. Kelly, and is inscribed "Saml. L. Clemens, Hartford, 1875" (*A1911*, p. 38).

31. Tale 52 tells of a joke played on a greedy gentleman by an apothecary, who wraps a lump of frozen human feces to resemble a sugar-loaf (a great delicacy at a time when sugar was scarce), drops it in the gentleman's path, and enjoys his discomfiture when the package, taken into a coffee house, begins to thaw. Immediately after the story, a remark on the smuttiness of the language inspires a discussion of how much ladies enjoy such language, though they pretend to be shocked by it. The tone of Tale 12 and the nature of the talk which follows are more like that in *1601*. At the conclusion of the story, which repeats a sermon preached by a friar and full of *doubles entendres,* the ladies and gentlemen amuse themselves by continuing the salacious play on words as they discuss the tale.

32. For a fuller discussion, see *MT&HF,* p. 94. For notes on other sources and analogues for the "generating circumstance" and for other allusions, see Franklin J. Meine's edition of *1601,* privately printed for the Mark Twain Society of Chicago, 1939, pp. 57–65. Aubrey's *Brief Lives* (London, 1949, repr. Ann Arbor, 1957), p. 305, contains an additional instance of courtly flatulence at the Court of Queen Elizabeth. Aubrey's entry on Edward DeVere begins by noting that "this Erle of Oxford," in making his "low obeisance" to the Queen, "happened to let a Fart, at which he was so abashed and ashamed that he went to Travell 7 yeeres," and records that in welcoming him on his return, the Queen remarked, "My Lord, I had forgott the Fart." That passage, however, was probably not available to Clemens, for it does not appear in the 1813 edition of Aubrey, and in Andrew Clark's edition of 1898 (far too late, of course, for *1601*), Oxford merely "happened to. . . ." [editor's ellipsis].

33. Entry of 5/1/67. Another passage that mentions Bridgewater (7/30/67) goes on to discuss one of the King's quarrels with Lady Castlemaine (Barbara Villiers), another of the royal mistresses who so interested and infuriated Clemens. Probably the humorist would also have noticed the footnote to Pepys' entry of 11/19/66, which explains that Berkshire House, later "purchased by Charles II, and presented to the Duchess of Cleveland" was "of great extent, and stood on or near the site of Bridgewater House." The Duchess was the same Barbara Villiers, who received her new title from Charles in 1670.

34. Nbk 3, p. 7, quoted in *MT&HF,* p. 273; *RI,* II, 320 (Ch. XXXVI).

35. *MT&HF,* pp. 319–320.

36. On 12/20/83 Clemens outlined to Howells the plot for a play version of that story, saying that he had encountered the incident "in Carlyle's Cromwell a year ago," and had made a note about it which he had just rediscovered (*MTHL,* II, 455–458). See ibid., 458–459n. for his note and the passage from Carlyle which inspired his idea. Clemens ultimately turned the idea into an overly sentimental story (with a happy ending), which appeared in *Harper's,*

Dec., 1901, and the following year was dramatized and presented at Carnegie Hall.

A note from the summer of 1882 to the effect that Carlyle could not account for the fact that Frederick the Great was "a bad speller," shows also that Clemens by that time was reading, or had read, the biography of the German emperor (Nbk 16, p. 48). Clemens' library contained both *Frederick the Great*, 10 vols., London, n.d. [c. 1865], and *Cromwell's Letters, Etc.*, 5 vols., n.d. [c. 1865] with the inscription "S. L. Clemens, Hartford, 1882," on the flyleaf of Vol. II of the latter (*A1911*, p. 14).

37. A letter of 11/3/84 to a cousin of WDH (copy in MTP) indicates that Clemens had read Mrs. Carlyle's *Letters* when they appeared and that he accepted Froude's portrait. *C1951* lists Froude's biography, the last two volumes of which appeared in 1884. Paine's comment on the deathbed reading of *FrRev* quoted in Hartford *Courant*, 4/22/10 (the day following Clemens' death); on Carlyle as "stump speaker," *MTB*, III, 1535.

38. For a fuller discussion, see Walter Blair, "The French Revolution and *Huckleberry Finn*," *MP*, LV (Aug., 1957), 21–35. References to Carlyle, *FrRev*, II, 4, iv; III, 2, viii. Here, and later, the references are to volume, book, and chapter of *FrRev* (3 vols., New York, Frederick A. Stokes, 1890).

39. As Blair points out (Ibid., p. 23), Carlyle several times mentions the taking of solemn oaths (I, 5, ii; II, 1, vi, xii); he or Dickens (*TTC*), or both, could have provided Tom with the idea to "kill the *families* of boys that told the secrets" and perhaps the device of prisoners changing clothes in order to escape (*FrRev*, III, 5, iii; II, 4, iii; *TTC*, III, xiii), though of course most historians of the French Revolution recorded the fact that the royal family assumed disguises for the flight to Varennes.

40. *FrRev*, III 6, vii. Henry Fischer says that Clemens once told him that he had learned from various accounts of mob action that men in mobs did not act as they would as individuals; that "they don't think for themselves, but become impregnated by the mass sentiment uppermost in the minds which happen to be en masse" (*MT&EF*, p. 50).

41. In *FrRev* (as Blair notes), Mirabeau (II, 3, iii), Marat and Robespierre (III, 2, i), and Danton (III, 6, ii) all at times assume such a "haranguer's" role. The parallel to Sherburn's speech, however, is in II, 2, ii.

42. *FrRev*, II, 3, vii. For tribute to Burlingame, see *E&E*, pp. 17 29; *MTB*, I, 287; *MTBus* p. 86; *MTL*, I, 108; *MTF*, p. 31. For pilot: *LOM*, pp. 120–121; *MTBowen*, p. 13 (Burlingame mentioned in same letter).

43. See *MTA(P)*, I, 131; *SCH*, pp. 106–108. In later years Clemens did write (in "The United States of Lyncherdom" [1901]) that as a boy he had once seen "a brave man insult a mob and drive it away" (*E&E*, p. 245). But even if that recollection were accurate, similar events encountered in his reading very likely would have reminded him of his boyhood experiences and underscored their significance.

44. *FrRev*, III, 6, vi. Preceding quotation from *Cromwell's Letters and Speeches*, Part V, "The Levellers," which describes dissensions among the Puritan troops in 1647.

45. *FrRev*, III, 2, viii; III, 4, viii; III, 6, vii.

46. *FrRev*, I, 2, vii.

47. *MT& HF*, pp. 205–215; dating of Chs. XVII, XVIII, pp. 199–203. Along with the debt to Julia A. Moore, it is tempting to find in the title of one lugubrious drawing, "Shall I Never See Thee More Alas" (which depicts a mourning maiden under a weeping willow), an echo of Danton's farewell to his wife (*FrRev*, III, 6, ii). As Danton mounts the scaffold, Carlyle has him cry out, "Oh my Wife, my well-beloved, I shall never see thee more then!"

48. For fuller treatment of Dickens' influence see article by Walter Blair cited in n. 38, above. In addition, J. M. Ridland finds parallels between *HF* and *Great Expectations;* he compares Huck's struggle with his conscience and decision to help Jim with Pip's helping and then being ashamed of helping the convict Magwitch; and the destruction of Huck's raft and Pip's rowboat by the respective steamboats (*Nineteenth Century Fiction*, XX, Dec., 1965, 286–290).

49. *TTC*, II, i and xiv. (References to Dickens here and hereafter are to book and chapter.) The scene between Pap and Huck probably also owes something to *Our Mutual Friend* (I, vi), for Gaffer Hexam berates his son Charlie for his ability to read and write and for putting on superior airs. See Joseph Gardner, "Gaffer Hexam and Pap Finn," *MP*, LXVI (Nov, 1960), 155–156.

50. Leo Marx points out that in *The Lay of the Last Minstrel* (Canto IV, xxvii) "slogan" (which Tom calls his blazing stick) is used in an earlier sense to mean "a battle cry." In *The Lady of the Lake* (Canto III) the clans are called to battle by means of a "fiery cross" carried through the countryside (*Adventures of HF*, Indianapolis and New York: Bobbs Merrill, 1967, p. 23n). In *TSAbr*, Ch. I, Clemens uses Scott in much the same way when Huck specifically attributes Tom's grandiose scheme for delivering the Holy Land from the "Paynim" to "Walter Scott's book that he was always reading"—obviously *The Talisman.*

51. In a later attack upon Scott's faulty style and characterization, which he composed in the form of two letters to Brander Matthews (5/4/03, 5/8/03), Clemens described his attempt to reread Scott's novels, condemning *Rob Roy* and *Guy Mannering,* but praising *Quentin Durward.* After declaring that the experience with the latter was "like leaving the dead to mingle with the living," or like leaving "the infant class in the College of Journalism to sit under the lectures in English literature in Columbia University," he concluded ironically, "I wonder who wrote Quentin Durward?" (*MTL*, II, 738–739). See also notes to Chapter Four, *ante.*

52. *MT&HF*, p. 331.

53. Quoted in *NF*, p. 92. Clemens and Arnold had also met at a reception the night before at the home of Charles W. Clark. Though Howells was later to remember that Arnold had been charmed by Clemens' sparkling personality, Arnold does not seem to have referred to the meeting in letters or journals of the time (J. B. Hoben, "MT's *Connecticut Yankee*: A Genetic Study," *AL*, XVIII, Nov., 1946, 205).

54. Paper and ink place them among the mss. which resulted from an

editor's request for an answer to Arnold's "Civilization in the United States," which had appeared in the April, 1888, issue of *Nineteenth Century*.

55. SLC to WDH, 1/7/84. *MTHL*, II, 461.

56. Fred W. Lorch, "Hawaiian Feudalism and MT's *A Connecticut Yankee*" *AL*, XXX (Mar., 1958), pp. 56–57.

57. *EurMor*, II, 245. Lecky goes on at this point, also, to cite as one of the many services rendered to mankind by the medieval Troubadours, the ridiculing of the visions of hell stressed by the monks, which they did so effectively as to discredit and almost suppress those superstitions. This comment suggests, in part, the role that Clemens later envisioned for his Connecticut Yankee.

58. SLC to Mrs. Fairbanks 1/24/84, 1/30/84. *MTF* pp. 255–256; SLC to WDH, 2/13/84; 2/26/84, *MTHL*, II, 471–472, 476.

59. *MTSP*, p. 82.

60. *MTLec*, p. 210; SLC to Chatto, 12/4/84, quoted in *MTQ*, IV (Summer-Fall, 1941), 2. Business and family reasons prevented the trip. Cable's memorial tribute to SLC (11/30/10) places the incident on a Saturday evening in Rochester (*MT&GWC*, p. 135), and a letter to Olivia from Rochester is dated "Sunday, Dec 7/84" (*LLMT*, p. 222).

61. SLC to CLW, 3/16/85, *MTBus*, p. 307.

62. *MTN*, p. 181.

63. *MT&HF*, 377; 421, n. 22.

Chapter Six, THUNDER AND THE STORM

1. *MTB*, III, 1320; Nbk 19, p. 25; SLC to OLC, 2/4/85, *LLMT*, p. 230.

2. *MTN*, p. 171; bracketed phrases added from original passage, Nbk 18, p. 11.

3. Nbk 20, p. 33, quoted in my "The Course of Composition of *CY*," *AL*, XXXIII (May, 1961), 197. The nostalgic tone and reference to a lost love suggest that Clemens might have been remembering his legend of Dilsberg Castle, invented for *TA*, Ch. XIX (*MT&ER*, p. 135). The notion of the Yankee's eventual conflict with the Church was apparently stirring in his mind, for shortly after the "suicide" entry he noted: "Country placed under an interdict" (Nbk. 20, p. 34) Here he was possibly recalling the Pope's threat in Malory (Bk. XX, Ch. xiii) to use the Interdict against Arthur. The summer before, he had listed a description of England under the Interdict invoked against King John as one of the "Picturesque Incidents in History and Tradition" that he hoped to compile into a book (Nbk 19, p. 32).

4. SLC to CLW, 12/16/85, 2/13/86, *MTBus*, pp. 343, 355; WDH to SLC, 1/16/86, *MTHL*, II, 550. SLC to Charles C. Buel, an assistant editor of the *Century*, mentions on 2/26/86 that a chapter or two of the book he is working on will be good material for the magazine when he finishes (Berg).

5. *MTN*, p. 171. For a fuller discussion of the Governors Island reading, see my "The Autobiography of Sir Robert Smith of Camelot': MT's Original Plan for *A Connecticut Yankee*," *AL*, XXXII (Jan., 1961), 456–461.

6. *MTF*, p. 257, 11/16/86; *MTFP*, p. 48.

7. The tone of the original "dream" idea is very much in evidence as the Yankee awakes to be greeted by Sir Kay in words appropriated from Balin's challenge to Lanceor (Malory, II, v)—"Fair Sir, will ye just? [*sic*]"—and replies, "Will I which?" His lack of surprise at seeing a knight, his comments on the circus, and his mistaking the towers of Camelot for Bridgeport suggest also that Clemens was drawing some of the Yankee's characteristics from his interest in the great sensation-salesman, P. T. Barnum [Hamlin Hill, "Barnum, Bridgeport, and *The Connecticut Yankee*," *AQ*, XVI (Winter, 1964), 615–616]. Clemens and Barnum corresponded during the 1870's (MTP).

8. *Galaxy* (July, 1870), 135–136.

9. *MTF*, p. 258, 11/16/86. He hoped that Sir Galahad would still remain "the divinest spectre that one glimpses among the mists & twilights of Dreamland," that Arthur would "keep his sweetness & his purity," and that Launcelot would "abide & continue 'the kindest man that ever strake the sword,' yet 'the sternest knight to his mortal foe that ever put spear in the rest.'" He would be reluctant, too, to destroy the tears and pathos inherent in the dissolution of the Round Table and in the last great battle, which he termed "the Battle of the Broken Hearts."

10. My summary is from the Hartford *Courant*, 11/13/86 (reprinted from the New York *Sun*, 11/12/86) and the New York *Herald*, 11/12/86. Louisiana established a state lottery in 1886, which operated until it was outlawed in 1895.

11. For documentation of the chronology of work on the remainder of the novel, see my "The Course of Composition of *A Connecticut Yankee*," *AL*, XXXIII (May, 1961), 195–214.

12. DV 80, MTP, published in Paul J. Carter, "MT and the American Labor Movement," *NEQ*, XXX (Sept., 1957), 383–388; reprinted in *Twainian* (Sept.-Oct., 1960), 2, 4. In February, 1887, also, Clemens spoke again to the Monday Evening Club on "Machine Culture," praising the inventive skill of the American workman. (Parts of this address perhaps survive in *The American Claimant*, Ch. X, in one of the speeches at the Mechanics Club).

13. *MTSP*, p. 110.

14. Nbk 18, p. 23; 23 I, p. 11, quoted in *MTSP*, p. 122; see also pp. 120–121.

15. *MTN*, pp. 190–191. For mention of Trafalgar Square demonstrations and crofters' riots, see R. H. Gretton's *A Modern History of the British People*, 1880–1910 (Boston, 1913), I, 195. Gretton cites the files of the London *Times* as his chief source of "dates and facts" and *Punch* as his authority for some of "the popular interests of the moment." His book, therefore, is an excellent source for matters of current interest in England during the years covered by his study.

16. *MTS(P)*, p. 137. See also John Y. Simon, ed., *General Grant by Matthew Arnold with a Rejoinder by MT* (Carbondale, Ill., 1966).

17. Facts based on letters from George Standring to SLC, 1886–90, 1905. On the letter of 12/6/05 Clemens wrote (probably for his biographer's benefit) that he had known this printer and "radical in politics and religion" for thirty years and considered him "a fine man." Though the length of time was somewhat exaggerated, the compliment was doubtless sincere.

18. *The People's History of the English Aristocracy,* 2d. ed. (London, 1891), Chapter I, passim. Direct quotations in this and following paragraph: Introduction (unnumbered), and pp. 1, 6, 16, 165.

19. By this time, too, he had probably read such books as Andrew Carnegie's popular *Triumphant Democracy* (1886), which also urged the establishment of a republic in Britain. Clemens' gift copy from Carnegie, however, was from the 1888 edition. (*A1911,* p. 14).

20. In May, 1887, Clemens reminded himself to "Hand the nobility book to a publisher" (Nbk 21, p. 47) and in September thought of including a copy of *The People's History* as a bonus for purchasers of *A Connecticut Yankee* (Nbk 22 I, p. 5). Early in 1889 he saw Standring's views as "An Englishman on England" forming an eloquent contrast to those of "Englishmen on America" like Matthew Arnold and Sir Lepel Griffin (whom Arnold had cited in his criticisms of the U.S.). At the same time, presumably to make Standring's comments widely available, he proposed to publish companion volumes of Arnold, Griffin, and Standring in paper covers at twenty-five cents each (Nbk 23 II, pp. 54–55). That fall he even got so far as drafting a title page for an "Authorized American Edition" of *The People's History* to be called *English Royalty and Nobility* (*A1911,* p. 11). But again something interfered, and the project was shelved again, permanently, even though as late as November 24 Clemens was urging Fred Hall to "pile on the printers" so that copies could be on the booksellers' counters and in the hands of reviewers when *CY* issued on December 10 (SLC to Hall, 11/24/89, *MTLP,* p. 257).

21. Gretton, *Modern History of the British People,* I, 211.

22. In Ch. XL, Clarence facetiously argues that after Arthur's demise a royal family of cats should be established, whose obvious virtues would inspire other nations of Europe to request "catlings from our own royal house" for their rulers. In an attack on royal grants, added to Ch. XXV in the proof stage, the Yankee cites the excessive costs arising from the fact that these "royalties . . . were a long-lived race and very fruitful."

23. SLC to WDH, 8/22/87; 9/22/89, *MTHL,* II, 595, 613.

24. Reminding himself to "make an appendix in support of the assertion that there were no real gentlemen and ladies before our century," he cited besides "Standring's book," Madame Campan's memoirs of Marie Antoinette, Taine's *Ancient Regime,* St. Simon's *Memoires,* Cellini's *Autobiography,* memoirs of Madame du Barry and the Margravine of Beyreuth, Rousseau's *Confessions,* the writings of Lord Herbert of Cherbury and Emile Zola, "Fielding's chief novels, and Richardson's and Miss Burney's, and even Vicar of Wakefield." From these he would select "instances where printable" and explain "that others (note their places) are not" (Separate ms. sheet included with *Yankee* ms., Berg).

25. Standring, p. 61; Introduction; p. 42.

26. References in this paragraph: Eugene Tompkins, *History of the Boston Theater* (Boston, 1908), p. 262; *MTHL,* II, 554n.; interview in Sydney (Australia) *Morning Herald,* 9/17/95. Clemens may not have enjoyed the performance of the *Mikado* in 1886, for he wrote to a friend that he had seen only half of it and wished to be spared the rest (SLC to Mrs. Sage, n.d., T/S, MTP).

He would obviously enjoy much more the Bryn Mawr production of *Iolanthe* in February, 1891, in which his daughter Susy appeared as Phyllis (E. C. Salsbury *Susy and MT*, New York, 1965, p. 286). In 1902 he added to his library a copy of a newly published limited edition of *Patience,* inscribed "S. L. Clemens, Dec. 1902" (*A1911*, p. 31). See also his use of *The Mikado* in "The Man that Corrupted Hadleyburg," Chapter Eleven, *post.*

27. The allusion to "dudes and dudesses" suggests that Clemens was possibly remembering Andrew Carnegie's scorn for American "dudes" who aped English fashions. As James D. Williams has also noted (*PMLA,* LXXX, Mar., 1965, 107), Carnegie hoped for the day when "royal families are extinct as dodos" and thought that a royal family was "an insult to every other family in the land" (*Triumphant Democracy,* p. 9). In 1888, Clemens' notebook exclaims: "Royalty and nobility in *our* day!—These Dodos and pterodactyls!" (Nbk 23 I, p. 11). In Ch. XIII of *CY*, Hank cites the irrationality of conferring rank and privilege on "a certain hundred families . . . to the exclusion of the rest of the nation's families." All of these, however, could just as easily have been inspired by similar remarks in *The People's History.*

28. SLC to WDH, 8/5/89, *MTHL,* II, 609.

29. Quoted by Arthur L. Scott, "*The Innocents Adrift,* Edited by MT's Official Biographer," *PMLA,* LXXVIII (June, 1963), 230–237. Standring, too, attacked British game laws, and Taine made much of French nobility's misuse of hunting rights in *The Ancient Regime.* See also Gretton, I, 221.

30. Paine 91; Nbk 24, p. 15.

31. *MTF*, p. 262. As late as September, Clemens had made tentative plans to issue the novel the following spring, predicated upon finishing it by Nov. 15 (Nbk 22 I, p. 2).

32. Nbk 22 II, pp. 37, 64; five items after the latter reference, recalling a dream in which Americans greeted the Archangel Michael "with a hearty and friendly 'Hello Mike!'" he ironically admitted: "No, there *is* no reverence with us." (All quoted in my "Course of Composition of *CY*," p. 206, as is quotation from Nbk 22 II, p. 69 in the following paragraph). For Metcalf's request see *MTHL,* II, 600–601.

33. Hartford *Courant,* 6/22/88, p. 5, col. 1. Arnold had died on April 15, hence the reference to the "late" Matthew Arnold.

34. *MTN,* p. 195. Many of these notes were preparations for a speech to be delivered the following Sept. 20 (in response to the toast, "The American Press") at an Encampment of the Army of the Cumberland in Chicago (Nbk 22 II, p. 67; 23 I, pp. 1, 2).

35. See "Mary Augusta Ward," *DNB;* W. L. Phelps, "The Novels of Mrs. Humphry Ward," *Forum,* XLI (1909), 325. No less a personage than former Prime Minister William Gladstone wrote a long essay-review for the May *Nineteenth Century.* Ironically, too, Mrs. Ward was a niece of Matthew Arnold.

36. Quoted by Kipling, *From Sea to Sea* (New York, 1899), II, 178.

37. Charles Kingsley, for instance, whom Clemens had known since his visits in the early '70's. Many of the fictional characters, too, were based on real people: Elsmere's college mentor Mr. Grey on Oxford philosopher Thomas

Hill Green; Squire Wendover on scholar-author Mark Pattison; Langham, probably on Walter Pater. Quotations in the following discussion are from *Robert Elsmere* (London and New York: Macmillan, 1888), pp. 198, 56, 74, 89, 107.

38. DV 24, MTP, a cancelled portion of the *Yankee* ms. carries a notation (I, 483) that space is to be left for a chapter on Hank's recuperation.

39. *FrRev*, III, 4, i; III, 3, vii. In a manuscript note at the beginning of Ch. XV, Clemens planned to have Hank and Sandy encounter some hermits and to borrow details of their "austerities" from Lecky. He also tentatively proposed to have his wanderers visit a convent and monastery before going on to Morgan le Fay's castle. Possibly the later decision to put monastery, convent, and hermits all together in the Holy Valley could have been inspired by Lecky's notation that in early Christian times the monasteries had spread rapidly even into "the secluded valleys of Wales and Ireland" (*EurMor*, II, 113). Marginal notes in the ms. (I, 413) indicate that Clemens found a parallel situation in J. R. Green's tale of the founding of the Abbeys of Crowland (monks) and Ely (nuns) in Lincolnshire's wild fen country (*Short History of the English People*, New York: Harper's, 1877, p. 67). Linked with Green in that note was James Anthony Froude's *Short Studies on Great Subjects*, a collection of essays (1867–83), several of which deal with conditions in medieval monasteries and other ascetic practices, one of which cites the legendary lives of the saints and the Arthurian legends as providing excellent examples for imitation (Series I, New York: Scribner's, 1887, p. 450). Though Clemens borrowed no specific details, Froude's treatment of monasticism and chivalry doubtless provided an additional stimulus to the satire. Nevertheless, the nature of the Valley itself seems to owe a good deal to *Robert Elsmere*. See also *EurMor*, II, 119.

40. In "The Small-Pox Hut" (Ch. XXIX) parallels occur to Mrs. Ward's description of one of the thatched huts on Squire Wendover's estate, the stench of the interior, the young girl who died after some six weeks of suffering, the parents who pled merely to be left alone. Langham's horror and Elsmere's questioning why "the old ways" were "so terribly long in dying" might well have been Clemens' own. Just as the epidemic and Elsmere's efforts finally cause the Squire to notice the awful situation of his tenants, so King Arthur gains understanding of his subjects' plight. Like Wendover on his inspection tour, Arthur ignores warnings about exposing himself to the disease raging among the peasants. The Yankee's vow to raise a statue to Arthur's true bravery and basic manhood, implicitly echoes Mrs. Ward's comment upon the Squire's fearlessness as he moved from hovel to hovel. Even closer is Langham's memory of Elsmere in the wretched hut. Comforting the mother, with one hand on the head of a small child, the minister became for Langham a symbol of "the modern 'Man of Feeling,' as sensitive, as impressionable, and as free from the burden of self, as his eighteenth-century prototype." The proposed statue to Arthur calls up much the same picture. The Yankee vows that it will not be the customary sort—"a mailed king killing a dragon"—but "a king in commoner's garb bearing death in his arms that a peasant mother might look her last upon her child and be comforted." The Yankee's tribute: "He was great now; sublimely great" also implicitly reflects Langham's feeling for Elsmere.

Yet, in the additional implication that Arthur's increased understanding of human suffering cannot withstand the pressures of traditional attitudes, there is a further reflection of Wendover's reactions. Though appalled by the hideous conditions (which his unscrupulous overseer had kept hidden from him for many years) the Squire never developed any sort of real compassion for his tenants. Similarly, Arthur's sympathy did not extend very far. Learning that the peasant family's two sons had escaped from their unjust imprisonment by the lord of the manor, he immediately proposes to return them to the lord's dungeons.

Finally, the Yankee's picture of his life with Sandy and his concern over the illness of their daughter (whose recuperation sends them to France and allows the Church to reestablish its control over England) probably owes something to the domestic felicities portrayed in *Robert Elsmere* as well as to Clemens' affection for his own wife and daughters. Both Hank's worries and the trip to France closely parallel Elsmere's anxieties during the birth of his child and also his own illness and attempted recuperation on the Mediterranean seacoast near Algiers. (See *Robert Elsmere*, pp. 200–205; 256, 258; 282–295; 264, 593ff.)

41. Other details: the supplies requisitioned from Clarence for the "restoration" of the fountain, and the appearance of the "West Pointer" at the competitive examination.

42. See Gretton, I, 210, 220, 228, 243.

43. Emily A. Acland, "A Lady's 'American Notes,'" *Nineteenth Century*, XXIII (Mar., 1888), 412. For English developments in electrification and telephone service, see also Gretton, I, 236, 279.

44. Gretton, I, 240.

45. Nbk 22 I, p. 4; *MTN*, p. 195 (note in Nbk 23 I, p. 3, indicates that the paragraph quoted was added at a later date).

46. Henry Labouchere had waxed especially eloquent in an 1886 speech in the House of Commons (Alger L. Thorold, *Life of Henry Labouchere*, New York and London, 1913, pp. 239–240.

47. Nbk 24, p. 3, quoted in *MTSP*, p. 128.

48. *Eighteenth Century*, I, 227. Clemens was reading this work in 1888. See notes to Ch. VII, *post*.

49. They would also doubtless identify the two other members of the Board as the two other ruling members of the College: Garter King of Arms and Clarenceux King of Arms.

50. *FrRev*, II, 2, ii. Taine also briefly mentions the rule (*Ancient Regime*, p. 64), and Clemens, in a note for an appendix, cites both Taine and Carlyle as supporting sources (Nbk 24, p. 15).

51. *People's History*, p. 29. He doubtless also noticed Standring's reference (p. 145) to the bastard son of the Duke of Clarence—"this offspring of a prostitute actress"—who, at fourteen, was not only a Cornet in the Tenth Regiment of Light Dragoons, of which the Prince of Wales was Colonel, but was *"senior to four other Cornets"* [Standring's italics].

52. *People's History*, pp. 149, 161–163, and passim. See also *MTN*, p. 207. Clemens may also have known some of Standring's shorter pamphlets like

Court Flunkeys: Their Work and Wages (London: Freethought Publishing Co., n.d.) and "Does Royalty Pay?" *The Atheistic Platform,* X (1884), 174–160). The "pensions" passage was a late addition to *CY,* for sometime during the proof stage of the novel Clemens reminded himself to "Insert royal grant" (Nbk 24, p. 13) immediately following the discussion of how Hank planned to increase military efficiency by establishing the King's Own Regiment. This, too, is where he pointed directly at Victoria, blaming the vast expense of the royal grants on the fact that the rulers of the "Pendragon stock" were so "long-lived" and "fruitful."

In view of all these contemporary implications, one wonders if the great English stock booms of 1886–88 did not influence the Yankee's stock-manipulations as much as Clemens' knowledge of financial activities in the U.S. Some of the arguments advanced in England during the mid-80's by the proponents of bimetallism, also, seem reflected in Hank's substitution of new nickels for the old and worn goldpieces traditionally given to participants in the Royal Touch ceremony. Even more likely, the emphasis on the savings which resulted from Hank's financial reforms may have resulted from the publicity accorded the success of G. J. Goschen, Chancellor of the Exchequer, in converting the greater part of Britain's funded debt to a lower rate of interest in 1888. See Gretton, I, passim.

53. Gretton, I, 239.

54. SLC to Thedore Crane, 10/5/88, *MTL,* II, 500. A letter from Webster & Co. dated 4/16/89 (MTP) reports the completion of two typewritten copies of the ms.

Chapter Seven, A CONNECTICUT YANKEE

1. See Nbks. 20–24, passim. Many are also mentioned in subsequent notes to this chapter. Some are also discussed by James D. Williams, "The Uses of History in MT's *A Connecticut Yankee, PMLA,* LXXX (Mar., 1965), 102–110, and by James R. Russell, "The Origin, Composition, and Reputation of MT's *A Connecticut Yankee,*" unpublished doctoral dissertation, Chicago, 1966, both of which appeared after these chapters were written.

2. "Malory in the *Connecticut Yankee,*" *HTSE* (1948), pp. 185–206. See also Harold Aspiz, "MT's Reading," unpublished doctoral dissertation, UCLA, 1950, pp. 348–359. Often Clemens adapted hints from Malory into dominant characteristics, as in the case of Sir Dinadan, whose fame as "the Humorist" derives from the fact that Sir Tristram once referred to him as "the best joker and jester," and Malory several other times refers to his scoffing and jesting (Bk. X, Chs. LVI, XXV, XLII, XLVII). On the other hand, the *Yankee* ms. validates Wilson's conjecture that the author merely skimmed index or chapter headings for names to fit characters he had introduced. One of the most notable instances was the penciled addition of the very appropriate name Sir Breuse Sance Pité to identify the "neighboring lord" who sent the young couple to Morgan le Fay's dungeons for refusing him his *droit du seigneur* (Ch. XVIII).

3. In "A Word of Explanation" from Bk. VI, Chs. XI, XII, XIII; Merlin's

story of Excalibur in Ch. III from Bk. I, Ch. XXIII; story of the tournament in Ch. IX from Bk. X, Ch. LVI. In each of these cases Clemens, in the *Yankee* ms., directed the printer to the appropriate passages in Malory.

4. The report of the tournament in Ch. IX is a pretty dull account of "How the knights bare them in battle." Hence, as Wilson suggests, Clemens is almost certainly being ironic when the Yankee notes the "quaint and sweet and simple" wording and other "fragrances and flavors" that made up for "more important lacks." See Wilson's article for analysis of the satire on Malory's style in Sandy's tale (Chs. XV, XIX).

5. *Ivanhoe* probably also helped underscore the humorist's conception of artistocratic ignorance and ineptitude, for few of his sources contain more striking comments than the witty, sophisticated DeBracy's admission that he could neither read nor write (Ch. XXVI).

6. Ms. I, 235, Berg.

7. Besides the typical Protestant bias of his youth and an early enthusiasm for Tom Paine, Clemens had (from the late 1870's) admiration for Robert Ingersoll, one of the most vigorous of the many voices protesting the efforts of clergymen (especially Roman Catholics) to influence political matters and to impede the progress of scientific investigation. He perhaps also knew such works as John W. Draper's *History of the Conflict Between Religion and Science* (1874), Henry C. Lea's several studies of Catholic faults, and various recent discussions in the *North American Review*. (Louis J. Budd discusses these possible influences at greater length in *MTSP*, pp. 116–117). Clemens owned a copy of Draper's *Human Physiology* (1st published, 1856), interesting for its pioneering use of microphotographs (*C1951*).

8. *EurMor*, II, 16. Two pages later Lecky all but enunciates the sort of difficulties that would plague Hank Morgan: "In medicine, physical science, commercial interests, politics, and even ethics, the reformer has been confronted with theological affirmations which barred his way. . . ." All references to marginalia in Clemens' copy of Lecky are based on Chester L. Davis' analysis (*Twainian*, XIV [May-June; July-Aug.; Sept.-Oct.; Nov.-Dec., 1956]).

9. *EurMor*, I, 389, 399, and passim.

10. On the same page as the underlined phrase concerning the "spirit of belief" Lecky comments that through the ages "eclipses were supposed by the population to foreshadow calamity." Other sources, however, could have furnished the initial suggestion. The Yankee's remark that Columbus or Cortez had once "played an eclipse as a saving trump" possibly points to an episode in Washington Irving's *Life of Columbus* (Bk. XVI, Ch. iii) as the source of some of the effects. The *Sun* report of the Governors Island reading indicates that the Yankee was to determine the date of his arrival in Arthur's England "by watching for a total eclipse of the sun that he remembered the almanac of 1884 had spoken of as having occurred in 528. . . ." Though notices of eclipses were featured prominently in the almanacs of the day, the author may well have remembered a scene from Emerson Bennett's popular novel, *The Prairie Flower* (1849). In *TA* (Ch. XIX), while discussing the Goshoot Indians, he mentions in the same sentence Bennett's works and New York's Bowery Theatre. Since he had been in New York from December 10-17, 1870, he may

well have seen the stage version of *The Prairie Flower*, played at the Bowery Theatre during the 1870–71 season. In both play and book, the heroine, captive of a villainous Indian chief, recalls that years ago in an almanac she had read of a solar eclipse to occur at that very moment; she "invokes" the eclipse, and refuses to "lift it" until her safety is guaranteed. (I am grateful to Franklin R. Rogers for calling this source to my attention).

11. *EurMor,* II, 198. The complete sentence (near the end of the discussion from which Clemens later borrowed details for the hermits in the Valley of Holiness) reads: "When men have learnt to reverence a life of passive, unreasoning obedience as the highest type of perfection, the enthusiasm and passion of freedom necessarily decline."

12. In the account of the National Assembly's deliberations shortly before the Feast of Pikes, for instance, Carlyle remarks that difficulties with the clergy constituted "a most fatal business . . . a weltering hydra-coil . . . which cannot be appeased, alive; which cannot be trampled dead!" (*FrRev,* II, 1, ii). The style of Clemens' revised passage suggests that he may have found a more immediate stimulus in Taine's summary of clerical activities and achievements of the early Church (*Ancient Regime*, pp. 2–5). Taine, however, was complimenting those activities. Thus, in using the latter's style and approach in presenting Lecky's arguments *against* the Church, Clemens gave his satire an added dimension.

13. See especially *EurMor,* I, 235, 310–311. Quotations on "divine right" in this paragraph: II, 275, 285.

14. A few pages before Lecky's discussion of the treatment of suicides (II, 62) Clemens wrote: "I can quite easily imagine myself giving an unhappy person something to kill himself with, but I cannot imagine myself trying to prevent an unhappy person from committing suicide. It gives me a very real pang to read of a prevented suicide, and a very real feeling of gratitude to read of a successful one" (II, 56). The Forfeiture Act abolished all forfeitures for felony in 1870, but self-destruction remained a felony in England until the Suicide Act of 1961 abolished criminal penalties for suicide or attempted suicide.

15. *EurMor,* I, 299; marginalia, II, 72, 394.

16. *EurMor,* I, 136–142.

17. *MTF,* p. 258, 11/16/86.

18. SLC to Clara, 7/20/90, *LLMT,* p. 257.

19. This comment is reminiscent of Carlyle's report of Marat's statement (just after the Frenchman's demand for "Two Hundred and Sixty thousand Aristocrat heads" as the only way to rid France of the nobility): "Give me two hundred Naples Bravoes, armed each with a good dirk . . . : with them I will traverse France, and accomplish the Revolution" (*FrRev,* II, 1, ii).

20. That rationalizing and the Yankee's remark about the freedom of masters to kill slaves, reflect Lecky's discussion of the Roman law regarding slaves (*EurMor,* II, 66–67), a passage which Clemens was also to cite (Nbk 24, p. 15) as pertinent to the hanging of the slave-band in Ch. XXXVII.

21. See also Taine, *The Ancient Regime,* Bks. I, V, and notes; Baring-Gould, *In Exitu Israel* (London, 1870), 2 vols., I, 52–53. Lest anyone interpret the Yankee's comment that each head of a family and each son owed three

days of service on the road, with "a day or so added for their servants" as a sign of Clemens' ignorance or a lack of social consciousness in suggesting that these peasants had servants, it should be noted that the *corvée* was required of *all* tenants on a noble's land, not just of peasant farmers, and that the Yankee specifically refers to "small 'independent' farmers, artisans, etc." Furthermore, Clemens probably got the detail directly from Baring-Gould, who notes among other duties that the tenant worked three days a year "for himself, three days for each of his sons and servants" (p. 52).

22. *FrRev*, III, 1, i (See also III, 2, i); III, 7, vi.

23. Tennyson, "Merlin and Vivien"; Strachey, ed., *Le Morte Darthur*, p. xiii. The Yankee's sneer about Merlin's "working" the weather perhaps also derives from the first *Idyll*, "The Coming of Arthur," where Merlin is pictured as "riddling" about "Rain, rain, and sun."

24. *FrRev*, II, 1, ix–xii; Nbk 19, p. 34.

25. Carlyle elsewhere describes France as a powder-tower (I, 1, ii) and as a "monstrous Galvanic mass" filling twenty-five million Leyden jars (the French people) with electricity, with future explosions almost certain (II, 3, ii). Taine also saw pre-Revolutionary France as a house with a powder magazine in its cellars (*Ancient Regime*, p. 328).

26. *FrRev*, I, 5, vi; III, 4, v. Some of the details perhaps came also from Baring-Gould's *In Exitu Israel*, I, 59.

27. Planning notes for *CY* indicate that part of the satire was aimed indirectly at the genteel picture of Arthurian England in *Idylls of the King*. Possibly Tennyson's acceptance of a peerage in 1884 had irked Clemens, as it had some of the English Liberals (even though it was Gladstone who had urged Tennyson to accept the title). Whatever the impetus, the humorist certainly did not object to Dan Beard's putting the poet laureate's head on his portrait of Merlin. Originally, too, passages from Tennyson's poems were to appear in the novel, for one note outlines an episode in which Hank was to impress the court with renditions of "Break, Break, Break!" and "The Fair Maid of Astolat," and to seek Guinevere's favor by recounting "some exploit of Launcelot" from the *Idylls*. To expose a rival bard's charge that his performance was "prepared" rather than impromptu, he would expose the bard's faulty memory and then "whirl in some more Tennyson," add a touch of Shakespeare and Browning, and "take the cake" (Nbk 23 I, pp. 21–22).

28. SLC to "Dr. Parker," n.d. (paper indicates early 1880's), Barrett. Other references in paragraph: "The Love Letters of MT," ed. Dixon Wecter, *Atlantic*, CLXXX (Nov., 1947), 38; Nbk 32 II, p. 43. In "Queen Victoria's Jubilee" (1897) he played with a variation of his favorite lines in a way that both implied considerable respect for Tennyson's poem and took a humorous swipe at literary pirates. The flash from shields lifted in salute during the "spirit-correspondent's" description of the pageant following Henry V's victory at Agincourt "lit up that dappled sea of color with a glory like 'the golden vortex in the west over the foundered sun.'" Commenting on the alleged quotation, the humorist then added parenthetically, that its presence in the account was very interesting, for it showed that "our literature of to-day has a circulation in heaven—pirated editions, no doubt" (*E&E*, p. 201). In "3000

Years Among the Microbes," written in 1905, the narrator recalls his human sweetheart's "fairy form transfigured by the golden flood of the sinking sun!" (*MTWWD*, p. 464).

29. Clemens seems also to have echoed Dickens' description of the Marquis almost twenty years earlier in his "Open Letter to Commodore Vanderbilt," *Packard's Monthly*, I (Mar., 1869), which describes the Commodore's driving recklessly through the park, looking neither to the right nor to the left, "with a bearing which plainly says, 'Let these people get out of the way if they can; but if they can't, and I run over them and kill them, no matter, I'll pay for them.'" This echo likewise suggests that Clemens had read *TTC* by 1869.

Many other sources provided details for the actions and attitudes of the nobility described in the episodes at Morgan le Fay's castle. The noble who "walled up the only Fountain of the Township" is mentioned in *FrRev*, i, 6, iii. Other allusions (direct or indirect) point to St. Simon's *Memoires*, Casanova, Dumas' *Count of Monte Cristo* (which implicitly carries the Yankee's notice of the use of *lettres de cachet* up into the nineteenth century), and the enjoyment of bawdry by Queen Elizabeth and Marguerite of Navarre (which in turn reminds the reader of *1601*).

30. In Ch. XXIII of *AmCl*, too, there is an echo of Manette's denunciation of the Evrémondes and their posterity "to the last of their race" when Sally Sellers, thinking that Viscount Berkeley had died in the hotel fire, promises Howard Tracy (who is actually Berkeley under an assumed name) that she will make sure that the Viscount will never make trouble for them again, by teaching herself "to detest that name and all that have ever borne it or ever shall bear it."

31. This detail, too, probably derives from *TTC*, for in II, xv, just after referring to Damiens' attempt on the life of Louis XV (an incident also mentioned by Clemens in this chapter of *CY*), Dickens speaks of his "mender of roads" as being thirty-five, though he looked sixty. Both Taine and Carlyle cite British historian Arthur Young's mention of a similar peasant who looked sixty or seventy, though only twenty-eight; but this was a woman.

32. For Kennan's probable influence on the picture of the slave-band and the pilgrims, and on the latters' journey to the "holy fountain," see my "The Course of Composition of *CY*" *AL.*, XXXIII (May, 1961), 207–211.

33. *EurMor*, I, 295 (in a discussion of gladiatorial games, parts of which Clemens marked in his own copy); Ball, *Slavery in the United States: A Narrative of the Life and Adventures of Charles Ball, A Black Man* (Pittsburg: J. T. Shryock, 1853), p. 331. (*A1911*, p. 63, lists a much-worn copy of the 1837 edition, which is inscribed "S. L. Clemens, 1902.") Of the numerous details derived from Ball for first meeting with the slave-band, the most important were the number in the group, the kinds of chains (with a detail borrowed from Kennan's Siberian exiles), the separation of the slave family, the slave being stripped and whipped (Ball, pp. 30ff., 12, 49). For the future adventures when Hank and King Arthur "join" the group, Clemens borrowed the haggling over prices, the granting of a bargain price for two slaves, the prototype of the orator who lauds "our glorious British liberties" in the presence of the slaves

(Ball, p. 59ff. Ball's orator, of course, is American, and his speech is delivered, ironically, on July 4); and the demand that Hank and the King *prove* they are freemen (Ball, p. 419). In the *Yankee* ms. on the top of a page near the first description of the slaves, Clemens wrote and then crossed out: "Autobiography of Charles Ball" (ms. I, 416); in a notebook list for an appendix, " '*Prove* that ye be free.' Rich II and Ch. Ball" (Nbk 24, p. 15). "Rich II" probably refers to a passage at the end of the chapter on "The Peasant's Revolt" in Green's *History of the English People* (Bk IV, Ch. iii), in which Richard sneers at the peasant's claims that they are free men.

34. For the story of the "holy fountain" (actually a well), the description of the hermits, and a possible inspiration for the author's concept of the knights as missionaries, see *EurMor*, II, 114–120, 261–262, and note 39 of Chapter Six here, *ante*. In addition, he could have been reminded of the "fountain" passage by Kennan's discussion of Russian reverence for the shrine and famous well at the monastery of St. Sergius (*Century*, XII, June, 1887, 253–254); and his having Sir Ozana le Cure Hardy deliver the news of the "fountain's" failure suggests that he perhaps also recalled Sir Ozana's presence among a group of knights who ate a meal by a well, or his defeat at the hands of Sir Palamides by another well two chapters later (Malory, Bk X, Chs. xi, xiii). For the Yankee's "miraculous" restoration of the damaged well, the author combined his own memories of a fireworks display at Heidelberg Castle (*TA*, Appendix B) and details borrowed from a storm scene in Baring-Gould's *In Exitu Israel* (I, 59–61), one of his favorite novels of the French Revolution. In the latter, Baring-Gould presents the superstitious populace chanting the *Magnificat*, while church bells peal in the "popular belief" that their sound would dispel the tempest, and then notes that with a momentary pause, and a lightning-flash, "the water began to flow down the hill, collect into a stream in the churchyard, and to pour in a turbid flood down the steps into the nave." So, too, the Yankee describes tolling bells and a Latin chant, and invokes not one, but two flood images, when the masses "pour . . . like a vast black wave" into the area where the "miracle" is to occur, and again when the "freed waters" flow *out* of the chapel door.

For ceremony of the "Royal Touch," see *EurMor*, I, 386–388n. For clairvoyant magicians, I, 395–397. Lecky's mention in the same passage of similar powers attributed to Apuleius (author of the famous satire, *The Golden Ass*, and an "indefatigable student of the religious mysteries of his time") and to various beliefs in guardian "daemons" points to two other borrowings. Clemens' decision to accompany "Peterson's Prophylactic Tooth-brushes" with *Noyoudont* tooth-wash (the name of which echoes that of a much-advertised nineteenth-century cure-all, *Sozodont*) was probably reinforced by Lecky's later notation (II, 157–158) that Apuleius was once forced to answer charges of promoting luxurious living after he had praised the use of tooth-powder. More significantly, in a passage in which Sandy was to be visited by a "maniac" who claimed to be brother to the Recording Angel (DV 22, MTP), Clemens employed almost the identical device for describing the "petitions," their answers, and the totalling of "debits" and "credits" in the Office of the Recording Angel as that outlined in Lecky's summary of Apuleius' discussion of the activities of "daemons" (I, 343). [The relation between the "maniac" and the Recording

Angel also again recalls Lecky's account of the Spanish lunatic (II, 92), who probably was the model for the crazed hermit in *P&P*.] Clemens adapted this episode from a previously written satire directed at Olivia's cousin, Andrew Langdon. Though it was ultimately deleted from *CY* (it would have been ms. I, 371–396), the piece on which it was based has been published as "Letter from the Recording Angel" by DeVoto in *Harper's*, Feb., 1946, and (as "Letter to the Earth") in *LE*, pp. 117–122; and by Wecter in *RP*, pp. 87–94. In *LE*, DeVoto uses the fictitious name of the *Yankee* ms., "Abner Scofield"; Wecter uses Andrew Langdon's name but incorrectly identifies him (p. xxv) as Livy's *uncle*.

35. All references here and hereafter are to the Cabinet Edition, 7 vols. (New York: D. Appleton, 1892). Clemens owned the six-volume edition of 1887–88 (*A1911*, p. 44). He referred to this work specifically in a note at the top of one page of what became Ch. XXIII (ms. I, 464). Along with "Boiling in oil in Blue Laws" (a reference to the book by J. Hammond Trumbull) he wrote "Witch-lynchings in 18th cent." (He used both incidents in Ch. XXXVI.) Specific sources as follows: *Mansion House,* IV, 291.

Small-pox Hut: Cf. Lecky's description of condition of agricultural workers as "purely animal" well into the nineteenth century (VII, 257), and discussion of penalties for excommunication (IV, 288–290). The latter probably inspired the priest's invoking "the curse of Rome," though Clemens later proposed to quote the "curse" itself in an appendix and to get it from the "Cyclopedia"— probably *Appleton's;* see Nbk 24, p. 13). In that same note of sources for his Appendix Clemens cited "Ophelia's burial" as an appropriate example of the Church's attitude toward a young girl who had died a "doubtful" death. (See comments of the grave-diggers and the reluctant priest, *Hamlet*, V, i).

Argument with Dowley: Though details concerning prices, trades, and working conditions were derived largely from articles by Edward Jarvis in the *Atlantic Monthly* (October, November, December, 1869), Clemens, in laying Hank's trap for Dowley, drew on Lecky's discussion of how sixteenth and seventeenth century laws were extended to regulation of industry in the eighteenth. Besides combining Lecky's citation of a law of James I (permitting justices and town magistrates to fix wages) with the further information that during the eighteenth century employers were fined for paying more or less than the going rate and employees were forbidden to organize to seek higher wages (VII, 299–301), he added the penalty of the pillory (for the employer), at the same time expanding upon Lecky's mention in another place (II, 137) of the cruelties inflicted upon prisoners in the pillory.

Witch-burning: II, 331–333. In Lecky's discussions of the gruesome execution of Jane Corphar and those of other alleged witches, Clemens was doubtless also impressed by the summary comment that as late as 1736, Scotland's associated Presbytery "solemnly denounced the repeal of the laws against witchcraft as an infraction of the express word of God." He used details of these cases again in *The Mysterious Stranger* (see notes to Ch. Eleven, *post*).

Hanging for theft: IV, 343; VII, 322. This episode arose from the historian's discussion of hardships resulting from British practice of impressing soldiers and sailors. Though Clemens originally planned an episode in which the Yankee would cause the abolition of the practice in Arthur's kingdom by impressing some nobles, allegedly by mistake (Nbk 23 I, p. 19), he ultimately settled on combining two cases in Lecky, which besides dramatizing the tragic results that sometimes followed impressment of the head of a family, provided additional illustrations of the incredible harshness of English law. Again, Lecky's comment (VII, 322–323) that the "scandal of English executions was not wholly removed until our own day" must have provided fuel for Clemens' fire.

36. *Ibid*, VI, 472; see also I, 10 and passim.

37. See Nbk 23 I, pp. 15, 18, MTP. Clemens actually wrote and later deleted one passage in which Hank's forcible conversion of hermits to various protestant sects caused "immense trouble" with the Church.

38. *Eighteenth Century*, VII, 16, 17 (cf. also II, 321); 103–104, 54. Lecky may even have been responsible for the number and ages of boys who remained faithful, for his story of the "September Massacres" of 1792 notes among the victims "more than forty boys who were not yet seventeen" (VII, 46).

39. *FrRev*, Petition: I, 2, ii; "Insurrection of Women": I, 7, i–x. The reference to the people being driven back to their "dens," probably also provided the imagery for the Earl Grip's command (Ch. XXXIV): "Lash me these animals to their kennels!" Clarence's vivid figure of speech—"Dismember me this animal and return him in a basket . . ." originally read "Disembowel me this animal and convey his kidneys to the baseborn knave his master" (ms. II, 376). The phrase was changed at suggestion of Howells and Stedman (*MTHL*, II, 620). In *Slavery in the United States,* Charles Ball, describing the slaughtering of a beef, records his master's order to "cut off the head, neck, legs, and tail, and lay them together with the empty stomach and the harslet, in a basket" and then send them to the kitchen of the great house (p. 171).

40. This detail probably derives from Malory, and possibly also from some of the legends that Arthur and his knights had not died but lay sleeping in a cave, awaiting a signal to return to activity in the world (See Everyman's Library *Malory*, p. xv).

41. SLC to Stedman, 5/18/89, Yale; Stedman to SLC, 7/7/89, Stedman, *Life in Letters* (New York, 1910), II, 320–321; *MTHL*, II, 608–619 passim. Completed page proofs were ready by November 15 (Hall to SLC, 11/11/89, *MTLP*, p. 258n.).

42. *MTE,* p. 211.

43. See both *EurMor* and *Eighteenth Century*, passim. It is important to note that *CY* implies the importance of education as well as of technology. Though mechanistic terms like "teacher-factory" and "Man-Factory" are entirely appropriate to the vocabulary of the "practical" Yankee, the Yankee's school system was not to be limited to technical education. References to that system and to the purposes of the Man-Factory indicate that instruction there would emphasize the importance of the individual in a democratic society and the means by which men might develop their individual capacities.

44. *MTS(P),* p. 271.

45. Stedman, *Life in Letters*, II, 320.

The several prefaces written at different times during the novel's composition (mss. in MTP) all stress the fact that the author chose his details of "medieval" abuses from many periods of history and that these "superstitions" and abuses had lasted into eras much later than the novel's setting. But whereas two of the earlier prefaces inject the positive note that hope might be derived from the progress of the nineteenth century, the one finally adopted merely admits the anachronism of laws and customs depicted in the story, and explains that since they existed "in the English and other civilizations of far later times," one is safe in believing that no injustice is done to the sixth century in supposing that they were in practice then also. Less specific, that statement is at the same time more consistent with the broader view that the book carried a message for the present as well as for the past. Dan Beard's illustrations, highly praised by Clemens (See *MTB,* II, 888; New York *Times* interview, 12/10/89) consistently point up contemporary implications (sometimes stretching the text to do so). Not only were some of the vestments in the drawings more Anglican than Roman, but Beard explicitly attached the punning label "High Church" to his picture of a monk being blown up by Hank's dynamite. Besides giving Merlin the features of Tennyson, the artist put the faces of the Prince of Wales (later Edward VII) and Kaiser Wilhelm II in his gallery of royal "chuckleheads." But the picture that Clemens especially praised suggests again that he considered the novel's major focus to be on the *underlying principles* that permitted tyranny to exist in any age. In that one Beard gave the cruel slave-driver the face of the notorious American financier, Jay Gould.

46. SLC to Baxter, 11/20/89, MTP; *MTHL,* II, 621. The preceding summer Clemens and Fred Hall had agreed that the canvassers should not mention the political and religious bearing of the book but should play up to the American public's interest in "whatever makes fun of royalty and nobility and government by aristocracy" (Hall to SLC, 7/30/89, 8/16/89, MTP). But the intensity of emotion in the letters to Baxter and Howells and the agitation noted by the N. Y. *Times* reporter (12/10/89) further indicates that all this was not merely aimed at increasing sales.

47. *MTN,* p. 198.

48. Clemens was to express the same view, indirectly, in one of Puddn'head Wilson's maxims in *FEq* (II, Ch. XV): "Let me make the superstitions of a nation and I care not who makes its laws or its songs either." [Here he was adapting the famous comment of Andrew Fletcher of Saltoun (perhaps encountered through Carlyle's quoting it in his essay on Robert Burns): "Give me the making of the songs of a nation and I care not who makes its laws."] Moreover, Isabel Lyon, Clemens' secretary, has reported that in 1907 the author told her he intended *A Connecticut Yankee* to serve as "an eternal example of the sameness of . . . the God-damned Human Race" (letter to W. T. H. Howe, 1933, Berg). Though Miss Lyon's recollections in her series of letters to Howe are not always wholly trustworthy, this one gains validity in the light of the foregoing considerations.

Chapter Eight, THE ROAD BACK

1. SLC to Chatto and Windus [Fall, 1889], *MTL,* II, 524–525; Hall to SLC, 1/17/90, MTP.

2. Clemens almost certainly had not seen the one most favorable British

review, "MT's New Book. A Crusher for Royalty," Sydney (Australia) *Bulletin*, 3/8/90 (See Joseph Jones, "MT's *CY* and Australian Nationalism," *AL*, XL, May, 1968, 227–231).

3. SLC to Andrew Lang, erroneously dated "1889" in *MTL*, II, 525–528. DeVoto (without explanation) assigns a date of "Early 1890" (*Portable MT*, New York, 1946, p. 770). *Late* 1890 is more likely, for in the letter to Lang, Clemens speaks of "Kipling's far-flung bugle-note." His first acquaintance with Kipling's works (as he later remembered it) came "about a year" after Kipling's visit to Elmira in August, 1889, on his way from India to England via the United States (*MTE*, p. 311). Kipling was relatively unknown outside of India until 1890, when *Departmental Ditties* (1886) and *Plain Tales from the Hills* (1888) were republished in London. A reprinting in the New York *Herald*, 8/17/90, of Kipling's account of the Elmira visit (Allahabad *Pioneer*, 3/18/90) may have been Clemens' first reminder, and it was probably sometime in September, after the Clemenses returned from their summer stay at the Onteora Club in Tannersville, New York, that Charles Dudley Warner's brother George loaned him the copy of *Plain Tales* which thenceforth made him an avid reader of Kipling's books. The later date of Clemens' letter would also help account for the fact that Lang's article did not appear until February, 1891.

4. Rodney, p. 118. As Rodney indicates (pp. 152–154), the book became more popular as the years went on, running to thirteen editions by 1940, and thus surpassing *FEq, RI,* and *GA* in popularity, though the critics never wholly appreciated it.

5. SLC to WDH, 8/24/89, *MTHL*, II, 610–611.

6. DV 344, "Letters From a Dog, Etc." and DV 313a, "A Defence of Royalty and Nobility," MTP. Clemens used (or planned to use) pp. 24–35 of DV 344 as the "magazine article" referred to on p. 4 of DV 313a. Hence DV 344 was obviously written first. Nbk 25, p. 20, sometime between Jan. 8 and Feb. 7, 1891, lists the title of "Letters From a Dog," perhaps as a projected work or perhaps to suggest one recently done. Both DV 344 and 313a are on the same paper, with the same color ink, as the ms. of *AmCl.*

7. Clemens' secretary, C. W. Stoddard, collected six large scrapbooks of newspaper clippings, now in MTP. The humorist was reminded of the Tichborne case again in 1887 when Orton tried to interest Webster & Co. in publishing his autobiography. Though much interested, Clemens insisted on seeing the ms. first (*MTBus*, pp. 380–381). Either it did not come, or it was not good enough, for there is no record of Webster having published it. When news came in May, 1895 that the "Tichborne Claimant" had confessed to being "Arthur Orton, son of a Wapping Butcher," Clemens recalled his own meeting with Orton in 1873, remembering that Orton had had a remarkable memory and had played his role well, and that the claimant, after serving a fourteen-year prison term, "came over here and was a bartender in the Bowery" (*MTN*, p. 242). See also *FEq*, I, Ch. XV, and the English edition, *More Tramps Abroad*, Ch. XVII. The latter contains additional discussion, which publisher Frank Bliss omitted from the American edition, apparently on his own volition. (See Dennis Welland, "MT's Last Travel Book," *BNYPL*,

LXIX, Jan. 1965, 34, 43). For Webster's comment on "rival show" see *MTBus,*
p. 381.

8. Clemens' correspondence with Leathers is summarized in *MTHL,* II,
869–870.

9. Nbk 15, p. 6 provides approximate date and identifies Olivia as speaker.
Incident recounted in "Mental Telegraphy," first published, *Harper's,* Dec.
1891, though written earlier. Perhaps the possibility that his own family had a
claim upon a place in the British peerage influenced his lifelong fascination
with "claimants" of various sorts and with the closely related characters wandering in "disguise" throughout his works, some of whom, too, were denied
their rightful ranks.

10. *MTN,* p. 357.

11. For the story of Clemens' and Howells' collaboration on the play see
W. J. Meserve, *Complete Plays of WDH* (New York: NYU Press, 1960), pp.
205–208. Written chiefly in 1883, the play was actually produced in September,
1887, at Clemens' own expense. Titled *The American Claimant, or Mulberry
Sellers Ten Years Later,* it played one-night stands in New Brunswick, N.J.,
and Syracuse and Rochester, N.Y., and then on September 23, a matinée at
New York's *Lyceum Theater.*

12. *AmCl,* Ch. V. Samuel Ward McAllister (1827–95) was a self-appointed
social arbiter of New York and Newport society, especially from about 1872
until his death. Though the term "The Four Hundred" had been used earlier
to describe the "cream" of society, McAllister's list of those to be invited to a
dance at the home of Mrs. William Astor in 1892 (capacity of ballroom—400)
popularized the phrase.

13. Quotations from *AmCl,* Chs. I, VII, XX, XXI. The description of his
literary tastes and his occupation as journeyman chairmaker link Tracy's friend
Barrow with Clemens' St. Louis boarding-house friend, J. H. Burrough. If Barrow's interest in Darwinian evolution (suggested in *AmCl,* Ch. XII) also reflects an interest shared by Burrough, it may be that Burrough was at least
partially the model for Clemens' "Macfarlane" (See Ch. Five, *ante,* and Eleven,
post).

14. *MTN,* p. 217. Clemens retained some of his concern for the inequities
he saw in the British legal system, proposing in Sept., 1893, to do a book
entitled "English Justice," and the following Jan. to put Arthur Stedman to
work on such a book (Nbk 27, pp. 37, 46). Somewhat later, inspired by a column
in Henry Labouchere's *Truth,* he drafted an essay, "Labouchere's 'Legal
Pillory' " (DV 72) and, in 1895, returned to his old charge that commoners received far harsher treatment than aristocrats in the courts, since judges were
almost invariably from the upper classes (Nbks 28, p. 25; 28a II, 57–58).

15. Quoted in *A1911,* p. 33. The book was *The Heavenly Twins* (1893) by
Mme. Sarah Grand (pseudonym of Mrs. David C. M. Fall). Other notations
indicated that the comments were written Mar. 9 or 10, 1894, when Clemens
was returning to Europe after a business trip to America.

16. *MTN,* p. 220. In 1895 Clemens himself credited the remark about meeting God to his daughter Jean (*MTN,* p. 242), but it was actually made by Olivia
(SLC to Annie Trumbull, 3/8/92, TS, MTP). Of the dinner with the emperor

he also wrote that "the Imperial lion and the Democratic lamb shall sit down together, and a little General shall feed them" (*MTB*, II, 940). Those who cite that note as evidence of Clemens' antipathy toward monarchy ignore much evidence to the contrary.

17. *MFMT*, p. 206; Nbk 36, p. 7. Clemens' pride in aristocratic associations remained strong. In Aug., 1906, he would say: "Scoffing democrats as we are, we do dearly love to be noticed by a duke, and when we are noticed by a monarch we have softening of the brain for the rest of our lives." He himself was now able, by great effort, to remain calm while a traveling American bragged of the earls he had met: "I can look on, silent and unexcited, and never offer to call his hand, although I have three kings and a pair of emperors up my sleeve" (*MTE*, pp. 46–47).

18. *MTN*, p. 218. For opinions of Edward, see "At the Shrine of St. Wagner," *WIM*, pp. 221–222; SLC to Orion, 8/23/92, *MTL*, II, 566. In 1896 Clemens illustrated his altered opinions of Edward's accomplishments by calling him the "hardest-working" man he knew, whose job was not affected by any of labor's newly won rights. "He does not get the benefit of the eight-hour law and ought to strike" (*MTN*, p. 323).

19. "The Composition of MT's *Puddn'head Wilson and Those Extraordinary Twins:* Chronology and Development," *MP*, LV (Nov., 1957), 93–102.

20. *IE*, p. 188.

21. SLC to OLC [1/27/94], *MTL*, II, 607; date from check-list, *LLMT*, p. 371.

22. The real Louis de Contes (called "de Coutes" in Regine Pernoud, *The Retrial of Joan of Arc,* tr. J. M. Cohen, New York, 1955) became Joan's page at 14 or 15.

23. See *TIH*, pp. 172, 188.

24. In the Comtesse de Chabannes, *La Vierge Lorraine: Jeanne D'Arc* (Paris, 1890), MTP, for instance, when the author tells of Joan's confessing to the Franciscans on a visit as a young girl to Neufchateau, Clemens writes: "Think of this heroic soul in such company—and yet nothing but this base superstition could lift her to that fearless height." Again at the beginning of the chapter describing Joan's trial at Poitiers: "Persecution by these mitred donkeys," and a little later: "There the question wasn't 'Can this soldier win victories?' but 'Is he a sound Catholic?'" (Quoted in *TIH*, pp. 175, 178). Remark about changing religion quoted in *MFMT*, p. 100.

Chapter Nine, WORLD TOUR AND AFTER, 1895–97

1. SLC to OLC, 9/13/93, MTP.

2. Quoted in *Journals of Arnold Bennett,* ed. Newman Flower (London, 1932–33), I, 188.

3. *MTA(P),* I, 258–259.

4. SLC to JHT, 5/24/96, *MTL*, II, 633; *MTN*, p. 293; SLC to WDH, 4/5/99, *MTHL*, II, 690. For the completest accounts of the world tour, see Coleman O. Parsons, "MT in New Zealand," *SAQ*, LXI (Winter, 1962), 51–76;

"MT in Australia," *Antioch Review*, XXI (1961), 455–468; "MT: Sightseer in India," *Mississippi Quarterly*, XVI (Spring, 1963), 76–93; "MT in Ceylon," *Twainian*, Twenty-second Year (Jan.–Feb.; Mar.–Apr., 1963).

5. D. Welland, "MT's Last Travel Book," *BNYPL*, LXIX (Jan., 1965), 36.

6. *LE*, p. 229. See also Paul Baender, "The Date of MT's 'The Lowest Animal,' " *AL*, XXXVI (May, 1964), 174–179.

7. SLC to WDH, 2/23/97, *MTHL*, II, 665. In June, 1896, he had noted that "uncourteousness" was *the* American characteristic (*MTN*, p. 298).

8. Welland, op. cit., p. 38.

9. *FEq*, I, Chs. VI, XXI, XXVII; II, Chs. XXX–XXXII.

10. Clemens drew most of his information on Tasmania from James Bonwick, F.R.G.S., *The Lost Tasmanian Race*. The omitted passage is part of an eighty-six page deletion from a typescript of the *FEq* ms. (in Berg).

11. In 1888, shortly before beginning his summer's stint on *CY*, he had reminded himself to look up a *Nineteenth Century* article about British rule in India, presumably as ammunition for his attacks on England (Nbk 22 II, p. 64). On shipboard off New Zealand, he had mused over the fact that if England had not prevailed, India would have been French, and Australia would have fallen to some nation other than England. But, he said, though "England has made it hard for India's natives—we must believe they would have fared still worse in other hands" (Nbk 28, p. 44). Little more than a month later, during the voyage from Australia, news arrived that Siam had acknowledged her almost complete dependence on France, he noted that all Asian nations would probably be "grabbed" by European powers. But then he said that he wished England might be the "grabber" rather than France, since her "yoke" was lighter than others—the lightest, for instance, in India's 800 years of foreign domination (Nbk 28b, p. 16).

12. Clippings, 1895–96, MTP.

13. *FEq*, Vol. II, Chs. IV, XI, XXII. Most of the material on the Thugs, Clemens derived from Major W. N. Sleeman's report to the British Indian Service (Calcutta, 1840), and on the Great Mutiny, from G. O. Trevelyan's *Cawnpore* (1865).

14. DV 345, MTP; date of *Mysterious Stranger*, Ch. X: *MTSatan*, p. 50.

15. "Love Letters of MT," *Atlantic* CLXXX (Nov., 1947), 38; *IA*, I, 349 (Ch. XXVI); II, 245 (Ch. XX); *CY*, p. 314 (Ch. XXXIV). See also Chester L. Davis, "MT's Marginal Notes on Macaulay," *Twainian*, X (July-Aug., 1951), 1–2.

16. "The Derelict" was first published in full in Arthur L. Scott's *On the Poetry of MT* (Urbana, Ill., 1966), pp. 105–107. For comment on Hastings see *FEq*, II, Ch. XVI. Clemens also quoted from Macaulay's essay on Hastings in II, Ch. VII, and in his notebook reminded himself to "see Macaulay's Clive" for information on famine in India. (Nbk 28, p. 44). In 1901 Clemens was to be much less complimentary to Hastings, associating him and his organization in India with Richard Croker and Tammany Hall in New York, and then adapting Edmund Burke's denunciation of Hastings to his own attack on Croker and Tammany [*MTS(H)*, pp. 114–117].

17. *MT As Critic* (Baltimore, 1967), pp. 227–245. Though Macaulay, too,

may have influenced Clemens' concern with "realization" of the historical past as Krause suggests, the passage from Lecky which I have discussed in Chs. Five and Seven, *ante,* seems the more likely source. Macaulay, of course, exerted a great influence on Lecky.

18. All details and quotations concerning Kipling's Elmira visit are from Kipling, *From Sea to Sea* (first published, 1899), Ch. XXXVII, and from *MTE,* pp. 309–312. Kipling's interview itself was first published in two Allahabad, India, papers: *The Pioneer,* 3/18/90, and *The Pioneer Mail,* 3/19/90, and reprinted in the New York *Herald,* 8/17/90. The last paragraph of the *Herald* article, which comments unfavorably on *CY,* is omitted in *From Sea to Sea.*

19. Kipling to SLC, dated "Summer 1890" (perhaps by Paine), TS, MTP. Dinners: Apr. 5, 7, 1893; Tea: 1/16/94, Nbk 27, p. 5; SLC to OLC, 1/12/94, *MTL,* II, 601.

20. Nbk 25, p. 23; *C1951;* quotations in paragraph, *MTE,* p. 312.

21. Quotations from Adelaide *South Australia Register* and *Advertiser,* 10/14/95. Other comments appear in Minneapolis *Penny Press,* 7/23/95, and *Times,* 7/24/95; Sydney *Morning Herald* and *Daily Telegraph,* 9/17/95; and Bombay *Times of India,* 1/24/96 (Clippings, MTP).

22. *Portable MT,* ed. DeVoto (New York, 1946), p. 774; Carlyle Smythe, "The Real MT," *Pall Mall,* XVI (1898), 31; T. S. Eliot, ed., *A Choice of Kipling's Verse* (New York, 1943), p. 11.

23. SLC to Doubleday, 10/12/03, *MTL,* II, 746.

24. See especially Elizabeth Wallace's account of readings in Bermuda in 1908, *MTHI,* pp. 93–100, which cites specific poems mentioned in these paragraphs; "Mandalay" as "most fascinating," *MTL,* II, 610. Clemens also liked Kipling's word-play in "Soldier an Sailor Too," and at one point jotted down some of the coinages applied to the marines—"herumphrodite," "cosmopolouse," "procrastitute," noting with amusement that William E. Benjamin (H. H. Rogers' son-in-law) had accused him of playing "herumphrodite billiards," a mixture of the British and American games; and also had called Clemens' secretary, Isabel Lyon, a "procrastitute," i.e., a "woman who promises then fools along and doesn't perform" (Nbk 38, p. 18). In "Was the World Made for Man?" the author, describing the amazing pterodactyl as "a kind of long-distance premonitory symptom of Kipling's marine," quotes the poem: " 'E isn't one o' the reg'lar line, nor 'e isn't one of the crew, / 'E's a kind of a giddy harumfrodite—soldier an' sailor too!" (*LE,* pp. 214–215).

25. Paine 217, MTP, dated "about 1902"; "Affeland," Paine 100; a fragment of this piece is published by F. R. Rogers, ed., *MTS&B,* pp. 170–171, who assigns it "probably" to 1892. Clemens' interest in Rhodes was more intense in 1896–97.

26. Clemens may not have known "The Last of the Stories" by 1898, however, for it was not collected in a volume until *Abaft the Funnel* (1909), a copy of which he did own (*C1951*). Another story, "My Platonic Sweetheart," written in July or early August, 1898, may owe something to Kipling's dream-fantasy, "The Brushwood Boy." The latter story of George Cotter's wanderings with his dream-companion (which first appeared in the *Century* for December, 1897) would surely have appealed to Clemens' fascination with dreams. Even if the similarities in Clemens' "little short story" (as he described

it to Howells, 8/16/98, *MTHL*, II, 676, 678n.) are purely coincidental and its details based solely on the author's own dreams, "The Brushwood Boy" may well have inspired him to put the tale on paper. Isabel Lyon's journal records that on 6/11/06, the humorist read aloud "A Fable," written that afternoon (TS, p. 164, MTP). "Refuge of the Derelicts" (DV 309a, TS, p. 26; Lyon, TS, p. 44, MTP).

27. Clemens wrote "bandar-log" next to the second line of the paragraph in St. Simon, beginning "One of the misfortunes. . . ." (*Memoires*, II, Ch. XXXII); *MTHI*, p. 16.

28. Copy dated 8/16/95, *MTN*, p. 248.

29. Quotations from *FEq*, II, Chs. XVIII, X, XXVI. "For to Admire" later helped Clemens add a touch of eloquent pathos to his speech thanking those honoring his seventieth birthday with a banquet at Delmonico's restaurant in December, 1905. Concluding his humorous recital of the advantages of reaching the "scriptural statute of limitations," he turned more serious: "After that you owe no active duties . . . ; you are a time-expired man, to use Kipling's military phrase. You have served your term, well or less well, and you are mustered out. . . . You are emancipated, compulsions are not for you, nor any bugle call but 'lights out.'" [*MTS(P)*, pp. 260–262].

30. J. R. Clemens, "Meeting Newman and Kipling," *MTQ*, III (Winter, 1938), 12. Clemens also thought of one of Kipling's novels while compiling notes for a eulogy of Susy early in 1897: "This is the history of a promise—a Light that Failed—[to borrow]" (Nbk 31 II, p. 58).

31. C. F. Carrington, *Life of Rudyard Kipling* (New York, 1956), pp. 213–214.

32. Edward Shanks, *Rudyard Kipling: A Study in Literature and Political Ideas* (New York, 1940), p. 114.

33. See, for example, "The Masque of Plenty" (first published, Allahabad *Pioneer*; first collected in *Departmental Ditties, Etc.*, 4th ed., 1890), which deals with deplorable economic conditions in India, and "The Captive" (*Illustrated London News*, 1903; *Traffics and Discoveries*, 1904), which satirizes British conduct of the Boer War.

34. SLC to WDH, 1/25–26/1900, *MTHL*, II, 716; SLC to JHT, 1/27/1900, *MTL*, II, 695.

35. Quoted by D. M. McKeithan, "A Letter from MT to Francis Henry Skrine in London," *MLN*, LXIII (Feb., 1948), 134–135. Clemens' draft of the poem in MTP (DV 152, I) adds another variant of a line from Kipling's poem as a last line of the stanza: "Pay, pay goddam you, pay."

36. SLC to WDH, 10/19/99, *MTHL*, II, 709.

37. *Kipling*, p. 372.

38. Howard C. Rice, *Kipling in New England*, rev. ed. (Brattleboro, Vt., 1951), p. 9.

39. "News and Notes," *Kipling Journal*, XXVI (Dec., 1935), 107.

Chapter Ten, RECONCILIATION AND REMINISCENCE (1897–1900)

1. Nbk 31 I, p. 21.

2. *MFMT*, p. 113; *LWMT*, p. 158. Wilde's "On the Decay of Lying" (*Nineteenth Century*, Jan., 1889) did *not* influence MT's "On the Decay of the Art of Lying," first published in *The Stolen White Elephant, Etc.*, 1882.

3. *A Victorian Diarist: Later Extracts*, ed. E.C.F. Collier (London, 1946), p. 23.

4. *MTB*, II, 1041 and note. See "Statistics," *MTS(H)*, pp. 276–278, for the impromptu speech which he probably gave on this occasion, erroneously dated 1899 (instead of 1897), and Sir Ian MacAlister, "MT: Some Reminiscences," *Landmark*, XX (Mar., 1938), 141–147.

5. "Queen Victoria's Jubilee," *E&E*, pp. 193–210; *MTN*, p. 248; *MTS(H)*, pp. 238–239.

6. *MTN*, pp. 337, 367.

7. Evening at Lecky's mentioned in SLC to JHT, 3/4/1900, *MTL*, II, 697. Clemens also saved the newspaper report of the annual meeting of the Savage Club, which mentions that Lecky was among the evening's speakers (Clippings, 1899, MTP).

8. Kingsley to SLC, 11/26/73; OLC to Mollie Clemens, 7/29/77, MTP. In 1881 Clemens was strongly reminded of Kingsley when he noticed a "laboring man" whose face was "beautiful because of its sweetness." (SLC to OLC, 8/25/81, *LLMT*, p. 205). When the Kingsleys were in America in 1874, Clemens invited them to spend a few days in Hartford, regretting that a dinner in Boston (honoring another English novelist, Wilkie Collins) prevented his being with Kingsley in New York "to-morrow night" (2/13/74, TS, MTP). On the evening of the seventeenth, he introduced Kingsley to a Boston lecture audience, and a few weeks later (3/14/74), the clergyman and his wife paid their "long-promised visit" to the Clemenses ("MT's Introduction of Charles Kingsley," *Twainian*, Thirteenth Yr., Mar.-Apr., 1954, 2; *Charles Kingsley: His Letters, Etc.*, p. 459). On *Hypatia*: SLC to OLC, 11/28/69, *LLMT*, p. 126. For other MT anecdotes involving Kingsley (not cited in text), see *A1911*, p. 20, and C. O. Parsons, "MT in New Zealand," *SAQ*, LXI (Winter, 1962), 51.

9. *MTF*, 8/6/77, p. 209. For significance of burlesque *Weekly Occidental* novel in *RI*, see Postscript III, Nineteenth Century Fiction, *post*, and *MTBur*, pp. 77–78. Letters from Reade to Clemens, 2/3/76 and 8/6/76, MTP. See also, *Simon Wheeler, Detective*, ed. F. R. Rogers, New York, 1963, pp. xii, xvi. Reade further suggested that Clemens put the "detecting plot" into a story rather than a play, which he later did, although not until Howells, too, urged the change.

10. Quoted in *MT&HF*, p. 129. Phillip H. Highfill notes an analogue to this incident in *Literary Anecdotes . . . of Professor Parson and Others; from the Manuscript Papers of the Late E. H. Barker* (London, 1852), p. 82, in which a farmer unmasks by the same method used by Judith Loftus two thieves disguised as women. (*MTJ*, X, Fall, 1961, 6). Clemens' acknowledged admiration, however, makes Reade's novel the more likely source.

11. *MTE*, p. 333. In that same autobiographical dictation Clemens says that the dinner was in Miller's honor, but both Miller and Trollope indicate that it was given for both writers [Hartford *Courant*, 1/9/83, p. 1, col. 6; Michael Sadlier, *Anthony Trollope: A Commentary* (Boston and N. Y., 1917), p. 285.]

12. Cited by Bradford Booth, *Anthony Trollope: Aspects of His Life and Art* (Bloomington, Ind., 1958), p. 99. Reference to Trollope novels in following paragraph is from Nbk 32b, p. 23.

13. *MTA*, II, 43, 236–237.

14. RLS to SLC [4/16/93], *Twainian*, IX (Sept.-Oct., 1950), 1; *MTA(P)*, I, 247–248. The *Twainian* dates this letter which reminisces about the New York visit, "sometime between 1888 and 1893." The actual date was doubtless 4/16/93, for on that date Stevenson wrote his friend and lawyer, Charles Baxter of Edinburgh, that he was writing to Clemens by the same post [*LS: Stevenson's Letters to Charles Baxter*, ed. DeLancey Ferguson and Marshall Waingrow (New Haven, 1956), p. 329].

15. John A Steuart, *Robert Louis Stevenson: A Critical Biography* (Boston, 1924), II, 135; *MTA(P)*, I, 248.

16. *Twainian,* loc. cit.; RLS to SLC, 8/12/93, MTP.

17. *MTML*, p. 229; J. A. Hammerton, ed. *Stevensoniana* (London, 1903), pp. 293–294; *Twainian*, loc. cit. For other Stevenson compliments to Clemens and his books, see Hammerton, p. 88; Steuart, II, 135, and *MTB*, II, 794, 859–860.

18. *Travels with a Donkey:* Nbk 30 II, p. 54. The 1898 Chatto and Windus edition of *A Lowden Sabbath Morn* in MTP is inscribed "To Livy on her next birthday, S. L. Clemens, Kaltenleutgeben, Aug. '98." *Prince Otto: MTN*, pp. 266–267.

19. Paine dated first entry erroneously as 1897 (*MTN*, p. 348; see Nbk 32 I, p. 1). He printed the 1904 entry (*MTN*, p. 292) without the final question, and with Clemens' original phrase, "sacred romance." The word "fiction" is a later addition by the author (Nbk 37, p. 18).

20. *FEq*, I, 89–90 (Ch. VII): *MTN*, pp. 227–228: *MTE*, p. 331; Barrie, *Who Was Sarah Findlay? by Mark Twain, etc.* (London: privately printed, 1917), p. 7.

21. *MTN*, p. 372, *MTS(II)*, p. 217. In *MTS(P)*, pp. 375–377, the reference to Kipling in the Authors Club speech is included, obviously by mistake, in "Booksellers," delivered 5/20/08.

22. Clippings, 1895–96, MTP. One suspects that Clemens was hardly pleased when in the following May, 1897, the U.S. Senate failed to approve the Olney-Pauncefote Treaty that he had hailed so jubilantly the preceding January.

23. Quoted in *MTB*, II, 1063–64.

24. *MTE*, pp. 330–331.

25. DV 101, MTP. This version of the speech, the longest of several extant, was first published as "Now We are Kin in Sin," *American Heritage*, XII (Aug., 1961), 112.

26. Churchill, *My Early Life* (London, 1930), quoted in *MTSC*, p. 265. Clemens and Churchill met at least once more, for on 1/22/01, the author signed all twenty-five volumes of Churchill's set of his works, inscribing the first, "To be good is noble; to teach others to be good is nobler, & no trouble" (R. S. Churchill, *Winston S. Churchill*, 2 vols., Boston, 1966, I, 525).

27. Nbk 36, entry in front dated "Jan. 22" [1903].

Chapter Eleven, Literary Efforts—The Later Years

1. *MTA(P)*, I, 143–147, article dated "about 1898." Paul Baender has shown that it was written in 1895 ("Alias Macfarlane: A Revision of MT Biography," *AL*, XXXVIII, May, 1966, 187–197).

2. Clemens included "The Character of Man" as part of his autobiographical dictation of 1/23/06 [published first in *MTA(P)*, II, 7–13]. The fact that Susy's death interrupted work on "The Lowest Animal" rather than inspired it (as Paine believed) further indicates that the author was merely expressing ideas he had been considering for a long time.

3. SLC to WDH, 4/2/99, *MTHL*, II, 689; *MTN*, pp. 360–363. The 1906 autobiographical dictations of June 19, 20, 22, 23 and 26 were first published as "Reflections on Religion," ed. Charles Neider, *Hudson Review*, XVI (Autumn, 1963), 329–352, and "Letters from the Earth" as the title-piece of *LE* (1962), which also contains "The Lowest Animal" and similar sketches from the late 1890's and early 1900's.

4. Besides those works cited in Ch. Five, Clemens found important supplementary materials in Thomas Henry Huxley's *Evolution and Ethics* (first published in book form in 1894), Sir John Lubbock's studies of ants and bees, William James' *Principles of Psychology* (1890), and the reports of the English Society for Psychical Research collected in *Phantasms of the Living* in 1886 (see Sherwood Cummings, "*What is Man?:* The Scientific Sources," *Essays in Determinism in American Literature*, Kent, Ohio, 1965, pp. 108–116). He apparently also knew the work of French psychologists like Jean M. Charcot; and marginal notes in his copy of James Mark Baldwin's *Story of the Mind* (1899) contain an echo of one of the passages in *WIM* (See *MTSatan*, pp. 26, 27; *IE*, pp. 239–241. *MTHL*, II, 659).

5. Nbk 26, pp. 37–38. Slight variations in wording and capitalization suggest that Clemens was quoting from memory.

6. Nbk 32a II, p. 44. Millet's gift copy in MTP.

7. Nbk 32 II, pp. 46a, 47. Ms. of "bawdy quatrains" (Yale). Any account of Clemens' outlook during these late years must take into account the author's keen sense of his own advancing age. (See especially his letters to Howells, 1/22/98; 12/30/98, *MTHL*, II, 670, 685, 686n.) One of his favorite stanzas was No. 48 which begins "A Moment's Halt . . ." and ends, "And Lo!—the phantom Caravan has reached / The Nothing it set out from—Oh make haste!" Besides an echo in "AGE–A Rubaiyat," an interesting early reference occurs in a letter to Clara Spaulding (copy in MTP), on the occasion of her marriage to John B. Stanchfield in 1886. Admonishing her not to hold onto "words spoken in debate" he comments that "There isn't *time*—so brief is life—for bickerings, apologies, heart-burnings. . . . There is only time for loving—and but an instant . . . for that" and then quotes Stanza 48, "(which is the admonition of the divine Omar—adopt the rule!)"

8. *Hadleyburg*, pp. 246–254. Of the 20 stanzas, 17 contain specific echoes of the *Rubaiyat*. On 4/10/99, before leaving Vienna for England and Sweden, Clemens had asked Chatto and Windus to send him a copy of FitzGerald's poem (Berg).

9. He apparently did some planning as early as 1897 for the story that became "3000 Years Among the Microbes" written in 1905 (unfinished). That story in turn contains an echo of Omar, for the microbe-narrator quotes Horace to a friend—"Well, Franklin, . . . Carpe diem—quam minimum credula postero," and translates: "Be thou wise: take a drink whilst the chance offers; none but the gods know when the jug will come around again" (*MTWWD*, p. 455).

10. Quotations (in order) from *Hudson Review*, XVI (Autumn, 1963), 351, 346–347, 352.

11. *MTA(P)*, I, 146.

12. For an account of the complicated stages of composition, see Paul Baender's forthcoming volume of *Religious and Philosophical Writings* in the Iowa-California edition of MT's works. The portion written in 1898 contained somewhat more than half as much material as was ultimately published, including two short chapters, "The Moral Sense," and "The Quality of Man," both later deleted. Shortly thereafter, Clemens wrote what Baender calls the "God" section (also later deleted), and the remainder at intervals during the next eight years, transposing, adding examples and sections, and continuing to revise even in printer's copy and galley proof.

13. I am pleased to note that Sherwood Cummings' "*WIM:* The Scientific Sources," (see note 8), which I read after this chapter had already been written, agrees that *EurMor* was an important influence. To Cummings, of course, goes the credit for the first published identification of this source for *WIM*. This conjecture of debt to Lecky is further strengthened by the fact that *EurMor* was certainly on Clemens' mind during the period when he was writing both *WIM* and *MysStr*, and thereafter. Besides reflections in "Hadleyburg" and *MysStr* (to be discussed later), he obviously drew on Lecky's discussion of Stoic attitudes toward death as "the end of all sorrow . . . the last and best boon of nature" (I, 215) for "The Five Boons of Life" (*Harper's* Dec., 1902). In one of the humorist's last efforts—the unfinished "International Lightning Trust," probably written in 1909—his character Jasper Hackett, after quoting Lecky's description (I, 390) of how even the great Roman emperors cowered in fright during thunderstorms, explains that this passage had given him the idea of establishing the "Lightning Trust" (DV 374a, TS, p. 10, MTP).

14. SLC to Sir John Adams, 5/12/98, quoted by Adams, "MT, Psychologist," *Dalhousie Review*, XIII (Jan., 1934), 418.

15. *WIM*, p. 5.

16. *EurMor*, I, 27–28. Other quotations from and summaries of Lecky's points in the following discussion are (in order) from pp. 30, 68, 36, 70–72, 35, 32, 45n., 85, 89–93, 55, 125–126; 38, 35.

17. *WIM*, pp. 45, 43. Clemens says the same thing in almost the same words in a notebook entry, 1/17/97 (*MTN*, pp. 348–349). Other quotations from and summaries of Clemens' points in the following discussion are from *WIM*, pp. 11–12, 21 and passim, 45–47, 54, 55, 59, 24–29, 105–109.

18. Still another of Lecky's objections is removed by the Old Man's continued insistence that *all* motivation derives from this "desire to content one's spirit." Lecky contends that the utilitarian philosophy fails to account for the

fact that though men generally agree that some pleasures are of a "higher" nature, than others (e.g. mental pleasures as opposed to physical) they almost invariably seek the "lower" ones; if utilitarian theory were valid, one should prefer the "higher pleasures." But since by the Old Man's definition, *all* pleasures become mental, or "spiritual," the distinction between "higher" and "lower" disappears.

19. At one point Lecky says, "Pure disinterestedness is presupposed in all our estimates of virtue. . . . This is the highest prerogative of our being, the point of contact between human nature and the divine" (I, 72; see also p. 35). It is difficult, also, not to see a reaction to Lecky's contention (e.g. I, 97) that military action often involves self-sacrifice of the highest order, for the Old Man frequently uses examples from military action to illustrate his argument that bravery and self-sacrifice are merely products of training and *do not* arise from an innate sense of duty or selflessness.

20. See *EurMor*, I, 53–54 for somewhat similar examples of loss of faith.

21. Here, almost as if directly stimulated by Lecky's admission that "the selfish instinct that leads men to accumulate confers ultimately more advantage upon the world than the generous instinct that leads man to give" (I, 38), the Old Man says, "Without [self-approval] . . . no one would do anything, there would be no progress, the world would stand still" (*WIM*, p. 29).

22. *EurMor*, I, 35; *WIM*, p. 105. Shortly thereafter, in asking if it might not be better to suppress the facts of the Old Man's philosophy, the Young Man seems to be echoing Lecky's remark (I, 54) that one cannot reasonably deny that man's happiness may often be increased by "diffusing abroad, or at least sustaining pleasing falsehoods," nor can he deny that suffering must commonly result when those falsehoods are dispelled.

23. This brighter outlook possibly gained emphasis in the portions written in late 1901 or early 1902 (including the "Admonition"), and perhaps also with the revisions of late 1905 or early 1906, when the author put the first two chapters in their present position (they had been reversed) and extensively revised Ch. II, replacing "selfishness" and similar terms with less "negative" phrases like "self-approval," "spiritual comfort," and "self-contentment." My thanks to Paul Baender for these facts of composition (letter to me, 11/8/62).

24. Cited in *MTSP*, p. 199.

25. Clemens wrote the first draft of *WIM* between April and July, 1898; the last page of the "Hadleyburg" ms. (Morgan Library) is dated "Vienna, October, 1898"; SLC to J. M. Touhy, 11/2/98 (copy, MTP) says that the story on which he had worked "for several months" is now finished.

26. *EurMor*, I, 114–115, 117. Clemens drew a heavy line next to Lecky's quotation from Cardinal Newman's *Anglican Difficulties*, citing the Church's contention that one should endure any sort of calamity rather than commit "one single venial sin . . ." (p. 115n.). In 1901 the humorist specifically dramatized in the short story, "Was it Heaven or Hell?" (*Harper's*, Dec. 1902), the moral quandary that such a principle could create. Some scholars have traced the inspiration for "Hadleyburg" to Clemens' unpleasant personal experiences with actual towns. Fairly convincing is the case made by Leslie F. Chard for

Fredonia, New York, MT's 'Hadleyburg' and Fredonia, N.Y., *AQ*, XVI, Winter, 1964, 595–601). See also Russel B. Nye, "MT in Oberlin," and Guy F. Cardwell, "MT's Hadleyburg," *Ohio State Archaeological and Historical Quarterly*, XLVII (1938), 69–73 and LX (1951), 257–264. As John S. Tuckey has shown, however, various details also parallel the humorist's observations of the disgraceful proceedings in the Austrian Reichsrath during the fall of 1897, suggesting that Hadleyburg might be seen as "a microcosm of the Austrian empire, and by extension of the entire world" (*MTSatan*, p. 37). Obviously Clemens was drawing heavily upon his own experiences and memories (as he did in all of his writings), but whatever the exact initial impulse, his subject again was the character of man.

27. Sydney *Morning Herald*, 9/17/95

28. Sometime close to the time Clemens saw the *Mikado* in New York in 1886 (see notes to Ch. Six, *ante*), he wrote in his notebook "Mikado music" and then, "Photo of 3 little maids f'm school" (Nbk 21, p. 6).

29. See *MTSatan*, passim, and William M. Gibson's volume in the Mark Twain Papers series (to be published in 1969), which will contain all three.

30. *Eighteenth Century*, II, 331–333. In adapting his source, Clemens further emphasized the overwhelming pressures to conform by having the woman's daughters (unlike the two in Lecky who begged the mob to let them speak with their mother before she died) merely stand "looking on and weeping, but afraid to do anything." He also toned down some of the more gruesome details of the stoning and beating, perhaps in order to concentrate more fully on the reactions of Theodore and the others. Besides the items mentioned in the text, Theodore's comment that the Eseldorfers had taken to witch-hunting on their own initiative because of impatience with the relative inactivity of the witch-commission seems to reflect the fact that Jane Corphar had been released by the magistrate for insufficient evidence, whereupon the minister, on his own authority, arrested her and later turned her over to the people to do whatever they pleased with her. Obviously intrigued with the Corphar case, Clemens again referred to it, indirectly, in "Bible Teaching and Religious Practice" (1st published *E&E*, 1923), noting that in Scotland "the parson" not only "killed the witch after the magistrate had pronounced her innocent," but when the legislature proposed to repeal the laws against witches, "came imploring" that they be allowed to stand (p. 392). Lecky mentions that in 1736 the Associated Presbytery of Scotland denounced the repeal of such laws. Other sources: Theodore's reference to questions written down for the use of the witch-commission, points to Jacob Sprenger's *Malleus Maleficarum* (the "Witches' Hammer," first published about 1486, and reprinted in many editions), which remained a sort of official "witch-trial" handbook (See *MT&EF*, pp. 179, 181, for evidence that Clemens knew the book). For the case of Gottfried Narr's grandmother in the same chapter, several details came from Sir Walter Scott's *Letters on Demonology and Witchcraft* (1830). But even so, Lecky was probably at least indirectly responsible, for a footnote on the page immediately preceding the Corphar incident cites Scott's volume as an excellent source of information about Scottish practices in those areas. (Coleman

O. Parsons, "The Background of *The Mysterious Stranger*," *AL*, XXXII, Mar., 1960, 67–68, mentions Sprenger's volume and describes the exact passages borrowed from Scott).

31. For comments on Mrs. Eddy, see *MTSatan*, pp. 64, 68. Parsons (op. cit.) also examines the possible influences of Voltaire's *Zadig* and *Micromegas*, the *Apochryphal New Testament*, *Paradise Lost*, *Gulliver's Travels*, Prospero's speech (*Tempest*, IV, i), and Jane Taylor's "The Mysterious Stranger" (a moral tale, reprinted in McGuffey's *Rhetorical Guide and Fifth Reader* and *Eclectic Sixth Reader*). Parsons sees "corroborative influences" in Carlyle, the writings and speeches of Robert Ingersoll, Goethe's *Faust*, Wilbrandt's *Master of Palmyra*, Lecky's *European Morals*, and possibly Michelet's *La Sorcière* and Louis François Clairville's comédie-vaudeville, *Satan ou Le Diable à Paris* (tr. by Charles Selby, and sub-titled "The Mysterious Stranger" when published in Boston, 1855); and he conjectures that certain episodes derived from G. Macdonald's *At the Back of the North Wind* (1871), Verne's *Cinq Semaines en Ballon* (1862, tr. N.Y., 1869), and L. M. Alcott's *Little Men*. Martin Klotz, "Goethe and MT," *N&Q*, n.s., VII (1960), 150–151, adds *Werther* to the list of possible sources.

32. WDH to SLC, 3/13/76, *MTHL*, I, 127; Jervis Langdon, *Some Reminiscences, Etc.*, pamphlet, n.d., p. 22.

33. Another ironic discussion of "enchantments" in *CY* (Ch. XX) also seems related to the *Tempest* passage, and at the same time enhances the novel's satire of royalty. When Sandy says that the "princesses" appear to be hogs only to the Yankee, Hank explains that it is fortunate, for if she, too, saw them as hogs, the enchantment would have to be broken—a hazardous undertaking, since "without the true key, you are liable to err, and turn your hogs into dogs, and dogs into cats . . . and so on, and end by reducing your materials to nothing, finally, or to an odorless gas which you can't follow. . . ."

34. *Is Shakespeare Dead?* (New York and London, 1909). In that same essay, Clemens quoted some nine lines of "sailor-talk" from the first scene of *The Tempest* to show the futility of surmises based on anything which could not be documented. Noting that at the present time the language would confuse even a mariner, he argued that any discussion of Shakespeare's nautical knowledge was pointless since there remained no documented body of nautical language with which to compare the dramatist's usage. This discussion follows one in which he had agreed with critics like Sir George Greenwood (*The Shakespeare Problem Restated*, 1908) that the actor from Stratford could hardly have had the legal knowledge represented by the language of the plays (a knowledge which *could* be verified by comparison with the large body of legal terminology that had been documented through the ages). Still other echoes of *The Tempest* crept into such diverse writings as an 1880 letter to the joys of piloting, and a discussion of cigars in the story "Sold to Satan" (1904). Both echo Ariel's first-act song, "Full fathom five thy father lies," the first to enhance a mood of nostalgic melancholy, and the second to inject a piece of heavy-handed nonsense. In "Sold to Satan," after noting that the statesman Cavour had invented a new brand of cigar by inadvertently laying his in a pool of ink, the narrator comments that ever since then, "the brand passes through the ink-

factory, with the great result that both the ink and the cigar suffer a sea change into something new and strange" (*E&E*, p. 330). The 1880 letter, however, captures some of the music and magic of Ariel's song. To twelve-year-old Watt Bowser, who had asked if Clemens ever wished to be a boy again, the humorist wrote that he would like to, but only if he could become a cub-pilot and remain one permanently, on a boat whose crew "would never change." Recalling one group of shipmates, he reflected sadly on the impossibility of his terms, for, he said, "two decades have done their work on them and half are dead, and the rest scattered, and the boat's bones are rotting five fathom deep in Madrid Bend" (Quoted in *MT&HF*, p. 257).

35. SLC to Munro [early Feb., 1905], Berg. On verso of ms. p. 5, "The Czar's Soliloquy" (MTP), Clemens has written: "Somewhere in the foregoing suggest Teufelsdroeckh, Sartor Resartus, Carlyle—anything will answer, to indicate that one is aware that these ancient ideas are not fresh," and reminds himself to make the change in galley proof. At the end of the ms., a penciled notation reads, "Feb. 5." Clemens owned a volume containing *Sartor, Past and Present,* and *On Heroes and Hero-Worship,* inscribed "S. L. Clemens, 1888" (*A1911,* p. 14).

36. *MT&EF*, p. 160.

37. Other possible echoes of Carlyle occur in the notebooks of August or September, 1897, just before he began the "Eseldorf" ms. Playing with the idea that would dominate "The Czar's Soliloquy" seven years later, he wrote: "What is Civilization? . . . What is back of all political powers (thrones, popedoms, etc.)? Clothes" (Nbk 32b I, p 98), and immediately thereafter the comment (quoted in Ch. Nine, *ante*), that only in nakedness lay "real democracy" (*MTN,* p. 337). A few pages later he commented even more explicitly that a prince's "artificialities" make and keep him what he is. "Without them he is as other men" (32b I, p. 36). He was at least reminded of Carlyle again in 1901, when he turned the play based on the "death-wafer" incident (which he had found in Carlyle's *Cromwell*) into a short story (See *MTHL,* II, 455–459, and notes to Ch. Five, *ante*).

38. See also III, ix, for another quotation of these lines.

39. Satan's revelations do not exactly parallel Omar's picture (in the next two stanzas) of an external Master of the Show directing a "moving row of Magic Shadow-shapes" or manipulating "helpless pieces" on a cosmic checkerboard. Yet Theodore, as creator of the dream, symbolically plays just such a role, and the skeleton-procession of the 1908 "Print-Shop" fragment presents a kind of "Magic Shadow-shapes."

40. DV 327c, MTP, cited in *MTSatan,* p. 64. Interestingly, Carlyle, too, had described Teufelsdröckh as one whose "humour" it was to see "all Matter and Material things as Spirit" (I, iii).

41. SLC to Muriel Pears, 5/9/05, Yale, quoted in *MTSatan,* p. 62.

42. On August 22, 1897, four days after the first anniversary of Susy's death he had referred to the calamity as "not a reality, but a dream which will pass—*must* pass" (to Wayne MacVeagh, TS, MTP); the letter to JHT was almost exactly seven years later. Again shortly after his seventieth birthday celebration in 1905, Clemens borrowed almost the identical language of letter and

novel to describe the emotions of one who reviews his life from the mountain-top of old age (See *MTB*, III, 1256).

43. All along, Carlyle stresses the Professor's gaining of freedom as he increasingly penetrates the "Shows of things." Deep in the "Everlasting No!" (II, vii) he sees the universe much as Satan describes it to Theodore: "void of Life, of Purpose, of Volition, . . . one huge, dead, immeasurable Steam-engine, rolling on, in its dead indifference. . . ." The Professor himself feels banished to a "vast, gloomy, solitary Golgotha . . . companionless. . . ." His only explanation for such a universe is that the Devil must be the ruler. But at the end of the chapter, the emergence from despair begins; Teufelsdröckh's "whole Me" denies the Devil's claim that "thou art fatherless, outcast, and the Universe is mine." "I am not thine," he says, "but Free. . . ." It is tempting also to see in Carlyle's association of poetic creativity and the Phoenix image (mentioned several times in *Sartor*) the source of Clemens' inspiration for "44's" spectacular "destruction" by fire and his subsequent rebirth (in the "Print Shop" version, DV 328, p. 261, MTP).

44. Except for Ceres' comment on Cupid, references in this paragraph are from SLC to Clara, 8/3/05, 7/27/07, MTP; *MTE*, 198–199; *NAmRev* (Aug. 2, 1907), p. 689; all quoted or paraphrased in *MTSatan*, pp. 69–71.

Chapter Twelve, THE FINAL HONOR

1. Ambassador Reid sent the message at the request of Lord Curzon, who had written on May 2 that he wished to name Reid a Doctor of Civil Law. Because time for planning was short, and candidates must be present in person, Curzon hoped Reid might also be willing to cable Clemens ("whose influence upon public life seems to me to have been uniformly healthy and pure and who is one of the conspicuous literary figures of our time") and Thomas Edison ("who enjoys a world-wide scientific reputation") concerning his intention to honor them that June. Edison was apparently too busy with his inventions to make the voyage (Royal Cortissoz, *Life of Whitelaw Reid*, New York, 1921, II, 380–381; SLC to Reid, 5/3/07, TS, MTP). Clemens was thrilled, too, by Curzon's follow-up letter, which declared that acceptance of the degree "by one who has always set before himself the highest of literary work, and for nearly half a century has made an incomparable addition to the pleasure of the English-speaking race" would, in reality, honor the University (quoted in SLC to Jean, 5/26/07, TS, MTP). Unfortunately, records at Oxford contain no additional information regarding Curzon's choice of Clemens, save for the minutes of the Hebdomadal Council which approved the list of nominees, and the Chancellor's note of thanks for that approval (Letters to me from Douglas Veale, Registrar, Oxford, 10/25/52, 11/21/52).

2. *AMT(N)*, p. 349; see also his comments which imply that he merited the award. An entry in one of Isabel Lyon's secretarial notebooks (dated at the back "July 24/07 & 08," MTP) reveals why Clemens wrote to Moberly Bell, editor of the London *Times*, that "Your hand is in it! and you have my best thanks" (*MTL*, II, 806). Miss Lyon notes that Clemens told her "with satisfac-

tion" of a luncheon with Bell, "probably in 1906." Bell had asked when the humorist was coming to England again; Clemens had replied, "When Oxford bestows its degree upon me," whereupon Bell "said he 'would arrange that' and he did." For Miss Lyon, the Oxford robe was "cheapened . . . because it was asked for." This fact did not, apparently, reduce the thrill for Clemens.

3. Quoted by Cortissoz, II, 380. For additional facts about the Embassy party, see Sidney Brooks, "England's Ovation to MT," *Harper's Weekly,* LI (July 27, 1907), 1086; *MTB,* III, 1384.

4. "MT and the Pilgrims," London *Times,* 6/23/07, p. 3, col. 2; *MTS(P)*, pp. 373–374, except for exit-line which was quoted in Providence (R. I.) *Journal,* 6/26/07, p. 14, col. 4. The *Journal* also noted that the committee in charge of the luncheon had to refuse "nearly 1000 persons of prominence who were anxious to attend." My thanks to my father-in-law, John K. Cheesman, of Providence, for providing the *Journal* excerpt.

5. As listed in the official program, *Convocation/Encaenia, June 26 1907/ The Right Hon./Lord Curzon of Kedleston/Chancellor/Presiding* (slashes indicate title arrangement).

6. SLC, "Chapters from My Autobiography," *NAmRev,* CLXXXVI (July 26, 1907), 169–173; Carrington, *Kipling,* p. 307; SLC to J. M. Touhy, 3/3/99, TS, MTP; Carrington, p. 226; SLC to Doubleday, n.d., *MTL,* II, 760. Clemens had also attempted to provide aid of a more material sort by giving evidence for Kipling in the latter's long but futile copyright battle (1899–1901) with the Putnam publishing house (Carrington, p. 307; SLC to Kipling, 4/23/01, TS, MTP).

7. Kipling's comment about Cervantes quoted in *MTL,* II, 747n. Thrilled by Kipling's praise, Clemens replied to Doubleday: "It makes me proud and glad—what Kipling says. I hope Fate will fetch him to Florence while we are there. I would rather see him than any other man" (10/12/03, *MTL,* II, 746). Clemens' compliment: *MTE,* pp. 309, 311. He indirectly reiterated that praise at a banquet of the Associated Press that same year (1906), coupling the Associated Press on earth with the sun "in the heavens" as the "only two forces that can carry light to all corners of the globe" and concluding: "No one can reach so many hearts and intellects as you—except Rudyard Kipling, and he cannot do it without your help" [*MTS(P)*, p. 315]. Hope to meet: Kipling to SLC, 6/11/07, MTP.

8. Quoted in J. Langdon, *Some Reminiscences, Etc.,* p. 18.

9. Quoted by O. G. S. Crawford, *Said and Done: The Autobiography of an Archaeologist* (London: Wiedenfell and Nicholas [1955]), p. 37. Crawford says that he heard the anecdote from C. B. Gull, the young editor to whom Clemens addressed the question.

10. Quoted in *MFMT,* p. 271.

11. Treloar, *A Lord Mayor's Diary* (London, 1920), p. 188.

12. Quotations from *Punch: Its History, Its Humour, Its People* (London, 1951), p. 12 (my thanks to William A. Dyer, Jr. of Indianapolis for calling my attention to this information) and Sir Henry W. Lucy, *The Diary of a Journalist* (London, 1920), p. 271. As of 1962 *Punch*'s "sanctum" had been violated" only twice since 1907 (though at luncheons rather than at a dinner)–

by H. R. H. Prince Philip in March, 1958, and by James Thurber in June of the same year. In 1907 Clemens had declined to follow the custom of carving his initials in the Table, saying that the second two-thirds of the stylish "W. M. T." inscribed by Thackeray would serve for him. As the *PUNCH Diary* for 6/2/58, put it: "No one could find a monogram to provide a ready-made Thurber autograph, so he put his 'Th' signature alongside that of Shirley Brooks. He also did a Thurber dog in the visitor's book. 'I can feel Mark Twain looking over my shoulder right now,' he said" (Quoted in a letter to me from Mrs. W. M. Ashton, Librarian of *Punch*, 7/23/62).

13. Cortissoz, II, 381. Reid did admit, however, that Clemens' last sentence had helped redeem the rest of the speech. As Reid describes the remarks, Clemens concluded by expressing the hope that his light tone would not be mistaken for lack of appreciation of the great honor he had received. In Reid's words, "It impressed him all the more when he realized that in receiving it he had been bracketed between a Prince of the Blood (here he turned and bowed to Prince Arthur of Connaught) and a Prince of the Republic of Letters, whose fame envelops the world like an atmosphere, Rudyard Kipling, and with that he sat down."

14. Whibley, quoted in Arthur L. Scott, *MT: Selected Criticism* (Dallas, 1955), p. 89ff. Beerbohm's cartoon, reproduced (facing p. 95) in Marquess of Zetland, *Life of Lord Curzon* (New York and London, 1938). At the luncheon with Shaw, Beerbohm was fascinated not only with Clemens' conversation, "but also with his Southern charm, his beautiful hands, and 'his benign blue eyes'" (Alan Dent, "Max is Eighty," *Saturday Review*, XXXV, Aug. 30, 1952, 20).

15. Henderson says that Clemens knew "little or nothing" of Shaw ("MT and Bernard Shaw," *MTJ*, IX, Summer, 1954, 1–3). On the other hand the not-always-reliable Henry Fischer recalls that Clemens once complained to him (facetiously) of the injustice of Shaw's plays enjoying world-wide popularity while his own dramatic efforts were relegated to obscurity (*MT&EF*, p. xviii). Paine reports that in 1906 the humorist read him one of Shaw's lectures on religion, praising it as "a frank breath of expression" and heartily agreeing with its scepticism concerning human morality and established creeds (*MTB*, III, 1335–36). Quotations: GBS to Cyril Clemens, *MTQ*, XIX (Winter, 1951), 30; SLC to Shaw, 7/4/07, TS, MTP.

16. Autobiographical dictation, pp. 2183–84, MTP, quoted in *MTSC* p. 316n.

17. Quoted in *MTB*, III, 1398. Shaw was referring to Act II of *John Bull's Other Island* (1904), where the speech actually reads "My way of joking is to tell the truth." Shaw also once praised Clemens to Henderson in much the same terms, saying that he regarded MT more as a sociologist than as a humorist, and adding that MT was in much the same position as himself in having to "put matters in such a way as to make people who would otherwise hang him, believe he is joking" (Henderson, *Mark Twain*, New York, 1911, pp. 199–200). Henderson suggests, too, that Shaw's story "Aerial Football, The New Game" (*The Neolith*, Nov., 1907; *Collier's Weekly*, Nov. 23, 1907) was inspired by "Captain Stormfield's Visit to Heaven." It was not, however, unless in the way that Clemens himself discusses in an unpublished sketch, "Mental

Telegraphy?" (DV 254, MTP), written that same November, while he was preparing "Captain Stormfield" for publication in *Harper's* (Dec., 1907; Jan., 1908). The sketch tells how Clemens sensed resemblances to "Stormfield" when reading Shaw's story "last night," but then realized that the details bore even more resemblance to another story, "The Late Rev. Sam Jones's Reception in Heaven," written "seventeen years ago" in Germany, but never published. His only conclusion from all this was that perhaps the idea had been transmitted from his mind to Shaw's the summer before—though they had not spoken of such matters during their conversation. Citing his firm belief in such a possibility, he went on to develop the suggestion that almost all seemingly original ideas result from just such "unconscious and uninvited thought-transferrence." My thanks to Ray Browne for calling this item to my attention.

18. See *MTE*, pp. 323–328.

19. *MTS(P)*, pp. 373–374, with corrections based on autobiographical dictation (MTP). In *MTS(P)*, the first reference to the ship erroneously reads "*Begum*, of Bengal." (Either Paine or a compositor mistook the top of an exclamation point in the line below for a comma after *Begum*). Nbk references: 22 II, p. 60 (1888): 25, p. 4 (1890); 36, p. 34 (1903).

20. SLC to J. Henniker-Heaton, 1/18/09, *MTL*, II, 829.

Postscript I, THE EIGHTEENTH CENTURY AND EARLIER

1. *RP*, p. 78. See *A1911* for other books named. Reference to "Pilgrimage to Canterbury" in following paragraph: Nbk 31 II, pp. 41–43; titled in Nbk 32, p. 1 (1/7/97). *Canterbury Tales* is listed in *C1951* among items containing marginal notes. John D. McKee sees possible sources of the arming scene in *CY* (Ch. XI) in Chaucer's story of Sir Thopas, as well as in *Sir Gawaine and the Green Knight* ("Three Uses of the Arming Scene," *MTJ*, XII, No. 4, Summer, 1965, 18–19, 21).

2. *LOM*, Ch. LI, *MTLMusc*, pp. 22, 25; *MTSM*, p. 214. The unpublished portions of the notebooks (MTP) contain numerous references to attendance at Shakespeare's plays.

3. *WIM*, p. 8; *MTN*, pp. 206, 325; Nbk 33, p. 8; Nbk 36, p. 34

4. *Julius Caesar* was obviously a favorite. Nbk 13, p. 18, on 10/31/78, mentions Clemens' entertaining his family by reading it aloud. Some twenty-eight years later (10/12/06) he wrote Mary Rogers of reading part of "that tremendous poem" to Jean and his secretary—"a poor preparation for sleep, certainly." (*MTLMary*, p. 71).

5. *TJS*, p. 33; *MTH*, pp. 367–368. One wonders, also, what prompted Clemens to note in Sept., 1866: " 'Give thy thoughts no tongue'—Polonius to his Son" (Nbk 4–5, p. 57) or in late summer, 1887: "Say the kind word for it, Horatio—Hamlet Act 2, Sc v" (Nbk 22 I, p. 15).

6. Nbk 32a I, pp. 14–15, 12/22/97. "Burlesque *Hamlet*" now published in *MTS&B*, pp. 49–87.

7. See also notes, Ch. Six, *ante*, for allusion to "Ophelia's burial to illustrate Church's attitude toward excommunication, "Small-Pox Hut" episode.

8. *MT&HF*, p. 302.

9. As Dewey Ganzel points out in "Twain, Travel Books, and *Life on the Mississippi*" (*AL*, XXXIV, Mar., 1962, 51), Clemens cites the particular passage from Fearon's *Sketches of America* (London, 1819) in one of the deletions from *LOM*, though with acknowledgment only to "a sorely disgusted English eye-witness" (See Heritage *LOM*, pp. 404–405); Sol Smith, *The Theatrical Journey Work and Anecdotal Reminiscences of Sol Smith* (Philadelphia, 1854), pp. 118–119. Clemens had also used the same device in a different way in Chapter XXVIII of *LOM*, where "Uncle Mumford" interjects fierce orders to the boat crew into his conversation with Mark Twain about the U.S. River Commission.

10. *MT&HF*, p. 303.

11. *LSI*, p. 94; DV 114, MTP, 14 pp., with about twenty-five words or phrases per page, chiefly from Shakespeare; *E&E*, pp. 200–201. Minor details in several other works also reflect Clemens' interest in Falstaff. Sir John's vivid reference to man as a "forked radish with a head fantastically carved" seems to have stuck in the humorist's mind, though he was perhaps reminded of it by Carlyle's occasional use of the metaphor in *The French Revolution* and elsewhere. In *Joan of Arc* (Bk II, Ch. XXIII) King Charles, seated on his throne in tight-fitting breeches, resembles "a forked carrot." In a *Connecticut Yankee* (Ch. II) Hank Morgan first sees the page Clarence as "an airy slim boy in shrimp-colored tights that make him look like a forked carrot." Falstaff's dying motions as described by Mistress Quickly (*Henry V*, II, iii) seem echoed in those of Hank Morgan ("Final P.S. by M.T.") and in *LOM* (Ch. XX) those of Clemens' brother Henry. Like Sir John, who "fumbled with the sheets" before expiring, both Henrys feebly "picked at the coverlet."

12. Besides those instances mentioned in subsequent paragraphs and notes, interesting borrowings occur as follows, though this list does not pretend to include *all* of the humorist's allusions to and quotations from Shakespeare. *King John:* In *RI* (I, 153, Ch. XVIII) the narrator says that to describe the thirst of the mule-team after a twenty-three mile haul "would be to 'gild refined gold or paint the lily'" (*KJ*, IV, ii). Immediately admitting that the quotation does not seem to fit in that context, he says he will let it stay, for he had long been trying to work this "really apt and beautiful" phrase into some appropriate description. Here, as elsewhere in the book, the humorist implicitly satirizes efforts of writers to be "literary."

King Lear: A prosaic echo of Lear's "How sharper than a serpent's tooth . . ." (I, iv) occurs in *CY*, Ch. XVI, when Hank reacts to Morgan Le Fay's fussy insistence on absolute cleanliness just after callously murdering the page, with: "Often how louder and clearer than any tongue, does dumb circumstantial evidence speak." In "*The P&P and King Lear*" (*MTJ*, XII, Spring, 1963, 16–17), Robert Gale finds a number of parallels, some rather tenuous. The most likely one suggests that in having Edward name Hendon the Earl of Kent, the author was remembering, perhaps unconsciously, the friendship of Kent for the outcast Lear.

Richard III: Besides the line in the Duke's garbled soliloquy in *HF*, Clemens paraphrased the play's opening lines to applaud (and to make a pun on) the defeat of Tammany Hall by Seth Low, president of Columbia University and Fusion Party candidate for mayor of New York. On seeing the victory notice in the *Sun*, 11/6/01, he wrote (with more enthusiasm than logic, since

Low seems to be causing the clouds): "Now is the winter of our discontent made glorious sumr by this sun of New York; and all the clouds that Seth Lowered o'er our housetops are in the deep bosom of the ocean buried" (Nbk 34, p. 17).

Titus Andronicus: During Clemens' last years, visitors signing the Stormfield guestbook were greeted by Clemens' own hand-written quotation of the six-line passage from Act I, Sc. i, beginning "In peace and honor rest you here . . ." (Guestbook, MTP).

13. *Merchant of Venice:* Nbk 15, p. 9. For *MV* (and *Othello*) see also *IA*, I, 283–284 Ch. XXII), where the author proclaims the power of nighttime Venice to evoke visions of "Shylocks in gaberdine and sandals, venturing loans upon the rich argosies of Venetian commerce, . . . Othellos and Desdemonas, . . . Iagos and Rodrigos. . . ." In *RI* (Appendix A) Clemens borrows Shylock's comment about Antonio (I, iii) to note that Mormon hatred had "fed fat its ancient grudge" against the sect's persecutors. See also Margaret Duckett, *MT and Bret Harte,* Norman, Okla., 1964, p. 317.

Macbeth: SLC to OLC, 8/29/96, *LLMT*, p. 327. Cf. also the image of the dead Duncan's "silver skin lac'd with his golden blood" (III, iii) and of the murdered page in *CY* (Ch. XVIII), with his "little silken pomps and vanities laced with his golden blood." In *IA* (I, Ch. XVII) the author borrows Macbeth's comment about his own castle (V, v), remarking that the houses of Genoese nobility seemed well able to "laugh a siege to scorn."

Antony and Cleopatra: MTA(P), II, 317.

14. "The Indignity Put Upon the Remains of George Holland . . ." *Galaxy* (Feb., 1871), p. 320. As Robert Gale observes (op. cit. in note to *Lear,* above), when the author says of Tom Sawyer's quarrel with Becky Thatcher (*TS*, Ch. XII) that Tom had "tried to 'whistle her down the wind,' but failed," he is misquoting Othello's comment (III, iii) that if he proved Desdemona faithless, he would "whistle her off and let her down the wind / To prey at fortune." And how appropriate for Raleigh's crepitation in *1601* is the apparent echo of Montano's remark on the fierce storm (II, i) that "a fuller blast ne'er shook our battlements," when "Shakspur" comments that "heaven's artillery hath shook the globe in admiration of it." Comment on "intellectual snow-summits" is in "About Play-Acting," *Hadleyburg,* p. 215.

15. Sidney: Nbk 27, p. 44. Evelyn: *A1911,* p. 28. Bessus: "Some Reminiscences of MT," *Overland Monthly,* LXXXVII (Apr., 1929), 125. In the article, however, the play is erroneously credited to John Ford. Clemens owned a copy of Bacon's *Promus of Formularies and Elegances . . . Illustrated and Elucidated by Passages from Shakespeare,* ed. Mrs. Henry Pott (Boston, 1883), but *A1911* lists it as "Uncut" (p. 29). In Feb., 1908, the humorist was enchanted by one of Ben Jonson's masques performed at New York's Plaza Hotel (autobiographical dictation, 2/19/08, MTP).

16. Clemens also owned a two-volume edition of Samuel Butler's satire of Presbyterians and Independents, *Hudibras,* London, 1847 (*A1911,* p. 13), but I have found no specific evidence of its influence.

17. *MTB*, I, 146; SLC to OLC 1/12/69, "Love Letters of MT," ed. Wecter, *Atlantic,* CLXXX (Nov., 1947), 38; *MTF,* 10/31/77, p. 212; *MTS(P),* p. 210.

18. *E&E,* pp. 333–334.

19. *AL* XXXII (Mar., 1960), p. 62.

20. Shakespeare-Bacon controversy: In a letter to Orion, 9/7/87 (MTP), Clemens criticized Samuel Webster for failing to secure Ignatius Donnelly's book, *The Great Cryptogram* (1888). Apparently he had conveniently forgotten that on July 9 he had written Fred Hall about the possibilities of getting the rights to Donnelly's book and had then crossed out the question, adding, "No— we don't want it" (*MTBus,* p. 384). "Southey's Bunyan": Nbk 22 I, p. 22; "Stereoptical panorama": *MTN,* p. 192.

21. The previously unpublished note on Bunyan's "Tower of London" immediately follows one in the published *MTN* (p. 328) which comments that modern conveniences have made earthly life so pleasant that no one would now go to Bunyan's heaven, adding however, "but it was a superior place in its day." In one of his copies of *The Pilgrim's Progress,* a facsimile of the first edition published in 1875 and now owned by the MT Research Foundation, Perry, Mo., Clemens' only marginal note (on p. 6, probably next to the passage where Pliable leaves Christian to struggle alone in the Slough of Despond) reads "Correct picture of selfishness & baseness." According to the inscription, Clemens acquired this copy in the year of its publication (*Twainian,* May-June, 1959, p. 1). In 1882, he received a two-volume edition published in the Cantonese dialect (Canton, 1870–71) and noted in the cover that it had been sent by "the Rajah of Ambong and Morocco in the Island of Borneo . . . a full-blooded Yankee . . . born in Boston" (*A1911,* p. 13). He also owned a copy of the *Visions of John Bunyan* (New York, 1806) [Redding].

22. *MTSM,* pp. 225–253.

23. *MTMusc,* 2/18/54, p. 19. Preceding quotations in paragraph: *SCH,* p. 141; *MTSM,* p. 119.

24. SLC to OLC, 3/1/69, *LLMT,* p. 76. Clara Clemens remembers that during the Hartford years Clemens did relate parts of Gulliver's story to his three daughters (*MFMT,* p. 56).

25. Quotations of marginalia are from Coley B. Taylor, *MT's Margins on Thackeray's "Swift"* (New York, 1935), pp. 39, 55. Clemens continued to resent Swift's treatment of women, apparently, for Henry Fischer says that Clemens in the late 1890's once called the Dean's attitudes those of a sadist and masochist in one (*MT&EF,* p. 184).

26. SLC to JHT, 3/14/87 quoted in *NF,* p. 52.

27. *TSAbr,* 16, 59, and passim; *MTWWD,* pp. 433–553; *CY,* Ch. VIII.

28. SLC to OLC, 7/8/89, *LLMT,* p. 253.

29. *MTN,* p. 337.

30. *LLMT,* p. 34; DV 36, TS p. 2, MTP; *CY,* Ch. IV, and ms. plan for appendix (Berg); *MTS(P),* p. 152. Of Smollett's works he mentions specifically only *Roderick Random* (*CY,* Ch. IV; Nbk 14, pp. 10, 12), from which he borrowed the name Tom Bowling for an "ancient whale-ship master" who tells a story in "Some Rambling Notes. . . ." (*TSAbr.* pp. 259–261). Richardson's *Pamela* he cites in several notebook entries (e.g. Nbk 21, p. 30) and on 1/14/84, in a letter to E. H. House, he wrote that he had recently read "all of Clarissa Harlowe" and "the closing chapters of Pamela" (Barrett). *Clarissa Harlowe* is also listed in *C1951.*

31. SLC to Osgood, 3/30/81, Berg, quoted in *MTHL*, II, 869.

32. *CY*, Ch. VII. Clemens had originally worked another reference to *Crusoe* into the *Yankee* ms. as an illustration of human stupidity. In Ch. XXXI, after expounding upon "real" wages and the American devotion to the protective tariff, Hank was to despair of ever making men understand that real wages depended on purchasing power, and add that the average man, in Crusoe's place would not have "kicked the bag of gold aside" in order to carry "more hoop-iron and other really valuable stuff ashore." Because the "gold coin was *money*, . . . he would have lugged it ashore sure. . . ." (Ms. II, 130, Berg). For some reason—possibly because the same passage praised England's policy of free-trade as opposed to "protection," and hence clashed with the book's general attack on England—Clemens deleted the segment sometime during the novel's proof-stage. Earlier he had listed the doubloon episode as a possibility for his "Picturesque Incidents in History and Tradition," calling it "a fine literary point, but untrue," since "no man would have done that" (Nbk 19, p. 37).

33. WDH to SLC, 8/9/85, *MTHL*, II, 536.

34. Quoted by C. O. Parsons, "MT in New Zealand," *SAQ*, LXI (Winter, 1962), p. 74.

35. Ms. plan for appendix of *CY*, Berg. Most of Clemens' objections to *The Vicar*, however, focused on what he considered its faulty character-drawing and false sentimentality (See *MTN*, pp. 240, 262, 266; *FEq*, II, 312).

36. SLC to Orion, 3/18/60. *MTL*, I, 45; Letter I, *Galaxy*, IX (Oct., 1870), p. 569. Letters II–IV appeared in the same issue, V–VI in Nov., and VII in Jan., 1871.

37. See "Beau Tibbs and Colonel Sellers," *MLN*, LIX (1944–45), 310–313. It also seems a little more than coincidental that Goldsmith's Letter LV, which immediately follows the two Tibbs episodes, deals largely with Russia.

38. *MTBus*, p. 60.

39. *MTLec*, p. 39; *MT&HF*, pp. 330–331; *Vicar*, Ch. XIV.

40. Friedrich Schönemann has suggested some possibilities (*MT als Literarische Persönlichkeit*, p. 94ff), but they are general ones. See also S. Krause, *MT as Critic*, pp. 118–127, and passim. *C1951* lists *She Stoops to Conquer* and *The Good-Natured Man* among books belonging to Jean or Clara, and *The Deserted Village* among those bearing Olivia's autograph.

41. *MTS(P)*, p. 185. Clemens' set of Walpole's letters is listed in *A1911*, p. 68. Volume IX, with his marginalia, is in the Yale collection. Most of the marginal comments agree with Clemens' views during the 1870's (see Ch. Three, *ante*) rather than opinions in the late 1880's when he glorified the French Revolution.

42. Walpole, *Letters*, IX, 462 (Yale).

43. SLC to WDH, 2/25/06, *MTHL*, II, 800.

44. *MTF*, 10/31/77, p. 212.

45. Quoted in *PRI*, p. 35.

46. *MTA(P)*, II, 51. Comments on Tam O'Shanter, statement by Burns' mother are from *MTEnt*, p. 56; *IA*, I, 185 (Ch. XIV) and II, 118 (Ch. IX).

47. SLC to A. A. H. Dawson, 1/24/80, MTP (not sent); *LE*, pp. 35–36.

Clemens had used these lines from Burns' poem to make this same point directly rather than ironically in a notebook entry late in 1897, by changing the initial word to "God's" (*MTN*, p. 344).

Postscript II, NINETEENTH-CENTURY POETRY

1. Clemens' copy of the "Ancient Mariner," illustrated by J. Noel Paton (New York, 1875), is inscribed "Saml. L. Clemens, Hartford, June, 1875"; Livy's copy (New York, 1876) bears the legend, "To Livy L. Clemens, Nov. 27, 1876, from S. L. Clemens." (*A1911*, pp. 20, 24). References to waiter, Riley, and Carnegie: Nbk 11, p. 3; *TA*, I, 272 (Ch. XXVI); *MTE*, p. 37; "The Enchanted Sea Wilderness," *MTWWD*, pp. 83-85. The ending of *P&P* also seems to echo the "Ancient Mariner." There the king addresses Hugh Hendon "with wrathful voice and kindling eye" and later is moved to tell and retell the story of his own experiences in order to teach compassion to his courtiers and subjects.

2. R. L. Brooks, "A Second Possible Source for MT's 'The Aged Pilot Man,'" *Revue de littérature comparée*, XXXVI (1962), 451-453. As Brooks notes, representative stanzas of the two poems immediately reveal differences in meter and rhyme scheme. "The Raging Canal" begins: "Come list to me, ye heroes, ye nobles, and ye braves, / For I've been at the mercy of the winds and the waves. . . ." "The Aged Pilot Man's" second stanza starts: "From out the clouds at noon that day / There came a dreadful storm."

3. Quoted in Nbk 32a II, p. 32, 6/20/97. "In Memoriam" is reprinted in *LitE*, pp. 311-313.

4. *MTL*, II, 808.

5. *SN&O*, p. 66. This story first appeared in *Galaxy*, IX (May, 1870), 724-726. Clemens echoed Wordsworth's epigraph to the "Intimations" ode, "The Child is father of the Man" at the conclusion of his speech at the banquet honoring General Grant, November 13, 1879 (*MTB*, II, 657).

6. *TIA*, p. 235. In the same letter he recorded that Byron's lines had come back to him with a "new excellence" by the shore of the Sea of Galilee. The description of spears shining "like stars on the sea / When the blue wave rolls nightly on deep Galilee" evoked for him a vision of "Long files of burnished spear-heads stretching rank upon rank, far away till they are lost in the mists that brood over the further shore." Probably this was meant as a typical tourist effusion, and since it did not come off well, the author wisely omitted it when revising the passage for *IA*.

7. *SN&O*, p. 86; *MTB*, I, 290. He played with "Sennacherib" again as late as November, 1895. While lecturing in New Zealand, among other notes for a poem, he wrote: "The Moa came down like a sheep on the fold, and his glance was stern and high, and he fetched the Maori a lift with his foot that landed him in the sky" (Nbk 28a II, p. 63).

8. *IA*, I, 310, 279 (Chs. XXIII, XXII). May Welland first pointed out the similarity to *Beppo* ("MT, the Great Victorian," *Chicago Review*, Fall, 1955, 102). Clemens' knowledge of the career of Marino Faliero mentioned in the same chapter of *IA* could have come from Byron's dramatization (1821) of the

fourteenth-century doge's attempt to overthrow the Venetian constitution, but a more likely source was one of the many guide-books he doubtless knew. So also, his knowledge of "the doge Foscari, whose name . . . Lord Byron has made permanently famous" [i.e., in the play, *The Two Foscari* (1821)], *IA*, I, 302.

9. *IA*, I, 361 (Ch. XXVII); 78 (Ch. VI).

10. *AmCl*, pp. 478–479. Chillon reference: *TA*, II, 180 (Ch. XIII). There he also noted Byron's name among others "of the first celebrity" scrawled on the columns of the cell (p. 181).

11. Quotations in this and preceding paragraph: Buffalo *Express*, 2/18/69, 2/11/69, 2/24/69, 2/25/69, and Paine 260, MTP, quoted by Paul Baender, "MT and the Byron Scandal," *AL*, XXX (Jan., 1959), 479–482.

12. Baender, op. cit., p. 485.

13. Nbk 26, p. 13; Baender, p. 478n. As Baender points out in the same note, Clemens once implied considerable sympathy with Byron in his marginal comment in Greville's *Journal* of the reigns of George IV and William IV: ". . . what a man sees in the human race is merely himself in the deep and honest privacy of his own heart. Byron despised the race because he despised himself. I feel as Byron did, and for the same reason" (*MTB*, III, 1539).

14. *SN&O*, p. 68; *TSAbr*, pp. 302–303, 257; Nbk 31 II, p. 58. See also *SSix*, pp. 208–209 for a burlesque poem combining "This world is all a fleeting show" with three other lines from Thomas Campbell's "Hohenlinden," Gray's "Elegy," and S. Foster's "Old Dog Tray," respectively.

15. These and preceding quotations from Arnold's essay are all from DV 49, MTP, quoted by J. B. Hoben, "MT's *Connecticut Yankee*: A Genetic Study," *AL*, XVIII (Nov. 1946), 210.

16. E. Hudson Long, *MT Handbook* (New York, 1958), p. 223n. In the "Defence," Clemens also echoes Arnold's famous description of Shelley as "a beautiful and ineffectual angel beating in a void his luminous wings in vain," when he calls the Shelley portrayed by Dowden "a fallen and fettered angel who is ashamed of himself; an angel who beats his soiled wings and cries. . . ." (*LitE*, pp. 50–51).

17. *MFMT*, p. 66; *C1951; MTHI*, pp. 131–132. On 2/14/07 he read Shelley's "To a Skylark" at a Shelley-Keats memorial celebration at the Waldorf-Astoria (Lyon Journal, TS, p. 24, MTP).

18. Nbks 19, p. 25; 15, p. 10. In the parody, after changing Hunt's first line to "May his tribe *decrease!*" Clemens followed the original until line 5, when instead of "peace," he wrote "Exceeding *cheek* had made Ben Butler bold." For "love" in lines 9 and 13 he substituted "The names of those who *serve* the Lord," and "Write me as one who *serves* his fellow men [italics mine]. Finally, he concluded the poem with: "And showed the names whom God's firm trust [Hunt: "dear love"] had blessed—/And lo! It was distinctly manifest that Abou Ben B had 'got left.' "

19. M. A. DeWolfe Howe, *Memories of A Hostess* (Boston, 1922), p. 254; *A1911*, p. 65, inscribed "Saml. L. Clemens, Hartford, 1875"; *MTHL*, II, 654n. Of *Becket* he wrote Twichell that "you must see it . . ." (11/20/93, TS, Yale). "Break, Break, Break!": SLC to OLC, 9/29/96, *LLMT*, p. 327; "In Memoriam": OLC to J. Y. W. MacAlister [4/6/97]; SLC to Ibid., 6/28/97 (both

Barrett); "Locksley Hall": *MTN*, p. 373: "Mariana," *MTA(P)*, II, 228. There is also an allusion to "The Charge of the Light Brigade" in *AmCl*, Ch. XVII, when the author describes Howard Tracy surrounded by "Saltmarsh-Handel" portraits, with each subject leaning on a cannon, and says, "It was Balaklava come again."

20. TS of *FEq* (3 vols.), I, 73 (Berg). The lines quoted from *Enoch Arden* began with "The mountain wooded to the peak, the lawns. . . ." and continued to "The scarlet shafts of sunrise—but no sail," omitting one passage of three lines and another of four, both of which describe Enoch's actions.

21. Written in the margin of p. 1, original ms. of *TS*, Riggs Memorial Library, Georgetown University, quoted by Hamlin Hill, "The Composition and Structure of *TS*," *AL*, XXXII (Jan., 1961), 386.

22. See *MTN*, p. 212; *MTW*, p. 49. The "man-at-his-own-funeral" idea appears also in "The Mysterious Chamber" (begun in 1876) and in the play and novel versions of *Simon Wheeler, Detective* (1877–79). I am grateful to Walter Blair for reminding me of those latter instances.

23. Hill, *AL*, XXXII, 387–388.

24. "Mark Twain," *Yale Review*, XXV (1935–36), 302. See Louise Greer, *Browning in America* (Chapel Hill, 1952), pp. 168–169, 295, n. 97.

25. *MTF*, 11/16/86, 3/22/87, pp. 258–259, 260–261, 261n. In preparing the reading Clemens marked the poems extensively, indicating varying stresses and emphasis by underlinings and other notations. Sometimes he included stage directions, as when he wrote, "He's choking," in the margin of "Mr. Sludge, 'The Medium'" and sometimes he wrote glosses to help him clarify some of the obscure passages for his listeners. For examples of notes and underlinings, see *MTB*, II, plate facing p. 846; Phelps, *Yale Review*, XXV (1936), 305–306.

26. *MFMT*, p. 57.

27. The copy of *Men and Women*, MTP, is inscribed "Livie L. Langdon, 1864" on the flyleaf. *A1911*, p. 12, lists Vols. II, III, and IV of the 1887 Riverside edition (*Dramatic Lyrics, etc.; The Ring and the Book;* and *Red-Cotton Nightcap Country, etc.;* Vols. I (*Paracelsus, etc.*) and VI (*Parleyings*) are at Redding, as is a separate copy of *Ferishtah's Fancies* (1886), inscribed "Livy L. Clemens, 1887." *C1951* lists 8 vols. of Browning, but since no publishers or dates are given, it is impossible to tell whether some of these are the same volumes listed in *A1911*. *C1951* also lists William Sharp's *Robert Browning* [London, 1890]. The inscription in *Asolando* (Redding) is dated "Venice, 1892."

28. M. B. C., "MT as a Reader," *Harper's Weekly*, LV (Jan., 7, 1911), 6.

29. Phelps, *Yale Review*, p. 303; Grace King, *Memories of a Southern Woman of Letters* (New York, 1932), p. 84; M. B. C., op. cit., p. 6.

30. In Sept., 1888, for instance, some 130 people gathered at a neighbor's home to hear him (*MTN*, p. 200). For a program at Smith College the following November, he made no fewer than three lists of selections to be read, each of which contained a number of Browning's poems. A reading for a group of friends at Danieli's Hotel in 1892 was remembered as "remarkable" for its "sympathetic interpretation of the poet" (R. U. Johnson, *Remembered Yes-*

terdays, Boston, 1923, p. 321). Isabel Lyon recalls that he read Browning's "Memorabilia" as well as Shelley's "To A Skylark," at the Shelley-Keats memorial celebration, 2/14/07, and "Rabbi Ben Ezra" at the Whitmores' on 3/8/07 (Lyon Journal, TS, pp. 224, 229, MTP).

31. *MTB*, II, 847; SLC to WDH, 8/22/87, *MTHL*, II, 596.

32. In *Men and Women* (Boston, 1856), MTP. All poems cited in the discussion of Browning are those actually mentioned by Clemens or his listeners (in notebooks, letters, and the magazine articles already cited). Besides those, the following are marked, most of them extensively, in the same copy of *Men and Women:* "Love Among the Ruins," "A Lover's Quarrel," "An Epistle . . . of Karshish, the Arab Physician," "Mesmerism," "The Last Ride Together," "The Patriot," "Old Pictures in Florence," "Cleon." In various notebook lists appear also "Soliloquy of the Spanish Cloister," "In a Gondola," and "The Lost Leader."

33. *MTN*, p. 297. Reference to "Clive": Nbk 29 II, p. 36; to Barrett Browning: Cyril Clemens, *My Cousin MT* (Emmaus, Pa., 1939), p. 109.

34. On 5/26/99, for instance, he wrote from Vienna to Sidney G. Trist, Secretary of the London Anti-Vivisection Society, citing various experiments he had read about. That letter was later published by the London Society as "The Pains of Lowly Life" in 1900, and ca. 1905 was reprinted by both the New York and New England Anti-Vivisection Societies (*BAL*, 209, 215).

35. *BAL*, II, 212, 213.

36. First published in full in Arthur L. Scott, *On the Poetry of MT* (Urbana, Ill., 1966).

Postscript III, Nineteenth-Century Fiction

1. *MTB*, III, 1500–01.

2. Paine notes that Olivia was once embarrassed to admit to the Russian visitor Stepniak that Clemens did not like Thackeray's novels (*MTB*, III, 1500); Carlyle Smythe recalls unsuccessful attempts by Howells and Brander Matthews to interest the humorist in *Barry Lyndon* and *Henry Esmond* (*Pall Mall*, XVI, 1898, 31). Thackeray's pioneer collection of "condensed novels" was entitled "Mr. Punch's Prize Novelists" (1847); reprinted as "Novels by Eminent Hands" in *Miscellanies* (1856). Clemens did read *Esmond* in October, 1906, and wrote Clara that he had never read it before, but had confused it all these years with *The Virginians* [its sequel]. As his one compliment to Thackeray, he also said that on the whole he had liked it and had found the ending "dramatically great" (Lyon Journal, 11/7/06, TS, p. 191, MTP). For discussion of further influence of "condensed novel" form see *MTBur*, passim.

3. *MTBur*, p. 171, n. 55. The most famous of these composite burlesques was *Chikken Hazzard*, by the "Sensation Novel Company, Ltd"; announced by *Punch*, 3/7/68. Besides Charles Reade's *Foul Play* (1868), it burlesques such authors as Dickens, W. E. Sutner, Julia Kavanaugh, Wilkie Collins, and Eugéne Sue.

4. The foregoing discussion of *RI* is based largely on *MTBur*, pp. 76–78.

5. SLC to Pamela and Jane Clemens, 2/8/62; *MTL*, I, 65; *MTH*, pp. 186–187; SLC to OLC, 10/31/71, *LLMT*, p. 162; *C1951*.

6. SLC to *WDH*, 1/18/09, *MTHL*, II, 841; DV 201, MTP, quoted in *MTHL*, II, 770n. In *Feq*, II, 312 (Ch. XXVI), he had commended the ship's library for the absence of Jane Austen's books from its shelves: "Just that one omission alone," he said, "would make a fairly good library out of a library that hadn't a book in it." Much earlier, he had written to Twichell that though he often wanted to criticize Jane Austen, her books maddened him so greatly that he couldn't conceal his "frenzy" from the reader (SLC to JHT, 9/13/98, *MTL*, II, 667).

7. SLC to WDH, 7/21/85, *MTHL*, II, 533–534; Notebook entry, 8/11/78, quoted in *MTB*, II, 627. Clemens mentions specifically that he was reading the Tauchnitz edition of *Romola*. His library ultimately contained two other editions of the novel (one published in New York, in 1869, and the other in Philadelphia in 1890) and also *The George Eliot Birthday Book* (*A1911*, pp. 6, 27).

8. Nbk 22 II, p. 65; *MFMT*, p. 61. In one discussion of *Diana of the Crossways* (1885) he objected that the heroine did not live up to Meredith's description of her. Though the author kept telling the reader "how smart she is, how brilliant" Clemens could not see that she ever said anything smart or brilliant and challenged the others to read him some of her "smart utterances." (*MTB*, II, 847).

9. Schreiner: *FEq*, II, Ch. XXXII. Clemens noted the title of her novel in late November or early December, 1888 (Nbk 23 II, p. 37) and on 12/24/96 wrote Chatto for a copy of "Olive Schreiner's (and her husband's) little book (political) . . ." (Berg). He was referring to *The Political Situation* (1895). Steel: *MTMWI*, p. 42. Robbins: *MTB*, II, 1089. Glyn, *MTE*, pp. 312–319; *MTL*, II, 809.

10. John Dickson Carr, *Life of Sir Arthur Conan Doyle*, p. 199. Doyle was one of the guests at Whitelaw Reid's Embassy dinner in 1907 (autobiographical dictations, 7/25/07, MTP). Foner quotes from SLC's letter to "the author of *The Crime of the Congo*," but without identifying Doyle (*MTSC*, p. 297); letter in MTP dated "early 1900's," probably by Paine. Clemens also owned a copy of Doyle's *The War in South Africa: Its Cause and Conduct* (New York, 1902) [*A1911*, p. 25, misprinted p. 28].

11. SLC to WDH, 1/21/79, *MTHL*, I, 246, 247n. For both play and novel versions of the Simon Wheeler story, see *MTS&B*, pp. 205–454.

12. Nbk 30 II, p. 32, quoted in *IE*, p. 191.

13. SLC to JHT, 9/8/01, Yale. This same letter both identifies the book loaned by Twichell as the "seed" for the story and refers to the "recent resurrection" of Holmes—obviously in *The Hound of the Baskervilles*.

14. Besides noting sometime in May, 1886, that he would "write an account of the man with a blood-hound's marvelous scent" (Nbk 21, p. 7), Clemens actually attempted in the late 1890's (possibly 1899) a sketch called "A Human Bloodhound," whose main character, Godkin, possessed such a sense of smell. Though the original idea thus preceded publication of *A Study in Scarlet* (1887), the concept nevertheless is still appropriate both to a burlesque

of Jefferson Hope's quest and to a satire of some of Doyle's actual descriptions of Holmes (e.g. in "The Red-Headed League," the author calls his protagonist "Holmes the sleuth-hound, Holmes the relentless, keen-witted . . . criminal agent"). In turn, *A Study in Scarlet* perhaps owed a debt to Clemens. In having Jefferson Hope scrawl "RACHE" on the wall of Drebber's death-chamber, Doyle echoes *TA,* Appendix C, which describes inscriptions on the wall of Heidelburg College prison, among which was the same word. The humorist called it "an inscription well calculated to pique curiosity," since there was no indication of the deed, the nature of the revenge desired, or of whether the writer had ever achieved his goal. (For further details see, Maria Von Krebs: *"Rache* is the German for Revenge," *Baker Street Journal,* Jan., 1960, 12–14.)

15. The satire here and later of Holmes' ability to rise from the dead is actually somewhat anachronistic, for whereas Doyle plunged his hero to death in Reichenbach Falls in "The Final Problem" (the concluding story in *Memoirs of Sherlock Holmes,* 1894), he did not actually resurrect him until October, 1903, when "The Adventure of the Empty House" (in that month's *Strand* magazine) explained that Holmes had miraculously escaped drowning. But although the events of both *The Hound of the Baskervilles* and the episodes of the popular play that Clemens' friend William Gillette had rewritten from an 1897 play by Doyle were supposed to have been "reminiscences" of adventures that had occurred *before* the Reichenbach Falls mishap, Clemens obviously considered both the play and the *Hound* to be "resurrections" of the detective. The miners' remarks also strike at characteristic actions and situations, like that in "Silver Blaze" (first story in *The Memoirs*), where Holmes recites the background of the case "leaning forward, with his long, thin fore finger checking off the points upon the palm of his left hand." (Cf. "Now he has rose up standing, and is putting his clews together on his left fingers with his right finger. See? he touches the forefinger—now the middle finger—now ring finger—." Then, smiling "like a tiger," he proceeds to "tally off the other fingers like nothing.") Amazed at such intellect, the miners then recreate how Holmes would have attacked the case of Mrs. Hogan's lost child, satirizing the detective's characteristic collecting of insignificant scraps of clothing, soil samples, etc. Finally the awestruck Ferguson asks, "I wonder if God made him?" To which his companion replies, "Not all at one time, I reckon."

16. The existence of a somewhat similar description, composed as a discarded opening paragraph for *GA* (quoted in *MT&EB,* p. 73) does not necessarily contradict the supposition that Clemens had *A Study in Scarlet* in mind in 1901. The device is the same, but the details of the later sketch seem very pointedly designed to parallel and, at the same time, to contrast with Doyle's description.

17. *TJS,* Letter 1, 11/18/56; Letter 3, 3/14/57; *Galaxy* (May, 1870), reprinted *SN&O,* pp. 121–131. In the case of the Irish widow it is possible that Clemens was remembering a similar Irish widow from Carlyle's *Past and Present* (1843), who with her three children was refused help "at this Charitable Establishment and then at that . . . ; referred from one to the other, helped by none"; and finally died of typhus (Bk. III, Ch. ii).

18. In addition to subsequent references, "Daniel in the Lion's Den—and

Out Again All Right" (*Californian*, 11/5/64, reprinted *SSix*, 143–150) contains some fifteen names either borrowed from or similar to those of various Dickens' characters.

19. SLC to Orion, 2/6/61, *MTBus*, p. 57. Webster, following Paine (*MTN*, p. 183) identifies the girl as Laura Dake. Dake was Laura Wright's married name.

20. *MTS(P)*, p. 44. Bernard Poli sees parallels to the relationships and experiences of Martin Chuzzlewit and Mark Tapley in those of Mark Twain and Mr. Brown in *LSI* and *MTTB* (*MT, écrivain de l'Ouest: Regionalisme et humour*, Paris, 1965, p. 102).

21. *MTEnt*, p. 92, 12/5/63.

22. Letter dated 11/30/61, Keokuk (Iowa) *Gate City*, 3/6/62 (quoted *PRI*, p. 30); SLC to W. H. Claggett, 2/28/62, MTP, partially quoted *MTBur*, pp. 103–104. [In this letter Clemens also quoted Sarah Nipper's line: "I hope I'm not an oyster though I may not wish to live in crowds" and characterized by means of typical phrases "Cap'en Cuttle," Walter Gay, Mr. Toots, Jack Bunsby, Florence, and "the Biler" (Robin Tootle, also nicknamed Rob the Grinder)]; MT to Sacramento *Union*, 3/18/66, quoted in *MTH*, p. 262. On the Hawaiian trip, too, he once noted a passenger leaning with the ship's roll "like Capt. Cuttle" (Nbk 5, p. 6b). There seems to be an echo of the Captain's urging Walter Gay several times (in Ch. X) to "Go on," and also of Mr. Toots' constant references to his "state of mind" or "state of feelings" in Clemens' letter (8/11/57) to Belle Stotts (Orion's wife's sister), *MTBus*, pp. 34–35.

23. Quoted in *LSI*, pp. 110–111.

24. *MTF*, p. 65, 1/7/69. Other quotations in paragraph: *MTH*, p. 367; *W1868*, p. 11. Clemens probably read *Our Mutual Friend* in the *Golden Era*, where it was still appearing in Jan., 1866 (the last English number was Nov., 1865). I am grateful to Joseph Gardner for pointing out this fact.

25. Nbk 19, pp. 33, 28, 36.

26. Clemens probably read *Bleak House* (1852–3) shortly after its publication, for Wecter says, though his dating seems to be in error, that Orion published excerpts from the novel in the Hannibal *Journal* presumably during the fall and winter of 1851 (*SCH*, p. 240). Besides borrowing Snagsby's name, the author seems to echo the repeated orders to poor Jo, the crossing sweeper, when in Ch. XVIII of *P&P*, the little king in Tom Canty's rags is "called hard names and . . . promised arrest as a vagrant except he *moved on* promptly" [italics mine]. He was possibly remembering Mrs. Rouncewell (Lady Dedlock's housekeeper) and her son George, when he named one of the story-tellers in "Some Rambling Notes, etc." (1877), Captain Rounceville. In 1880 a notebook entry reminded him to "buy Bleak House" for Anna Dickinson, whom he wished to "educate" (Nbk 15, p. 53).

Snodgrass: *SN&O*, p. 89; *SSix*, p. 60; *TSAbr*, pp. 328–330. For evidence that Quintus Curtius Snodgrass was *not* a Clemens pseudonym, see Allan Bates, "The Quintus Curtius Snodgrass Letters: A Clarification of the MT Canon," *AL*, XXXVI (Mar., 1964), 31–37; and Claude Brinegar, "MT and the Q. C. Snodgrass Letters . . . ," *Journal of the American Statistical Assn.* LVIII (Mar., 1963), 85–96, which argues against MT's authorship on the basis of a word-frequency test.

27. *MTE,* pp. 266–267. Clemens names Bret Harte as being especially guilty of exploiting Dickensian sentimentalism and also of imitating other qualities. In the margin of "Tennessee's Partner" (p. 62 of his copy of *The Luck of Roaring Camp and Other Sketches.* 1872), he wrote: "This is much more suggestive of Dickens & an English atmosphere than 'Pike County' " (Bradford A. Booth, "MT's Comments on Bret Harte's Stories," *AL,* XXV, Jan., 1954, 494). The *Californian* sketch about l'il Addie is reprinted in *SSix,* pp. 191–193. It is possible that Clemens also had the shrewish Jenny Wrenn's care of her alcoholic father in mind (*Our Mutual Friend*), but the burlesque has more bite when compared with *The Old Curiosity Shop.*

28. *MTA(P),* II, 103; *MTE,* p. 213. For correction of the date and a fuller account, see my "MT's 'First Date' with Olivia Langdon," *Mo. Historical Society Bulletin,* XI (Jan., 1955), 155–157.

29. Quotations from the 1868 account are from a photostatic copy of the original *Alta* article (Brownell), and the 1907 reminiscences from *MTE,* pp. 213–214.

30. "A Memorable Midnight Experience," *E&E,* pp. 4–5.

31. My discussion of those details is based chiefly on *MTBur,* pp. 101–107. For parallels to Aldrich's *Story of a Bad Boy,* see *MT&HF,* pp. 64–65. "Boy's Manuscript" was first published in *MTW,* pp. 25–44.

32. Nbk 32 I, p. 26. Actually, Clemens wrote the name and then later deleted it.

33. These parallels occur especially in Chs. XXVI, XXXIII, and XLIII of *David Copperfield.*

34. *MTML,* p. 168.

35. *MTMWI,* p. 270n. Minnie Brashear notes resemblances between another work of the 1870's, the "Carnival of Crime in Connecticut," and Dickens' *The Haunted Man* (*MTSM,* p. 213n.). A few parallels exist but there is no additional evidence that Clemens knew *The Haunted Man.*

36. *American Notes,* Chs. XI, XII; *LOM,* Chs. XXXVIII, XXV. On the trip itself, in May, 1882, he reminded himself to "See Dickens for a note on Cairo" (Nbk 16, p. 33). The tradition that Marion City, Missouri, was the model for "Eden" (cited in *MTSM,* pp. 68–71, and *SCII,* pp. 51, 55) seems to have no basis in fact. For a consideration of this matter, see my "What Place was the Model for Martin Chuzzlewit's 'Eden'? A Last Word on the 'Cairo Legend'," *Dickensian,* LV (Autumn, 1959), 169–175.

37. *MT&EF,* pp. 59–60.

38. *MTBus,* p. 58; other references: *MTN,* p. 183, entry dated 5/26/85; *AMT(N),* pp. 79–82. I am pleased that Bryant M. French's study, which appeared after this chapter was written, further supports the suggestion that the fictional Laura Hawkins owes a good deal to Clemens' memories of Laura Wright (*MT and* The Gilded Age, pp. 154–157).

AFTERWORD

1. Carlyle, *On Heroes, Hero-Worship, and the Heroic in History,* Lecture VI.

2. *Sartor Resartus,* Bk III, Ch. VIII.

Academy: on *Prince and Pauper*, 67; *Life on Mississippi*, 77; *Yankee*, 163
Albert (Saxe-Coburg-Gotha, Prince Consort of Gt. Britain), 20–21
Aldrich, Thomas B., 52, 203, 313
Allsopp, Sir Samuel, baronet, 126
Alta California: SLC in, 280, 308–09, 313, 314
Arnold, Matthew, 40–41, 75, 97–98, 110, 119, 159, 161, 182, 284, 338n53, 338–39n54, 341n20, 342n33,35, 377n16
Athenaeum: on *Prince and Pauper*, 67; *Life on Mississippi*, 334n20
Athenaeum Club, London, 19
Atlantic Monthly, 33, 351n35; SLC in, 24–25, 44, 51 58
Aubrey, John, 336n32
Austen, Jane, 294, 296–97
Australia, 179; SLC on, 183
Authors Club, London, 198, 273

Bacon, Sir Francis, 262, 373n15
Baconian heresy, 262
Baender, Paul, 282, 364n23, 377n13
Bain, Adam, 218
Ball, Charles: *Slavery in the United States*, 131–32, 151, 349–50n33, 352n39
Baring-Gould, Sabine, 30, 347–48n26, 348n26, 350n34
Barnum, Phineas T., 340n7
Barrie, James M., 206, 214, 241
Bass, Richard Arthur, bart., 126
Beard, Daniel Carter, 318, 348n27, 353n45
Beaumont and Fletcher, 262
Beecher, Henry Ward, 267
"Beer Peerages," 126, 129
Beerbohm, Max, 248, 250, 370n14
Belfast *Northern Whig*, 19, 24
Bell, Moberly, 368–69n2
Bermuda, 31, 51
Bigelow, Poultney, 197
Birrell, Augustine, 242
Blackwood's magazine, 75, 248

Blair, Walter, xiii, 45, 54, 83, 91, 93, 96, 273, 331n16, 337n39,41
Blamire, Joseph, 3, 4
Bliss, Elisha, 3
Boer War, 185, 193–94, 209
Boers, 185, 208–09
Bolingbroke, Henry St. John, 153
Booth, Edwin, 256
Bowen, Will, 69, 333n6
Bowser, David Watt (Wattie), 366–67n34
Brashear, Minnie Mae, 265
Breen, H. H., xiii, 330n6
British Museum, 10, 20
Brown, Dr. John, 203
Browning, R. Barrett, 289, 291
Browning, Robert, 9, 188, 288–93
  SLC readings of, 288–90; 348n27, 378n25,27,30, 379n32
Budd, Louis J., 109, 346n7
Buffalo *Express*, 4, SLC on Byron in, 281–82
Bulwer-Lytton, Edward G. E L., 295–96
Bunyan, John, 262, 264–65, 374n21
"Burial of Sir John Moore," 280
Burke, Edmund, 153, 357n16
Burney, Frances, 270, 341n24
"Burning Shame, The," 86
Burns, Robert, 274, 275–76, 353n48, 375–76n47
Burrough, J. H. 56, 355n13
Butler, Benjamin F., 285, 556n18
Butler, Nicholas Murray, 195
Butler, Samuel: *Hudibras*, 373n16
Byron, George Noel Gordon, Lord, 280–83, 376n6–8, 377n10,13

Cable, George W., 100, 102, 339n60
Campbell, Thomas, 377n14
Carlyle, Jane Welsh, 87, 337n37
Carlyle, Thomas: 27–28, 65, 71, 89, 91, 131, 136, 143, 147, 160, 196, 318, 319, 327n33, 336–37n36,37, 353n48, 372n11

—*Cromwell*, 87, 336–37n*36;* in *Huckleberry Finn,* 80, 90–91, 92
—*Frederick the Great,* 87, 336n*36*
—*French Revolution,* 27–29, 30, 42–44, 80, 87, 112, 113, 196; in *Connecticut Yankee,* 128, 144–51, 151–57, 344n*50,* 347–49n*12,19,25,29,31;* in *Huckleberry Finn,* 87–90, 91, 92, 337n*37,39,* 338n*47*
—*Past and Present,* 381n*17*
—*Sartor Resartus,* 233, 319, 367n*35,37,40;* in *Mysterious Stranger,* 233–36, 239, 367n*40,* 368n*43*
Carnegie, Andrew, 277, 341n*19,* 342n*27*
Carroll, Lewis (Charles Lutwidge Dodgson), 36
Castlemaine, Lady (Barbara Villiers), 336n*33*
Cellini, Benvenuto, 341n*24*
Century magazine, 339n*4,* 75, 132, 151
Cervantes, Saavedra, Miguel de, 71, 245, 271, 282–83
Charles II, of England, 81, 83–85, 336n*33*
Charles L. Webster & Co., 68, 100, 158, 180
Chatto, Andrew, 67, 100, 111, 162, 164, 183, 197
Chatto & Windus, publishers. *See* Chatto, A.
Chaucer, Geoffrey, 255, 371n*1*
Cheesman, John K., 369n*4*
Chicago *Republican:* SLC in, 306
Churchill, Winston Leonard Spencer, 207–09, 361n*26*
Civil Service. *See* SLC on
Classical Dictionary of the Vulgar Tongue, 52, 53
Cleland, John: *Fanny Hill,* 269
Clemens, Clara Langdon, 139, 196, 240, 246–47
Clemens, Jane Lampton, 166
Clemens, Jean, 177, 242, 246
Clemens, Olivia L., 3, 10, 56, 196, 200, 245, 286, 289, 308, 309; SLC letters to, 6–7, 18, 175, 179, 262, 266, 267
Clemens, Olivia Susan (Susy), 11, 180, 203, 275, 283, 285; her death and its influence on SLC, 181, 245, 278–79, 293, 359n*30,* 367n*42*
Clemens, Orion, 262, 270, 305
Clemens, Samuel Langhorne; SLC and acquaintance with British authors: M. Arnold, 97–98, 338n*53,* 342n*33;* J. M. Barrie, 206, 214, 241; Max Beerbaum, 248, 250, 370n*14;* Augustine Birrell, 242; Dr. John Brown, 203; Browning, 9, 288; Lewis Carroll, 36; Winston L. S. Churchill, 207–09, 361n*26;* Wilkie Collins, 326n*14,* 360n*8;* Marie Corelli, 251; Darwin, 37; Conan Doyle, 241, 298,

380n*10;* Thomas Hughes, 202, 326n*14;* Kingsley, 9, 200, 360n*8;* Kipling, 187–95 passim, 206–07, 245–46, 353n*3,* 369n*6,7,* 370n*13;* Andrew Lang, 164; Lecky, 200, 360n*7;* Sidney Lee, 244; George Meredith, 326n*14;* Arthur Pinero, 326n*14;* Charles Reade, 9, 14, 200–01, 360n*9;* G. B. Shaw, 250–51, 370n*15,17;* Herbert Spencer, 326n*14;* Standring, 111, 340n*17;* R. L. Stevenson, 203–06; 361n*14,* 17; Bram Stoker, 197; Tennyson, 18; A. Trollope, 202, 326n*14,* 360n*11;* Oscar Wilde, 196
SLC and: Anglo-American relations, 39–40, 67, 72–76, 119, 163–64, 206–07, 247, 334n*19,* 361n22; Australia, 182–83; "chivalry," 70–74, 105–06, 133–34, 146, 283, 333n*9;* civil service, 25, 26–27, 73, 76, 127–29, 327n*31;* conscience, 57–59, 61–62, 69–70, 97, 143, 203, 205, 219–25 passim, 336n*6;* communism, 43, 108, 329n*19;* Deity, 205, 210, 211–12, 215–17, 276; determinism, 54–62 passim, 66, 69–70, 97, 99, 115–16, 142–43, 210, 216–26 passim, 230, 238, 319; "discussion with Lecky," *see* Lecky; education, 59–66 passim, 142, 158–59, 352n*43*
—and England: attitudes toward, 10, 13–26 passim, 78–79, 102, 108–30 passim, 162, 165, 172, 174, 177–78, 196–207 passim, 209, 241–52, 340n20; reception and sales of books in, 4–5, 40, 66–67, 77, 100, 101, 162–64, 188, 204, 353–54n2,4, 355n*14;* visits to, 1–10, 11, 15–19, 35–37. *See also* SLC and: Established Church, India, monarchy and aristocracy, rank and caste, royalty and nobility
—and English characteristics, 9–10, 15, 19–23, 31, 35, 38–39, 40–41, 76, 109, 113, 119, 172, 182, 244; English clubs, 6, 19, 197, 198, 202, 242–44, 247, 273, 360n4,7; English law, 6–7, 62–64, 118, 342n29, 351n35, 355n*14*
—and English tradition, 15–16, 20, 21, 65, 77, 78, 246–47, 252
—and Established Church, 110, 116, 117, 123, 126, 127–30, 132, 135–38 passim, 151, 154–55, 158, 172, 176–77, 182, 339n3, 346n7, 353n45
—and France and the French, 16, 29, 35, 38, 42–44, 45, 184, 357n*11*
—and French Revolution, 27–31, 42–44, 87–89, 113–14, 141, 143–156 passim, 337n*39,41,* 375n*41*
—and Germany, 35, 160, 173, 181
—and human nature, human race, 26, 45, 66, 72–73, 78–80, 84–91 passim, 93–94, 96–97, 100–01, 160, 161, 165, 166, 171,

Clemens, Samuel Langhorne—*Cont.*
172, 174–75, 181–83, 191, 209, 210–12, 214, 215–16, 218–29 passim, 268, 319, 377n*13*
—and imperialism, 182–86 passim, 191–195, 207, 208–09, 357n*11*
—and India, 179, 180, 183–85, 191–92, 193, 357n*11*
—and manners and morals, 19, 37–41, 82, 114–15, 117, 119, 172, 182, 267, 268–69, 327n*28*, 341n*24*, 357n7
—and monarchies and republics, 41, 44–45, 65–66, 76, 77–80 passim, 109, 136–37, 159, 162, 172–73, 198, 327n*33*, 328n*43*, 356n*16*
—and New Zealand, 179, 183
—and pessimism, 34, 69–74 passim, 97, 100–01, 161, 165, 171, 174–178 passim, 210, 214, 225–26, 239, 263, 290–91, 318
—and publishers, 3–9 passim, 68, 73, 100, 111, 158, 180, 182–83, 204, 269, 325n9
—and rank and caste, 10, 78, 79, 116–17, 127, 128, 129, 165, 169, 170–71, 342n27; romanticism and sentimentalism, 91–92, 278, 279–80, 283, 284, 294, 295–96, 307, 312, 338n47
—and royalty and nobility, 23–24, 35, 76, 77–80 passim, 112, 113–16 passim, 120, 125–26, 129, 132, 140–41, 145, 146, 151, 158, 166, 169, 170–74 passim, 198, 341n*20,22*, 342n27, 353n*46*, 356n*17*. *See also* monarchies and republics; rank and caste
—and slavery, 108, 132, 137–38, 151–54 passim, 159, 160, 161, 174–75, 276, 347n20; the South, 73, 70–75, 154; South Africa, 180–81, 185–86, 193–94, 206, 208–09, 312; suffrage, 12–13, 23, 24–26, 28–29, 31, 108, 182, 327n*24,26*; "superstition," 62–64, 98–99, 128, 132, 152–55 passim, 158–59, 353n*48*, 100, 108; technology, 40, 158, 161, 124
—and U.S. government, 11, 12, 13, 22, 24–32 passim, 76, 334n*19*
—and utilitarianism, 55–56, 57–59, 69–70, 142–43, 218–31 passim (*See also* Lecky).
—lectures, 16–18, 24, 180
—literary opinions (*See also* main entries for individual authors), 30, 39, 40, 49, 54, 57, 71–72, 87, 120, 188–92 passim, 200, 201, 232, 261–62, 269, 270–71, 273–75, 285, 290, 294, 296–317 passim, 331n*23*, 338n*51*, 340n9, 371n*3*, 375n*35*, 379n2, 380n*8*, 380n*6*
SLC reading: 27–31, 41–42, 48–64 passim, 74–75, 80–97, 102–07 passim, 111–123 passim, 131–161; 189–95 passim, 213–39 passim, 254–317; T. B. Aldrich, 313;

M. Arnold, 40–41, 110, 119, 284, 338–39n*54*, 341n20, 377n*16*; Jane Austen, 294, 296–97, 380n*6*; Francis Bacon, 373n*15*; James Mark Baldwin, 362n*4*; Charles Ball: *Slavery in U.S.*, 132, 151–52, 349–50n*33*; 352n*39*; Baring-Gould, 30, 347–48n21,26, 350n*34*; J. M. Barrie, 206; Beaumont and Fletcher, 262; James Bonwick, 357n*10*; H. H. Breen, xiii, 330n*6*; Dr. John Brown, 203; Browning, 188, 288–93, 348n27, 378–79n*25,27,30,32*; Bulwer-Lytton, 296; 378–79n*25,27,30,32*; Bunyan, 264–65, 374n*21*; Edmund Burke, 357n*16*; Fanny Burney, 270, 341n*24*; Burns, 274, 275–76, 375–76n*47*; S. Butler: *Hudibras*, 373n*16*; Byron, 280–83, 376n*6–8*, 377n*10*; Thomas Campbell, 377n*14*
—Carlyle (For specific works, *see also* main author entry), 27, 65, 71, 87, 90–91, 92, 128–29, 131, 136, 143, 147–48, 233–36, 239, 327n*33*, 336–37n*36,37,44*, 367n*35,37,40*, 368n*43*, 381n*17*; Jane Welsh Carlyle, 87, 337n*37*; Andrew Carnegie, 341n*19*, 342n27; Lewis Carroll, 36, Cellini, 341n*24*; Cervantes, 71, 271, 282–83; Chaucer, 255, 371n*1*; *Classical Dictionary of the Vulgar Tongue*, 52, 53; Cleland: *Fanny Hill*, 269; Coleridge, 277–78; Comtesse de Chabannes, 356n*24*; Darwin, 56, 213; Defoe, 269–70, 375n*32*
—Dickens (For specific works except TTC, *see* main author entry), 294, 304–17, 381–82n*18*, 382n*20,24,26*, 383n*27,36*, 383n*35*; *Tale of Two Cities*, 42, 80, 126–28, 131, 143, 149–51, 153–54, 294, 304–07, 315–16, 317, 337n*39*, 349n*30*; Ignatius Donnelly, 374n20; Edward Dowden: *Shelley*, 284–85; Conan Doyle, 298–304 passim, 380n*10,13,14*; 381n–*15,16*; John W. Draper, 346n7; Dumas, Alexandre, 30, 294, 349n29; George Eliot, 296, 380n7; John Evelyn, 262; Henry B. Fearon, 258, 372n9; Fielding, 39, 114, 268, 269, 341n*24*; FitzGerald: *Rubaiyat*, 57, 213–18 passim, 236–38, 331–32n23, 362n7,*8*, 363n9, 367n*39*; J. A. Froude, 51, 52, 87, 337n*37*, 343n*39*; Mrs. Gaskell: *Cranford*, 296–97; Mme. de Genlis, 30; W. S. Gilbert, 115–16, 127, 228–29, 241, 341–42n26, 365n*28*; Elinor Glyn, 298; Goldsmith, 270–73, 314, 341n*24*, 375n*35,37,40*; Sarah Grand: *Heavenly Twins*, 355n*151*; J. R. Green, 343n*39*, 350n*33*; Sir George Greenwood, 366n*34*; Charles Greville, 377n*13*; E. Gurney, et al.: *Phantasms of the Liv-*

Clemens, Samuel Langhorne—*Cont.*
ing, 362n4; Basil Hall, 72; Thomas
Hardy, 334–35n21; Head and Kirkman:
English Rogue, 52,53; Henry of Huntingdon, 254; Lord Herbert of Cherbury, 341n24; O. W. Holmes, 56, 331n-
20; Victor Hugo, 330n3; D. Hume, 51,
52, 61, 65; Leigh Hunt, 51, 52, 285,
377n18; T. H. Huxley, 362n4; Ingulph:
Chronicle of Abbey of Croyland, 254;
William James, 362n4; Edward Jarvis,
351n35; J. Heneage Jesse, 52; George
Kennan, 132, 151; Kingsley, 200
—Kipling (*See also* main entry), 187–92
passim, 194; 353n3, 358–59n24,26,27,-
29,30,35; William Langland, 255
—W. E. H. Lecky (For specific works *see
also* main author entry), 27, 54–65, 70,
123, 131, 134–43, 152–53, 155–56, 218–28
passim, 230, 238, 331n16, 332n29,30,
339n57, 343n39, 346–47n8–10, 347n11,-
12,14,20, 350–51n31, 351–52n35,38, 363–
64n13,18, 364n19–22,26, 365n30; Sir
John Lubbock, 362n4; John Lyly, 262;
Macaulay, 186–87, 357n16, 358n17;
Malory, 100, 104, 105, 106, 131, 132–33,
339n3, 345–46n2,3,4, 352n40; Marguerite of Navarre, 82–83, 336n31; Marryat,
72; Meredith, 294, 296, 297, 380n8;
Michelet, 175; Milton, 262–64; Thomas
Moore, 283–84, 377n14; Wm. Morris,
130; J. L. Motley, 91, 92; Tom Paine,
55; Pepys, 52–53, 80–87, 335–36n27–29,
33; Pope, 274–75; Rabelais, 82; Charles
Reade, 200–01, 295; S. Richardson, 268,
341n24, 374n30; Elizabeth Robbins,
298; Rousseau, 341n24; Saint-Simon,
112, 113, 131, 143, 191, 341n24, 349n29;
O. Schreiner, 298, 380n9
—Sir Walter Scott (For specific works *see
also* main author entry), 49, 50, 71, 80,
94–96, 169, 330n5,7; 338n50–51, 346n5,
365n30
—Shakespeare (*See also* main author
entry), 81, 254–62; 304, 306, 348n27,
351n35, 366–67n33,34, 371–73n4–14;
G. B. Shaw, 370n15,17; Shelley, 284–85;
Sir Philip Sidney, 262; Smollett, 39,
114, 268, 269, 374n30; Southey, 264;
Jacob Sprenger, 365–66n30; Standring,
111–15, 117, 125, 126, 127, 129, 341n20,-
24, 342n27,28; 344–45n514–2; Flora A.
Steel, 298; Sterne, 201, 268; R. L.
Stevenson, 205; Harriet B. Stowe, 281;
Swift, 201, 265–68, 374n24; Taine, 30–
31, 112, 113, 131, 136, 143, 147, 255,
341n24, 344n50, 347n12, 348n25, 349n-
31; Tennyson, 118,132,145, 148–49, 285–

–88, 348n27,28, 377–78n19,20; Thackeray, 266, 268, 294, 295, 379n2; F.
Thompson: *Shelley*, 285; G. O. Trevelyan, 186, 357n13; A. Trollope, 202–03,
360n11; Frances Trollope, 72, 74; J.
Hammond Trumbull, 52, 351n35;
Horace Walpole, 29, 273–74; Mrs.
Humphrey Ward, 120–23, 296, 342n35,
343–44n40; A. Wilbrandt, 231; Charles
Wolfe, 280; Wordsworth, 278–80,
376n5; Charles D. Yonge, 30,43; Charlotte M. Yonge, 48, 49, 52; Zola, 341-
n24
SLC speeches: "American Press," 342n34;
at Army of Tennessee banquet, 46,
376n5; at Authors Club, 273; at Holmes
breakfast, 46–47; at Lord Mayor's dinner, London, 247; at Oxford, 246, 248;
at Pilgrims Club, 242–44; at Savage
Club: 1872, 23; 1897, 523n4; "Day We
Celebrate," American Society, London,
247; "Edmund Burke on Croker and
Tammany," 357n16; farewell speeches:
Liverpool, 1907, 251–52; London, 1873,
16, 18; "General Grant's Grammar,"
110–11; "License of the Press," 14, 28;
"Machine Culture," 340n12; "New
Dynasty," 108; "Now We Are Kin in
Sin" (intro. Churchill), 208–09, 361n25;
"On Foreign Critics," 268; on Macaulay,
186; "Our Fellow Savages of the Sand-
wich Islands," 16, on women's suffrage,
24; "Roughing It on the Silver Fron-
tier," 18; Seventieth birthday, 359n29;
"What is Happiness?" 218; Whittier
Birthday Dinner, 24, 33–34
SLC works (*See also* SLC speeches for un-
titled speeches):
"Abou Ben Butler," 285, 377n18
"About All Kinds of Ships," 281
"About Magnanimous Incident Litera-
ture," 307
"AGE–A Rubaiyat," 214
"Affeland," 190, 358n25
"Aged Pilot Man," 277–78, 295, 376n2
Ah Sin (with B. Harte), 33, 51
"Albert Memorial," 20–21
American Claimant, 97, 166–172 passim,
179, 354n6; sources, 56, 166–67, 271,
272, 307, 340n12, 349n30; 377–78n19;
theme, 170–72
"American Press" (speech), 324n24
"Answers to Correspondents," 307
"Approaching Epidemic," 310
Autobiography, 56, 203, 240
"Awful German Language," 46, 263–64
"Bible Teaching and Religious Prac-
tice," 365n30

Clemens, Samuel Langhorne—*Cont.*
SLC works—*Cont.*
  Book on England (projected), 19; contents, 20–23
  "Boy's Manuscript," 312–14
  "British Benevolence," 14–15
  Burlesque Autobiography, 4
  [*Burlesque Hamlet*], 257, 371n6
  Captain Stormfield's Visit to Heaven, 65, 255, 367, 371n17
  Celebrated Jumping Frog, 4, 22
  "Character of Man," 211, 225, 362n2
  "Colonel Sellers as a Scientist," 97, 99, 166, 169–70, 355n11
  Connecticut Yankee, 64–65, 66, 102–65; composition, 104, 107, 118, 130, 339n4, 340n11, 342n31, 343n38, 344n41, 344–45n52,54, 348n27, 352n37, 375n32; SLC reactions to British reviews, 163–64; SLC readings from, 104–05; genesis, 45, 64, 98, 100, 102–07, 108–18, 339n57,60,3; publication, 157–58, 159, 352n41; reception, 162–63, 164, 188, 353–54n2,4; sources: 102–57 passim; 131–61, 335n3, 340–43n7,24,27,39,40, 344–45n52, 345n1, 346–52n5,7,10,12, 21–35 passim,39, 366n33, 371n1, 372n-11–13; 375n32; Carlyle, 128, 141–51, 151–57, 344n50; 347–49n12,19,25,29–31; Dickens, 126–28, 131, 143, 149–51, 153–54, 337n39; Lecky, 127, 131, 134–43, 152–53, 155–56, 230, 339n57, 343n39, 346–47n10, 347n11,12,14,20, 350–51n34,35,38, 365n30; Malory, 102–06 passim, 131, 132–33, 339n3, 340n7, 345–46n2,3,4, 352n40; Standring, 111–17 passim, 126–129, 344–45n51,52; theme and structure, 104–16 passim, 131–32, 134, 138–42, 149, 151, 154–57 passim, 158–161, 352–53n45,48; mentioned 169, 171, 173, 174, 186, 228, 269–70, 315
  "Creatures of Fiction," 190, 313
  "Curious Republic of Gondour," 24–25, 26, 28, 52, 66, 266
  "Czar's Soliloquy," 233, 367n35,37
  "Daniel in the Lion's Den," 381–82n18
  "Day We Celebrate" (speech), 247
  "Death Disk," 87, 336n36
  "Defence of Royalty and Nobility," 166, 170, 354n6
  "Dog's Tale," 292–93
  "Double-Barrelled Detective Story," 299–304, 380–81n13–16
  "Edmund Burke on Croker and Tammany" (speech), 357n16
  "Enchanted Sea Wilderness," 277

"English Criticisms of America" (projected), 119
"English Justice," 355n14
"Fables For Good Old Boys and Girls," 267
"Facts Concerning the Recent Carnival of Crime," 58, 69–70, 383n35
"Facts in the Case of the Great Beef Contract," 305
"Five Boons of Life," 363n13
Following the Equator, 98, 181, 182–87 passim, 193, 205, 207, 277, 353n48; composition, 181–82, 197, 286; sources 186–87, 191–92, 298, 357n9,-13, 357n16; theme, 182–87
"French and the Comanches," 42
"General Grant's Grammar" (speech), 110–11
Gilded Age, 11–14, 15, 22, 381n16; sources, 12, 270–73, 314–15, 326n3
"Goldsmith's Friend Abroad Again," 271, 375n7
"Great Revolution in Pitcairn," 44–45
"Heidelberg Castle," 350n34
Huckleberry Finn, 22, 31, 74, 78–97; composition, 49, 68, 81; publication, 99, 100; reception, 100, 101, 164, 204; sources, 22, 58–59, 80–97, 255, 257–58, 265, 269, 273, 284, 337n39,41, 338n47–49; theme and structure, 58–59, 79–80, 84, 87, 88, 201–02, 258, 265; mentioned, 149, 169, 174, 188, 203, 315
"In Defence of Harriet Shelley," 284–85, 377n16
"Indignity Put Upon the Remains of George Holland," 261
"In Dim and Fitful Visions" (poem on death of Susy), 293
"In Memoriam: Olivia Susan Clemens," 278–79
Innocents Abroad, xii, 29, 186, 376n6; publication, 4–6; reception, 5, 40; sources, 264–65, 275, 280, 285, 294, 296, 310–12, 373n13; theme, 280, 312
"International Lightning Trust," 363n-13
Is Shakespeare Dead?, 186, 258, 366n34
"Jungle Discusses Man," 190, 358n25
"Killing of Julius Caesar Localized," 256
"King Leopold's Soliloquy," 298
"Labouchere's 'Legal Pillory'," 355n14
"Late Rev. Sam Jones' Reception in Heaven," 371n17
"Legend of Count Luigi," 294
"Legend of Dilsberg Castle," 339n3
"Legend of the Spectacular Ruin," 105

Index

Clemens, Samuel Langhorne—*Cont.*
SLC works—*Cont.*
  "Letter from the Recording Angel," 351n34
  "Letters from A Dog . . . ," 165–66, 211, 353n6
  "Letters from the Earth," 212, 262, 276, 362n3
  "Letters of Quintus Curtius Snodgrass" *not* by MT, 382n26
  "Letters of Thomas Jefferson Snodgrass," 256, 304, 301n17
  Letters to the Muscatine Journal, 266
  Letters to the *Sacramento Union. See* Sandwich Islands letters
  "License of the Press" (speech), 14, 28
  Life on the Mississippi, 68–77 passim, 75, 79, 119, 169, 333n1, 334n12,14; reception, 77; sources, 90, 282, 315, 333n6, 37an11
  "Lowest Animal," 181, 211, 214, 225, 362n2,3
  "Macfarlane," 56, 210–11
  "Machine Culture" (speech), 340n12
  "Man That Corrupted Hadleyburg," 45, 226–29, 364–65n25,26
  "Marjorie Fleming, the Wonder Child," 203
  "Memorable Midnight Experience," 20, 200, 232
  "Mental Telegraphy?", 370–71n17
  "Methuselah's Diary," 80, 328n43
  "My Boyhood Dreams," 214
  "My Platonic Sweetheart," 358n26
  "Mysterious Stranger," 45, 122, 185, 213, 214, 216, 229–39 passim, 299; sources, 230–39, 262–63, 268, 330n7, 351n35, 365–66n30,31, 367–68n37,39, 40,43; theme, 233, 234–39 passim
  "New Dynasty," 108
  "Noble Red Man," 312
  "Now We Are Kin in Sin" (speech intro. Churchill), 361n25
  "Old Saint Paul's," 20, 21
  "On Foreign Critics," 269
  "Open Letter to Commodore Vanderbilt," 349n29
  "O'Shah," 15
  "Our Fellow Savages of the Sandwich Islands" (speech), 16
  Personal Recollections of Joan of Arc, 165, 175–78, 259–61, 372n11; theme, 260–61
  "Picturesque Incidents in History and Tradition," 146, 335n27, 339n3, 375n32
  Prince and Pauper, 48–67, 68, 81, 99

  (play), 138; composition, 34, 47, 50–52, 65, 331n11; genesis, 48–50; reception, 66–67; sources: 48–64 passim, 71, 259, 329n3, 330n7, 331n14, 372n12; Lecky, 54–64 passim, 332n29,30; theme and structure, 59–66, 332n33
  "Property in Opulent London," 20, 22–23, 25
  Puddn'head Wilson, 165, 202, 270, 299; theme, 174
  "Queen Victoria's Jubilee," 197, 259, 348n28
  ["Reflections on Religion," from autobiography], 216–17, 362n3
  "Rogers," 20, 22
  Roughing It, 4, 85, 201, 325n3; sources, 266–67, 273, 277–78, 295–96, 312, 372–73n12,13; theme, 267, 278, 295–96
  "Roughing It on the Silver Frontier" (speech), 18
  "Royalty and Nobility Exposed," 112
  Sandwich Island letters, 256–58, 280, 306, 382n20
  Sandwich Islands novel (and play), 98–99, 155
  "Shem's Diary," 80, 335n27
  Simon Wheeler, Detective (play, novel), 33, 51, 201, 298–99
  1601, 38, 50; sources, 81–83, 258, 335n29, 336n31,32; 373n14
  Sketches New and Old, 49, 267, 283
  "Sold to Satan," 263, 366–67n34
  "Some Rambling Notes," 51, 283, 374n30, 382n26
  "Story of the Good Little Boy," 279–80
  "Stolen White Elephant," 299
  "Stupendous Procession," 185–86
  "Those Annual Bills," 283
  "3000 Years Among the Microbes," 267, 348n28, 363n9
  Tom Sawyer, 49, 99 (play), 204–05, 280, 299; sources, 51, 94, 286, 312–16 passim, 373n14; theme and structure, 286–88, 312, 314, 315–16
  Tom Sawyer Abroad, 165, 175, 267, 318, 338n50
  "To the Above Old People," 214–15, 362n8
  "Tournament in A.D. 1870," 105
  Tramp Abroad, 35, 41, 71, 105, 269; composition, 46, 47, 51; sources, 42–44, 263–64, 277, 281; reception, 67; theme, 329n26
  "U.S. of Lyncherdom," 230, 337n43
  Upon the Oddities and Eccentricities of the English (projected book), 19; contents, 20–23

Clemens, Samuel Langhorne—*Cont.*
SLC works—*Cont.*
  "Was It Heaven or Hell?" 364n26
  "Was the World Made for Man?",
    359n24
  "What is Happiness?" 69–70, 218
  What is Man? 70, 229, 238, 239; compo-
    sition, 211, 218, 363n12, 364n23,25;
    sources: 56, 70, 218–26 passim,
    331n20, 362n4; Lecky, 218–28 passim,
    363–64n13,18, 364n19–22
  Which Was the Dream, Etc., 239
  Whittier Birthday speech, 22, 24, 33–
    34, 46, 328n1
Cleveland, Grover, 100, 108
Clifford, Rosamond ("Fair Rosamund")
  85, 86
Clive, Robert, 186, 289, 291
Coleridge, Samuel T., 277–78
Collins, Wilkie, 326n14, 360n8
Commons, House of (Eng.), 112, 123
Conservative Party (Eng.), 110, 123, 124
Corelli, Marie, 251
Crane, Susan, 4, 10
Crane, Theodore, 10, 165
Credit Mobilier scandal, 12
Crofter movement (Scot.), 110, 118
Cromwell, Oliver, 76, 80, 87, 90, 318,
  336n36, 337n44
Cummings, Sherwood, 363n13
Curie, Marie and Pierre, 263
Curtis, George William, 75
Curzon, G. N., Marquess of Kedleston,
  241, 246, 248, 368n1, 369n5

Darwin, 37, 56, 213
Davis, Chester L., 357n15
Defoe, Daniel, 269–70, 375n32
DeVoto, Bernard, 45, 351n34; corrected,
  65, 354n3
Dickens, Charles, 16, 40, 131, 232, 304–17,
  381–82n18, 383n27; *American Notes*,
  75, 315, 383n36; *Barnaby Rudge*, 317;
  Bleak House, 307, 314, 382n26; *David
  Copperfield*, 271, 306, 308–10 312–15;
  Dombey and Son, 305–06, 382n22; *Great
  Expectations*, 338n48; "Haunted Man,
  The," 383n35; *Little Dorrit*, 313; *Mar-
  tin Chuzzlewit*, 305, 317, 382n20, 383n-
  36; "Noble Savage," 312; *Old Curiosity
  Shop*, 307, 383n27; *Our Mutual Friend*,
  306, 338n49, 382n24, 383n27; *Pickwick
  Papers*, 305, 306–07, 313, 315–16; *Pic-
  tures from Italy*, 310–12; *Tale of Two
  Cities*, 42, 80, 126–28, 131, 143, 149–51,
  153–54, 294, 304–307, 315–16, 317, 337n-
  39, 349n30,31

Dickens, Charles (the novelist's son), 119,
  310
Dilke, Sir Charles, 9
Disestablishment, 117
Disraeli, Benjamin, 25
Dodgson, Charles Lutwidge (Lewis Car-
  roll), 36
Dolby, George (impresario), 16
Dollis Hill, England, 111, 200
Doré Gallery, London, 10, 21
Doubleday, Frank, 245, 369n7
Dowden, Edward, 284, 377n16
Doyle, Sir Arthur Conan, 206, 241, 298–
  304 passim, 380n10,13,14; 381n15,16
Dumas, Alexandre, père, 30, 294, 349n29
D'Urfey, Thomas, 83
Durham, Earldom of, 166, 269, 271,
  355n9

Ealer, George, 231, 255, 258, 270
Edison, Thomas A., 124, 361n1
Edward IV, of England, 85
Edward V, of England, 76, 198
Edward, Prince of Wales. *See* Edward
  VII
Edward VI, of England, 51, 53, 61
Edward VII, of England, 174, 197, 242,
  356n18, 353n45
Eliot, George (Mary Ann Evans), 296,
  380n7
Eliot, Thomas Stearns, 186
Encaenia (Oxford), 1907, 244–45, 246
England. *See* SLC and
Established Church. *See* SLC and
Evelyn, John: *Diary*, 262

Fairbanks, Mary M. (Mrs. Abel W.) 9,
  10; SLC letters to, 15, 99, 105, 106, 107,
  118, 139, 201, 288, 306
Fairbanks, Mollie, 32
Falstaff, Sir John, 258–61
Fatout, Paul, 24, 273
Faulkner, William, 319
Fearon, Henry B.: *Sketches of America*,
  258, 372n9
"Feast of Pikes," 146–48
Fielding, Henry, 39, 114, 268, 269, 341n24
Fields, Annie, 26
Finlay, Frank, 19, 24, 109
Fis[c]her, Henry W., 234, 315, 337n40,
  374n25
FitzGerald, Edward: *Rubaiyat*, 57, 213–
  18 passim, 236–38, 331–32n23 362n7,8,
  363n9, 367n39
Ford, John, 262
Forum magazine, 119
France. *See* SLC and
Franz Josef, of Austria, 173

Frederick II, of Prussia (the Great), 87, 336–37n*36*
French Revolution, 27–31, 42–44, 113–14, 131–32, 136, 143–57 passim, 337n*39,41,* 375n*41*
Froude, James Anthony, 51, 52, 87, 337n-*37,* 343n*39*
Fun, 294

Galaxy magazine: *SLC* in, 105, 261, 270, 282, 305, 310, 312, 333n*9,* 376n*5*
Gardner, Joseph, 338n*49,* 382n*24*
Garrick Club, London, 202
Gaskell, Elizabeth: *Cranford,* 296
George IV, of England, 20
Germany. *See* SLC and
Gilbert and Sullivan operas: *See*
Gilbert, William Schwenck, 115–16, 127, 228–29, 241, 341–42n*26,* 365n*28*
Girondins, 27, 113
Gladstone, William, 24, 109, 200, 342n*35*
Glyn, Elinor: *Three Weeks,* 298
Goethe, Johann Wolfgang von, 264
Goldsmith, Oliver, 270–73, 314, 341n*24,* 375n*35,37,40*
Gould, Jay, 353n*45*
Grand, Mme. Sarah (Mrs. David C. Fall); *Heavenly Twins,* 355n*15*
Grant, Ulysses S., 46, 68, 100, 110, 376n*5*
Great Mutiny (India), 184
Green, John Richard: *History of English People,* 343n*39,* 350n*33*
Greenwood, Sir George, 366n*34*
Greville, Charles, *Memoirs,* 377n*13*
Griffin, Sir Lepel, 341n*20*
Ground Game Act, 1835 (Brit.), 118
Guinness, Sir Arthur E. (Lord Ardilaun, 1880), or Edward Cecil (baronet, 1885), 126
Gwyn, Nell (Eleanor), 81, 129

Hall, Basil, 72
Hardy, Thomas, 77, 241, 334–35n*21*
Harper's magazine, 179; SLC in, 293, 299, 336–37n*36,* 355n*9*
Harris, Joel Chandler, 36
Harte, Francis Bret, 33, 40, 294, 295, 383n*27*
Hartford Monday Evening Club. *See* Monday Evening Club
Hartley, David, 218
Hastings, Warren, 186, 357n*16*
Hawaii, SLC on annexation of, 13
Hawthorne, Nathaniel, 40
Hayes, Rutherford B., 26, 27, 328n*43*
Hemingway, Ernest, 319
Henderson, Archibald, 250, 370n*15,17*
Henry VIII, of England, 23, 51, 64, 79, 85

Henry of Huntingdon, 254
Heralds' College, 127, 344n*49*
Herbert, Edward (Lord Herbert of Cherbury), 341n*24*
Hill, Hamlin, 287
Hingston, Edward P., 4
Hiroshima, 263
History of European Morals. *See* Lecky, W. E. H.
Holmes, Oliver Wendell, 34, 40, 46, 56, 331n*20*
Hood, Thomas (the younger), 6
Hotten, John Camden, 4, 5, 8–9, 326n*9*
House, Edward H., 374n*30*
House of Commons, 112, 123
House of Lords, 112, 126–27, 167
Howells, William Dean: xiii, 27, 33, 40, 75, 269, 338n*53,* 339n*2;* on literary matters, 52, 77, 158, 270; SLC letters to: 180–81; on literary matters, 35, 52, 98–99, 165, 175, 290, 296, 299, 330n*36,* on political matters, 32, 113–14, 159, 181, 194
Hughes, Thomas, 202, 326n*14*
Hugo, Victor-Marie, 330n*3*
Hume, David, 51, 52, 61, 65
Hunt, James Henry Leigh, 51, 52, 285, 377n*18*
Hunting, Robert, 335n*25*
Huxley, Thomas Henry, 124, 362n*4*

Idler magazine (Brit.), 179
Illustrated News (London), 164
India, 179, 180, 183–85, 191–92, 193, 357n*11*
Ingulph, 254
Ireland, 16, 19
Irving, Sir Henry, 6, 198
Irving, Washington, 75, 273, 346n*10*

Jackson, Andrew, 26, 333–34n*9*
James, Duke of York (later James II, of England), 81, 83–85, 110, 113–15
James, Henry, 36, 203
Jameson Raid, 181, 185
James, William, 362n*4*
Jesse, J. Heneage, 52
Joan of Arc, 175–78, 194, 356n*24*
Johnson, Samuel, 273
Jonson, Ben, 262, 373n*15*
"Junius," 282

Kellgren, Henrick, 214
Kennan, George, 132, 151, 349–50n*33,34*
Kingsley, Charles, 9, 200, 231, 360n*8*
Kipling, Rudyard: 186, 187–95, 196, 241, 289, 354n*3,* 358n*18,* 359n*33,* 361n*21,* 369n*6,7,* 370n*13;* on SLC, 187, 195, 245;

Kipling, Rudyard—*Cont.*
 influence, 206; MT's influence on, 195;
 SLC and poems, 187, 189–94 passim,
 246, 358n24,26, 359n39; stories and
 novels: 187–88, 190–91, 358n26,27,
 359n30; with SLC at Oxford, 245–46
Knights of Labor, 108
Krause, Sidney J., 186, 357–58n17

Labouchere, Henry, 344n46; 355n14
Lambton family, of Durham, England
 166–67
Lampton, James, 271, 272, 315
Lampton, Samuel, 166
Lampton, William, 166
Lang, Andrew, 164
Langdon, Andrew, 351n34
Langdon, Charles J., 187, 308
Langland, William, 255
Leary, Katy, 196
Leathers, Jesse M., 167–68, 269, 271
Lecky, William Edward Hartpole, xiii, 27,
 54–65 passim, 70, 97, 98, 99, 123, 131,
 134–43, 152–53, 155–56, 218–28 passim,
 238, 363n13, 365n30; SLC visit, 200,
 360n7; *England in the Eighteenth Century*, 127, 131, 152–53, 155–56, 230, 351–
 52n35,38, 365n30; *History of European
 Morals* and "discussion with Lecky":
 27, 70, 98, 99, 331n16; in *Huckleberry
 Finn* and *Prince and Pauper*, 54–55,
 57–59, 61–64, 97, 332n29,30; in *Connecticut Yankee*, 134–43, 152–53, 339n-
 57, 343n39, 346–47n10, 347n11,12,14,20,
 350–51n34,35,38, 365n30 in *What is
 Man?*, 218–28 passim, 363–64n13,18,
 364n19–22; in *Hadleyburg*, 226–28,
 364n26; in *Mysterious Stranger*, 283; relationship between "realisation," imag-
 ination, compassion, 59–66 passim,
 138–42
Leonardo da Vinci, 310–12
Liberal Party (Brit.), 24, 109–10, 123
Local Government Bill, 109, 118
London, Eng., 20–23, 125, 196–98
London newspapers, 18, 23, 125; on SLC,
 11, 16, 34, 40, 246
Longfellow, Henry W., 34
Lords, House of, 112, 126–27, 167
Lorne, Marquis of (J. D. S. Campbell,
 Duke of Argyll), 77, 173
Louis XVI, of France, 42–43, 44, 71, 88,
 91, 156
Louise, Princess (daughter of Victoria),
 77, 173
Louisiana lottery, 107, 340n10
Low, Seth, 372n12
Lubbock, Sir John, 362n4

Lucy, Sir Henry, 247
Luther, Martin, 101
Lyly, John, 262
Lyon, Isabel V., 353n48, 359n26, 368n2,
 379n30
Lytton. *See* Bulwer-Lytton

MacAlister, J. Y. W., 196
McAllister, (Samuel) Ward, 169, 355n12
Macaulay, Thomas B., 186–87, 357n16,
 358n17
"Macfarlane," 56, 210
MacVeagh, Wayne, 367n42
Malory, Sir Thomas: *Morte Darthur*,
 100, 102, 104–105, 106, 131, 132–33,
 339n3, 340n7, 345–46n2,3,4, 352n40
Marat, Jean Paul, 113, 123, 143, 144, 155,
 337n41, 347n19
Marguerite of Navarre; *Heptameron*; 82–
 83, 336n31
Marie Antoinette, 29, 30, 43, 44, 71, 91,
 341n24
Marryat, Captain Frederick, 72
Marx, Leo, 338n50
Matthews, Brander, 101, 338n51, 379n2
Meredith, George, 241, 294, 297, 380n8,
 326n14
Metcalf, Lorettus D., 119
Mill, John Stuart, 25, 218
Miller, Joaquin, 202, 360n11
Milton, John, 262–64
Monday Evening Club, Hartford, 14, 24,
 70, 100–01, 108, 340n12
Monkswell, Lady Mary, on SLC, 197
Moore, Julia A. ("Sweet Singer of Mich-
 igan"), 91
Moore, Thomas, 281, 283–84, 377n14
Morris, William, 250
Motley, John Lothrop, 31, 32, 40
Mugwumps, 109
Munro, David, ed. *NAmRev*, 234
Murray's magazine, 110

Nansen, Fridtjof, 197, 247
Napoleon I, of France, 43, 174
Newman, John Henry, 364–65n26
Newton, Sir Isaac, 153
New Vagabonds Club, London, 198
New York *Herald*, 188, 309; on *Yankee*
 104; SLC in, 15, 208
New York *Sun*, on *Yankee*, 104
New York *Tribune*, 241, 309; on *Yankee*,
 104; SLC in, 13, 14–15
New York *World*, SLC in, 19–20
New Zealand, 179, 183
Nineteenth Century magazine, 124–127
 passim; M. Arnold in, 75, 119, 294

North American Review, SLC in, 233–34, 284

Olney-Pauncefote Arbitration Treaty, 207, 361n22
Omar Khayyam. See FitzGerald
Orton, Arthur (Tichborne claimant), 166–67, 354n7
Osgood, James R., 73, 269
Oxford, University of, 21, 241–46, 368n1

Paige typesetter, 68, 158, 164, 179, 197, 256, 332n2
Paine, Albert Bigelow, 294, 304, 379n2; corrected, 18, 48, 56, 174, 201, 354n3, 361n19,21, 362n1,2
Paine, Thomas: *Age of Reason,* 55
Pall Mall Gazette, 162–63
Parker, Sir Gilbert, 207
Parsons, Coleman O., 231, 363, 365–66n-30,31
People's History of the English Aristocracy. See Standring
Pepys, Samuel, 52–53, 80–87, 335–36n27–29,33
Phelps, William Lyon, 288
Pilgrims Club, London, 242–44
Pinero, Sir Arthur, 326n14
Pinkerton, Allan, 298
Pond, Ozias, 102
Pope, Alexander, 153, 268, 274, 312
Progressive magazine, 111
Puck, 74
Punch, 18, 74, 247–48, 279, 294, 327n22, 369–70n12

Quarterly Review (Brit.), 67

Rabelais, François, 82
Ragsdale, Bill, 98
Raleigh, Sir Walter, 82
Reade, Charles, 9, 14, 200–01, 295, 360n9
Reform Act, 1885 (Brit.), 110
Reform Bill, 1867, 25–26
Reid, Whitelaw, 241–44 passim, 248, 361n1, 370n13, 380n10
Republican (later *Radical*), 111
Review of Reviews, on *Yankee,* 163
Rhodes, Cecil, 182, 185, 358n25
Richard II, of England, 350n33
Richard III, of England, 76
Richardson, Samuel, 268, 341n24, 374n30
Robbins, Elizabeth, 298
Robespierre, Maximilien, 89, 91, 337n41
Rodney, Robert M. 325n4, 354n4
Rogers, Franklin R., 60, 294, 295, 296, 329n3, 346n10
Rogers, Henry H., 179, 180, 189

Rosebery, Archibald P., earl of, 109
Rousseau, Jean Jacques, 91, 341n24
Routledge and Sons, 3–9 passim
"Royal Nonesuch," 86
"Royal Touch," 152
Russell, James R., 345n1
Russia, 160, 173, 181

Sacramento *Union,* SLC letters to, 258, 280. *See also* SLC works—Sandwich Island letters
St. Louis *Missouri Democrat,* 24
St. Nicholas magazine, 175
St. Simeon Stylites, 121–22
Saint-Simon, Louis, 112, 113, 131, 143, 191, 341n24, 349n29
Salomon, Roger B., 61, 176, 330n10
Sandwich Islands, 13; SLC letters from. *See* SLC works
San Francisco *Californian,* SLC in, 256, 280, 307, 383n27
San Francisco *Morning Call,* 307
Saturday Morning Club, 51, 186
Saturday Review (Brit.) on *Jumping Frog,* 4; *Innocents,* 5; *Prince and Pauper,* 67; *Huckleberry Finn,* 101; *Yankee,* 163
Savage Club, London, 6, 23, 197, 198, 247, 360n4,7
Schreiner, Olive, 298, 380n1
Scots Observer (Edinburgh), on *Yankee,* 163
Scott, Arthur L., 325n5
Scott, Sir Walter, 49, 50, 71, 77, 80, 105; SLC attacks, 49, 70–73, 282, 330n5, 338n51; works: *Ivanhoe,* 49, 50, 71, 133–34, 169, 282, 346n5; *Quentin Durward,* 94–96, 330n7, 338n51; others: 94, 330n5,7, 338n50,51, 365n30
Shakespeare, William, 20, 21, 37, 81, 254–62, 270, 348n27, 371–73n4–14; *Hamlet,* 86, 306, 351n35, 371n5,7; *Henry IV, V,* 52, 258–61, 372n11; *Julius Caesar,* 255, 304, 544n4; *Macbeth,* 261, 373n13; *Merchant of Venice, Othello,* 255, 261, 373n13; *Richard III,* 255, 256, 372–73n-12; *Tempest,* 231–33, 234–39 passim, 291, 366–67n33–34; Others: 256, 258, 261, 372–73n12–13
Shaw, George Bernard, 125, 250, 251, 370n15,17
Shelley, Harriet, 284–85
Shelley, Percy Bysshe, 284–85, 377n16,17
Shore, Jane, 85, 86
Sidney, Sir Philip, 262
Skrine, Francis Henry, 194
Smith, Sol, 258, 372n9
Smollett, Tobias, 39, 114, 268, 269, 374n30
Smythe, Carlyle, 291, 379n2

South Africa, 180–81, 193–94, 206, 208–09, 312

Southey, Robert, 264, 282

Southwestern Humorists, 265

Spanish-American War, 207

Spaulding, Clara, 11, 36, 362n7

Speaker (Brit.), on *Yankee*, 163

Spectator, 8–9; on *Prince and Pauper*, 67; *Yankee*, 163; *Gilded Age*, 314

Spencer, Herbert, 326n14

Sprenger, Jacob, 365–66n30

Standring, George, 111–15, 117, 125, 126, 127, 340n17; *People's History*, 111–113, 126, 129, 341n20,24, 342n27, 344–45n-51,52

Stead, William T., 163

Stedman, Edmund Clarence, on *Yankee*, 158–159

Sterne, Lawrence, 201, 268

Stevenson, Robert Louis, 203–06, 361n-14,17

Stewart, Alexander T., 299

Stoddard, Charles W., 18–19, 354n7

Stoker, Bram, 197

Stolberg-Wernigerode, Prince, 173

Stone, Albert E., 175

Stow, John, *Survey of London*, 51

Stowe, Harriet Beecher, 281

Strachey, Sir Edward, 145

Stratford-on-Avon, 21, 37, 262

Stylites, St. Simeon, 121–22

Swift, Jonathan, 24, 153, 374n25; *Gulliver*, 75, 201, 265–68, 374n24

Sydney (Australia) *Bulletin*: on *Yankee*, 353–54n2

Sydney (Australia) *Morning Herald*, 274, SLC on Dickens, 316–17

Taine, Hippolyte: *Ancient Regime*, 30–31, 112, 113, 131, 136, 143, 147, 341n24, 342n29, 344n50, 347n12, 348n25; 349n-31; *English Literature*, 255

Tammany Hall, 357n16

Tasmania, 183

Temple Bar, London, 22

Tennyson, Alfred (Lord), 18, 105, 285–88; 353n45; works: "Bugle Song," 148–49, 348n28; *Idylls*, 118, 132, 145, 148–49, 348n23,27. Others, 145, 285–88, 348n27, 28, 377–78n19,20

Thackeray, William M., 40, 266, 268, 294, 295, 370n12, 374n25, 379n2

Thorwaldsen (Thorvaldsen), Bertel: "Lion of Lucerne," 43, 46

Thugs, Thugee, 184, 192

Tichborne claimant, 166–67, 354n7

Timbs, John, 51, 52

Treloar, Sir William Purdie (Lord Mayor of London), on SLC, 247

Trollope, Anthony, 202–03, 360n11

Trollope, Francis, 72, 74

True Blue Laws (J. H. Trumbull), 52

Trumbull, J. Hammond, 52, 351n35

Truth (Brit.), review of *Yankee*, 163; 355n14

Tuckey, John S., 236, 240, 365n26

Turner, Justin G., 331n14

Twain, Mark. *See* Clemens, S. L.

Tweed, William Marcy, and Tweed Ring, 12, 13, 14

Twichell, Joseph H., 97–98, 305, SLC letters to: 18, 237; on literary matters, 46, 80, 82, 380n6,13; political-social matters, 180, 194, 267

Vanderbilt, Cornelius ("Commodore"), 349n29

Vanity Fair magazine, 294

Victoria, of England, 20, 21, 76, 77, 113, 125, 163, 184, 193, 197, 198, 341n22

Villiers, George (2nd duke of Buckingham), 115

Walpole, Horace, 29, 273–74

Ward, Artemus (C. F. Browne), 4

Ward, Mrs. Humphrey, 241; *Robert Elsmere*, 120–23, 296, 342n35, 343–44n40

Warner, Charles Dudley, xiii, 11, 75, 289

Warner, George, 188, 353n3

Webb, Charles H., 294

Webster, Charles L., 68, 100

Webster, Daniel, 275

Westminster Abbey, 10, 20, 113, 200, 231, 310

Whistler, James, 36

White, Newman Ivey, *Shelley*, 285

Whitefriars Club, London, 6, 198

Whittier Dinner, 22, 24, 33–34, 46, 328n1

Wilde, Oscar, 196

Wilhelm I, Kaiser, 35

Wilhelm II, Kaiser, 173, 353n45

Williams, James D., 342n27, 345n1

Wilson, Robert H., 132, 345–46n2,4

Wordsworth, William, 278–80, 293, 376n5

Yale University, 119

Yonge, Charles D., 30, 43

Yonge, Charlotte M., 48, 49, 52

Young, Arthur (British historian), 30

Zola, Emile, 341n24

Zulus, 39